The Apostolic Fathers

Wilhelm Pratscher, editor

The Apostolic Fathers

An Introduction

BAYLOR UNIVERSITY PRESS

Wilhelm Pratscher, Th.D., is Professor of New Testament Studies in the Evangelical Theology Faculty of the University of Vienna.

Cover Design by Pamela Poll

Originally published in German as *Die Apostolischen Väter: Eine Einleitung,* © 2009 Vandenhoeck & Ruprecht, Göttingen (ISBN 978-3-525-03637-2)

Library of Congress Cataloging-in-Publication Data

Apostolischen Väter. English
  The Apostolic Fathers : an introduction / edited by Wilhelm Pratscher ; translated by Elisabeth G. Wolfe.
    p. cm.
  Includes bibliographical references and index.
  ISBN 978-1-60258-308-5 (pbk. : alk. paper)
  1. Apostolic Fathers--History and criticism. I. Pratscher, Wilhelm. II. Title.
  BR60.A65A6613 2010
  270.1--dc22
                              2010022950

Printed in the United States of America on acid-free paper with a minimum of 30% pcw recycled content.

For Kurt Niederwimmer
on his eightieth birthday

Contents

Foreword

The Apostolic Fathers have enjoyed growing popularity over the last decades. The terminology and the boundaries are certainly disputed, but the selected writings represent foundational documents from the time of the transition from the New Testament to the early church. They show the variety of the emerging universal church from the late first century to the end of the second century.

These articles discuss the originating conditions and the intentions of the individual texts, especially considering their theological orientation.

I thank my student assistant Thomas Feldkirchner for drawing up the typeset copy, as well as the press Vandenhoeck & Ruprecht for including this volume in their series of Uni Taschenbücher (UTB) and the circumspect printing.

This volume is dedicated to my esteemed teacher, Professor Kurt Niederwimmer, on his eightieth birthday. He made a great contribution to the research on these writings through the initiation of the "Commentary on the Apostolic Fathers" (KAV).

Vienna, March 2009   Wilhelm Pratscher

The Corpus of the Apostolic Fathers

Wilhelm Pratscher

We find the first compilation of individual writings of the Apostolic Fathers already in the earliest manuscripts. Codex Sinaiticus (ℵ, 4th c.) contains the Epistle of Barnabas and the Shepherd of Hermas, Codex Alexandrinus (A, 5th c.) both epistles of Clement.[1] Both times the aforementioned texts, because Bible codices are at issue, are measured against a high, possibly canonical standard. Precisely why they were admitted to the aforementioned codices is beyond our knowledge. The occurrence shows in any case their esteem in the circles in question. A collection of "Apostolic Fathers" is naturally not yet in their sights.

That is already much more strongly the case in the Codex H (Hierosolymitanus) from the year 1056, discovered by Ph. Bryennios in the library of the Church of the Holy Sepulchre in Constantinople. Next to a few other (partly related) texts we find here the Didache, the Epistle of Barnabas, both epistles of Clement and the letters of Ignatius (rec. *longior*). The choice may have been based on the materials at hand. That the Epistle of Polycarp was overlooked is hard to reconcile with the reputation of the bishop of Smyrna. But since the knowledge of manuscripts has a well-known happenstance about it, it is not unlikely that it is still in some collection or other in as yet unknown manuscripts.

We first find ourselves on firm footing with the printed versions. An equivalent collection was first published in 1672 in Paris by Jean-Baptiste Cotelier.[2] He speaks only in the title of writings of fathers who flourished in the apostolic period, in the text itself of an "Apostolicorum Patrum Collectio" (S.VII).[3] He offers the Epistle of Barnabas, both epistles of Clement, the letters of Ignatius, the Epistle and the Martyrdom of Polycarp, the Shepherd of Hermas, and several more writings. The criterion for inclusion is the assumed historical connection to the time of the apostles. The named texts are supposedly "Apostolorum partim comites [. . .] partim discipuli" (S.X).[4] In addition to Barnabas (Gal 2:1; 1 Cor 9:6; Acts 4:36; and elsewhere), Clement (Phil 4:3) and Hermas (Rom 16:4) appearing as companions and disciples of Paul, Ignatius and Polycarp are brought into connection with the Johannine tradition in Asia Minor (cf. Eus HE III 36.1-2).

---

[1] Cf. Aland, *Text*, 117–18.

[2] The titles of the subsequent editions can be found in a chronological series list at the end of the book.

[3] After Fischer, 1st ed., 161.

[4] Fischer, 1st ed., 161.

William Wake took over Cotelier's selection in his 1693 edition and was thereby the first who spoke in the title of the "Apostolic Fathers." Thomas Ittig undertook a reduction of the same in 1699, in that he did not include the Epistle of Barnabas and the Shepherd of Hermas in his "Bibliotheca Patrum Apostolicorum." The historical argument here met a theological one: Apostolic Fathers are only those writings that show evidence of the apostolic spirit. Barn and Herm are understood as "a spiritu apostolico remotiores."[5] The historical argument also relates to both: Neither the writer of the Epistle of Barnabas is identical with the companion of Paul, nor Hermas with the person greeted in Romans 16:14. Ittig also discusses Papias and Quadratus. The first was, according to Irenaeus' Adversus Haereses V 33.4, someone who had heard John and a friend of Polycarp. The latter, according to Eusebius' Historia ecclesiastica IV 3.2, belongs to the early period and was (IV3.1) praised for his apostolic orthodoxy. Ittig nevertheless declined Papias on the judgment of Eusebius (HE III.39.12-13), and he did not include Quadratus because of his shortness.[6]

Ittig's restrictive position had only a limited history of reception. While Johann Ludwig Frey followed him in his 1742 edition (*Epistolae sanctorum Patrum apostolicorum*), Richard Russel returned again to the selection of Cotelier (*Ss. Partum apostolicorum Barnabae, Hermae, Clementis, Ignatii, Polycarpi opera*).

The now ever more usual number of eleven writings of the Apostolic Fathers appears first (without the still-unknown Didache) in Andreas Gallandi's *Bibliotheca Veterum Patrum* [. . .], published in Venice in 1765–1781. To the previously mentioned texts he adds here the work "To Diognetus."

In the following years the writings chosen by Cotelier proved to be a kind of foundation. With few exceptions they have appeared in all editions to date (as has the Didache since its publication in 1883). Papias and the text "To Diognetus" have appeared most often alongside them, Quadratus somewhat more seldom. The following table (which presents only a selection, despite its length) should make that plain:

Editions and Translations of the Apostolic Fathers[7]

	Did	B	1C	2C	I	Polyc	MP	Pap	Q	Dio	H
Cotelier 1672		■	■	■	■	■	■				■
Wake 1693		■	■	■	■	■	■				■
Ittig 1699			■	■	■	■	■				
Frey 1742			■	■	■	■	■				

---

5   Fischer, 1st ed., 178.
6   Fischer, 1st ed., 183.
7   The bibliographic information for the editions and translations can be easily found at the end of the book.

	Did	B	1C	2C	I	Polyc	MP	Pap	Q	Dio	H
Russel 1746		■	■	■	■	■	■				■
Gallandi 1765–81		■	■	■	■	■	■	■	■	■	■
Hefele 1839		■	■	■	■	■	■			■	■
Dressel 1857		■	■	■	■	■	■				■
Hilgenfeld 1866		■	■	■							■
Mayer 1869		■	■	■	■	■	■			■	■
Hoole 1872		■	■	■	■	■	■				
Ge/Ha/Za 1875–77		■	■	■	■	■	■	■		■	■
Ge/Ha/Za ed. min. 1877		■	■	■	■	■	■	■		■	■
Funk 1878–81		■	■	■	■	■	■	■		■	■
Lightfoot 1889–90 (incomplete)		■	■	■	■		■				
Lightfoot/Harmer 1891	■	■	■	■	■	■	■	■		■	■
Funk ed. min. 1901	■	■	■	■	■	■	■	■	■	■	■
Hennecke 1904	■	■	■	■	■	■					■
Hemmer 1907–1912	■	■	■	■	■	■	■				■
Lake 1912–13	■	■	■	■	■	■	■			■	■
Zeller 1918	■	■	■	■	■	■					■
Funk/Bihlm. 1924[8]	■	■	■	■	■	■	■	■	■	■	
Bosio 1940	■	■	■	■	■	■	■	■		■	
Gl/Ma/Wa 1947	■	■	■	■	■	■	■	■		■	■
Kleist 1948	■	■			■	■	■			■	
Goodspeed 1950	■	■	■	■	■	■	■	■	■	■	■

[8] The exclusion of Hermas in the edition by Funk and Bihlmeyer had only a technical basis.

Editions and Translations of the Apostolic Fathers (*cont.*)

	Did	B	1C	2C	I	Polyc	MP	Pap	Q	Dio	H
Ruiz Bueno 1950	■	■	■	■	■	■	■	■			■
Fischer 1956			■		■	■			■		
SUC I–III 1956–95	■	■	■	■	■	■		■	■	■	■
Grant 1964–68	■	■	■	■	■	■	■	■			■
Sparks 1978	■	■	■	■	■	■					■
Quéré 1980	■	■	■	■	■	■	■	■			
Klijn 1981–83	■	■	■	■	■	■	■	■	■	■	■
Balthasar 1984			■		■	■					
Lf/Ha/Ho 1990	■	■	■	■	■	■	■	■		■	■
Lind./Pauls. 1992	■	■	■	■	■	■	■	■	■	■	■
Holmes 1999	■	■	■	■	■	■	■	■		■	■
Ehrman 2003	■	■	■	■	■	■		■	■	■	■

A brief look at the corresponding secondary literature (introductions, commentaries, and helps) bears this out. In introductions to the Apostolic Fathers (Vielhauer 1975, Rebell 1992, Jefford 1996, Günther 1997, and Foster 2007) the writings already chosen by Cotelier (Barn, 1Clem, 2Clem, Ign, PolPhil, and Herm) and the Didache were consistently discussed, as well as the Martyrdom of Polycarp in Günther, Jefford, and Foster; Papias in Vielhauer, Günther, and Foster; Quadratus in Foster; and finally Diognetus in Jefford and Foster.

The situation appears similar with the commentary series. The "Handbook of the New Testament" (1920–1923) covers Did, Barn, 1Clem, 2Clem, Ign, PolPhil, and Herm (the new editions from 1982 on have already included Did, 1Clem, 2Clem, Ign, and PolPhil), and the "Commentary on the Apostolic Fathers" (1989ff.) includes Did, Barn, 1Clem, 2Clem, Ign, PolPhil, MartPol, and Herm. The series "Hermeneia" has included Did, Ign, and Herm to date.

This trend appears even in the indices: Goodspeed, *Index* (1907) has Did, Barn, 1Clem, 2Clem, Ign, PolPhil, MartPol, Pap, Diogn, and Herm broken down; Kraft, Clavis (1964) Did, Barn, 1Clem, 2Clem, Ign, PolPhil, and Herm.

The problem of defining the Apostolic Fathers has not appeared only since the first printing but has been pondered especially since the beginning of the twentieth century. So Otto Bardenhewer[9] shows them to be an unstandardized group of texts that neither are internally related nor hang together temporally. In regard to genre there is an unusually great variety. We find a community rule (Did), actual letters (1Clem, Ign, PolPhil), a tractate (Barn), an exhortation (2Clem), a martyrdom story disguised as a letter (MartPol), an instruction of apocalyptic, ethical, and kerygmatic character (Herm), a collection of the Lord's sayings (Pap), and apologetic pamphlets (Quadr, Diogn). One would be hard-pressed to postulate a unified group of writings from that.

The criteria applied since the seventeenth century to the chronological and dogmatic order are fundamentally sensible. However, the problem is how closely one follows them. Fischer (1956) restricts himself to 1Clem, Ign, PolPhil, and Quadr.[10] One ought to include Papias here as well.[11] But there too a direct apostolic discipleship is most questionable. Hubertus R. Drobner would absolutely not want to employ the collection of the Apostolic Fathers: according to literary and historical categories they are not a unified group of writings, since "on the one hand some of them belong to the biblical Apocrypha, while on the other hand postapostolic literature includes much more than just these works."[12]

The disparity of genres hardly presents a problem for a collection. That much the Apocrypha (or the New Testament) shows, where there is also no generic unity. The assembly does not rely on that, though.

The group becomes a collection (as it has since the 17th c.) only through the demonstration of historically and theologically belonging to the apostolic period. Both criteria do not underlie the necessity of the assumption of such a collection, however, but rather can only allow the already assembled selection to appear meaningful secondarily. Neither the historical connection with the apostles can be proven, nor is the theological connection limited to these writings.

Both criteria can therefore be understood meaningfully only in a further sense. Historically that would then be *writings from the postapostolic period*, which must be expanded quite broadly, to the late first century to the late second century. Theologically it would be *documents that accord with the universal church standard* (originating in the 2nd c.).[13] By that definition all writings from this period understood as heretical fall out. Also excluded from usefulness would be

---

9 Bardenhewer, *Geschichte* I:80.

10 Fischer, *Väter*, IX–X, understands the Apostolic Fathers to be "such authors of the early Christian period [. . .] who according to current scholarship have plausibly proven to be personal disciples or auditors of the Apostles, including Paul and the like, or also without personal acquaintance with the Apostles nevertheless in their common teaching to a high degree can be declared upholders and preachers of the apostolic tradition, but who do not belong among the authors of the New Testament." Altaner/Stuber, *Patrologie*, 44, also approve this definition.

11 Cf. Rahner, *Väter*, 763.

12 Drobner, *Patrologie*, 96.

13 Cf. similar judgments: Rahner, *Väter*, 762: "the authors of the immediate post-apostolic period"; Wegenast, *Apostelväter*, 458: "a group of Christian writers of the second century who still were or appear to be immediate students of the Apostles"; Altaner/Stuiber, *Patrologie*, 43: "The oldest Christian writings apart from the NT" (in relation to the epistles of the Apostolic Fathers); Schöllgen, *Väter*, 875: "Collective name for early writings outside the New Testament."

the body of the Apocrypha and the apologists, which shows a certain grey zone between the two groups (Barn on the side of the Apocrypha, Quadr, and Diogn on that of the apologists). Something similar appears to be the case for the early antiheretical literature.[14]

Altogether, not only objective, historical-theological criteria prove decisive in favor of the existing selection of the eleven aforementioned writings,[15] but so also do (perhaps even more strongly) traditional-pragmatic ones. They have gained acceptance, as the history of the editions shows, and appear therefore to possess a satisfactory (if perhaps also somewhat surprising) persuasiveness.[16]

Bibliography

Aland, K., and B. Aland. *Der Text des Neuen Testaments*. Stuttgart ²1989.

Altaner, B., and A. Stuiber. *Patrologie*. Freiburg/Basel/Vienna ⁹1980.

Bardenhewer, O. *Geschichte der altchristlichen Literatur I: Vom Ausgang des apostolischen Zeitalters bis zum Ende des zweiten Jahrhunderts*. Freiburg i.B. 1913.

Drobner, H. R. *Lehrbuch des Patrologie*. Frankfurt/Main ²2004.

Fischer, J. A. *Die ältesten Ausgaben der Patres Apostolici: Ein Beitrag zu Begriff und Begrenzung der Apostolischen Väter*. I, HJ 94, 1974, 157–90; II, HJ 95, 1975, 88–119.

———. *Die Apostolischen Väter*. Munich 1956.

Foster, P., ed. *The Writings of the Apostolic Fathers*. London/New York 2007.

Goodspeed, E. J. *Index Patristicus sive Clavis Patrum Apostoloricum Operum*. Leipzig 1907.

Günther, M. *Einleitung in die Apostolischen Väter*. ARGU 4. Frankfurt/Main et al. 1997.

Jefford, C. N., et al. *Reading the Apostolic Fathers: An Introduction*. Peabody, Mass. 1996.

Kraft, H. *Clavis Patrum Apostolicorum*. Darmstadt 1964.

Lindemann, A. *Apostolischen Väter*. RGG⁴ I, 1998, 652–53.

Rahner, H. *Apostolischen Väter*. LTK² I, 1957, 762–65.

Rebell, W. *Neutestamentliche Apokryphen und Apostolische Väter*. Munich 1992.

Schöllgen, G. *Apostolischen Väter*. LTK³ I, 1993, 875.

Vielhauer, P. *Geschichte der urchristlichen Literatur: Einleitung in das Neue Testament, die Apokryphen und die Apostolischen Väter*. Berlin/New York 1975.

Wegenast, K. *Apostelväter*. DKP I, 1979, 458.

---

[14] According to Lindemann, *Väter*, 652, the eleven texts exhibit "certain common characteristics": "they originate from the period ca. 90–170; they distinguish themselves from the writings of the apologists by form and theological structure, and in contrast to the New Testament pseudepigrapha and the Apocrypha, they do not use fictitious names of early Christian authors."

[15] The text "To Diognetus" has the least basis for inclusion among the Apostolic Fathers, not because of its apostolic character (cf. Quadratus), but because of its late origin. However, it has been numbered with them since Gallandi and has a firm place among them.

[16] The fact that the period of origin of the eleven writings presented in the following pages is frequently uncertain will be covered in the forthcoming edition of Lindemann/Paulsen, *Väter*.

The Didache

Jonathan A. Draper[1]

1. Textual Tradition

The text of the Didache was rediscovered by Archbishop Ph. Bryennios in the monastery of the Holy Sepulchre in Istanbul in a major manuscript collection of early Christian writings also containing the Epistle of Barnabas, 1 and 2 Clement, and the twelve letters of Ignatius. His publication of this text in 1883 caused a sensation, since it seemed to provide the missing pieces of the puzzle in the reconstruction of the evolution of early Christianity.[2] Its title, *The Teaching of the Twelve Apostles*, was known from the list of disputed texts (τὰ ἀντιλεγόμενα) to be distinguished from the genuine writings of the New Testament (τὰ ὁμολογούμενα) provided by Eusebius (HE III 25). He includes it among those which are "spurious" (ἐν τοῖς νόθοις) and rejects its attribution to the apostles, though he shows it not to be heretical and numbers it with texts used by many in the church. The Didache also figures among the New Testament apocrypha in the stichometry of Nicephorus, who attributes 200 stichs to it.[3] The manuscript was later moved for safety to the library of the Greek Orthodox Monastery in Jerusalem and given the number H54, by which it is usually known. It is carefully copied and precisely dated to 11 June 1056. Thus it is likely to preserve an ancient and accurate archetype, though a fragment preserved in *Oxyrhyncus Papyrus 1782* (4th c.) shows many variant readings, as do the partial texts found in Coptic (4th c.)[4] and Ethiopic (4th c.).[5] A redacted form is incorporated also in the *Apostolic Constitutions*

---

[1] This chapter contains the original English text that was translated into German by Susanne Pratscher for the German edition.

[2] In some respects it provided the inspiration for Harnack, *Mission*.

[3] The length of this "rounded number" is disputed. Zahn, *Forschungen*, 295–301, sees it as far shorter than H54, but Rordorf/Tuilier, *Doctrina*, 109n3, see it as matching almost exactly (204 stichs) an uncial text of Did. (Cf. Audet, *Didachè*, 111; Niederwimmer, *Didache*, 15–18.)

[4] This text covers 10.3 to 12.2 but is not a fragment, but possibly from a training exercise for an amanuensis to use up waste papyrus cut from the end of a scroll. See Jones/Mirecki, "Considerations," 47–87.

[5] This text is an insertion into the Ethiopic text of the Ethiopian Church Order and covers a form of the Apostolic Decree similar to 6.3, 11.3–13.7 and 8.1-2 in that order. The text and translation were published by Horner, *Apostles*. Audet argued that it derives from the fourth century, before Did and *Didascalia* were incorporated into the *Apostolic Constitutions*. This appears to have been confirmed by the discovery of a new and unpublished manuscript by Alessandro Bausi. See Bausi, "San Clemente," 13–55. A reexamination of Horner's evidence by Dr. Darrel Hannah and myself concluded that text is more reliable once the best witnesses are used and once the so-called "abbreviations" are seen to be the result of *homoioteleuton*.

VII 1–32 (4th c. from Syria, AposCon).[6] These texts provide important evidence for a stage of the text earlier than H54, especially when they agree against it.[7]

The textual problem is compounded by the existence of an independent text of the Two Ways teaching also entitled *The Teaching of the [Twelve] Apostles*, corresponding to Did. 1–6.1, but excluding the Jesus tradition 1.3-6. It is found in the Latin *Doctrina apostolorum* (DocApos), the *Ecclesiastical Canons* (Can), the *Epitome* (Ep), the *Vita Shenoudi*, and in a more attenuated form in the *Canones/Fides Nicaeni* and the *Syntagma doctrinae* of Pseudo-Athanasius; it is also incorporated in the Epistle of Barnabas 18–20 (Barn). It seems that Did is a compilation. It consists of four major sections: the Two Ways (1–6), the Liturgical Section (7–10), Rules Relating to Community Life (11–15) and the concluding Apocalypse (16). As we shall see, this makes it difficult to date Did, since a source may be considerably older than the collection. Nevertheless, Did in its final form has a coherence that one should not ignore.[8] The material was collected because it was used and continued to be used by a single community after its final editing, and that community found no contradictions between the sections (however it may appear to us). Our purpose in this study is to explore the text for meaning for that community.

2.   Dating

There is no direct evidence for the date and place of origin of Did. All that can be known must be garnered from the internal evidence of the text and its distribution. The dating rests above all on decisions about sources, namely, the *Two Ways*, Q, and the Synoptic Gospels. Harnack,[9] who published the first major text with translation and commentary in German, saw Did as dependent on Barn for the Two Ways and so dated it somewhere in the first quarter of the second century. Others contended that Barn utilized Did.[10] However, since the work of J.-P. Audet,[11] comparing DocApos to the *Manual of Discipline* (1QS 3.13–4.26) from

---

[6] This forms, with major redactions, omissions, and additions, the entire text of Did. However, its redactions have a consistent character and where its text agrees with other witnesses, it provides important evidence. For the text, see Metzger, *Constitutions*.

[7] For a discussion of the textual tradition and for an excellent critical text and translation, based on H54, see Rordorf/Tuilier, *Doctrina*, 102–9. Wengst, *Didache*, provides a composite text and attempts to reclaim the earliest available form.

[8] *Contra* Schöllgen, "Kirchenordnung," 5–26. The debate about the *Traditionsgeschichte* of the *Kirchenordnung* and its implications for Did continues (see Steimer, *Vertex Traditionis*, esp. 13–27; Mueller, "Ancient Church Order," 337–80. 1QS

also shows evidence of additions and editing; see Murphy-O'Connor, "Genèse Littéraire," 528–49, and Verme, *Didache*, 264–65). While this is true with respect to *genre*, it is not true with respect to theology, since an exhaustive comparison with the scrolls shows that Did is nearly always closer to Pharisaic Judaism than to the Essenism of the scrolls, except in the case of tradition common to both (so Draper, *Commentary*). A sustained, though not entirely convincing, attempt to read the text as an early, coherent (oral) composition is made by Milavec, *Didache*.

[9] Harnack, *Lehre*.

[10] Or knew an earlier form: Draper, "Barnabas," 89–113.

[11] Audet, "Affinités," 219–38.

Qumran, it has been widely agreed that the Two Ways derives from earlier Hellenistic Jewish tradition and has been incorporated into Did as a source, perhaps originating from *Hasidic* circles, similar to what survives in the rabbinic tractate *Derekh Eretz Zuta*.[12] In this case both Did and Barn would then be predicated on the same source so that this criterion fell away for their respective dating. Secondly, the redactor(s) of Did inserted material drawn mostly from the teaching of Jesus in Q in the Sermon on the Mount as a "first teaching" of the instruction to love God and one's neighbor,[13] and the negative form of the Golden Rule ("And whatever you do not want to happen to you, do not do it to another").[14] The original interpretation of the Two Ways consisting largely of expansions of the Decalogue then follows as a "second teaching."[15]

Significantly, this Jesus tradition is from the Q source, closest to Matthew and sometimes to Luke but not identical to either. Besides this, there are further parallels to Matthew in 8:1-2, 9:5 and various other places. For this reason, a dependence on Matthew and even Luke is posited by some commentators. Clearly the use of either gospel as a source would provide evidence for the date of the final edition of the whole text, but this cannot be established with any certainty. Helmut Köster has argued convincingly that it does depend on the orally circulating gospel tradition.[16] The debate over Did's use of synoptic material is by no means settled,[17] but what is decisive, in my opinion, is that only Q and special "M" material in a form closest to, but seemingly independent of, the final edition of Matthew is used. It is difficult to explain how only the material in Matthew and Luke that is not found in Mark is represented, unless it results from independent access to their sources. One can conclude from this that the final edition of Did originated in the period when the gospel material still circulated orally and in a relatively fluid form (see Just *Apol* I 15.9–16.1, 45–47).[18] However, it does suggest that the final date for the present text of Did should not be pushed too far into the second century (if at all). On the other hand, the language of 11.3 ("But with regard to the apostles and prophets, act in accordance with the precept of the Gospel"[19]) and 15.4 ("Your prayers and alms and all you do should be so

---

[12] See Sandt/Flusser, *Didache*. Indeed, they see this *chasidic* tradition lying behind Jesus' teaching in the Sermon on the Mount also (193–237).

[13] The twofold love command is ancient and probably predates the teaching of Jesus. Cf. TIss 5.2, 7.6; TDan 5.3; SifreDt 32.29. See Nissen, *Gott*.

[14] Cf. Tob 4.15; ArisEx 207; Philo, *Hypothetica* 7.7. This summary of the Law has a long history, especially in the negative form in which it is found here, and springs from the Jewish Wisdom tradition (see Dihle, *Regel*). There are indications of the combination of the double love command with the negative form of the Golden Rule as well. Cf. Philo, *Quod om. hom. lib. sit* 83 (cf. Josephus *BJ*

II.139);TgPsJ zu Lev 19:18; bSabb 31a. The Golden Rule appears in a positive form as a summary of the Law and the Prophets in Matthew 7:12, where it is followed by a form of the Two Ways teaching (7:13-14), though nothing here suggests literary dependence.

[15] Cf. Rordorf, "Beobachtungen," 431–32.

[16] Köster, *Überlieferung*, 159–241.

[17] For the arguments for independence, see Draper, "Jesus Tradition," 269–89. The debate is continued in papers in Sandt (ed.), *Matthew*.

[18] For a discussion, see Smith, "Justin," 287–90.

[19] All English translations from the German text of Did are based on Schöllgen, *Didache*, unless otherwise stated.

ordered as you have it in the Gospel of our Lord") may indicate, though not necessarily, a written text. My own view is that the text of Did comes from the same community(ies) as Matthew and that its earliest form predates that gospel, but that it has continued to evolve, in tandem with Matthew's gospel, which eventually replaces it.[20]

If Did is independent of Barn and the Synoptic Gospels, then there is no firm basis for dating the text beyond the contents, and they suggest a very early date. Here is a community which still knows of apostles and prophets traveling from community to community; in which elected bishops and deacons (no priests are mentioned) are in danger of being despised because of the high honor given to prophets and teachers. This is a community whose baptism makes no mention of forgiveness of sins through incorporation in the cross of Christ, whose Eucharist makes no mention of the body and blood of Christ or even the words of institution from the Last Supper. Its catechesis consists of traditional Jewish instruction based on the Decalogue, with only a small section providing (unattributed) material from the Jesus tradition in Q. It has strong concerns about ritual purity (7.1-3). Even if some of these sections derive from a period considerably earlier than the final redaction of the text, they still reflect the current life and practice in the life of a community no later than the end of the first century.

Such a supposition is supported by the widespread early attestation of the text in Egypt (*P. Oxyrh. 1782*; the Coptic version, Ps.-Cyprian, *De centesima, sexagesima, tricesima*), Ethiopia (Ethiopic Church Order) and Syria (Didasc., AposCon, and probably the *Liber graduum*) and perhaps Asia Minor (Lacantius, *Epitome*;[21] *Testamentum Domini*). Some of these sources indeed seem to consider it to be "scripture." This indicates the importance attached to the writing and its antiquity.[22] There is little consensus for the place of composition. Some have argued for Egypt on the basis of the use of τὸ κλάσμα (9.3-4) in the Eucharistic prayers,[23] but on the whole most scholars settle on Syria or Syria-Palestine, some seeing here a precursor to Syrian asceticism. A growing number of commentators have pointed specifically to Antioch, influenced particularly by its heavily Jewish

---

[20] Garrow, *Gospel*, argues plausibly that Matthew is dependent on every redactional layer of Did. I prefer to see the two texts as mutually interactive over time, with Did presenting the community rule of the Matthean community. Naturally this rule determines many aspects of the content, structure and text of Matthew's composition and redaction of Mark, but in the end it is superseded by the gospel. For an understanding of Did as "evolved literature" see Draper, "Modern Research," 1–42, esp. 19–22.

[21] See Draper, "Lactantius," 112–16.

[22] After Harnack, *Lehre*, 168–70. So, for instance,

Niederwimmer, "Entwicklungsgeschichte," 145–67, esp. 153. Kraft, *Barnabas*, 77. The grounds for a rural setting appear, usually on the basis of the first fruits, in ch. 13. This thesis has been decisively countered by Schöllgen, "Zeugnis," 140–43. Niederwimmer retreats from his earlier position in *Didache*, 80, while still rejecting Antioch.

[23] Harnack, *Lehre*, 159–60 initially. See also Kraft, *Barnabas*, 76–77, who favors Egypt on the basis of the early presence of texts there—hardly convincing, since climatic conditions in Egypt favored the preservation of manuscripts—but also on later uses of the tradition there.

character despite the address to Gentiles in its "longer title," and by the presence of a form of the Apostolic Decree in 6.2-3.[24] In the absence of conclusive evidence either way, this seems the most plausible venue for the origin of the text to me.

3.   Origin

The closeness to Matthew and also to the Epistle of James[25] is significant, since it places Did within the ambit of Christian Judaism.[26] By this I understand a community (or group of communities) of Diaspora Jews who saw Jesus as the Messiah but were receptive to Gentile Christians. They found themselves in competition with nascent rabbinic Judaism (see Did 8), even if they were closer in their beliefs to the Pharisees than to other Jewish groupings. This matches the self-designation of the text in its subtitle (or probably more accurately its *incipit*): "The Lord's Teaching to the Gentiles by the Twelve Apostles," which was probably added when the Two Ways was incorporated into the larger work.[27] The Two Ways teaching in chs. 1–6 is clearly intended as catechesis for baptismal candidates (7.1; but cf. 9.5). — RCIA model

What follows shows concern mostly about the "grades of purity" of water which may be used, in a manner similar to rabbinic discussions on the same topic (7.2-3). There is no reference in the context of baptism of "repentance for the forgiveness of sins," nor of the cross. The baptismal fast (7.4) provides the occasion to differentiate the community's teaching on fasting and prayer from another Jewish community designated "hypocrites," with Q material close to that found in Matthew 6:9-13/ Luke 11:2-4. This is followed by a eucharistic meal with prayers over the cup first and then the broken bread and further prayers after the meal in a style close to what is known of Jewish *berakoth*. I have argued elsewhere that these prayers are intended for a baptismal Eucharist, which determines their particular content.[28] In other words, like the *Manual of Discipline* from Qumran, Did has a concern with initiation into the community and its socialization at the core.

⌐→ Table fellowship

---

[24] Adam, "Erwägungen," 266–67 argues for its origin in Palestine. For Syria more generally, see Rordorf/Tuilier, *Doctrine*, 97–98; Wengst, *Didache*, 61–62, on the basis of envisaged lack of water in 7.2-3, "bread on the mountains" in 9.4 and its use of Matthew's gospel; Niederwimmer, *Didache*, 80, cautiously on the basis of the continuity between the wandering disciples of Jesus and the itinerant charismatics in Did. For Antioch, in particular, see Jefford, "Milieu," 35–47.

[25] See Kloppenborg, "Didache," and the various studies in Sandt/Zangenburg (eds.), *Matthew, James, and Didache*, 2008.

[26] There is today considerable agreement on this,

e.g., Rordorf/Tuilier, *Doctrine*, 21; cf. Niederwimmer, *Didache*, 67. Today the early "parting of the ways" between "Christianity" as a new "law-free and universalistic" religion and "Jewish orthodoxy," as a stable "law-bound" and particularistic religion has been problematized. Indeed, Boyarin, *Border Lines*, has argued that no such division occurred until the fourth century. For a helpful discussion of this new direction, see Jackson-McCabe, "Problem," 7–38.

[27] So Rordorf/Tuilier, *Doctrine*, 16–17.

[28] Draper, "Ritual Process," 1–38; cf. Just *Apol.* I 65–66.

In many ways, the instructions in Did 6.1-3 represent a crux for understanding the origin of the community of Did and the orientation of the text:[29]

> See that no one cause you to err from this way of the Teaching, since apart from God it teaches you. For if you are able to bear all the yoke of the Lord, you will be perfect; but if you are not able, what you are able that do. And concerning food, bear what you are able; but against that which is sacrificed to idols be exceedingly on your guard; for it is the service of dead gods.[30]

Many scholars have seen 6.1 as the original conclusion to the Jewish Two Ways and 6.2-3 as provided by the Christian editor in order to join the Two Ways to the liturgical section.[31] The question of "perfection" then relates to the impossible demands of the teaching of Jesus found in 1.3b-6 and in the Sermon on the Mount in the Synoptic tradition.[32]

Yet this interpretation depends first of all on the post-Reformation *sola fide* and the erroneous belief that the teaching of Jesus cannot be fulfilled; that belief creates a crisis for the conscience that can be resolved only by an acceptance of the good news that salvation is through grace alone appropriated by faith.[33] Second, the interpretation depends on the understanding of "perfection" as an ethical category rather than a code word for living according to the Torah. In the *Manual of Discipline*, for instance, walking in the Way of Light is the same as "walking perfectly" (cf. *halak betamim* in 1QS 1.8; 8.20; 9.6, 8, 19; cf. 1QSb 1.2; CD 1.21; 7.5). In my opinion, an instruction that says to new Gentile converts, "The teaching of Jesus we have presented to you is an intolerable burden, so you only have to keep as much of it as you can," would undermine their socialization. Besides, Did nowhere ascribes the Jesus tradition, as opposed to the Two Ways, to Jesus and it is not certain whether "Lord" refers at any one point to *Adonai* or to Jesus. Certainly, the phraseology of 6.2 relates in some way to the saying of Jesus found in Matthew 11:28-30. Indeed, Matthew's sense is the opposite: "Take my yoke on your shoulders, it's easy to carry!" Rather, "taking on oneself the yoke of the Lord" is a technical term for obedient observance of the Torah in both Did and Matthew[34] (cf. *m. 'Abot* 3.5; cf. 6.2; *b. B. Metsi'a* 85b; *t. Sotah* 14.4; *2Bar.* 41.3).

Like the "Apostolic Decree" in Acts, Did does not require that Gentiles get circumcised and take on themselves the whole Torah, but it does require them to keep as much as they can. In any case, the minimum required of them is that they

---

[29] See Draper, "Enigma," 106–23.

[30] This prohibition of food offered to idols is the central point also of the so-called Apostolic Decree in Acts 15 and 21, where it is cited three times in various forms, once in the form "the defilement of idols." Cf. Wedderburn, "Apostolic Decree," 362–89. [Translation by M. B. Riddle from Roberts/Donaldson/Coxe, *Fathers*, 379.]

[31] See Niederwimmer, *Didache*, 152–53; Rordorf/ Tuilier, *Doctrine*, 32, 80–81, 168n3.

[32] Niederwimmer, *Didache*, 157; cf. Rordorf/ Tuilier, *Doctrine*, 32–34.

[33] For a critique of this, see Stendahl, *Paul.*

[34] As argued by Stuiber, "Joch," 323–29; Flusser, "Opponents," 195–211; and Deutsch, *Hidden Wisdom.*

abstain from εἰδωλόθυτον, from food offered to "dead gods" (6.3). The position of a form of the Apostolic Decree next to the Two Ways in Did 6.2-3 is not arbitrary: The same thing appears in the fourth(?)-century representative of the Two Ways *Syntagma doctrinae* 1.6; it is found also immediately before the selections of Did itself in the Ethiopic version of the *Synodos*.[35] The text moves from its origin in catechesis of Gentiles to take its place in initiation of ascetics.

Did 3.1-6 presents a tightly constructed fivefold block of material, which may have come from an independent source. It finds close parallels in *Derekh Eretz Zuta*. The block is introduced with the instruction, "My child, avoid all evil and all that is like it" (3.1; cf. *Derekh Eretz Zuta* 2.7; *Avot de Rabbi Nathan* 2.2). In my opinion, it is this kind of affirmation of the Torah, ensuring the fulfillment of the major precepts by avoiding minor infringements, that also lies behind the "greater righteousness" in Matthew 5:17-48, rather than a rejection of the Torah in favor of the gospel.[36] Again, the signs point to a community that is concerned to preserve the observance of Torah but at the same time does not require Gentiles to put themselves under the whole Torah on their initiation into the community, but only under the "universal laws" set out in the Two Ways (7.1) and avoidance of εἰδωλόθυτον (6.3). However, there is the expectation that Gentiles keep "as much as they can" of Torah and also a hope that they will be "found perfect" on the last day when the Lord comes (16.2).[37]

4.   Theological Profile

In what follows, I have attempted to give a *description* of the theology which I observe in this obscure and much contested writing, following the lines familiar from New Testament theologies.[38]

4.1 God the Father

The fundamental understanding of God in Did begins with the concept of God as creator (1.2; cf. Deut 6:5), which is found already in the underlying Two Ways tradition (Can, Ep, DocApos, Barn with variant). Human beings are called to love God as the Creator and in turn their neighbors. A key mark of those on the way of death is that they "do not know their Creator," which stands parallel to "destroyers of God's creatures" (5.2). This is an essential safeguard against the danger of cosmic dualism in the Two Ways tradition, where the Two Ways are understood

---

35 The antiquity of this interpolation in the Ethiopic Church Order has been confirmed by its appearance in ch. 37 of a newly discovered Ethiopic text of the *Traditio apostolica* that appears to have been translated directly from Greek in the early period of the church in Ethiopia. See Bausi, "San Clemente," 13–55.

36 Draper, "Genesis," 25–48; Sandt/Flusser, *Didache*, 193–237.

37 Draper, "Torah," 347–72.

38 For a recent exploration of the nature of NT theology, which demonstrates a breadth of viewpoints, see the papers in Rowland/Tuckett (eds.), *Nature*.

to be under the control of the respective angels of light and darkness, truth and falsehood, as can be clearly seen already in the Dead Sea Scrolls (1QS 3.13–4.26). The influence of covenantal nomism of Deuteronomy 30:15-20 remains decisive.

This primary understanding of the goodness of God as Creator towards all his creatures continues in what follows, even though the material is drawn from various sources. God is viewed as a loving Father (1.5; 7.1, 3; 8.2; 9.2-3; 10.2) in the material deriving from the "Q" tradition and in the liturgy. Members of the community are urged to participate in the divine economy and to give to everyone who asks without asking that something be given back (1.5). This is why God will be "the good repayer of the loan." The same sentiment is found in the thanksgiving after the eucharistic meal. God the almighty Master has created all things for the benefit of human beings (10.3). Members of the community of believers receive spiritual food and drink and eternal life through Jesus, but clearly it is God's purpose in creation to bless all human beings. This is not to rule out the special blessing to Israel, since God is the God of his son David and of his Son Jesus. This is the basis of God's evenhandedness to all, rich and poor, slave and free (cf. 4.10).

This benevolent God of all human beings is also omnipotent, the source of all that happens. Thanks is thus given for all things because "You are mighty" (10.4; cf. 3.10). Nevertheless, the words of the Lord's Prayer express the hope of the community that God has done something radically new in his Son Jesus to usher in God's rule on earth as already in heaven, in conformity with God's will (8.2). This hope in the coming rule of God, associated with a restoration of the house of David through Jesus, is a constant thread (9.2, 4; 10.5, 6), as we shall see in our consideration of the Christology of the text. In the last days, God will intervene to save those members of the community who persevere (16.8).

The responses (or "seals") to the Lord's Prayer and the eucharistic prayers, probably given in reply to the president by the community, are usually variants of "for Thine is the kingdom [and the power] forever" (8.2; 9.2-4; 10.2, 4, 5). God's glory is the manifestation of his power and presence to his people, located in the tradition of Israel in the tabernacle and then in the temple in Jerusalem. The references to the name of God have the same background (e.g., indwelling the temple in Deut 12:11), particularly the idea of the holy name of God indwelling the community as a spiritual temple (10.2; 14.3, citing Mal 1:11, 14; cf. 1 Cor 3:16, 17; 6:19; 2 Cor 6:16).[39] The name manifests God's presence in the community. The community sanctifies God's name not only in prayer, but also by the manner of their communal life. It is thus vitally important that the "purification"

---

[39] The use of the "Name" to designate the manifestation of God in his ineffable holiness and glory, especially in the Temple, has been described by Danielou, *Theologie*, 200, as "un aspect essential de la théologie judéo-chrétienne." Nothing, however, suggests that the Name in 10.2 is understood as a designation for Jesus indwelling the believer, still less as an *epiclesis* in the Eucharistic prayers at the breaking of the bread, as argued by Peterson, "Didache," 3–13, esp. 5.

of the community should establish and maintain holiness, so that God's presence may be supported. The conditions for holiness are established by baptism and fasting, which serve ritual purity (chaps. 7, 8); therefore, only those baptized in the name of the Lord may partake of the eucharistic meal (9.5). The prayer for the church after the eucharist requires that it be "completed" in God's love and "sanctified" before it can be gathered into God's kingdom which he has prepared for it (10.5). "Holiness" is a prerequisite for the coming of the Lord (*maranatha!* 10.6). The preservation of the purity of the "sacrifice," namely, the spiritual sacrifices of prayer and Torah offered by the community as the spiritual temple, is the motivation for the confession of sins (against God) and exclusion of offenders for transgressions (against the neighbor) in chapter 14 and 15.3.[40] The spiritual sacrifices brought before God in the life of the community are also a witness to God's kingly rule and his holy name among the Gentiles (14.3).

It is never clear where, if ever, the word "Lord" refers to Jesus as opposed to the Father, but there is no evidence that it refers to Jesus, since there is only a brief section of sayings which are drawn from the "Q" tradition. In fact, the AposCon parallel here has θεός in place of κύριος.

4.2 Christology

The use of the word "Christology" to describe Did's understanding of the person and work of Jesus is in itself misleading, since the word "Christ" does not occur in the writing, except in one unsupported reading in H54: "For Thine is the glory and the power in Jesus Christ forever," which is unlikely to be original. The AposCon reads simply, "For Thine is the power forever," which is in line with the other "seals" to the eucharistic prayers. Another brief reference to the title may be found in 12:4. So the title was known in the community but did not receive any special emphasis. Instead, the understanding of Jesus is dominated by two related things: His association with David (9.2, 10.6) and the title παῖς, child/servant, in the eucharistic prayers (9.2 twice, 3; 10.2-3).

In the prayer over the cup, before the meal, the parallelism between David and Jesus is striking and deliberate: "We thank you, our Father, for the holy vine of David Your servant, which You made known to us through Jesus Your Servant" (9.2).[41] The "holy vine of David" cannot be taken as a reference to the sacrificial blood of Christ, since Did makes no reference to the death or the resurrection of Christ nor to the atonement on the cross. Instead, the allusion is more likely to the covenant people of Israel whom God brought up out of Egypt (as in Ps 80:8-16) and/or to the house of David as the "shoot/branch of David," which God has restored and made known to those who join the community by Jesus his successor. A similar understanding lies behind John 15:1-11. A prayer for the

---

[40] See Draper, "Sacrifice," 223–52.

[41] Translation by M. B. Riddle from Roberts/Donaldson/Coxe, *Fathers*, 380.

restoration of the "shoot of David" is also found in the fifteenth benediction of the *Shemoneh `Esreh*. That this understanding goes back to the Second Temple period of can be seen also in the hope for the restoration of the "shoot/branch of David" as expressed in 4QFlor 1.7-13.

While the reference to the vine of David in Did may be somewhat cryptic, it seems that its background lies in an expectation of the renewal of Israel through the restoration of the house of David in the last days.

This is supported by the second reference to David in 10.6. H54 has "Let grace come and let this world pass away. Hosanna to the God of David! . . . Maranatha. Amen," while the third- or fourth-century Coptic version has "Let the Lord come and let this world pass away. Hosanna to the house of David! . . . Maranatha!" Given the sensitive nature of any reference to the "house of David" after the two rebellions against Rome in 68–70 C.E. and 120 C.E., the Coptic text appears likely to offer the earliest text. AposCon at this point has the "Maranatha! Hosanna to the Son of David. Blessed be He who comes in the Name of the Lord! The Lord God, who became man," suggesting an independent modification of the tradition for the same reasons. Matthew 29:9, to which the AposCon version draws attention, provides an interesting parallel to this text in its account of Jesus' triumphal entry into Jerusalem (echoing Ps 117:25-26 LXX), but is unlikely, in my opinion, to be the origin of this prayer in Did. Either way, the conclusion of the eucharistic prayers with μαραναθά ("Come Lord!"—the Aramaic imperative is indicated by the opening imperative in the Coptic text, ἐλθέτω ὁ κύριος), seems to indicate that the reference to David again has Jesus in mind as the descendant and successor of David, who has made his house known to the community. In the light of the orientation of Did as "teaching of the Lord through the Twelve Apostles to the Gentiles," one can conclude that Gentiles are understood as coming to know eschatological Israel through their membership of the community. This goes no further than the eschatological expectation of Isaiah 55:3-5.

Supersessionism is not implied here, but instead a fulfillment of the hope for the homecoming of Israel from the Diaspora, which will also result in bringing the righteous Gentiles near to God.

The closeness of this concept to the prophecies of Isaiah is not accidental in the light of the use of the title παῖς θεοῦ for Jesus as well as for David. This παῖς-Christology seems most likely to derive from the Suffering Servant songs of Isaiah. The use of the title in Did seems to indicate that it was understood by this community as a reference to a Davidic figure. The well-known Psalm 2:7 sees David as υἱὸς θεοῦ, but the use of the παῖς points to the righteous servant of God in Isaiah whose sufferings and death have atoned for the transgressions of Israel (Isa 53:11-12). This indicates that Jesus' status as son of David is linked with his righteous suffering, through which he atoned for the sins of Israel and through which he has made known the "vine of David" to his people and now to the nations. He is the χριστός

one through whom God has restored the kingdom of David, although he is not addressed directly as king and the kingdom remains the kingdom of God (cf. the ambivalence in Ezek 34:25).

The clue here provided by the understanding of Jesus as the παῖς θεοῦ of the house of David, whose righteous sufferings atones for the sins of Israel, finds further support in the eschatological material in 16.7. As I have shown elsewhere, this text cited from Zechariah 14:5 is used also in rabbinic writings concerned with the resurrection of the righteous.[42] Jesus, the righteous suffering servant of God, will come with all the other righteous departed, the "holy ones," on the clouds of heaven, probably to judge the living, though that is unclear because the text breaks off here. A consistent picture is drawn of God as the all-powerful Creator who cares for all his creatures, although he gives particular spiritual gifts to those in the community. There is likewise a consistent picture of Jesus and his followers based on a Davidic reading of the παῖς θεοῦ. And just as God's Suffering Servant is raised through his righteousness, so too the community of those who believe are called above all to holiness, through which alone they will receive eternal life.

4.3 The Spirit

The first thing to observe with the Spirit in Did is that it is overwhelmingly seen as the Spirit of prophecy. Much is made of the "wandering charismatics" of Did, but in fact the Spirit is only brought into connection with prophets, who do indeed seem to come from outside but are also seen as settling in the community. Certainly, apostles are mentioned together with prophets (11.3), and fraudulent apostles are called "false prophets." Likewise, elsewhere teachers are mentioned together with prophets (13.1-2; 15.1-2). They can expect certain subsistence from the community if they are genuine, while bishops and deacons (patrons of the community) cannot.[43]

Characteristic of the prophets is that they are speaking the word of God and cannot be tested or judged by members of the community (11.7). To test a prophet speaking in the Spirit is an unforgivable sin (cf. Deut 18:18-22).

The prophet speaking in the name of God must be heard and obeyed, but not everyone who claims to be a prophet is in fact a prophet, as Did also recognizes (11.8). This creates a dangerous situation indeed, for any community. Deuteronomy institutes the test of the fulfillment of the prophecy, and this is interpreted by *Did* in terms of the lifestyle of the prophet (as also in Matt 7:15-23, "You will know them by their fruits"). The "way of life of the Lord" (τοὺς τρόπους κυρίου) differentiates the true from the false prophet (e.g., 11.9-10, 12). On the other hand, the tried and proven prophet may behave in a singular or bizarre manner

---

[42] Draper, "Resurrection," 155–79.   [43] See Draper, "Apostles," 139–76.

like the prophets of old and act out an "earthly mystery of the church."[44] This manner of dealing with the problem of prophecy on the basis of Deuteronomy 18:18 is found also in 11QT.

However, the Spirit does occur once in another enigmatic passage from the Two Ways (4.10), which is found also in Barn, DocApos, and the Can: "You shall not enjoin anything in your bitterness upon your bondman or maidservant, who hope in the same God, lest ever they shall fear not God who is over both; for he comes not to call according to the outward appearance, but unto them whom the Spirit has prepared."[45] Niederwimmer[46] sees this as "scarcely conceivable in the presumed Jewish production" and sees it as a Christian addition. He also thinks that the one who has come "to call" must refer to Jesus and hence that "the name of God implicitly refers to Jesus." This is quite uncalled for. The background seems to me to lie in the concept of the new covenant in Jeremiah 31:31-34 and more particularly Ezekiel 11:17-20. This understanding dominates the *Manual of Discipline* at Qumran also, where it occurs several times and, notably, in the Two Ways section in 1QS 3.13–4.26.

Did understands all the members of the community, high and low, slave-owner and slave, as entering the new covenant and so as being cleansed by the Spirit which God puts in their heart. Of course, the Spirit is found also in the Trinitarian baptismal formula, which is probably a later redaction, of which more will be said later.

4.4 Eschatology

There is no agreement among scholars as to the extent and intensity of eschatological expectation in Did. Key to any answer to this question is the eschatology of the eucharistic prayers, and whether the fervent prayer for the "coming of the Lord" (Jesus? *Adonai*?) refers to the presence of God in the sacrament or to his expected return to gather his people into the eschatological kingdom. There is nothing to suggest such sacramental theology in the nature of the prayers themselves. On the contrary, the additional material consistently presents a hope for the ingathering of the Diaspora of Israel, together with the righteous Gentiles, and the coming of the kingdom. As we have seen, this notion is in harmony with the Davidic Christology of the eucharistic prayers and with the prayer for the coming of the kingdom and the implementation of the will of the Father

---

44 The text is cryptic and there are variants in the ancient Coptic and Ethiopic versions which suggest that H54 may not contain the oldest text. Knopf, *Lehre*, 32–33 and A. Adam, "Erwägungen," 1–47, suggest that it refers to the practice of *syzygy*—a prophet traveling with a prophetess as a spiritual partner—or some other form of

asceticism, but there is no evidence for this in the text and it would run counter to the concessive spirit of Did ("do what you can").
45 Translation by M. B. Riddle from Roberts/Donaldson/Coxe, *Fathers*, 378.
46 Niederwimmer, *Didache*, 142–44.

"as in heaven so on earth" in Did's version of the Lord's Prayer in 8.2 (derived from Q material).

God has revealed the eschatological vine of David through Jesus his child/servant, symbolized by the cup of wine (9.2), and has opened up the way "for life and knowledge" that he has made known to the community, symbolized by the bread (9.3). This bread made into one out of the wheat scattered on the mountain is the ground for the hope expressed in the following prayer for the ingathering of the church "from the four corners of the earth" into God's kingdom (9.4). Likewise, in the parallel thanksgiving prayers after the meal, the thanksgiving for God's power as παντοκράτωρ is the ground for the hope and prayer that "You will free Your Church from all evil and complete it in love. And bring them together from the four winds, the sanctified, in Your kingdom that You have prepared for them" (10.5). The confidence in God's power to effect this is in turn the basis for the exclamation of praise: "Let the Lord come and let this world pass away! Hosanna to the House of David!" (10.6). Everything suggests a very "this-worldly" expectation for the restoration of Israel and the "house of David which is fallen," in line with the prophetic tradition, though it will be God who effects it and not a human military campaign.

The eschatological section of Did 16 begins in verse 1 with a reminder of the way of life, into which members were initiated in through the catechetical instruction, in a negative form appropriate to a warning against falling away and utilizing material found in the "Q" tradition in a form similar but not identical to Luke 12:35. Certainly, the eschatological teaching is designed to underscore the ethical instruction of the Two Ways, and indeed the Jewish Two Ways probably also ended with an eschatological warning, but it does not necessarily mean that eschatological expectation has now ceased or declined—otherwise the teaching could hardly be expected to reenforce ethical behavior! There does not seem to be any apology here for the delay of the παρουσία. Everything hinges on faithful fulfillment of that way of life.

At the heart of the eschatological teaching is the admonition, "Be prepared!" followed by a series of four γάρ clauses giving reasons for the urgency of their readiness in the present (16.2-4a) and a series of four τότε clauses giving predictions of eschatological events yet to come in the future (16.4b-8). The causal clauses are related to apostasy in the Christian movement and the quarrels of the community with other groups.

The warning of the hour of the coming of the Lord (in the first clause) points forward to the coming of the Lord on the clouds [to judge the living but not the dead] in the last of the τότε clauses in verse 6. No doubt the regular gathering[47] with other members of the community served to keep expectation alive by the

---

[47] Though Khomych, "Admonition," 121–41, has recently argued that πυκνῶς means "frequent" and not "numerous."

kind of invocation of the Lord (*maranatha!*) and the prayer for ingathering into the kingdom discussed already in chapters 9–10. However, it also points to the ongoing judgment of community members by their peers seen in 2.6-7, 4.3, 15.3 based on the archetype of Leviticus 19:17 and also based on the exclusion of those members who wronged others in 14.2-3. This involved confession of sins against God (4.14; cf. 14.1). It also involved acknowledging sins against one's neighbor and obtaining forgiveness (14.2-3). Whoever sinned in this regard risked exclusion from the community as a pure and holy temple for the offering of sacrifice (of prayer and righteousness) to God. Being gathered together frequently was thus a very real way of ensuring one was "made perfect" by the time of the coming of the Lord, as indicated by the second of the γάρ clauses.[48] The last two clauses emphasize the necessity of watchfulness against false prophets and corrupters, who used to be accepted members of the community—since these sheep "will be turned into wolves" (στραφήσονται) and love "will turn into hate" (στραφήσεται). This is linked to the increase in "Torah-breaking" (ἀνομία),[49] which leads the renegades from the community to persecute and betray them. It does seem to have a specific agreement with Matthew 24:9-12, where the corrupters come from outside, with regard to the present experience of the community.[50]

The three τότε clauses in 16.4b-8 are also interesting for their particular theological emphasis, compared with the Matthean text, with which it shares close affinities. The first three clauses lead up to the final τότε clause which envisages the Lord coming on the clouds with his holy ones.

Unfortunately, the final clause breaks off and H54 leaves a lacuna in its transcription, signaling that it was aware that there was further text. Probably it contained a judgment scene similar to that which remains in the parallel in the AposCon, but despite attempts to reconstruct the lost text, nothing can be said for certain here.[51] The picture envisages first the appearance of the "World Deceiver," secondly the purification of the saints in the fire of testing—as in Malachi 3:3-4, thirdly a series of signs indicates the approach of the end, and finally the coming of the Lord on the clouds with the saints [to judge the earth]. This is a traditional Jewish eschatological scenario, based on interpretation of the Hebrew Scriptures.

The resurrection of only the righteous is an important idea that originates in the Maccabean martyr cult. The righteous saints who were martyred will be vindicated when they are raised by God and return to accompany the Son of Man in judgment of the nations and of the wicked in Israel. It draws particularly on Zechariah 14:5, in a way parallel to 1 Thessalonians 3:13; 4:14-18 (cf. Matt 27:52-53).

---

[48] See Draper, "Sacrifice"; also Sandt, "Windows," 173–92.

[49] The word can have a more general sense, but I have chosen to see in it a reference to abandoning Torah, in line with my general hypothesis of the text's origin.

[50] See Draper, "Torah." Signals and warnings concerning the danger of seduction by renegades occur in 4.1-13, 11.1-2.

[51] For a discussion, see Aldridge, "Ending," 1–15.

This provides the clue to the absence from Did of any reference to the cross, death and resurrection of Jesus. The emphasis is not on the death as atonement, but on the coming on the clouds as vindication of Jesus, who is the Suffering Servant. His return in the company of all the suffering righteous of Israel will inaugurate the restoration of the kingdom with himself as its king, restoring the vine of David.

4.5 Ecclesiology

Like Matthew (16:18; 18:15, 17, 21), Did uses the word ἐκκλησία to describe its community. The first occasion in 4.14, attested only by H54, probably represents an interpolation into the Two Ways. It is important to note that, even if this occurrence of ἐκκλησία in 4.14 is genuine, it envisages no more than confessing in the *assembly*. The church is not envisaged as an "institution" nor as the "body of Christ" as Paul would describe it, but simply a gathering of the community. This aspect is even more prominent in the two occurrences of the word in the eucharistic prayers 9.4, 10.5, since in both cases the reference is to the ingathering of the dispersed ἐκκλησία "into your kingdom." What lies behind it is the concept of the assembly of Israel which is also the assembly of God (since it is "your ἐκκλησία"). It stands in continuity with the Jewish tradition found also in the early Jewish prayers, the *Shemoneh Esreh*, petition 10: "Sound the great horn for our freedom; raise the ensign to gather our exiles, and gather us from the four corners of the earth. Blessed art thou, O Lord, who gathers the dispersed of Your people Israel." I have argued elsewhere that the threefold series of the blowing of the *shophar*, the raising of the banner, and the gathering of the exiles comes from the holy war tradition of the Hebrew Scriptures and that it lies behind the three signs of Did 16.6.[52] The same series appears also in 1QM 4.9 (cf. 1QSa 1.25, 2.4).

The most significant aspect of the assembly is that it is holy and its members are the holy ones (e.g., 4.2).[53] Because God's holy name dwells in the hearts of the members as a spiritual temple, the community is holy also. His name is to be sanctified (8.2) through the sanctification of the community. As members of the ingathering of eschatological Israel, they are called to be holy. Therefore, they need to be perfected (τελειῶσαι αὐτήν) and sanctified (τὴν ἁγιασθεῖσαν) before they are gathered into the kingdom (10.5). Only those who are holy may "come" or else they need to repent. The holiness of God, present in the community in his holy name, and the holiness of the community as his eschatological spiritual temple are preserved by maintaining purity. While the full purity code of the Torah is not required of members, there is a concern with the purity of water (7.1-3); with eating food offered to idols (6.3); with the purity of those sharing the community meal (9.5); and with participating in the prayers of the community while quarreling with other members, which defiles "your pure sacrifice" (14.2).

---

[52] Draper, "Sign."

[53] The noun occurs eight times (4.2; 7.1, 3; 9.2, 5; 10.2, 6; 16.7) and the verb twice (8.2; 10.5).

A citation of Malachi 1:11, 14 (differing from LXX) sums up Did 14.3.[54] This holiness is expressed ethically, as we have seen, in life according to the Two Ways (1–6), in hospitality to those traveling "in the Name of the Lord" (12), in giving "firstfruits" to support the teachers and prophets (13), in living justly with other members of the community (14, 15.2-3).

The community also practices an intense common life, characterized by frequent meetings (e.g., 4.2, 16.2), love (e.g., 1.2-4; 2.7) and sharing. Sharing is the most significant, because in this way the member shares in God's own gracious generosity and receives God's blessing (1.5-6); giving, if one has anything to share, is an obligation because it is actually giving to God himself (4.7) and paying a ransom for one's sins (4.6).

The sacraments as understood by the community reflect the concern with purity: baptism is nowhere referred to as a baptism of repentance for the forgiveness of sins as in the Synoptic Gospels and Paul, but rather as conferring purity (7.2-3), and placing under the name of God (7.1, 3; 9.5). The Eucharist is a full meal in which the prayers give thanks to God for particular acts of salvation history, in the Jewish fashion.[55] There is no sign of the words of Institution. Indeed, there is even flexibility it would seem in the way the prayers offered in the text may be offered (10.7). There is no mention of the cross, death, resurrection, body and blood of Jesus. The cup comes before the breaking of bread and before a full meal, while prayers are offered in the same style after the meal (and may have included further cups of wine in the Jewish style; cf. Luke 22:17-20). The thanksgiving after the meal gives thanks for the name dwelling in their hearts and for the spiritual food and drink shared in the community. There has been a widespread attempt to defy the obvious absence of the words of institution by supplying them in the gap created by the final words, "If anyone is holy let that person come; if anyone is not let that person repent." However, it is in my opinion a matter of special pleading.[56]

Finally, it must be observed that there is no "threefold order of ministry." Instead, as 15.1-2 shows, there is a twofold local leadership of bishops, actually "overseers" with responsibilities for exercising control, and deacons, who are functionaries with some practical role in the community. They must be tested before they are appointed, unlike the prophets (11.7). The way they are installed is ambivalent, since χειροτονήσατε could refer to election by raising hands or to

---

[54]   See Gordon, "Parallels," 285–89.

[55]   The prayers are close enough to the much later *Birkath Hamazon* to have led some scholars to argue—improbably in my opinion—for *literary* dependence and *redaction* of a Jewish text. See Riggs, "Table," 83–102. There simply is no evidence for a fixed literary form of the *Birkath Hamazon* earlier than the mid-second century or even the fourth

century, and it is far more likely that it represented a broad and oral cultural tradition. For analysis of the rite, see Draper, "Ritual Process."

[56]   Most recently, Claussen, "Eucharist," 135–63, emphasizes the variety of forms of the Eucharist in the earliest communities; Schwiebert, *Knowledge*, traces its extensive influence from early Christian Jewish meal ritual to its final disappearance.

laying on of hands. In addition they must be "meek" men (πραεῖς) and honest (ἀληθεῖς), indicating that they will need to resolve the kind of quarrels in the community signaled by 14.2 and 15.3. In any case, the qualities required of them suggest that they are patrons of the community who would be wealthier members of the community respected in the broader society outside: they must not be "lovers of money" (ἀφιλάργυροι)—in other words, they must be prepared to share their resources as patrons in exchange for "honor" (τιμή) in the fashion of the ancient Mediterranean world. The honor accorded prophets and teachers jeopardizes their position and therefore the stability of the community. Did resolves this tension by advocating that they be given equal honor, since they share the same λειτουργία (15.1), by which I understand the performance of a public duty for the good of the community. However, there is clearly some tension around issues of leadership, in which there is no hierarchical order as yet.[57]

5.   Reputation

Did presents a theology that has consistently defied attempts to fit it into the usual evolutionary schemas of early Christian life. It remains firmly within the confines of first-century Judaism, albeit with its own emphasis and its own claim to represent the authentic tradition of Israel. In this it goes no further than the Essenes and the rabbis, among other Jewish groups in competition for dominance in the first century. The question as to who represented authentic Israel was intensified after the fall of Jerusalem, and the loss of the temple and sacrifice as points of reference, but it did not begin there since traditions of a spiritual temple and sacrifice were already promoted by these groups to some extent. Chapter 8 shows that the closest rivals of the Did community were the Pharisees, whom it designates as "hypocrites," but the theology presented by the text itself is close at most points to what we know from the rabbis who were heirs to the Pharisaic tradition.[58] The points at which they diverge, in my opinion, remain the question of the role of Jesus as son/servant of God in the line of David and the gift of the Spirit as a mark of the dawn of the eschatological age of the new covenant. Everything suggests that this enigmatic text preserves an insight into the earliest age of the movement that saw Jesus as the Messiah of Israel and that had taken the step of admitting Gentiles into the eschatological community on the basis of their understanding of the prophets of the Hebrew Scriptures and on the basis of their understanding of the universal laws and the role of Torah as binding only on Israel.

---

[57] For a more detailed discussion, see Draper, "Apostles."

[58] Draper, "Self-Definition," 223–43.

6.   Bibliography

Adam, A. "Erwägungen zur Herkunft der Didache." *ZNW* 46 (1955): 266–67; with the same title also: *ZKG* 68 (1957): 1–47.

Aldridge, R. E. "The Lost Ending of the Didache." *VC* 53 (1999): 1–15.

Audet, J.-P. "Affinités littéraires et doctrinales du 'Manuel de discipline.'" *RB* 59 (1952): 219–38.

———. *La Didachè*. Paris 1958.

Bausi, A. "San Clemente e le Tradizioni Clementine nella Letteratura Etiopica Canonico-Liturgica." In *Studi su Clemente romano: Atti degli Incontri di Roma, 29 marzo e 22 novembre 2001*, edited by P. Luisier, 13–55. OCA 268. Rome 2003.

Boyarin, D. *Border Lines: The Partition of Judaeo-Christianity*. Philadelphia 2004.

Claussen, C. "The Eucharist in the Gospel of John and in the Didache." In *Trajectories through the New Testament and the Apostolic Fathers*, edited by A. F. Gregory and C. M. Tuckett, 135–63. Oxford 2005.

Crossan, J. D. "The Resurrection of Jesus in its Jewish Context." *Neot* 37 (2003): 37–65.

Daniélou, J. *Théologie du Judéo-Christianisme I*. Paris 1958.

Deutsch, C. *Hidden Wisdom and the Easy Yoke: Wisdom, Torah, and Discipleship in Matthew 11:25-30*. JSNT.S 18. Sheffield 1987.

Dihle, A. *Die golden Regel: Eine Einführung in die Geschichte der antiken und frühchristlichen Vulgärethik*. StAW 7. Göttingen 1962.

Draper, J. A. *A Commentary on the Didache in the Light of the Dead Sea Scrolls and Related Documents*. Diss. Cambridge University 1983.

———. "A Continuing Enigma: The 'Yoke of the Lord' in Didache 6:2-3 and Early Jewish-Christian Relations." In *The Image of Judaeo-Christians in Ancient Jewish and Christian Literature*, edited by P. J. Tomson and D. Lambers-Petry, 106–23. Tübingen 2003.

———. "Apostles, Teachers, and Evangelists: Stability and Movement of Functionaries in Matthew, James, and the Didache." In Sandt and Zangenberg, *Matthew, James, and Didache*, 139–76.

———. "Barnabas and the Riddle of the Didache." *JSNT* 58 (1995), 89–113.

———. "Christian Self-Definition against the 'Hypocrites' in *Didache* 8." In Draper, *The Didache in Modern Research*, 223–43.

———. "Lactantius and the Jesus Tradition in the Didache." *JThS* 40 (1989): 112–16.

———. "Pure Sacrifice in Didache 14 as Jewish Christian Exegesis." *Neot* 42 (2008): 223–52.

———. "Resurrection and Zechariah 14.5 in the Didache Apocalypse." *JECS* 5 (1997): 155–79.

———. "Ritual Process and Ritual Symbol in Didache 7–10." *VC* 54 (2000): 1–38.

———. "The Development of the 'Sign of the Son of Man' in the Jesus Tradition." *NTS* 39 (1993): 1–21.

———, ed. *The Didache in Modern Research*. AGJU 37. Leiden 1996.

———. "The Didache in Modern Research: An Overview." In Draper, *The Didache in Modern Research*, 1–42.

————. "The Genesis and Narrative Thrust of the Paraenesis in the Sermon on the Mount." *JSNT* 75 (1999): 25–48.

————. "The Jesus Tradition in the *Didache*." In Draper, *The Didache in Modern Research*, 269–89.

————. "Torah and Troublesome Apostles in the Didache Community." *NovT* 33 (1991): 347–72.

Flusser, D. "Paul's Jewish Opponenets in the Didache." In Draper, *The Didache in Modern Research*, 195–211.

Garrow, A. J. P. *The Gospel of Matthew's Dependence on the Didache*. London 2004.

Harnack, A. von. *Die Lehre der zwölf Apostel nebst Untersuchungen zur ältesten Geschichte der Kirchenverfassung und des Kirchenrechts*. TU 2.1-2. Leipzig 1884.

————. *Die Mission und Ausbreitung des Christentums in den ersten drei Jahrhunderten*. Leipzig 1902.

Horner, G. *The Statutes of the Apostles*. London 1904.

Jackson-McCabe, M. "What's in a Name? The Problem of 'Jewish Christianity.'" In *Jewish Christianity Reconsidered: Rethinking Ancient Groups and Texts*, 7–38. Minneapolis 2007.

Jefford, C. N. "The Milieu of Matthew, the Didache, and Ignatius of Antioch: Agreements and Differences." In Sandt, *Matthew*, 35–47.

Jones, F. S., and P. A. Mirecki. "Considerations on the Coptic Papyrus of Did. (British Library Oriental Manuscript 9271)." In *The Didache in Context: Essays on its Text, History, and Transmission*, edited by C. N. Jefford, 47–87. Leiden 1995.

Khomych, T. "The Admonition to Assemble Together in Didache 16.2 Reappraised." *VC* 61 (2007): 121–41.

Kloppenborg, J. S. "Didache 1.1–6.1, James, Matthew, and the Torah." In *Trajectories through the New Testament and the Apostolic Fathers*, edited by A. F. Gregory and C. M. Tuckett, 193–221. Oxford 2005.

Knopf, R. *Die Lehre der zwölf Apostel, 2 Clemensbriefe*. HNT 1. Tübingen 1920.

Köster, H. *Synoptische Überlieferung bei den Apostolischen Väter*. TU 65. Berlin 1957.

Kraft, R. A. *Barnabas and the Didache*. Vol. 3 of *The Apostolic Fathers*, edited by R. M. Grant. New York 1965.

Metzger, M. *Les constitutions apostoliques III, Livres VII et VIII*. SC 336. Paris 1987.

Milavec, A. *The Didache: Faith, Hope, and Life of the Earliest Christian Communities, 50–70 C.E.* New York 2003.

Mueller, J. G. "The Ancient Church Order Literature: Genre or Tradition?" *JECS* 15 (2007): 337–80.

Murphy-O'Connor, J. "Genèse Littéraire de la Règle de la Communauté." *RB* 76 (1969): 528–49.

Niederwimmer, K. *Die Didache*. KAV 1. Göttingen 1989.

————. "Zur Entwicklungsgeschichte des Wanderradikalismus im Traditionsbereich der Didache." *WSt* 90 (1977): 145–67.

Nissen, A. *Gott und der Nächste im antiken Judentum: Untersuchung zum Doppelgebot der Liebe*. WUNT 15. Tübingen 1974.

Peterson, E. "Didache cap. 9 e 10." *EphLit* 58 (1944): 3–13.

Riggs, J. W. "From Gracious Table to Sacramental Elements: The Tradition-History of Didache 9 and 10." *Second Century* 4 (1984): 83–102.

Rordorf, W. "Beobachtungen zum Gebrauch des Dekalogs in der vorkonstantinischen Kirche." In *The New Testament Age: Essays in Honor of Bo Reicke* II, edited by W. C. Weinrich, 431–42. Macon, Ga. 1984.

Rordorf, W., and A. Tuilier. *La Doctrine des douze apôtres.* Paris 1998.

Sandt, H. v. d., ed. *Matthew and the Didache: Two Documents from the Same Jewish-Christian Milieu?* Assen 2005.

———. "Two Windows on a Developing Jewish-Christian Reproof Practice: Matt. 18:15-17 and Did. 15:3." In Sandt, *Matthew*, 173–92.

Sandt, H. v. d., and D. Flusser. *The Didache: Its Jewish Sources and Its Place in Early Judaism and Christianity.* CRINT 5. Assen 2002

Sandt, H. v. d., and J. K. Zangenberg, eds. *Matthew, James, and Didache: Three Related Documents in their Jewish and Christian Settings.* Symposium Series 45. Atlanta 2008.

Schöllgen, G. "Die Didache als Kirchenordnung: Zur Frage des Abfassungszweckes und seinen Konsequenzen für die Interpretation." *JAC* 29 (1986): 5–26.

———. "Die Didache—ein frühes Zeugnis für Landgemeinden?" *ZNW* 76 (1985): 140–43.

———. *Didache: Zwölf-Apostel-Lehre; Traditio Apostolica: Apostolische Überlieferung.* FC 1. Freiburg 1991.

Schwiebert, J. *Knowledge and the Coming Kingdom: The Didache's Meal Ritual and Its Place in Early Christianity.* London 2008.

Smith, E. C. "Did Justin Know the Didache?" In *StPatr* 7:287–90. TU 92. Berlin 1966.

Steimer, B. *Vertex Traditionis: Die Gattung der altchristlichen Kierchenordnung.* Berlin 1992.

Stendahl, K. *Paul among Jews and Gentiles.* Philadelphia 1977.

Stuiber, A. "Das ganze Joch des Herrn (Didache 6:2-3)." In *StPatr* 4:323–29. TU 79. Berlin 1961.

Verme, M. del. *Didache and Judaism: Jewish Roots of an Ancient Christian-Jewish Work.* New York 2004.

Wedderburn, A. J. M. "The 'Apostolic Decree': Tradition and Redaction." *NovT* 35 (1993): 362–89.

Wengst, K. *Didache (Apostellehre), Barnabasbrief, Zweiter Klemensbrief, Schrift an Diognet.* SUC II. Darmstadt 1984.

Zahn, T. *Forschungen zur Geschichte der neutestamentlichen Kanons und der altkirchlichen Literatur II: Der Evangeliencommentar des Theophilus von Antiochien.* Erlangen 1881.

The Epistle of Barnabas

Ferdinand R. Prostmeier

In his 1920 commentary, Hans Windisch summarizes the peculiarity and strangeness of the Epistle of Barnabas by saying that its content "really starts from only the most radical statements of the New Testament [. . .] and yet Barn. is also more conservative than all the others, insofar as it views the entire Old Testament, including the Pentateuch, as a still valid textbook from which the church takes the mysteries of the work of Christ and the instructions for its members."[1] Windisch thus expresses something of the attraction and the meaning of this early Christian document that does not readily disclose itself immediately.

1. Textual Tradition and Attestation[2]

The full text of the Epistle of Barnabas (Barn) survives only in the famous codices Sinaiticus (ℵ, 01)[3] and Hierosolymitanus 54 (H).[4] Four further textual witnesses[5]—including a Latin translation (L),[6] a papyrus (P)[7] and a Syriac fragment

---

[1] Windisch, *Barnabasbrief,* 395

[2] For more, see Prostmeier, *Barnabasbrief,* 11–46; idem, *Überlieferung,* 48–64.

[3] Cod. Sinaiticus (ℵ), 4th c., Barn 1.1–21.9 on fol. 334ʳ–340ᵛ.

[4] Cod. Hierosolymitanus 54 (H), 1056 in Byzantium, Barn 1.1–21.9 on fol. 39ʳ–51ᵛ.

[5] The Codex Vaticanus graecus 859 (v), 11th c., Barn 5.7–21.9 on fol. 198ʳᵃ17–211ᵛᵃ23, archetype of nine Greek Renaissance manuscripts that in three families constitute the witness G in modern editions. In eight of the Greek descendants Barn 5.7–21.9 is appended as in v to PhilPol 1.1–9.2 without transition. Funk, *Descendenten* 629–37, following Gebhardt/Harnack, *Barnabae Epistula,* uses the evidence to reach the sigil G for the codices he consulted. Funk, who was preparing his edition of the Letters of Ignatius and had preserved a copy of the epistles from H for that purpose, was primarily interested in the Ignatian corpus of the abovementioned Greek manuscripts, which is why he also noted manuscripts that did not uphold the textual connection between PhilPol and Barn, e.g., "Codex Paris, Suppl. gr. 341" (cf. *Codex Paris, Suppl. gr.* 633–34). The common result of his studies is also valid for the textual history of PhilPol and Barn, albeit not compelling for a linear descent, but rather leads to a branching descent. Cf. Lightfoot, *Apostolic Fathers* II.1.114 and his caveat: "But possibly a closer examination of other parts might show the relation is not quite so simple." Cf. Prostmeier, *Überlieferung,* 48–64. On the manuscript tradition of the Greek texts of 1/2 PhilPol cf. now Bauer, *Polykarpbriefe,* 13–15. A further descendent (Cod. Vat. Gr. 1909) is corrupted and now contains only Barn 10.3–21.9; cf. the collation in Prostmeier, *Barnabasbrief,* 611–20.

[6] Cod. Petropolitanus Q. v. I. 39 (L), 9th–10th c., in the nonbiblical portions 3rd or 2nd c. (Λ), Barn 1.1–17.2 on fol. 8ʳ6–20ʳ7.

[7] Papyrus PSI 757ᵇ (P), 3rd–5th c., Barn 9.31–36; the textual variants are similar to G.

(sy)[8]—are fragmentary; an Armenian translation is attested[9] but lost. The validation of the textual variants is in the case of Barn complicated on two fronts. First, the genesis of the textual witnesses is only settled from their roots. Despite their gaps and despite the translation, one manuscript or another of the fragmentary witnesses (G, L, sy, P) contains variants such as those drawn from א, which originates from the fourth century. Second, the indirect transmission is very sparse and the witnesses are controversial in their text-critical worth. Most notably the text construction varies. With good reason some editors rely on one of the four major manuscripts (א, H, G, L) or follow one of these four on a case-by-case basis.[10]

The evidence for Barn places it in the second half of the second century. Apparently Justin, the Valentinian Marcus, Irenaeus and Tertullian knew it. [11] The oldest of the four certain patristic witnesses for Barn is Clement of Alexandria (Cl). Not only does he cite the text repeatedly,[12] but he also frequently notes whence he takes the quote, namely, from the "Letter of Barnabas." Its author is for him the "fellow laborer with Paul" known from Acts, 1 Corinthians and Galatians (Strom II 20.116.3; V 10.63.1; fr. 70); he denotes him as an "apostolic man" (Strom II 20.116.3) as well as an "apostle" (Strom II 6.31.2, 7.35.5) and numbers him among the "seventy" (Strom II 20.116.3). Through Cl it is certain that this text was known to him as "the Letter of Barnabas" and that the argumentative power and dignity of an "apostolic writing" were granted to it at the turn of the third century. After Cl only three verses from Barn were quoted: Barn 5.9 appears in abridged form in Origen (Cels I.63);[13] in the second half of the third century the anonymous text Περὶ πατρὸς καὶ υἱοῦ quotes from Barn 5.4 and 6.12 and Didymus of Alexandria quotes from Barn 19.12. Barn obviously possessed some esteem in Alexandrian theology even at the end of the fourth century, which appears plausible from its inclusion in Cod. When Barn, after being excluded from the New Testament canon at the turn of the fourth century, is listed in

---

8   Cod. Cantabrigiensis Univ. Add. 2023 (sy), written by two copyists in Jacobite Syriac, 13th c., Barn 19.1-2, 8 and 20.1 on fol. 61ᵛ. The pattern reaches back to the sixth century and is closer to א and H than to G and L.

9   The manuscript (v) contains the following Armenian translator's note on fol. 211ᵛᵃ25–30, which presumably comes from Nerses IV of Klah (1166–1173) and refers to the textual association of PhilPol 1.1–9.2 with Barn 5.7–21.9: "I, Nerses, have translated this letter in the Armenian language, in the royal city, to the glory of Christ our God, to whom be ever praise. Amen."

10   Cf. Prostmeier, Barnabasbrief, 63–74; for more on the editions and modern translations cf. Barnabasbrief 12–34, 578–80; idem, Barnabasbrief, 108–10.

11   Cf. Tert Marc 3.7 and Spect 30 (to Barn 7.3-11). Here it occurred in Vir ill 5 that Tert Pud 20 falsely or mistakenly ascribed a quotation from Hebrews to Barn and called him "receptior apud ecclesias [. . .] illo apocrypho Pastore."

12   Of twenty-eight citations, Cl includes seventeen in five compositions. Verbatim Cl includes Barn 1.5; 2.2-3, 5, 7-8, 10; 4.11; 6.5, 8-10; 10.1, 3-3, 9-12; 11.4, 9; 16.7-9; 21.5-6, 9 and alludes to Barn 2.10; 4.8; 5.1, 11; 9.8; 10.3-4, 6-7, 11; 14.5; 19.4. A peculiarity is Barn 3.1-5, since Cl appears to have presented both Barn and Isaiah 58:4b-5, 7b-8. Cf. Prostmeier, Barnabasbrief, 34–46.

13   Barn 5.9 appears twice in Jerome (ca. 347–419/20), though scarcely independent from Or Cels I.63; for more, see Prostmeier, Barnabasbrief, 46–56; Lona, Kelsos, 112n489.

textual witnesses from the Eastern Church, the Greeks consistently classify it with ApcPetr; ActPaul, Herm, Did, as well as the Ignatian corpus, are further companion pieces, but not regularly or not included in the same class. While this tradition persists for the western Syrian-speaking realm until the eleventh century and for the Armenian church until the fourteenth century, the manuscript tradition of Barn shows that in the Greek East the combination with the Ignatian letters, 1 and 2 Clement, and the Didache already dominates (H), while a short time later the Greek tradition in the West (G) lost sight of Barn through a textual corruption. That no sign of Barn remains in the Western Church, apart from the Latin translations (Λ and L) that soon fell into oblivion, is evident from the fact that the Occident, although it knew of the Letter of Barnabas and had quotations from it, first became acquainted with the text of Barn through the editions of Ussher (1642) and Ménard (1645), but even then only fragmentarily in a Latin translation (L) and through manuscripts of the witness G until the discovery of א.[14]

2.   Structure, Composition, and Genre

2.1 Literary Integrity, Construction, Organization

The literary and form-critical analyses have turned out to be threefold. First, Barn contained from the beginning the text handed down in א and H. Second, one meets thereafter traditions in which two tradition complexes clash in Barn 17. Third, in stylistic similarity with Barn 17, Barn 1 presents itself as a greeting and introduction and Barn 21 as the conclusion of the work and as compositional cornerstones frame two sections of varying lengths (Barn 2–16, 18–20) with one profile regarding content, form and tradition history, in which 17 not only marks the division but also transitions from the first major section to the second. From these statements the following organization becomes apparent:

1	Greeting and Introduction
2–16	First Section
17	Transition
18–20	Second Section
21	Closing

The overall arrangement of Barn and the structure of its second section, which deals with a Two Ways teaching,[15] are easily reviewed. The introduction (18.1bf.) announces with the antonyms "light" and "darkness" a dichotomy, the use of which in 19.1 (ἡ οὖν ὁδός κτλ.; cf. Did 1.2) and 20.1(ἡ δὲ τοῦ μέλνος ὁδός κτλ.; cf. Did 5.1), referring to each other, contrast the "Way of Light" (19) with the "Way of Darkness" or "of the Black One" (20), and which following Barn 2–16

---

[14] For more, see Prostmeier, *Barnabasbrief,* 56–63.   [15] See below.

communicates a "knowledge and teaching" of a different sort (cf. 18.1a). This order, dictated by the form, is absent from the first section, but the choice and sequence of the quotations from the "Scripture" and their interpretation, which together make up the bulk of Barn 2–16, is in no way arbitrary or without a plan. Both forms of discourse constantly refer to each other and one theme or one point of view underlies them both, of which the uses, transitions, and boundaries are typical and make it possible to construct a *thematic order* for Barn 2–16.

1.1-8		Greeting and Introduction
	1.1	Greeting
	1.2-8	Thanksgiving, Commending of Self, Principles
		First Section: Knowledge from the Scriptures
2.1–16.10		
	2.1-3	Introduction
	2.4–3.6	Sacrifices, Feasts, and Fasts
	4.1-14	The Present and Salvation
	5.1–8.7	The Lord and Son of God—the Purpose of His Suffering
	9.1–10.12	Obedience to God—Circumcision and Food
	11.1–12.11	Water and Cross
	13.1–14.9	"Heir-folk" and Assurance of Salvation
	15.1-9	The Sabbath and the Eighth Day
	16.1-10	Right Understanding of the Temple
17.1-2		Transition
18.1–20.2		Second Section: Knowledge from the Two Ways Teaching
	18.1-2	Transition and Introduction
	19.1-12	The Way of Light
	20.1-2	The Way of the Black One
21.1-9		Closing
	21.1	Conclusion
	21.2-8	Closing Exhortation with Commending of Self
	21.9	Eschatological Collect

2.2 Arrangement

Both sections converge thematically in that Christian faith and behavior were passed forward from the prophetic tradition and are therefore binding. For that reason and because of the axioms that everything in prophecy has a meaning and Christians are exclusively capable of understanding them, all revelations always apply to Christians. Christians' faith and rules for behavior are therefore expressions of the prophetic tradition rightly understood. The basic theme and the communication structure are aligned on two fixed points. First, the readers are by their faith competent to grasp the theme and at the same time to know how to distinguish themselves from other Christians by their foundational beliefs. Second, the author is competent to expound the theme by exempla and in a way that points ahead (1.5, 4.9a, 17.1-2). Barn is intended to ground the faith and practice of its audience and to profile other Christians in contrast by proving that the Scripture is altogether Christian in origin and then reclaiming a dual ethical catalogue as a sign of typical Christian conduct. In content Barn is planned around questions about the eschatological salvation (cf. 2.10b, 4.1, 21.1-8b); this fact is clear from the choice and organization of the themes as well as from their treatment.

2.3 Literary Character and Purpose

The opening and closing give the piece the form of a letter. Epistolary framing (Barn 1 and 21), authorial impetus (Barn 1.5, 4.9, 12.2, 21.9), universal address (Barn 1.1), claim of authority (Barn 1.1-8, 4.9, 5.3, 6.5-10 *passim*), and didactic emphasis (Barn 6.5, 7.1-9, 9.7-9 *passim*), as well as intensive quotation and interpretation of Scripture, mark Barn as a *tractate framed as a letter* that seeks to build and secure the Christian identity of its readers on the foundation of authoritative evidence (Scripture) and definitive tradition (Two Ways teaching and Christian paradosis). The occasion of Barn is a dispute over the soteriological meaning of the Christ event. The purpose is the exegetical proof that Scripture as the undisputed authoritative basis (cf. Barn 1.7-8, 5.3, 7.1, 21.1-5) points exclusively to Christ and Christians and that through them all of its promises will be fulfilled.

3.   Intertextual Relationships

3.1 Scripture and Tradition

However, on the basis of Barn 1.5, 4.9a, and 17.1-2, it is also beyond question that in Barn 2–16 the author not only cites Scripture but also works from tradition on a broad front. Among these are on one hand—sometimes precisely, sometimes only in the basic tone—quotations from Greek translations of the Bible, mainly from Isaiah, Psalms, and the Torah, but also from extracanonical works whose common core is their prophetic standing (Barn 1.7-8, 2.4a, 3.6). Barn 1.5, 4.9a, and 17.1 belong on the other side, in that even the interpretation, that is to say the gnosis of all the quotations (Barn 1.5), has its basis in interpretation traditions with which the Christian paradosis could be associated. Barn 1.8 and more in the framing chapter, especially in the authorial pretention and the interjections related to the communication structure grounded therein, make it probable that these materials have earned their profile in the scholastic realm.

Next to the thematic accentuation and the commentary, the sequence of quotations and their interpretation determines the organization of individual themes. Both are introduced formally as a rule. Three observations are foundational. First, the author cites Scripture exclusively in Greek. Second, within thematically unified sequences one encounters both verbatim and very imprecise quotations.

Third, the precision of quotations is greatest in the biblical books that are most frequently included in Barn. The largest contingent comes from Isaiah, followed by the Psalter. Far smaller is the number of quotations from Jermiah, Ezekiel, and Daniel. From the Torah only the six quotations from Genesis and the passages from Deuteronomy are significant; of Exodus, Leviticus, and Numbers there are only echoes. The high number of quotations from Isaiah, Psalms, and Genesis is also a result of the prominence of these books in early Judaism and in early Christianity.

3.2 Testimonies

Barn 9.1-3 and 11.4-5 rest on testimonies. However, neither place proves the existence of one or more collections of testimonies, never mind their function as direct sources for Barn. The material is far more likely to have been present in the tradition, sometimes repeatedly, both orally and in writing, as well as in varying spoken coinage and in various literary forms. As far as the author was at home as a student of the Alexandrian school, it would come as no surprise if, in the framework of his profession, he adapted, varied, completed, and continued traditions, also by creating new works.[16]

3.3 Relationship to the Two-Ways Tractate

The Two Ways teaching is the most consistent piece of tradition in Barn, the traditional character and coherence of which are accented by Barn 18.1 and 21.1. Not a few allusions to it in the preceding chapters, the transition in Barn 17, which requires a continuation, and the conclusions to both sections place beyond question that this block is conceptually part of Barn. The conspicuous equation of this "knowledge and teaching" with any "gnosis" that the author mines on the basis of Scripture, leads to the conclusion that he became familiar with and learned to value this parenetic material in the same context in which the traditions for the first section were present and had been cultivated. In the conclusion of Niederwemmer's analysis of the Two Ways teaching in Did 1–6 "an independent, originally Jewish source" can be assumed, one that "existed in multiple recensions"[17] and the oldest Christian version of which serves as the source for Barn 18–20.

4.   Originating Circumstances

4.1 Time of Composition

Barn 16.3-4 refers to the destruction of Herod's Temple; the *terminus post quem* is thus 70 C.E. Because of the inclusion of Barn in the works of Cl written while

---

16 Cf. Prostmeier, *Barnabasbrief,* 101–6; idem, *Art. Testimonien,* LTK³ 9, 2000, 1356–57.

17 Niederwimmer, *Didache,* 63; cf. Prostmeier, *Barnabasbrief,* 106–11.

he was still in the metropolitan of the Nile Delta,[18] Barn must have been written before 190, but definitely before 202. For a precise dating Barn 4.3-5 and 16.3-4 come back into the discussion. No reliable conclusion can be drawn from Barn 4.3-5 because of the traditional character, the apocalyptic form, and the theological intent of the entry of ὑφ' ἕν in 4.4-5. Following the overall picture of Barn, Barn 16.3-4 can refer only to the time between the outbreak of the Jewish resistance and Hadrian's building campaign, reported in Cassius Dio 69.12.1-2, that included the refounding of Jerusalem as Aelia Capitolina and the building of a Temple of Jupiter. The composition would therefore have occurred between spring of 130 and February or March of 132.[19]

4.2 Place of Origin and Destination

Barn names neither its place of origin nor its destination. Suggestions for the place of composition include: 1. Egypt, specifically Alexandria; 2. Syria or Syro-Palestine, specifically Syrian Antioch; 3. Asia Minor, particularly the western regions; 4. Greece; and 5. Rome. Sometimes a geographical commitment is renounced. Alexandria is the most plausible for five reasons. First, the reputation of Barn through Cl points to a home in the spiritual and religious milieu of Alexandria, including a correspondingly ambitious theological language and with conflicting theological options. Second, rabbinic-sounding sequences reveal the presence and almost unavoidable influence of the literature of Alexandrian and Egyptian Judaism. Apparently the author collaborated on the multilayered Christian adaptation of this tradition in the scholastic atmosphere of Alexandria; possibly some came to his awareness already transformed in a Christian manner. Third, there are parallels to texts (JosAsen, SibOr, PrePet) that belong to Egypt with greater certainty. Fourth, the sparse and barely reliable information about the history of Alexandria and the region of the Nile before the episcopacy of Demetrius and before Cl, as well as the wealth of facts about second-century Christian literature, hardly allows Alexandria to be excluded as a possible place of composition, only on the grounds that Barn is missing supposedly typical Alexandrian theological formulae or includes something atypical. Fifth, literature originating in Syria or Asia Minor that sometimes appears similar to Barn could have come to the author's attention in Alexandria if he stood and worked as a teacher in a scholastic tradition. The Christianity that Barn represents may therefore be situated in an Alexandrian milieu until convincing reasons exclude this place of composition and destination. The interpretation meanwhile turns to the programmatic anonymity.[20]

---

18 Cf. the verbatim citation of Barn 2.5 in Paed III 12.90.3 as well as the meaningful allusions to Barn 10.6-7 in Paed II 10.83.4 and to Barn 10.11 in Paed III 11.76.1-2.

19 Cf. Prostmeier, *Barnabasbrief*, 111–19.
20 Cf. Prostmeier, *Barnabasbrief*, 119–30.

4.3 Author and Title

The author is unknown. The anonymity is as programmatic as the thoughtfully chosen indeterminacy of the place of origin and destination. His identity is that of the authentic champion of the paradosis (Barn 1.5-8, 4.9, 17.1, 21.7-9), the apostolic signature of which is inherent (Barn 5.9, 8.3a), on which he also bases his authority over the reader. The inscription ΒΑΡΝΑΒΑ ΕΠΙΣΤΟΛΗ is the oldest commentary on this anonymous text. The secondary naming occurred between 135 and the last quarter of the second century, since Cl presents it. Through the epistolary framing of the piece, the "genre designation" as letter is unavoidable. However, the choice of names, astonishing due to the anti-Jewish polemic (see below), and thereby the insistence on the authorship of the Cypriot Levite Joseph mentioned in Acts, 1 Corinthians and Galatians, assumes knowledge of these Scriptures as well as an imagination of the theological propria of the "apostle with Paul" (Acts 14:14). The basis for the choice of names may have been two personal traditions: on one side about James the Lord's brother for Egypt, on the other about John Mark for Alexandria. In this context a letter from Barnabas could be fabricated that assumed this prominent persona as author. So the inscriber would have corrected a perceived defect in the epistolary introduction to the piece, namely, the missing sender's name.[21]

5.   Theological Profile

The theological theme of Barn is soteriology; christological, ecclesiological, and eschatological themes are functionally ordered toward it and take their contours from the securing of soteriology. Three factors define the profile of this early Christian theology. First, the peculiarities and the function of the appeal to tradition, among which the christocentric Scripture interpretation and its intra-Christian thrust deserves first mention. Second, the use and meaning of theological terms, especially the κύριος-concept. Third, the *kairos* of church history, in which in view an intra-Christian dissent over the soteriological relevance of the Christ event anti-Jewish polemic[22] is driven with the help of Scripture interpretation toward the point that the image of faith constructed by the author is to be authorized as solely orthodox and relevant for salvation.

5.1 Christocentric Construction of Scripture

For Barn, Christology is the hermeneutical key to Scripture as well as the theological terminology and the proofs that he takes from biblical-Jewish tradition. Scripture announces Christ and Christians. To this understanding that gives direction to interpretation (cf. Barn 12.7c) is joined the idea that the κύριος

---

[21] Cf. Prostmeier, *Barnabasbrief*, 130–34.

[22] See below, "Anti-Jewish Polemic and Its Function."

has revealed that everything in Scripture is to be interpreted as allegory (cf. Barn 6.10). If the prophetic signature announcing Christ and Christians is absent, it is added by formulae. To this pattern belongs the introduction of quotations with ὁ προφήτης λέγει and its variations, the indication of a quotation as prophetic speech when the heraldic formula is placed ahead of it,[23] as well as the combined impression of ten stories, law texts, and cultic orders in a prophetic form.[24] Through these modifications Barn claims that everything that has rank and name for Jews, indeed Scripture itself from its very core is directed toward Christ and Christians.[25] The three-sided formula (1.7a, 5.3) and the eulogies in 6.10a and 7.1 therefore emphasize that the revelation is given to Christians, that it is complete and coherent, and that henceforth there are no prophecies about it. God's plan of salvation is thus presented in Scripture and becomes precisely accessible, that is to say relevant for salvation, in right Christian belief.

Because Scripture as a whole promises Christ and Christians, there is no salvation story that precedes God's investment of salvation in Christ. Everything that happened then, including circumcision, the Sabbath, and the Day of Atonement, and the like, exhausts itself pointing to the Christ event. That is exactly what the patriarchs, Moses, David, and the prophets, graced by God, understood and therefore through their words and deeds foreshadowed Christ and Christians. It follows that everything that Jews believe and do by faith is at best christocentric prophecy, at worst blasphemy. Scripture, especially the Torah of Moses, has thus always lacked any soteriological application. Whatever promise appears to have such an application (cf. Barn 2–3, 4.6, 9–10, 15–16) is based on a misunderstanding of Scripture that runs counter to God's intent (cf. Barn 9.4). While the author points out that Scripture announces Christ and Christians and in the

---

[23] In Barn 6.8 ἰοὺ τάδε λέγει κύριος ὁ θεός qualifies the promise of land through interpretation as prophecy, the *skopos* of which is consistent with the common foundation of Christ and the Church (cf. 9.2-5a).

[24] Moses shattering the tablets of the covenant (Barn 4.8 and 14.2-3), the two sacrifices of the Day of Atonement (Barn 7.3-5), Abrahamic circumcision (Barn 9.7-8), Moses crossing his hands in the battle with the Amalekites (Barn 12.2-4), Moses making the bronze serpent and raising it on wood (Barn 12.5-7), Moses changing the name of Nun (Barn 12.8-10a), Isaac's request for Rebecca (Barn 13.2-3), and Jacob's blessing (Barn 13.4-6). The principals are thus the patriarchs and above all Moses (five times) as well as the priests, especially the high priest, although in both of these sequences Moses is present in the background as the lawgiver. The transformation of the promise is—as technique and as strategy of the argumenta-

tion—founded on the two common goals of the allegoresis in Barn. First, proof that Scripture, and with it the covenant, the Torah, and the whole of salvation history, is to be understood as christocentric prophecy, just as are the offers of salvation tied to the following of the law to be understood as a promise. Second, proof and conclusion that all promises will be fulfilled through the Christ event.

[25] The identification of the law as prophecy, the following of which does not lead to salvation but only promises it, requires that its ethical portion must likewise be transformed. The interpretation of food regulations in Barn 10 is a perfect example of this process. In that case, inherent in the impression of salvation history stories, of law texts and cultic orders in prophecy as well as the ethical interpretation of the Law are the annulment of all Jewish prerogatives as well as the promise of Scripture as Christian property and the exclusive Christian competence to proper interpretation.

revealed will of God can be understood only by virtue of spiritual gifts and in an attitude of faith toward the Lord, he really makes of Scripture the book that contains all revelation for Christians, for which reason everything that Christians believe and do is to be grounded on the authority of Scripture. Scripture therefore does not testify to salvation history but is always only revelation for Christians. It is thus the bulk of Christian theology. If one cannot determine through the text of Scripture what Christian theology ought to say, however, the words of Scripture are modified and rearranged, and if necessary, fitting sequences are manufactured (cf. Barn 7.4) or else passages that are close to the subject but do not fit the argument are ignored (cf. Barn 4 and Exod 34). The *skopos* of all operations is that they adapt themselves to the composition made according to the stated intention and prepare a clue in Scripture about the kerygma "Jesus is Lord" and the dogma of the divinity of Jesus. "The Lord's demands of rights," which are cited from Scripture and interpreted in Barn 2–16, are therefore "proofs" for theological positions that are already firm. That goes especially for Christology. It is the hermeneutical key to Scripture, which Barn takes to Judaism with aradicalism like no other Christian writing before him.

5.2 The Term κύριος

The dominant and most meaningful christological term is κύριος.[26] The preexistence of the κύριος points to his divinity and similarly expresses the incarnational basis and bond of salvation on the basis of the story of his passion and its soteriological relevance. Thus the proof of the early Christian dogma[27] "Jesus is God" occurs as the founding revelation of Scripture and the Christ event as its fulfillment. From this fact the evidence gains the decisive meaning that the passion and death of Christ were foretold and that through them God's plan of salvation is fulfilled. This proof also secures the incarnation, since the passion and death follow from it. Barn does not reflect on the mode of the incarnation. One concludes from Barn 14.5 only that the Lord Jesus was prepared (ἡτοιμάσθη) to bear our sins. Barn 5.10-11 further establishes the character of grace and that with this salvation event the eschatological age and therefore also the time of crisis has begun. With the help of the κύριος term the author uses as a touchstone for the paradox that the Preexistent One and God has suffered and died the idea that this event is plausible first from the evidence of the fulfillment of the prophecies initiated by the κύριος himself, second on the basis of his will and third, above all, on the basis of the soteriological purpose of the event. Because the earthly Jesus, and thereby the Crucified, also comes into view through this relationship with the κύριος term, it is a constitutive element of the christological and soteriological as well as the ecclesiological concept.

---

[26] Cf. 1 Corinthians 12:3, Romans 10:9; Niederwimmer, *Theologie*, 107–12.

[27] Cf. John 20:28b.

Because in the view of Barn there is no salvation history prior to the Christ event, one must avoid formulas that place Christ in a continuum of salvation history. Not least for this reason the author, for example, in Barn 12.11, strictly rejects the naming and interpretation of Jesus Christ as the Son of David, which other Christians found revealing, in favor of the title Son of God. The expression τὸ σκεῦος τοῦ πνεύματος in 7.3c and 11.9b hides the same tendency of demarcation and strategy of denunciation. Because πνεῦμα in Barn should be taken as the Spirit of God, the genitive construction implies that in the "manhood" of Jesus (τὸ σκεῦος) the "Godhood" is present as well. The term πνεῦμα is meant similarly to refer to the fact that Jesus is part of the Godhead. These christological expressions make plain the anti-Jewish yet basically intra-Christian thrust: It is important, and the preexistence statements about the κύριος and the Son of God in 5.5 point to this fact, that an adoptionist Christology that could appear compatible with the confession of other Christians is reported as unthinkable. The insistence in 12.10 that Christ is not the son of a human goes hand in hand with that idea.[28] To securely mark and profile his own position, the author uses christological statements—for example, the appearance in the flesh—that, were their functional character left out of account, could also be taken as modalistic Monarchianism. This fact can be seen in connection with theological attributes.

5.3 Attributes of God

As the reader must think about the connection to Jesus with the use of the κύριος term in Christian theological speech, the same is true of the attributes of God that build their use in specifically Christian interpretations through the reader. Regarding the Old Testament attribute ὁ λυτρωσάμενος, which is included in Barn 19.2 and interpreted by ἐκ θανάτου, the reader must develop the christological meaning in connection with corresponding statements in Barn 14.5-9. According to those statements, the difference between God, the Savior, and Jesus is only that Jesus is the Savior come in the flesh. One can have the impression that for Barn the one God, the Creator and Savior, is revealed in the flesh, and like the "Spirit of the Lord" the "Son of God" is ultimately God. Standing against the unavoidable Monarchian classification of this view is the fact that the catalogue in Barn 19.2a is applied to ὁ θεός, God the Creator, and that the lexemes Ἰησοῦς and Χριστός do not occur in the Two Ways teaching or in the concluding chapter. The reader can conclude that Jesus is God and that God has appeared in him only if he connects the aforementioned dots. A similar qualification should be applied to the keyword δόξα. כְּבוֹד יְהוָה refers to the form of God's revelation, insofar as it expresses his Godhood, his power and might. When Barn 12.7c speaks of the δόξα Ἰησοῦ, especially in combination with an all-formula, the author doubtless wants to express God's presence in Jesus. However, these statements of the creed "Jesus is God" stand against statements in which a gradation is inherent.

---

[28] Cf. Niederwimmer, *Theologie*, 99–107.

First, Barn 14.6 establishes that the κύριος was prepared: ὃς εἰς τοῦτο ἡτοιμάσθη. The grammatical form is to be construed as divine passive, since the relative clause points to the previously named Lord Jesus. What he was prepared for is presented later and established with reference to his commissioning by the Father in this regard.

Second, Barn 3.6a uses unique names for God and Jesus, namely, ὁ μακρόθυμος for God the Father and, related to that, ὁ ἠγαπημένος αὐτοῦ for Jesus. Aside from this expression it is obvious that Jesus really appears as God's medium for calling the people.

Third, Barn 7.3c states, "the Lord has commanded that He Himself must offer the vessel of the Spirit as sacrifice for our sins." The offering is Jesus. One interpretation of this statement in the direction of a dynamic Monarchianism is ruled out on two sides. If Jesus is God in a modalistic sense, God would be offering himself to himself or, according to cultic terminology, the requested audience of the offering, namely God, would be missing. These three examples show that the Christology of Barn lacks the clarity of expression of later times, which is why the later dogmatic classifications are themselves minimally instructive in accurately understanding this early Christian discussion about God, which stays close to biblical usage and expression and has a significant soteriological *skopos* with a definite basis in church history.

5.4 Soteriology

Salvation in Barn is grace that works through the suffering of the cross and remains tied to the cross of Christ (Barn 7.11). Salvation always comes in Barn from the κύριος. The resurrection of Jesus seals the annihilation of death and grounds Christians' hope for their own resurrection from the dead, for which reason hope is the Christian life principle qualified by Christ's death and resurrection, both the core and the evidence of their faith. The individual experiences salvation through baptism (11.1-11). The benefits of salvation are remission of sin, freedom from the "curse of the Law," and competence for complete gnosis (1.7). This gnosis, which assumes and surrounds the believing attitude toward the κύριος, is the biblical basis of the faith. It does not lead to salvation, but it does signify salvation because only the knowledge of God's will creates the possibility of obeying his will. Thus the benefits of salvation, especially the gnosis, have the character of duties. Having a part in eschatological salvation depends on faith and on works, because the Law is not just prophecy but also ethical instruction; this aspect is emphasized by Barn 10, the Two Ways teaching, as well as the explanatory and unifying Barn 21.1. All present salvation stands with the eschatological reservation of the second coming and the Last Judgment. Herein lies the basis of ethics in Barn and from it ethics derives its motivation (cf. Barn 21.1).

5.5 Context in Church History

The context of this design in church history arises on the one hand from the statement in Barn 4.6, "The promise of salvation to them is ours as well," with which the author repeats the creed of other Christians, and on the other hand follows from the polemic that, despite its anti-Jewish nature, is directed at the other Christians that Barn 4 has in its sights. Barn develops its Christology in a situation in which it is essential to defend against a soteriology that seeks to establish a continuity in salvation history between the church and Israel and that in consequence represents a christological deficit. Christians who hold the principle in 4.6 assign salvific meaning to Israel, its institutions, and its cult and tangentially thereto the Christ event. Therefore the author shows first that all christological properties that are handed down to him and that matter to him can be shown to be scriptural, second that Scripture neither identifies modes of participation in salvation nor testifies to a salvation story but in every respect prophetically announces Christ and Christians as the locus of God's salvation, and third that the fulfillment of all promises of salvation is achieved by the incarnation, passion, death, and resurrection of Christ, as well as in the general resurrection and Last Judgment. Scripture therefore promises the Christ event and its soteriological consequences. It follows that the time of the church is salvation history. Because the salvation story is encompassed by the Christ event and the second coming of the Crucified as Son of God, high priest and kingly judge, the time of the church is the eschatological era. Salvation history in Barn's sense is exclusively church history, which implies that the Christians scolded in 4.6 as sinners do not belong to the church.

6.   Anti-Jewish Polemic and Its Function

In early Christian scholarship Barn is not seldom placed beside John 8:30-47 and Stephen's speech. In both texts that distancing of Christianity from Judaism seems to gain contours that appear as signs for Barn and allow it to be seen as the oldest document of an anti-Jewish polemic that states its intention formally and with regard to content in the Christian text *Adversus Iudaeos*. Barn is unique in the combination of elements of anti-Jewish polemic as well as in the radicalism of its argumentative development and the theological consequences, although none of its occasionally massive anti-Jewish statements were cited in the early church.[29] Granted, the author pours the heaviest polemic on Jews and Judaism, but he is not aiming it at them. The *skopos* of this anti-Jewish polemic develops against the background of the christological debate over the soteriological exclusivity of Jesus as a function within Christianity, namely, the construction of religious identity and the destruction of the identity of the other Christians that are in the sights of 4.6.

---

[29] For more, see Prostmeier, "Polemik," 38–58.

6.1 Elements of Anti-Jewish Polemic

The main elements of anti-Jewish polemic in Barn are openly polemical statements and expressions.[30] The *stylistic media of anti-Jewish polemic* are inconspicuous but effective. First, the Jews are never mentioned by name. They appear as an anonymous quantity, as a group, from which the author clearly distinguishes himself and his readers. Jews are often referred to disparagingly and excludingly as ἐκεῖνοι (2.9, 3.6, 4.7a, 8.7, 10.12a, 13.1-3; cf. πινῶν 19.4b.). Similarly Ἰσραήλ is spoken of only in a pejorative context (4.14, 5.2-8, 6.7, 8.1-3, 9.2, 11.1-2, 12.2a.c.5a, 16.5a). "Those people" and "Israel" are the keywords to which the author ties the picture of those opposed to Christians of his stripe. Second, the discriminating, bold allocation of Scripture citations, such as λέγει οὖν πάλιν περὶ τούτων πρὸς αὐτούς (3.1a) and πρὸς ἡμᾶς δὲ λέγει (3.3a) or ἃ μὲν πρὸς τὸν Ἰσραὴλ ἃ δὲ πρὸς ἡμᾶς (5.2a), although it is not just an artistic way of being able to direct threatening and judgmental words exclusively toward addressing the Jews. In addition to this open anti-Jewish tendency is the fact that the dedication of a quotation has the rank of an exegetical principle. The group-specific dedication of scriptural words is already interpretation; namely, he who knows to whom a Scripture verse applies already knows more than the Jews do.

There is nothing comparable in the epistolary framing chapters, in the transition between the two sections, or in the Two Ways teaching. Openly anti-Jewish statements and expressions therefore appear to cohere with the biblical interpretation of Barn. The author's appeal to Scripture, and especially the evidence of the patriarchs, Moses, David, and the prophets, as well as the representatives of Israel, foremost the high priests, sets the almost unbeatable polemic with irrefutable

---

[30] In reference to the prophetic criticism, Barn 2.9-10 and 3.6 warn against offering sacrifice, celebrating feasts, or keeping fasts in accordance with Jewish regulations. In connection thereto Barn 4.1-3 warns against the works of lawlessness, against the way of life and belief of the evildoer who misapprehends the present time. Barn 4.6b. 8 and 14.1-3 argue that the Jews have broken the covenant. With the alarming reference to God's rejection of Israel that occurred against all signs, Barn 4.14 seeks to impress on his readers as indispensable the duty to live in accordance with the Christian calling. Barn 7.9-10 predicts that the Jews at the Eschaton will fearfully see the one they crucified as Son of God, high priest, and kingly judge. According to Barn 8.7 and 10.12, the meaning of the prescriptions for the water of purification as well as the sense of the food regulations remain hidden from the Jews because of their disobedience and their refusal to follow God's will. Barn 9.4-5 downgrades the Jewish circumcision to no more than an ethnic phenomenon and traces it to the deception of an evil angel. According to Barn 10.9b, the "carnal desires" of the Jews are the reason for their following the food regulations to the letter. Barn 11.1 explains that Israel stands under eternal punishment because of its sins unless it comes to the faith through which alone it can receive salvation. Barn 12.8-11 strictly rejects the view that Christ is the successor of David, if only because this sovereign title would concede to the Davidic-messianic name the rank of a salvation history datum. Barn 13 attempts to prove that the Jews were never God's people and therefore cannot be heirs of God's eschatological promise of salvation. Barn 15.6 argues that at present no one is able to fulfill the command to keep the Sabbath holy, and Barn 15.8 states that the present Sabbath displeases God. Barn 16 aims to expose the hope of the Temple as blasphemy and equates Jewish veneration of God with that of the heathens.

authority against everything on which Jews base their identity, worth, and hope. This line of argument corresponds to the thesis of *Jewish misunderstanding of Scripture*. While the author pursues the proof of this thesis by means of his allegoresis and sophisticated interpretation strategies, massive anti-Jewish polemic takes place.[31] The consequences are therefore first: The misunderstanding of Scripture on the part of the Jews determines their inability to obey God. Second: The Jews have therefore become, including their history and present, together with their writings, sudden signs against their own hope for salvation (7.5b). Jewish practices of faith and life are not ways of life that lead to salvation (11.7). Both are at best signs that point to Christ and the church, at worst blasphemy insofar as, according to the evidence of Scripture, they underlie God's judgment of rejection (9.4, 10.2, 13.6). That means that everything analogous that happens to Jews, including suffering, stands uniquely under this sign. An indication that the author takes all events into account are the remarks about Israel's being attacked in Barn 12, the destruction of the temple, the handing over of the city and the people, as well as the rejection of Israel in the distance from God, without any hope of salvation and abandoned to ungodly influence. Third: The Torah and all promises of Scripture are fulfilled in a grace-filled way in and through the church.

Again under appeal to Scripture, the author shows that the Jews have never received the assurance of God's salvation (4.6b-8, 14.1-3).[32] Through the Christ event the church becomes the eschatological heir of the assurance of God's

---

[31] From the examples of the promise of land (6.8-19), the regulations for the Day of Atonement (7.3-11) and for purification by water (8.1-6) as well as circumcision (9.4-8) and the dietary regulations (10.1-11), the author presents the Jewish understanding of Scripture as unsuccessful from the ground up. The Jewish interpretation of Scripture is accordingly not simply deficient; far more often the Jews do not understand Scripture at all. The author claims that this disability has its roots in unbelief (4.8a, 6.10b), disobedience and stiff-necked refusal (8.7) that can be traced to a destructive, ungodly influence (9.4). In the author's view, this fact points to a constitutional inability of the Jews to understand Scripture (6.10b, 7.9). They lack what Christ exemplifies: the remission of sin 1.1, 5.1, 8.3, 11.11, 14.5-6, 16.8-9) and the blessing of the *pneuma* (1.2). This defect and the lack of a believing attitude toward the Lord deny Jews the ability to recognize the will of God revealed in Scripture (10.12). God namely lets everything ἐν πνεύματι be known through the prophets, including the patriarchs, Moses, and David. Scripture carries an exclusive prophetic signature. Everything in it is—as the Lord Himself has revealed—to be

taken as a likeness (6.10), and that with an exclusive *skopos* of content: Scripture uniquely promises the Christ event (5.6) and the church (6.14) as well as the second coming of the Crucified as the Son of God with the insignia of the high priest and kingly judge (7.9-10)

[32] The working out of this nonreceipt of the assurance of salvation as prophetic sign functionalizes the people of Sinai-Horeb, basically the Jews, nearly to accessories for Moses' prophetic hint toward the Christ event and baptism. In addition, the "tablets of the covenant" were also furnished with "deeper spiritual meaning," namely as a prophetic indication of the church. The meaningful retelling of the events at Sinai-Horeb as well as their argumentative use seek to make clear that all things Jewish, including the Law, lack the soteriological basis. Cf. Prostmeier, *Barnabasbrief*, 329–30, 498–500. With the same impetus and argumentative strategy, Barn 13.6 denies that the Jews were ever the people of God and heirs of the promises or that they ever will be. Whatever happened to Israel is only meaningful with regard to its prophetic function pointing to Christ and the church.

salvation, and that in accordance with Scripture. Taken together, these ideas have three consequences:

First, there is no salvation history prior to the Christ event. Although the revelation of the power of the Lord's grace that ran through the words and deeds of the patriarchs, Moses, David, and all the prophets (in Israel) gave proof of God's plan of salvation, it does not possess soteriological dignity with the rank of salvation history on the basis of the exclusively prophetic signature. The prophetic sign through which God revealed His δικαιώματα (1.7, 5.3, 17.1) expends itself with regard to its soteriological relevance in pointing to the Christ event and the church.

Second, the Jews block their own way to salvation by rejecting baptism (11.1), and that has eschatological import.

Third, Christ is not the successor of David (12.10-11). The Jews thus have nothing in common with salvation history under this threefold consideration. Therefore the Jewish prerogatives are void, the faith and hope that they call upon are mistaken, and all Jewish ways of life and belief, especially the cult and the institutions, are expressions of a blasphemy characterized by idleness (4.10, 16.2) and error (2.9-10, 4.1b, 12.10, 14.5b, 15.6b, 16.1).

Barn 1.7a states that Scripture has always and only applied to Christians; they possess Scripture and with it all revelation. Through the functional equation of the gnosis that comes from Scripture (Barn 2–16) with that which is handed down in the Two Ways teaching (18.1a, 21.1), as is the case with Scripture, the morality that alone leads to salvation is reclaimed as typically Christian. The process of this twofold use formally resembles the process in Christian Gnostic scriptures, namely, selection (e.g., Barn 4 and 14 deliberately skip over the renewal of the covenant according to Exod 34) and reinterpretation. Aside from allegoresis as an exegetical method for developing Christian properties as the will of God, which is coupled with the interpretation of Scripture as Christian property, the interpretation in Barn leads one to the shaping of salvation history stories, of law texts, and of cultic ordinances in a prophetic form (see above). The guideline for this shaping as well as for the reinterpretation is the thesis that Scripture is prophetic to the core and is always directed toward the Christ event and the church. The annulment of all Jewish prerogatives on the basis of the christocentric signature of Scripture has made the inherited "Scripture of the Jews" indispensible for the church and has made the theological development of Jesus from Scripture and tradition to an expression of the identity of the church.

6.2 Functionalization of the Jews and the Irreconcilability between Judaism and the Church

Apart from the open anti-Jewish polemic, fixed on appropriate statements and expressions and sharpened with the help of typical argumentation strategies, there appears in Barn a programmatic devaluing of all things Jewish. With his explanation, the author wants to present as succinctly as possible the fact that the belief of Christians of his stripe is scriptural (Barn 2–16) and that their practice fulfills the high moral standards of the tradition (Barn 18–20). With this intention the author uses the sharpest criticisms on Christians who profess a binding salvation rule and salvation history that predates the Christ event. According to the author, their faith makes the Christ event relative because it makes Christ's soteriological exclusivity tangential. In his view such faith and such hope can come only from a deficient understanding of Scripture, which is ultimately a sign of a lack of grace. Because the author traces the cause of this Christianity to a literal understanding of Scripture, which he also diagnoses as the basis of all Jewish properties, these Christians appear to him to be basically Jewish. This view gives him the possibility of using Jewish properties only pejoratively to profile and denounce the other Christians. Everything Jewish is suitable to expose the error, vanity, and sinfulness of these Christians, since in the author's view nothing that Jews exemplify possesses dignity before God. Everything is blasphemy born of error, vanity, and disobedience. This polemical demarcation against other Christians not only takes its contours and sharpness from its anti-Jewish form; it is at the same time a functionalization of Judaism—and Jews—that paves the way for the programmatic anti-Judaism.

Characteristic of this criticism of all things Jewish with the goal of an intra-Christian polemic against heresy is its legitimization by appeal to Scripture. Just as the author shows that the preexistence and sonship of the κύριος, the soteriological import of the Christ event, and the promise of God's grace to the church are the basic revelations of Scripture, the interpretation of Genesis 2:2-3 in Barn 15 shows that God's will revealed from the beginning is that Judaism and the church have nothing in common. The theological paralysis of a salvation history that predates the Christianity is the reason for this functionalization of Jews and Judaism. This fact explains both the extent and the vehemence of the anti-Jewish polemic. The expression of cultic community coupled therewith has consequences for all of church history. The church not only believes something different from Judaism, it prays and celebrates otherwise. The worship of the church has a different goal because its liturgy is grounded in God's eschatological promise of salvation in Jesus. In contrast to Did, which presents keeping the Sabbath as still a communal reality and freely opts for the Lord's Day,[33] Barn 15 holds Sabbath-keeping to be incompatible with Christianity. According to Barn, the church and Judaism are mutually exclusive. The Christianity that Barn propagates differentiates its exegesis from that of Marcion.

---

[33] Cf. Prostmeier, "Unterschiedenes Handeln," 55–75.

7.   Bibliography

Bauer, J. B. *Die Polykarpbriefe.* KAV 5. Göttingen, 1995.

Carleton Paget, J. *The Epistle of Barnabas: Outlook and Background. WUNT* 2.64. Tübingen, 1994.

Funk, F. X. "Der Codex Vaticanus gr. 859 und seine Descendenten." *ThQ* 62 (1880): 629–37.

Gebhardt, O. de, A. von Harnack, and T. Zahn, eds. *"Barnabae Epistula* graece et latine.— Papiae que supersunt—Prebyterorum reliquias ab Irenaeo servatas—vetus Ecclesiae Romanae Symbolum—Epistulam ad Diognetum." *Patrum apostolicorum opera: Textum ad fidem codicum et graecorum et latinorum ahibitis praestantissimis editionibus.* Fasc. 1.2. Leipzig ²1878.

Holmes, M. W., ed. *Apostolic Fathers* (Early Christian Collection). Translated by J. B. Lightfoot and J. R. Harmer. Grand Rapids, ²1990.

Hvalvik, R. "Barnabas 9:7-9 and the Author's Supposed Use of Gematria." *NTS* 33 (1987): 276–82.

————. *The Struggle for Scripture and Covenant: The Purpose of the Epistle of Barnabas and Jewish-Christian Competition in the Second Century.* WUNT 2.82. Tübingen 1996. (Same as Diss., Masch. Oslo 1994.)

Kraft, R. A. *The Apostolic Fathers.* Vol. 3: *Barnabas and the Didache: New Translation and Commentary.* New York/Toronto 1965.

Lightfoot, J. B. *The Apostolic Fathers.* I 1.2: *S. Clement of Rome: A Revised Text with Introductions, Notes, Dissertations and Translations.* Hildesheim/New York 1973 (reprinted from ²1890 ed.).

Lindemann, A., and H. Paulsen, eds. *Die Apostolischen Väter: Griechisch-deutsche Parallelausgabe auf der Grundlage der Ausgaben von Franz Xavier Funk, Karl Bihlmeyer und Molly Whittaker, mit Übersetzung von M. Dibelius und D.-A. Koch.* Tübingen 1992.

Lona, H. E. *Die Wahre Lehre des Kelsos.* KfA.Erg.1. Freiburg 2005.

Niederwimmer, K. *Die Didache.* KAV 1. Göttingen 1989, ²1993.

————. *Theologie des Neuen Testaments: Ein Grundriß.* Vienna 2003.

Prigent, P., and R. A. Kraft, eds. *Épître de Barnabé: Introduction, traduction et notes par P. Prigent, texte grec établi et présenté par R. A. Kraft.* SC 172. Paris 1971.

Prostmeier, F. R. "Antijüdische Polemik im Rahmen christlicher Hermeneutik: Zum Streit über christliche Identität in der Alten Kirche." *ZAC* 6 (2002): 38–58.

————. "Barnabasbrief." In *Geschichte der antiken Text: Autoren- und Werklexicon,* edited by M. Landfester, 108–10. DNP.S 2. Stuttgart/Weimar 2007.

————. "Unterscheidenes Handeln: Fasten und Taufen gemäß Did 7,4 und 8,1." In ΦΙΛΟΦΡΝΗΣΙΣ, edited by J. B. Bauer, 55–75. GThSt 19. Graz 1995.

————. "Zur handschriftlichen Überlieferung des Polykarp- und des Barnabasbriefes: Zwei nicht beachtete Dszendenten des Cod. Vat. gr. 859." *VC* 48 (1994): 48–64.

Rhodes, J. N. *The Epistle of Barnabas and the Deuteronomic Tradition: Polemics, Paranesis, and the Legacy of the Golden Calf Incident.* WUNT 2.188. Tübingen 2004. (Same as Diss., Washington, D.C.: Catholic University of America, 2003.)

Scorza Barcellona, F., ed. *Epistola di Barnaba: Introduzione, testo critico, traduzione, commento, glossario e indici.* CorPat 1. Turin 1975.

Wengst, K. *Tradition und Theologie des Barnabasbriefes.* AKG 42. Berlin 1971.

———, ed. *Didache (Apostellehre), Barnabasbrief, Zweiter Klemensbrief, Schrift an Diognet.* SUC II. Darmstadt 1984.

Windisch, H. *Die Apostolischen Väter* III: *Der Barnabasbrief.* HNT proceedings, edited by H. Lietzmann. Tübingen 1920. 299–413.

The First Epistle of Clement

Andreas Lindemann

The text traditionally known as "First Clement," written from the Roman fellowship to the Corinthian, is probably the oldest surviving text of the early church outside the New Testament. In contrast to most other Christian texts that were written around the end of the first century C.E., however, this letter is neither anonymous nor pseudonymous; rather, "the church of God that lives as strangers in Rome" writes to "the church of God that lives as strangers in Corinth." The connection to a (Bishop) "Clement" was made later.

1.   Textual Tradition

The oldest textual witness is the biblical Codex Alexandrinus (A) from the fifth century; it contains a number of small lacunae apart from a missing page with the text of 57.7–63.2 (the final chapter is preserved).[1] The full Greek text appears in the miniscule Codex Hierosolymitanus graecus 54 (H), written in 1056.[2] A manuscript with a Latin translation was discovered by Germain Morin and edited by him in 1894; this codex from the eleventh century, which offers a version of the text that may stem from the second century,[3] appears on the one hand to be a Latin "interpretation" of 1Clem, but on the other hand it is reliable throughout and occasionally (e.g., in 1.3) better than the Greek manuscripts.[4] Two codices with Coptic translations survive: C, handed down in Codex Berolinensis from the fourth or fifth century, is nearly complete; only the portion 34.6–42.2 is missing. In comparison, C[1] from the fifth to eighth century is a collection of fragments with considerable lacunae; only 1Clem 1.1–26.2 is somewhat better preserved. The Syriac translation (S) exists, along with 2Clem, in a manuscript of the New Testament from the year 1170 between the Catholic Epistles and the *Corpus Paulinum*; the composition date of the translation is uncertain, possibly seventh or eighth century.

---

1   Overview in Lightfoot, *Fathers* I/2, 263–67.
2   The 1875 edition of Codex H by Ph. Bryennios also includes Did and Barn as well as 2Clem; autotypy in Lightfoot, *Fathers* I/1, 425–62.
3   Cf. Mohrmann, *Origins*, 78–85, and Lona, *Clemensbrief*, 14–15.

4   Examples in Lona, *Clemensbrief*, 19. The edition of the text of 1Clem by Gerhard Schneider in the "Fontes Christiani" offers the Latin side by side with the Greek text.

2.   Reception in the Early Church

1Clem may be attested to already by Ignatius, although any reference is quite vague.[5] The Letter of Polycarp to the Philippians contains numerous parallels to 1Clem, even in the inscription,[6] but these are at least uncertain signs of literary dependence because there is no explicit reference to 1Clem. Irenaeus mentions and refers in part to the content of 1Clem: During the time of the episcopacy (*episcopatum*) of Clement, whom Irenaeus mentions earlier, "there was once a great controversy among the brothers in Corinth. Then the church in Rome wrote a very meaningful letter (*potentissimas litteras*) to the Corinthians in order to reconcile them in peace, renew their faith, and proclaim the tradition that they had recently received from the Apostles" (Haer III 3.3).[7] Important for the reception history and for textual criticism are the broad citations of 1Clem in the works of Clement of Alexandria, especially in Strom IV 105–19.[8] Clement of Alexandria even denotes the Roman Clement as an "apostle" (Strom IV 105.1) but speaks on the other hand of "the letter of the Romans to the Corinthians."[9]

1Clem is then referred to more frequently in the *Ecclesiastical History* of Eusebius. In the time of Domitian, "Clement"[10] wrote a letter "in the name of the Roman fellowship to the fellowship in Corinth because at that time quarrels had broken out there" (στάσεως [. . .] γενομένης, Eus HE III 16).[11] In HE III 38.1-2. Eusebius writes that 1Clem includes numerous allusions to and quotations from Hebrews.[12] According to HE IV 22.1 Hegesippus (ca. 110–180) refers to 1Clem in his ὑπομνήματα, and in HE IV 23.11 Eusebius quotes from a letter by Dionysius of Corinth (ca. 170)[13] that refers to the reading of 1Clem during worship in Corinth.[14]

In AposCon VIII 47 canon 85, 1Clem (together with 2Clem) is counted among the "holy Scriptures." Whether this fact as well as the survival of the letter

---

5   IgnRom 3.1 (ἄλλους ἐδιδξατε) recalls 1Clem 1.3 (τὰ κατὰ τὸν οἶκον σεμνῶς οἰκουργεῖν ἐδιδάσκετε).

6   Indicated by Lightfoot, *Fathers* I/1, 149–52, and by Lona, *Clemensbrief,* 91–92. Lona concludes that 1Clem "was already highly esteemed in Smyrna in the first half of the second century" (90).

7   Quoted from *Irenäus von Lyon: Adversus Haereses: Gegen die Häresien* III, translated and introduced by N. Brox, FC 8/3, 1995, 33. Irenaeus names numerous themes that are treated in 1Clem, which recalls 1Clem 62.1: "We have briefly taught you enough about that which is appropriate to our religion (θρησκεία) [. . .]." Irenaeus names the Roman church and not Clement as the sender of the letter.

8   A synopsis appears in Lona, *Clemensbrief,* 94–104.

9   In Strom V 80.1, where he quotes 1Clem 20.8.

10   Eus HE III 4.9 identifies the Clement who held the Roman ἐπισκοπή with the Clement mentioned by Paul in Philippians 4:3.

11   Quoted from *Eusebius von Caesarea Kirchengeschichte,* 1967. The translation by Ph. Haeuser was newly checked through by H. A. Gärtner.

12   This fact, according to Eusebius, shows that Hebrews was "not of a recent date" (ὅτι μὴ νέον ὑπάρχει τὸ σύγγραμμα).

13   According to Eus HE II 25.8, Dionysius was bishop of Corinth.

14   For further development of the reception history of 1Clem, see Lona, *Clemensbrief,* 104–9. A broader overview of quotations and allusions through the tenth century appears in Lightfoot, *Fathers* I/1, 148–200.

in a Greek and a Syriac Bible manuscript can be taken as an indication of canonical recognition is questionable. According to Eus HE VI 13.6, Clement of Alexandria counted 1Clem among the writings of debatable authenticity ("antilegomena"), along with Wis, Sir, Heb, Barn, and Jude, among others. Augustine speaks of Clement as the "third bishop" of Rome after Peter and Linus (Epist 53.2), but he does not refer to the letter.

3.　Authenticity and Literary Unity

The authenticity and literary unity of 1Clem need not be doubted, despite its unusual circumstances. The sender is ἡ ἐκκλησία τοῦ θεοῦ ἡ παροικοῦσα Ῥώμην, for which the corresponding "we" is strictly used throughout the entire text; nevertheless all signs point to the text having a single author (see below). Apart from the numerous and sometimes very substantial biblical quotations (see below), no literary predecessors are evident in 1Clem; only the prayer in 59.3–61.3 is obviously not formulated ad hoc but probably taken from church tradition.[15]

4.　Genre

According to its prescript, 1Clem is the letter of one congregation to another fellowship (τῇ ἐκκλησία τοῦ θεοῦ τῇ παροικούσῃ Κόρινθον); there are no direct parallels for such a correspondence (but cf. 2Macc 1.1: "The Jews in Jerusalem and in Judea" write to "the Jewish brethren in Egypt"). The author uses the early Christian, more specifically Pauline, letter formula; the fellowship as sender thus appears obviously in the traditional role and function of the apostle, but without claiming apostolic authority.[16] Conspicuously both the Roman and the Corinthian fellowships are referred to as ἡ ἐκκλησία ἡ παροικοῦσα, as "strange" in their present cities.[17]

On the basis of the use of συμβουλευτικὸν γένος in 58.2, W. C. van Unnik[18] has classified the letter as an advisory speech, with which an author gives advice to the audience;[19] but this classification captures only a partial aspect of the goal of the letter. In review of the whole letter, 63.2 says that the audience should "eradicate the wicked anger born of your envy in accordance with the plea for peace and harmony that we have made in this letter" (κατὰ τὴν ἔντευξιν, ἣν ἐποιησάμεθα περὶ εἰρήνης καὶ ὁμονοίας ἐν τῇδε τῇ ἐπιστολῇ). ἔντευξις can refer to "a petition to the king as the source of justice";[20] if a similar juristic connection should be made to the expression in 63.2,[21] the letter would almost see itself as an "official

---

[15] On this point, see Löhr, *Studien*.
[16] Contra Powell, *Clemens*, 117.
[17] Cf. on this point Schmitt, *Paroikie*, 135–37, which already derives a tone of "exile" in 1Clem from the formulation of the prescript.

[18] van Unnik, *Studies* I, 33–56.
[19] Lona, *Clemensbrief*, 21–22, is critical of this view.
[20] Mitteis-Wilcken, *Grundzüge* II/1, 14–15.
[21] Cf. Mikat, *Bedeutung*.

order," through which peace and harmony should be restored to the situation in Corinth marked by στάσις and ἀπόνοια.[22] To be sure, the word ἔντευξις is used in 2Clem 19.1 in the sense of "petition,"[23] and Justin denotes his apology as ἔντευξις (with προσφώνησις, Apol I 1.1); but the sermon known as "Second Clement" and Justin's apology directed to Caesar have a different character than the more "official" 1Clem, which recommends the possibility of understanding ἔντευξις in the sense of "judicial decree."[24] The Corinthian church would then clearly not simply stand under indictment but would be addressed as judge of its own affairs,[25] since the letter appeals to its ability to reason and allows the Roman church no possibility of enforcing its recommendations. It is worth noting that 1Clem claims at the end to have fully presented the norms of Christian existence (62.1-2); in fact the content of the letter does go beyond the present occasion (see below), even if the theme shines through almost universally. This fact is related to the unusual circumstances of the letter.[26]

5.   Construction and Content

1Clem consists of two major sections, namely, chapters 1–38 and chapters 40–65; chapter 39 serves as a transition. A clear organization in the parts is not readily recognizable. The contemporary theme, the situation in Corinth, is stated explicitly at the beginning (1–3) and then again at the end (44–54, 57, 62ff.). Apart from these statements, however, there are excursive remarks on totally different themes and problems; the description of the order of the cosmos (20), the statements about the resurrection of the dead (24–26), the picture of the *militia Christi,* and the church as a body (37–38), as well as the prayer in 59–61, all stray far from the concrete occasion of the letter. It is not always easy to order these statements according to the overall theme.

The first section following the prescript (1.1–38.4) can be understood as a broadly intended examination of the theme; the second section (40.1–65.2) essentially contains the content-wise implementation of the theme. Sometimes broadly developed doxologies occur frequently; they are not placed arbitrarily but should be understood as signals that show that the author sees a problem as having been sufficiently discussed. Thus the doxologies are always expressly mentioned in what follows.

---

[22] H.-J. Vogt, "Frühkirche," 167 in the edition of my commentary, is critical of this claim; cf. also Lona, *Clemensbrief,* 633.

[23] Cf. Pratscher, *Clemensbrief,* 221.

[24] Cf. Bauer, *Wörterbuch,* s. v. ἔντευξις. The Latin translation uses *denuntiatio* for this word.

[25] Lona, *Clemensbrief,* 633, contradicts this; but at the same time he affirms, "The decision stands out as self-evident as to whether or not the Corinthians accepted the opinion of the Roman fellowship: Only they could satisfy it, but there is no doubt as to the judgment."

[26] At approximately 9,800 words long, 1Clem is almost half again as long as Paul's Epistle to the Romans (ca. 7,100 words).

The letter begins in 1.1 with a short description of the situation with regard to the sender (there were "misfortunes and disagreements among us") and then the audience; here the keyword στάσις ("turmoil") used throughout for the situation in Corinth is given immediately. However, after that the letter speaks in a detailed *captatio benevolentiae* of the former excellent condition of the fellowship (1.2–3.1a); only then, introduced by the quotation from Deuteronomy 32.15, is there any reference to the present rupture, the consequences of which are "jealousy and envy, quarrel and turmoil, persecution and disorder, war and captivity" (3.1b-2).[27] Section 3.3–6.4 points to concrete biblical and contemporary examples of the dangers that arise therefrom, chief among which is the fate of the apostles Peter and Paul (5.3-7).

The call to leave this way follows in 7.1–8.5. In 7.1a the senders interpret their own action by showing solidarity with the audience: "We write not only to admonish you but also to remind ourselves" (ἀλλὰ καὶ ἑαυτοὺς ὑπομιμνήσκοντες).[28] After the indication that one finds himself on the same battlefield and in the same ἀγών follows the call to the audience that they should return to the known rule (κανών) of the tradition (παράδοσις) (7.1b-4); to this request are then added relevant biblical examples and quotes from Scripture (7.5–8.5).

In 9.1–19.1 the letter deals with the theme of "obedience" (9.1: διὸ ὑπακούσωμεν, 19.1: διὰ τῆς ὑπακοῆς). Again one reads a recounting of biblical examples of people who served God—from Enoch to Noah and Abraham to Rahab (9.2–12.8). Section 13.1a concludes, "Let us then be humble" (ταπεινοφρονήσωμεν οὖν), explained by examples from the Jesus tradition and the Old Testament (13.1b-4). Section 14.1–15.7 shows the consequences: "It is therefore right and pleasing to God that we obey Him" (δίκαιον οὖν κτλ., 14.1), and: "Let us therefore follow those who maintain peace" (τοίνυν κολληθῶμεν τοῖς μετ᾽ εὐσεβείας εἰρηνεύουσιν, 15.1), again with applicable biblical foundations. Section 16.1-17 names Jesus as example and quotes the text of Isaiah 53 in verses 3-16. At the end of this passage (16.17) stands the rhetorical question: "If then the Lord Himself is so humble, what should we do who through Him have come under the yoke of His grace?" The answer follows in 17.1–19.1 in the form of the recounting of yet more biblical examples (17.1: μιμηταὶ γενώμεθα κἀκείνων), including Elijah and Elisha, Moses, and David, among others (Ps 50:3-19 is quoted in 18.2-17). The statements are tied together in 19.1: Such examples enable us to improve.

A new aspect of the theme is introduced in 19.2a: "Therefore, since we have been so blessed [. . .], let us return [. . .] to the goal of peace." A description of the κόσμος created by God follows as an example of peace and harmony (19.2b–20.11), and at the end a doxology appears for the first time, directed toward Christ (20.12: ᾧ ἡ δόξα καὶ ἡ μεγαλωσύνη εἰς τοὺς αἰῶνας τῶν αἰώνων).[29]

---

[27] The keywords ζῆλος καὶ φθόνος as well as ἔρις καὶ στάσις recur frequently throughout the letter.
[28] ὑπομιμνήσκω occurs again in 62.2.

[29] According to Lona, *Clemensbrief,* 249, a new section begins with 20.1 (20.1–26.3: "the power of God in creation"); but a division after the doxology in 20.12 and the new entrance in 21.1 is still clear.

Consequences are then named in 21.1–22.8. Introduced with ὁρᾶτε κτλ. ("See to it that that His many benefits do not become a judgment against us"), the letter then points to the nearness of God in 21.1-3 and concludes in 21.4: "It is therefore right (δίκαιον οὖν, cf. 14.1) that we do not forsake His will." After further admonitions (21.5-9) everything that has been said is summarized with an indication toward belief "in Christ" (ταῦτα δὲ πάντα βεβαιοῖ ἡ ἐν Χριστῷ πίστις); as evidence, the author quotes Psalm 33:12-18 in 22.1b-7 and then Psalm 31.10 in v. 8.

Section 23.1 creates a transition: "God has a heart for those who fear him," and 23.2 concludes with: "Therefore we do not want to doubt," connected in 23.3-4 with the mention of the "shortness of the time."[30] This statement introduces the new theme of "eschatology" (23.5–26.3); at the beginning stands a mention of the second coming,[31] followed in 24.1–26.3 by statements about the certainty of the resurrection, evidenced by the resurrection of Jesus (24.1), by the everyday experience of day and night and the cycle of crops (24.2-5), and by the phoenix (25.1–26.1); at the end stand three short biblical quotes (26.2-3). The conclusion is drawn in 27.1: "In this hope our souls should be bound," followed by examples from Scripture that speak of God's power (27.2-7).

Another conclusion appears in 28.1a: "Therefore, since all things are seen and heard [sc. by God]," we cannot escape judgment (28.1b-4). From this statement follow admonitions about Christian conduct (29.1: "Let us therefore approach Him with a devout spirit"), explained with more biblical reasoning in 29.2–30.5 and connected with the concluding warning against "audacity and arrogance and daring" (30.8). After two interjections (31.1a: "Let us then strive for His blessing"; 31.1b: "Let us consider again") comes a reminder of the example of the patriarchs (31.2-4); after a renewed appellative comment in 32.1 ("When one considers this, he will recognize") and in conclusion to a mention of the patriarch Jacob (32.2) follows a statement on justification by faith (32.3), which closes with a doxology for God.

In 33.1, in a manner similar to Paul in Romans 6:1, the author poses a rhetorical question with regard to what has been said previously: "What should we then do, brothers? Should we cease to do good?" In answer, beginning with a comment on "every good work," the author speaks in detail in 33.2–35.12 about God's deeds as an example for humans under the testimony of more biblical texts; this section closes, after a further comment in review ("This is the way [. . .] in which we found our salvation," 36.1a), with a christological excursus (36.1b-6), the statements of which are clearly similar to the New Testament Epistle to the Hebrews (see below).

---

[30] There is here a word introduced as γραφή, the source of which is unknown; it recalls the προφητικὸς λόγος in 2Clem 11.2-4; on this, see Pratscher, *Clemensbrief*, 151–55.

[31] Here there is a citation that combines Isaiah 13:22b and Malachi 3:1, which the author probably found already in that state.

A conclusion appears in 37.1: "Let us therefore achieve our military service" for God (στρατευώμεθα); after the example of military discipline comes a remark that everyone has something important to do in his or her respective place (37.2-4).[32] The order of the human body (σῶμα, 37.5) speaks to this fact and leads to an ecclesiological conclusion: "Our whole body should thus be preserved in Christ" (38.1-2), from which comes the concluding request: "Let us therefore consider who we are" (38.3). The first section ends with the request to give thanks to God for all that we have (38.4a), connected in 38.4 with a doxology.

Chapter 39 contains an interjection that marks the transition to the second section at the same time: The author condemns the arrogance of the ἄφρονες (39.1), evidently the originators of the events in Corinth that are criticized in the following portion of the letter. To underscore the urgency of the exhortation in 38.2, Job 4:16–5:5 is quoted in 39.3-9.

The second section begins after a review (40.1a: "Since these things are obvious to us") with the assertion that we are "obliged to do everything in accordance with order (πάντα τάξει ποιεῖν ὀφείλομεν) that God has ordered to be completed at established times" (40.1b). In the first portion (40.1b–45.8) the next topic is disciplined service for God (40.2–41.1), but then the real theme is introduced without transition, namely, the appointment of "apostles, bishops, and deacons" in connection to the thought of succession (42.1-5, with Isaiah 60:17 as concluding biblical witness[33]). The biblical story of the miraculous establishment of Aaronic priesthood follows in 43.1-6a as a foundational explanation; the statements are concluded in 43.6b with a doxology.

In 44.1-3a the content of the letter finally turns to its actual occasion, the "strife over the office of overseer" (ἔρις [. . .] περὶ τοῦ ὀνόματος τῆς ἐπισκοπῆς)—clearly foreseen by the apostles. The senders state that they "do not hold it to be right" (οὐ δικαίως νομίζομεν) to remove such appointees from their office (44.3b), and the reasons are given in more detail in 44.4-6. In 45.1 the alternative is stated directly: The audience should indeed be "quarrelsome" (φιλόνεικοί ἐστε)—but for that which leads to holiness (εἰς σωτηρίαν)! Again reference is made to examples from Scripture (45.2-7a); at the end are a doxology for God (45.7b) and a further doxology for those who are acknowledged by God (45.8).

The following portion (46.1–50.7) consequently contains yet another admonition: "Therefore we must hold to such examples" (46.1); biblical and other reasons are given for this statement (46.2-7), apart from which 46.8 quotes a saying of Jesus that recalls Mark 9:42; another reproachful reference to the ongoing στάσις follows in 46.9. A very pointed reference to "the letter of Paul" (1 Cor)

---

[32] The question as to whether this passage refers to biblical statements (cf. Exod 18:21-25, 1Macc 3:55) or whether the author is thinking of the Roman army has been hotly debated, but there is little in the subject because the picture is understandable in any case. On the discussion, see Schmitt, *Paroikie*, 26–36; he assumes that this passage speaks of a "messianic" military.

[33] See below.

concludes the passage (47.1-4); the comparison between the situation then and the far worse current situation serves to judge the present actions sharply (47.5-7). Supported by biblical and other foundations, the conclusion "Let us therefore quickly put a stop to this!" (48.1-16) includes as an excursus a detailed macarism of love, connected with the call to repentance and humility (49.1–50.7a). Another doxology forms the conclusion (50.7b).

The request to recognize transgressions and to ask for forgiveness follows in 51.2–53.5; whoever does not do so risks the fate of Korah's gang (Num 16) and of the Egyptians in the Red Sea (Exod 14). The promise cited from the Psalms in 52.1-4 applies to the others; Moses is named as a further example because he asked God to forgive the people's outrages. The author then calls directly on the originators of the Corinthian conflict to leave the fellowship and "emigrate" (54.1-4; ἐκχωρῶ, ἄπειμι), for which a variety of exempla are given (55.1-6). There follows an exhortation to accept punishment (56.1-2), based in 56.3-15 on a quotation from Job 5:17-26. Further concrete admonitions appear in 57.1–58.1 ("Order yourselves under the presbyter"), again connected with a biblical example quoted in detail (Prov 1:23-33) and the call to heed the holy name of God (ὑπακούσωμεν κτλ.). These statements lead in 58.2 to the direct instruction "Take our advice" (δέξασθε τὴν συμβουλὴν ἡμῶν), and again the train of thought closes with a doxology.

The opposite warning appears in 59.1-2: Whoever does not obey will bring himself into danger—with regard to which the senders assert at the same time: "We, however, will be innocent of this sin." The long prayer for the community follows in 59.1–61.3, which closes with a doxology in keeping with the style.[34]

The end of the letter creates a broadly conceived conclusion. The content and intent of the whole letter are reviewed in 62.1-3, and there is even a *captatio benevolentiae* in 62.3 that seeks to contribute to ensuring the letter's success with the audience. A renewed, final call to obedience follows in 63.1, connected in 63.2 with a reference to an expected positive reaction from the audience and the self-interpretation of the letter as an "urgent petition (ἔντευξις) for peace and harmony." Section 63.3-4 makes the first reference to the emissaries of the community, who are probably to be thought of as those who delivered the letter. Chapter 64 is finally (λοιπόν) a concluding judgment with a final doxology, which on the one hand sounds very formal but also includes expressions like εἰρήνη and ὑπομονή and so picks up the theme of the letter. The messengers from Rome are referred to again in 65.1, this time by name; they should report the success of the letter as quickly as possible, namely, of those who prevail over εἰρήνη and ὁμόνοια. The letter concludes in 65.2 with a blessing formulated as a closing and a final doxology that recalls 64.

---

[34] On the structure and content of the prayer cf. Lindemann, *Clemensbrief,* 165–68, and above all Löhr, *Studien.*

6. Structure

Prescript

1.1–38.4		*First Section*
	1.1	The present for the senders and the audience: misfortune and turmoil
	1.2–3.1a	The previously excellent state of the fellowship
	3.1b-	The rupture
	3.3–6.4	Examples of the self-imposed dangers
	4.1-13	Biblical examples
	5.1-7	Peter and Paul
	6.1-4	The example of the women
	7.1–8.5	Call to repentance
	7.1-4	Call to return to the "canon of tradition"
	7.5–8.5	Biblical examples
	9.1–19.1	Call to obedience
	9.1–12.8	Biblical examples
	13.1–19.1	Exhortation to humility
	13.1-4	Conclusion: Jesus tradition and Old Testament
	14.1–15.7	Conclusions
	16.1-17	Jesus as exemplar (Isa 53:1-12)
	17.1–18.17	Further biblical examples
	19.1	Summary
	19.2–20.12	The cosmos as exemplar of peace and harmony. 20.12: Doxology
	21.1–22.8	Conclusions
	21.1-3	Application of statements made thus far
	21.4	Conclusion
	21.5-9	Further admonitions
	22.1a	Summary
	22.1b-8	Biblical examples
	23.1	Transition
	23.2-4	Conclusion
	23.5–26.3	On the theme of "eschatology"
	23.5	The coming judgment
	24.1–26.3	Resurrection
	24.1	Jesus
	24.2-5	Everyday experience
	25.1-26.1	The phoenix
	26.1-3	Biblical examples
	27.1	Conclusion: Relationship with God
	27.2-7	Scriptural examples of God's power

7.   Intertextual Relationships

H. E. Lona has presented a careful analysis of the language and style of 1Clem.[35] The language of the letter moves at a comparatively high level, with a rich vocabulary and recognizable care with regard to rhetorical quality. The numerous, often very extensive biblical quotations are characteristic;[36] they follow the LXX more or less verbatim, aside from 28.3, where Psalm 138:7-10 is quoted from an obviously different version.[37] As a rule quotations are introduced with a quotation formula,[38] but occasionally one is missing.[39] A relatively firm canon of biblical texts thus appears to be assumed, with the rare exception of quotations from or allusions to "apocryphal" texts.[40] The author freely retells the Rahab episode from Joshua 2 in chapter 12 and the interpretation of Aaron's budding staff from Numbers 17:16-26 in 43.2-6.

---

[35] Lona, *Clemensbrief*, 30–41.

[36] See on this Hagner, *Use*, 21–132. According to Lona, *Clemensbrief*, 31, quotations make up 28 percent of the text.

[37] The other variations can be understood as corrections of the LXX text; see Hagner, *Use*, 64–68. On 28.3, cf. Lona, *Clemensbrief*, 322–23.

[38] On this, see Hagner, *Use*, 26–29; Lona, *Clemensbrief*, 43–44.

[39] So, e.g., in 27.5, which is an obvious reference to Wis 12.12.

[40] A possible quotation from the "Apocryphon of Ezekiel" appears in 8.3; the same quote appears in the text "Exegesis on the Soul" (NHC II/6). The origin of the quotation in 23.3 is unknown, and the attribution to the text "Eldad and Modad" followed by some scholars is unfounded; the quotation also occurs in 2Clem 11.2-4. The statement in 46.2 recalls Psalm 17:26-27 LXX; but this passage is quoted in 46.3, where the author plainly writes that it comes from "another place."

The most frequently cited biblical texts are the Pentateuch, followed by the Psalter, the wisdom literature, and the book of Isaiah. The Bible provides mostly parenetic examples of both exemplary and blameworthy behavior; Rahab's red thread (Josh 2:18) is allegorically interpreted in 12.7 as the blood of Christ. In 22.1-7 the author quotes Psalm 33:12-18 LXX as the words of Christ "through the Holy Spirit" without reflecting on the hermeneutical question. By contrast, biblical texts are explicitly understood in 50.4-7 as eschatological reports of salvation, and μακαρισμός is pointed to as applying to Christians' present day (50.7).

Biblical texts are not cited as "law" (the word νόμος is completely absent from 1Clem[41]) nor as ἐντολή;[42] they are far more generally "the" Holy Scriptures, containing all instructions necessary for the Christian life. In 42.1-5, the argumentation that is most important for the occasion and the theme of the letter, a biblical quotation appears only at the very end;[43] before that the consideration of the succession is derived entirely from Christian tradition.

Explicit references to (later so called) "New Testament" writings or to early Christian tradition are few.[44] On the basis of 47.1, there is no doubt that the Romans knew 1 Corinthians and assumed its availability in Corinth;[45] in this regard the statements about σῶμα (37.5, 38.1) are probably to be read against the background of 1 Corinthians 12, and the encomium on love in 49.5 may show at least the influence of 1 Corinthians 13. The Pauline epistle to Rome is plainly referred to directly in 35.5-6 (cf. Rom 1:29-32), and the presentation of justification theology (32.4–33.1) is scarcely imaginable without the influence of Romans.[46] By contrast, there is no real evidence of knowledge of the other Pauline Epistles.[47] The apparent similarity to the pastoral letters, especially to their understanding of offices and their presentation of the role of women in the fellowship,[48] would be easily explained if the pastoral letters were written in Rome at about the same time as or slightly later than 1Clem.[49]

The citation of the Jesus tradition in 13.2 recalls the Sermon on the Mount (tradition) (Matt 7:1-2/Luke 6:37-38), but no textual source can be ascertained. Similarly, the logion cited in 46.8 coincides with Matthew 26:24b and 18:6 (cf.

---

[41] In 1.3 A and H read ἐν τοῖς νόμοις, but the editions rightly follow Cl and L (*in legitimis Dei*).

[42] ἐντολή is used only in 13.3 in reference to an instruction from Jesus.

[43] The quotation is from Isaiah 60:17, not insignificantly different from the LXX and introduced with the imprecise expression οὕτως γάρ που λέγει ἡ γραφή (cf. 28.2).

[44] Here the examples in Hagner, *Use*, 135–350, depart from the actually recognizable references, sometimes quite significantly.

[45] No conclusion can be drawn about 2 Corinthians; the context makes immediately clear which

epistle the phrase ἀναλάβετε τὴν ἐπιστολήν κτλ. means.

[46] Cf. Lindemann, *Paulus*, 185–87.

[47] Lindemann, *Paulus*, 185–87. For other opinions, see chiefly Hagner, *Use*, who finds references to all but 1 and 2 Thessalonians and Philemon in 1Clem.

[48] In 1Clem 1.3 the subordination of women is strongly advocated, and in 21.7 the silence of women is referred to as their special adornment; that recalls 1 Timothy 2:11ff. For more, see Lindemann, *Clemensbriefe*, 29 (Excurs: Frauen im 1 Clem).

[49] On linguistic indications of similarity to the pastoral letters, see Lona, *Clemensbrief*, 50.

Mark 9:42) without there being a recognizable literary relationship. So the question of whether 1Clem knew the Gospels as well as the aforementioned Pauline Epistles must remain open.[50] Relationships to other "New Testament" texts, except maybe Hebrews (see below), cannot be traced back to literary dependence with sufficient plausibility.[51] There is a certain relationship between 1Clem and the milieu of the Johannine writings; but there is no literary connection.[52] With the exception of 1 Corinthians, no early Christian writing is explicitly referenced.

8.   Relationship to Hebrews

The special similarity between 1Clem and Hebrews was recognized even in the early church. Eusebius writes (HE III 38.1-3) that the fact that the author of 1Clem cites Hebrews means that Hebrews cannot be a "young" text; he also refers to the similarity of style and thought. Origen concluded from Eus HE VI 25.14 that people saw Clement of Rome (or even Luke) as the author of Hebrews.

To be sure, neither agreement by citation nor other references to the text allow for the assumption of a direct literary relationship.[53] But the similarity of 1Clem 36.2-5 to Hebrews 1:3-5, 7, 13 is so great that the use of Hebrews by 1Clem must still be considered possible.[54] The discussion of Christ as the ἀρχιερεύς (1Clem 36.1, 61.3, 64) is by contrast clearly independent of Hebrews; both texts present the expression as a familiar concept, but 1Clem uses the title in connection with the term προστάτης, while the specifically priestly meaning characteristic of Hebrews appears only once (36.1).[55] 1Clem apparently owes the use of this title to a milieu similar to that of Hebrews,[56] but the intellectual form is independent of Hebrews.[57] It is possible that the author of 1Clem did not directly know and make use of all of Hebrews, but only Hebrews 1.

9.   The Situation in Corinth and the Motive for Roman Intervention

The occasion for the composition of 1Clem can be deduced reasonably accurately from the text itself; apparent uncertainties exist chiefly because it was not

---

[50] Hagner, *Use*, 171–332, comes to a similar conclusion; cf. further Köhler, "Rezeption," 60–72.

[51] Contra Hagner, *Use*, 271, who thinks it probable that the author of 1Clem used 1 Peter, James, and Acts directly.

[52] Compare, e.g., 60.2 with John 17:17 and 15:3; on this, see Jaubert, "Sources," 53–54.

[53] Lona, *Clemensbrief*, 54, speaks of a shared basis that "extends to a broad but heterogenous linguistic field."

[54] Cf. the synopsis in Lindemann, *Clemensbriefe*, 19, for more on the literature named there.

Theissen, *Untersuchungen*, 36–37, reckons with a common pattern for both. Lona, *Clemensbrief*, 55, thinks that "the possibility of a special origin cannot be concluded" in 1Clem 36.2-5 but that one should not consider the passage "in isolation."

[55] In 61.3; 64 presents a liturgical connection to the title.

[56] Lona, *Clemensbrief*, 58–61, reckons with a strong influence of Alexandrian Judaism on both texts.

[57] Cf. Ellingworth, "Hebrews," 266–67.

necessary for the senders to describe the audience's own situation in detail. In Corinth, as is already established in 1.1, a "disgraceful and godless στάσις" had arisen that lead to the once good ethos of the fellowship veering into "jealousy and envy," even "war and captivity" (3.1-4). The letter's statements become more precise in 44.1-6: The Corinthian holders of the ἐπισκοπή had been relieved of their offices; there was a σχίσμα that led many into error; and "your rebellion (στάσις) continues" (46.9). The (whole?) ἐκκλησία of the Corinthians, according to 47.6, rose against their presbyter "because of one or two people" (στασιάζειν πρὸς τοὺς πρεσβυτέρους).

The grounds for the στάσις are not apparent in 1Clem; the frequent references to misbehavior such as "jealousy and envy" are polemical and do not really address the actual motive. On the other hand, the very precise argumentation in 44.3-6 makes sense only on the premise that the Roman senders assumed that the dismissed presbyter in Corinth was not accused of official misconduct.[58] The recommendation in 54.1-3 that the "rabble-rousers" should go into exile assumes that they are not simply heretics or "teachers of error";[59] apparently, outside Corinth they could be respected as Christians without hesitation.

Because 1Clem never states that the originators of the στάσις sought the presbytery for themselves (or were chosen for office by the fellowship), it is possible that the στάσις—apparently participated in by the majority of the congregation—resulted in the elimination of the office and not simply to a change of personnel[60]—possibly due to the rationale that the office had not existed in Paul's day.[61] One point in favor of this argument is the fact that the letter does not primarily defend the individuals appointed as presbyters but above all argues in favor of the office, in that he pleads for the maintenance or reinstatement of the order established by the Bible and the instructions of the apostles (44–47). The goal is

---

[58] Lona, *Clemensbrief*, 79–80, presents what scholars believe might be the grounds for the conflict: tension between Jewish and Gentile Christians; disputes over Christian teaching; tension between "spirit and office, i.e., between charisma and structure"; power struggles "without a particular background." Welborn, "Clement," 1059, names another aspect: "Money seems to have been involved," which emerges from the reference to the previously accepted "provisions" (2.1): "From the Roman point of view of Clement, the younger generation of leaders at Corinth are dissatisfied with the provisions for their church." Welborn refers to the fact that "the unrest of the 1st and 2nd centuries almost always had economic causes." However, this notion cannot be proven from the text, with at most the exception of the expression τοῖς ἐφοδίοις τοῦ Χριστοῦ ἀρκούμενοι in 2.1, which is more likely meant metaphorically.

[59] Bauer, *Rechgläubigkeit*, 104–8, sees them as "Gnostics."

[60] The speculation that the leaders of the στάσις had "enthusiastically" appealed to the πνεῦμα (so Knopf, *Lehre*, 42, who refers to 13.1, 38.1-2, 48.5-6) or that they "most likely" espoused "the same present-focused eschatology that Paul had already had to fight in Corinth" (so Weiss, *Amt*, 80, who sees this as the only way to read the "eschatological block" in chaps. 23–26) cannot be verified. Weiss also states that "the opponents [were not fully aware of] the connection between present-focused eschatology and a false understanding of the office" (82).

[61] Lona, *Clemensbrief*, 81, assumes that the conflict could have had more causes; "the common basis could even be the refusal of a number of Corinthian believers to accept all the consequences of the institutionalization of the office without protest."

the regaining of peace and harmony, which for 1Clem directly accompany the reinstatement of the previously serving presbyter (57.1).

The motive for the Roman fellowship's intervention in Corinth[62] that is evident from the letter itself lies first in the fact that some in Rome had perceived that the στάσις would cause the long-esteemed "name" of Corinth (and with it Christianity overall) to be "blasphemed" and so endanger the church as a whole (1.1; cf. 3.2ff.); however, the idea that the Roman church feared state persecution because of an intramural στάσις is not readily apparent in the text.[63] The Roman fellowship seeks by its writing to "exhort" the audience (7.1) to return to the "rule of our tradition" (κανὼν τῆς παραδόσεως ἡμῶν) (7.2); this entails above all the recognition of the τάξις that goes back to God via Christ and the apostles (40–44). The audience is constantly called to εἰρήνη (15.1, 19.2, 63.2, 65.1), which is in accord with the whole of God's creation (20). Repentance (57.1, 62.1; cf. 7.7) and humility (13.1, 21.8, 48.6) are demanded, but at the same time God's readiness to receive the rueful sinner is promised (21.8, 22.1–23.1). The Roman fellowship expects that the admonition will be heeded in Corinth and that the fellowship there will therefore quickly repent (63.1-2, 65.1). 1Clem gives no evidence that anyone from Corinth had requested this advice.

In what way did the Romans learn of the situation in Corinth? H.-J. Vogt believes that it could not have been a matter of mere rumor; it is best to assume "that the dismissed Corinthian presbyter complained to Rome, i.e., lodged something like an appeal."[64] 1Clem makes no explicit statements about such a thing. Such an "appeal" would require that Rome, at least in the eyes of the plaintiff, had jurisdiction in Corinth as well, that the Roman church thus not only claimed but already possessed something like "primacy" in Christendom.[65] There is no indication of this state of affairs in 1Clem or in any of the texts that date from around 100 C.E. The Roman letter to Corinth is certainly not simply an instance of Christian solidarity in practice,[66] but it also does not prove that the Roman fellowship had any intention of exercising a controlling function over other fellowships.[67] It is conspicuous that 1Clem mentions no officials by whom, for example, the binding nature of the conveyed argumentation would be certified.[68] Not once in 63.3-4 and 65.1 is there any discussion of an "official" function of the

---

[62] The letter does not have other addressees in mind; contra Peterson, "Praescriptum," 135, who understands 1Clem as a καθολικὴ ἐπιστολή.

[63] Contra Dibelius, *Rom*, 198.

[64] Vogt, "Frühkirche," 169.

[65] For an overview of the scholarship on the question of primacy and the understanding of office until c. 1980, see Fuellenbach, *Ecclesiastical Office*.

[66] So van Cauwelaert, "L'intervention," 282.

[67] So, in criticism of van Cauwelaert, Altaner, "Clemens." Vielhauer, *Geschichte*, 538 concludes

from the "casual way in which the Roman church interferes in Corinth" that "such self-assurance and striving for power can be seen only as primatial."

[68] Welborn, "Clement," 1059, argues that the Roman intervention in Corinth is oriented toward the model of "the actions of the Roman senate and the emperor." "In adopting the ideology and strategy of the government, Clement endorsed the Roman imperium," which (according to Welborn) is shown primarily by the reference to military discipline. On this point, see n. 32 above.

fellowship's emissaries. The letter obviously wants to work through the force of its internal line of argumentation; it thus appeals to traditional authorities, chiefly the Bible; but it claims no special authority for the Roman fellowship.[69]

Whether the letter had any direct effect immediately cannot be determined; but it can be concluded from the fact that it was regularly read in Corinth in much later times that, at least in the longer term, its argumentation was successful.[70]

10. Theological Profile

1Clem represents the Christianity of the Roman fellowship at the end of the first century. Notable on the one hand are the intensive use of the Greek Bible and the relatively strong connection to Paul,[71] but also on the other hand the impartiality with which non-Christian and non-Jewish traditions and terminology are used.[72]

In the center of the theology of 1Clem stands the discussion about God. God is the παντοκράτωρ (prescript, 2.3, 32.4, 60.4, 62.2), the δεσπότης (7.5, 8.2, and elsewhere), the κτίστης (19.2, 59.3, 62.2) or δημιουργός (20.11, 26.1, 33.2, 35.3, 59.2; cf. 38.3), and the πατήρ (19.2, 29.1, 62.2). This language about God corresponds in expression and imagery with that of Greek-speaking Judaism.[73] God is the Giver of the προστάγματα and the δικαιώματα, which are self-evidently to be kept by Christians (2.8). Therefore the sinful abandonment of the φόβος τοῦ θεοῦ leads to the loss of righteousness and peace (3.4); but God always gives people the opportunity to repent (7.4-7, 8.2-5), and this fact is constantly announced anew by preachers authorized by God (8.1, 57.1). God bestows grace on those who obey him and abandon their own vanity (9.1), recognizing that God knows the thoughts of humans (21.3, 9).

Inextricably linked with faith are obedience and penitence (10.1-2, 11.1, 14.1, 22.1; cf. 34.5, 62.2). Therefore judgment threatens those who as in Corinth incite ἔρις and στάσις (14.2), just as it does those who doubt (23.1-5; cf. 27.1–28.4). However, God's will aims at the healthful ordering of the cosmos he created (19.3–20.11, 33.2-7), and this will for salvation shows itself in everyday

---

69 Contra Lösch, *Brief*, 187, who argues that the intervention makes sense only if it arose "from an awareness of a duty to watch over the tradition" and if it was therefore meant to be "an act of an authoritative manner to save the κοινὸν τῆς ἐλπίδος [51.1]."

70 Schmitt, *Paroikie*, 2: "The intervention was successful." This fact may have had two different but not mutually exclusive reasons: "Either the audience had such a high opinion of the senders at the time that they bowed to their instruction, or the letter succeeded on the persuasive strength of the arguments it contained." Schmitt concludes with good reason that both possibilities are correct (5).

71 Cf. Lindemann, *Paulus*, 72–82, 177–99; further idem, "Paul's Influence." Lona, *Clemensbrief*, 62, states that the Christianity of the letter "cannot be derived from Paul" and can therefore "not be measured with regard to its similarity or distance from Pauline theology." But it is immediately obvious that Paul plays a very fundamental role.

72 Lona, *Clemensbrief*, 61: The influence of Greco-Roman culture is slighter than Jewish or Christian tradition, but still "greater than that of the New Testament."

73 Cf. Marcus, *Names*, 43–120. See further Zimmermann, *Namen*, 159–60, 311–12.

experience (24.1-5) and also, for example, in the wonderful events surrounding the phoenix (25.1–26.3).[74] 1Clem takes from Paul the thought that all people at all times will be declared righteous before God only by faith (πίστις) and not by their own works (32.3-4). The recognition of the God-given order (τάξις, 40.1, 42.2) is plainly decisive; here the theological center of the letter links itself to the goal of its composition (40–45). In 59.3–61.3 the author cites a long prayer for community; it is set up by christological statements (59.2) and also structured by christological formulae, but it addresses God alone with manifold epithets.[75]

God is the Father of Jesus Christ (36.4-6), in whom God has obtained our salvation for us (36.1) and "taught kindness and long-suffering" (13.1). "Christians' relationship to God is grounded in Him, since God has chosen (50.7) and called (59.2, 65.2) us through Him and has given us the right knowledge of God through Him (36.1-2)."[76] The discussion of the Spirit has by contrast less weight: The author uses triadic formulas in two places (46.6, 58.2); according to 8.1, the "servants of God's grace" (διά πνεύματος ἁγίου) have preached of repentance, and in 13.1 an Old Testament quotation is introduced with the remark that here "the Holy Ghost" speaks (cf. 16.2, 45.2). According to 42.3, the apostles accomplished their world mission "with the fullness of the Holy Ghost" (μετὰ πληροφορίας πνεύματος ἁγίου). Such statements do not exceed the understanding of πνεῦμα apparent in the New Testament; on the other hand, the idea that Christians are endowed with the Spirit through baptism is missing, as is the discussion of spiritual gifts characteristic of Paul (χαρίσματα or πνευματικά). The statement in 63.2 that the Roman congregation has written the letter διὰ τοῦ ἁγίου πνεύματος does not mean that the text claims to be "inspired"; however, it may well mean that the expressions here are not simply of personal convictions.

Important for the theology (and also for the ecclesiological argumentation) of 1Clem is the (apocalyptic or future-focused) eschatology. God will bring about the resurrection of the dead (24.1), obviously only for those who "served [Him] well in the confidence of pious belief" (26.1); those who persist in evil deeds remain reserved for the future judgment (μέλλοντα κρίματα, 28.1). The letter speaks of the second coming of Christ indirectly in 23.5 and then explicitly, if in an unusual way, in 50.3 (φανερωθήσονται ἐν τῇ ἐπισκοπῇ τῆς βασιλείας τοῦ Χριστοῦ); the formulation in 42.3 of the sermon on the coming kingdom of God recalls Luke's use of language (cf. Acts 8:12, 20:25). The strictly future-oriented eschatology implies that the world God created is nearly immortal—the end times are no longer hoped for concretely, but rather are basically conceived abstractly and in any case not near the goal of history.[77] There is no reason to

---

[74] 1Clem offers an unusual setting for this mythos, namely that it can be seen as an unusual source of religious history; see Lindemann, *Clemensbriefe*, 88–89 (Exkurs: Die Überlieferungen vom Vogel Phönix). Numerous texts are printed in the same book, 263–77.

[75] Cf. Lona, *Studien*.

[76] Bultmann, *Theologie*, 538.

[77] On this Knoch, *Eigenart*, 452–55, who criticizes 1Clem for this reason; cf. the objections to Knoch by Räisänen, "'Werkgerechtigkeit,'" 98n77.

derive a doubt about the second coming from the "doubt" criticized by the author of 1Clem (11.2, 23.2-3).

The occasionally advanced thesis that 1Clem teaches a Christianity understood only as moral does not capture the kernel of its thought. 1Clem pursues an ecclesiological goal as ἔντευξις (63.2); the moral instructions, somewhat in the form of the catalogue of vices or even of the recounting of examples, without exception serve as argumentative support for the demand for "peace and harmony," understood as ecclesiological, that is to say social, values. The author wants to show the fact that and in what ways the God-ordained order of the church must be (re)established. To this idea corresponds the anthropology: The letter understands the person as a rational being that with proper instruction is capable of deciding for itself to do the good; only in hindsight does it become clear to a person that only God makes him capable of actually doing it. Only under these premises can 1Clem grasp people as creatures capable of being spoken to from the μετάνοια; "sin" is consequently the isolated offence against God (the word ἁμαρτία appears mostly in quotations anyway) and not a power that keeps the person enslaved under its rule.

11.   Authorship and Dating

Even the earliest express reference to 1Clem by Dionysius of Corinth (see above) connects the letter with "Clement," who was the third bishop of Rome (after Linus and Anenkletus) according to the lists of Roman bishops; Tertullian passes on the tradition (Praescr 32.2) that Clement was directly "ordained" by Peter (*a Petro ordinatum est*), as Polycarp was by the Apostle John.[78] To be sure, according to its prescript, 1Clem is a text by the (entire) Roman ἐκκλσία, and this aspect is maintained throughout the letter. In reality, though, the letter may have been composed by a single author, as the unified linguistic style and method of argumentation prove; the congregation probably authorized the letter later. The author was probably a leader of the Roman congregation, certainly a man; he might have been an office-holder, but beyond that we cannot say anything more accurate. Efforts to identify the author with the Clement referred to by Paul in Philippians 4:3 (Eus HE III 15-16) or even with the Clement referred to in HermVis II 4.3[79] presuppose that the connection of the letter with the name "Clement" is reliable; but that cannot be proven. It is always possible that in reality a man named Clement had a leadership role in the Roman fellowship and that the "anonymous"

---

[78] On this, see Bevenot, "Clement," 98–107, who also sees Clement as a direct disciple of Peter and Paul in the list in Irenaeus (Haer III 3).

[79] So Harnack, *Einführung*, 11.50, who connects him to the consul Titus Flavius Clemens who was condemned for "atheism" under Domitian (see Suet Dom 15.1; Dio Cass LXVII 14.1-2); he supposes that the author could have been a slave or freedman of the consul.

letter was therefore connected with his name.[80] P. Lampe had undertaken the attempt to characterize the author's persona, especially the philosophical and literary education that can be reconstructed from the letter;[81] he makes it probable that the author was not a Jewish Christian, especially since his biblical interpretation does not recall Jewish self-understanding.[82] On the other hand, the author was certainly familiar with Jewish and Jewish Christian tradition.[83]

The time of composition of 1Clem is often connected with the end of the reign of Domitian, who was murdered on September 18, 96; according to this view, the introduction in 1.1 looks back at a recently ended persecution of Christians in Rome, which cannot in any case mean the persecution by Nero. However, reports of a persecution of Christians by Domitian, even in Rome, are late and uncertain.[84] The statement in 41.2 about the "constant sacrifice in the temple" does not allow the deduction of either a dating of the letter to before the year 70 or the assumption that the temple cult in Jerusalem was continued after 70.[85] So a dating of 1Clem is at best made possible through the analysis of the presumed church structure; evidence for a not-too-late origin (in any case still before 100) is the fact that 1Clem, like the Pastoral Epistles, does indeed recognize ἐπίσκοποι but still no monepiscopate; evidence against a significantly earlier date[86] is the apparently long-accepted existence of the office of presbyter.[87] At any rate, the dating of the letter to the last decade of the first century is widely accepted in scholarship,[88] while earlier dates (to the time of Nero) and later dates (to the time of Trajan or Hadrian) have been rightly discarded.[89]

---

[80] Lona, *Clemensbrief,* 71. Lona asks whether "the 'canon law' moment in 1Clem is not a consequence of the judicial thought and feeling of a Roman author who represented the thought of a leading portion of the congregation at the same time."

[81] Lampe, *Christen,* 172–82.

[82] Lampe, *Christen,* 59.

[83] Cf. Lona, *Clemensbrief,* 58–61.

[84] Cf. Vogt, "Christenverfolgung," 1167–70; then he himself still freely judges 1Clem 1.1 and 7.1 to be a reference to such a persecution. On the problem of a "Domitianic persecution," see Erlemann, *Datierung,* 595–97. What can be historically proven, says Erlemann, are "simply reprisals against individual nobles of the Roman society" (597).

[85] So Clark, "Worship," 269–80. Rightly critical of this view is Schmitt, *Paroikie,* 117–22.

[86] Powell, *Clemens,* 117: "most likely during the reign of Vespasian," also 69–79.

[87] Erlemann, *Datierung,* 607: "The internal evidence of the text point—with all due caution—to the last third of the first century, to a time in which

eyewitnesses of the Apostles and thus of these founding leaders of the Corinthian church still lived." Erlemann reaches this conclusion primarily from 44.3, which assumes that "some of the presbyters of the first generation" still lived (605–6). But 44.3 does not say *when* these presbyters were "established"; the reference to Stephen as the firstborn of Achaia (1 Cor 16:15) does not mean that there were already "leading officials in Corinth" (so Erlemann, 606) in the sense of the office of presbyter in the mid-50s.

[88] Lona, *Clemensbrief,* 77–78.

[89] Advocates of both positions appear in Lightfoot, *Fathers* I/1, 346; cf. Fuellenbach, *Ecclesiastical Office,* 2–3. A plea for a late date (middle of the 2nd c.) in recent scholarship appears only in Eggenberger, *Quellen,* who holds the Corinthian situation described in 1Clem to be deliberate fiction; his critics include von Campenhausen, "Rez. Eggenberger," 38–39. In view of the apparent testimony, Welborn, *Clement,* 1060, does not want to agree to a time of composition more definite than "between A.D. 80 and 140."

12.   Bibliography

Altaner, B. "Der 1. Clemensbrief und der römische Primat." In *Kleine patristische Schriften* by B. Altaner, edited by G. Clockmann, 534–39. TU 83. Berlin 1967.

———."Neues zum Verständnis von I Clemens 5,1–6,2." In *Kleine patristische Schriften* by B. Altaner, edited by G. Clockmann, 527–33. TU 83. Berlin 1967.

Bakke, O. M. *"Concord and Peace": A Rhetorical Analysis of the First Letter of Clement with an Emphasis on the Language of Unity and Sedition.* WUNT II/143. Tübingen 2001.

Barnard, L. W. "Clement of Rome and the Persecution of Domitian." *NTS* 10 (1963–1964): 251–60.

Bartsch, H.-W. "Röm 9,5 und 1Clem 32,4." *ThZ* 21 (1965): 401–9.

Bauer, W. *Rechtglaubigkeit und Ketzerei im ältesten Christentum.* BHT 10. Tübingen ²1964 (with an afterword by G. Strecker).

Baumeister, T. *Die Anfänge der Theologie des Martyriums.* MBTh 49. Munich 1980.

Bevenot, M. "Clement of Rome in Irenaeus' Succession List." *JThS* NS 17 (1966): 98–107.

Beyschlag, K. "1. Clemens 40–44 und das Kirchenrecht." In *Reformatio und Confessio* (FS Wilhelm Maurer), edited by F. W. Kantzenbach and G. Müller, 9–22. Berlin 1965.

———. *Clemens Romanus und der Frühkatholizismus: Untersuchungen zu I Clemens 1–7.* BHT 35. Tübingen 1966.

———. "Zur EIPHNH BAΘEIA (1Clem 2,2)." *VC* 26 (1972): 18–23.

Blum, G. G. *Tradition und Sukzession: Studien zum Normbegriff des Apostolischen von Paulus bis Irenäus.* AGTL 9. Berlin 1963.

Brandt, W. "Die Wortgruppe λειτυργεῖν im Hebräerbrief und bei Clemens Romanus." *JThSB* 1 (1930): 145–76.

Brennecke, H.-Ch. "Danaiden und Dirken: Zu 1Clem 6,2." *ZKG* 88 (1977): 302–8.

Brunner, G. *Die theologische Mitte des ersten Klemensbriefes: Ein Beitrag zur Hermeneutik frühchristlicher Texte.* FThS 11. Frankfurt/Main 1972.

Bultmann, R. *Theologie des Neuen Testaments.* Tübingen ⁴1961.

Bumpus, H. B. *The Christological Awareness of Clement of Rome and Its Sources.* Cambridge 1972.

Camenhausen, H. von. *Kirchliches Amt und geistliche Vollmacht in den ersten drei Jahrhunderten.* BHT 14. Tübingen ²1963.

———. "Rez. von C. Eggenberger, *Die Quellen der politischen Ethik des 1. Klemensbriefes*, 1951." *TLZ* 77 (1952): 38–39.

Chadwick, H. "Justification by Faith and Hospitality." *StPatr* 4.2. *TU* 79:281–85. Berlin 1961.

Clark, K. W. "Worship in the Jerusalem Temple after A.D. 70." *NTS* 6 (1959–1960): 269–80.

Cockerill, G. L. "Heb 1:1-14, 1Clem 36.1-6, and the High Priest Title." *JBL* 97 (1978): 437–40.

Cullmann, O. "Les causes de la mort de Pierre et de Paul d'apres le témoignage de Clement de Rome." *RHPhR* 10 (1930) : 294–300.

Dibelius, M. "Rom und die Christen im ersten Jahrhundert." In *Botschaft und Geschichte: Gesammelte Aufsätze II*, 177–228. Tübingen 1956.

Eggenberger, C. *Die Quellen der politischen Ethik des 1. Klemensbriefes*. Zürich 1951.

Ellingworth, P. "Hebrews and 1 Clement: Literary Dependence or Common Tradition?" *BZ* NF 23 (1979): 262–69.

Erlemann, K. "Die Datierung des ersten Klemensbriefes—Anfragen an eine Communis Opinio." *NTS* 44 (1988): 591–607.

Faivre, A. "Le Systeme normative dans la Lettre de Clement de Rome aux Corinthiens." *RevSR* 54 (1980): 129–52.

Fisher, E. W. "Let Us Look Upon the Blood of Christ (1Clem 7.4)." *VC* 34 (1980): 218–36.

Fuellenbach, J. *Ecclesiastical Office and the Primacy of Rome: An Evaluation of Recent Theological Discussion of First Clement*. SCA 20. Washington, D.C. 1980.

Gerke, F. *Die Stellung des ersten Clemensbriefes innerhalb der Entwicklung der altchristlichen Gemeindeverfassung und des Kirchenrechts*. TU 47.1. Leipzig 1932.

Hagner, D. A. *The Use of the Old and New Testaments in Clement of Rome*. NT.S 34. Leiden 1973.

Harnack, A. von. *Einführung in die alte Kirchengeschichte: Das Schreiben der römischen Kirche an die korinthische aus der Zeit Domitians (1. Clemensbrief)*. Leipzig 1929.

———. *Militia Christi: Die christliche Religion und der Soldatenstand in den ersten drei Jahrhunderten*. Tübingen 1905.

———. "Über die jünst entdeckte lateinische Übersetzung des ersten Klemensbriefes." *SAB* 1894:261–73.

Jaeger, W. "Echo eines unerkannten Tragikerfragments in Clemens' Brief an die Korinther." *RhMus* 102 (1959): 330–40.

Jaubert, A. "Les Sources de la Conception Militaire de l'Eglise en 1 Clement 37." *VC* 18 (1964): 74–84.

———. "Thèmes Lévitiques dans la Prima Clementis." *VC* 18 (1964): 193–203.

Knoch, O. *Eigenart und Bedeutung der Eschatologie im theologisches Aufriß des ersten Clemensbriefes*. Theoph 17. Bonn 1964.

———. "Im Namen des Petrus und Paulus: Der Brief des Clemens Romanus und die Eigenart des römischen Christentums." *ANRW* II.27.1:3–54. Berlin/New York 1992.

Knopf, R. *Die Lehre der Zwölf Apostel: Die zwei Clemensbriefe*. Die Apostolischen Väter I, HNT-distributed volume. Tübingen 1920.

Köhler, W.-D. *Die Rezeption des Matthäusevangeliums in der Zeit vor Irenäus*. WUNT II/24. Tübingen 1987.

Köster, H. *Synoptische Überlieferung bei den Apostolischen Vätern*. TU 65. Berlin 1957.

Lampe, P. *Die stadtrömischen Christen in den ersten beiden Jahrhundereten: Untersuchungen zur Sozialgeschichte*. WUNT II/18. Tübingen 1987.

Leder, H.-G. "Das Unrecht der Presbyterabsetzung in Korinth: Zur Interpretation von 1. Cl. 44,1-6." *ThV* 10 (1979): 107–27.

Lightfoot, J. B. *The Apostolic Fathers* I 1.2: *S. Clement of Rome: A Revised Text with Introductions, Notes, Dissertations and Translations*. Hildesheim/New York 1973. (Reprinted from the ²1890 ed.)

Lindemann, A. *Die Clemensbriefe*. Die Apostolischen Väter 1. HNT 17. Tübingen 1992.

———."Paul's Influence on 'Clement' and Ignatius." In *Trajectories through the New Testament and the Apostolic Fathers*, edited by A. F. Gregory and Chr. M. Tuckett, 9–24. Oxford 2005.

———. *Paulus im ältesten Christentum: Das Bild des Apostels und die Rezeption der paulinischen Theologie in der frühchristlichen Literatur bis Marcion*. BHT 58. Tübingen 1979.

Lohmann, H. *Drohung und Verheißung: Exegetisches Untersuchungen zur Eschatologie bei den Apostolischen Vätern*. BZNW 55. Berlin 1989.

Löhr, H. *Studien zum frühchristlichen und frühjüdischen Gebet: Untersuchungen zu 1 Clem 59 bis 61 in seinem literarischen, historischen und theologischen Kontext*. WUNT 160. Tübingen 2003.

Lona, H. E. *Der erste Clemensbrief*. KAV 2. Göttingen 1998.

Lösch, S. "Der Brief des Clemens Romanus: Die Probleme und ihre Beurteilung in der Gegenwart." In *Studi dedicati alla memoria di Paolo Ubaldi*, 177–88. PUCSCV/16. Milan 1937.

Luschnat, O. "Griechisches Gemeinshaftsdenken bei Clemens Romanus." In *Antiquitas Graeco-Romana ac tempora nostra*, edited by J. Burian and L. Vidman, 125–31. Prague 1968.

Marcus, R. "Divine Names and Attributes in Hellenistic-Jewish Literature." *PAAJR* 3 (1932): 3–120.

Mees, M. "Die Hohepriester-Theologie des Hebräerbriefes im Vergleich mit dem Ersten Clemensbrief." *BZ* NF 22 (1978): 115–24.

Meinhold, P. "Geschehen und Deutung im Ersten Clemensbrief." *ZKG* 58 (1939): 82–129.

Mikat, P. "Der 'Ausweisungsrat' (1 Clem 54,2) als Schlüssel zum Gemeindeverständnis im 1. Clemensbrief." In *Geschichte, Recht, Religion, Politik (GAufs) I*, 361–73. Paderborn 1984.

———. *Die Bedeutung der Begriffe Stasis und Aponoia für das Verständnis des 1. Clemensbriefes*. AGF-G 155. Cologne 1969.

———. "Zur Fürbitte der Christen für Kaiser und Reich im Gebet des 1. Clemensbriefes." In *Festschrift für Ulrich Scheuner*, 455–71. Berlin 1973.

Mitteis, L., and U. Wilcken. *Grundzüge und Chrestomathie der Papyruskunde, I, II*. Leipzig/Berlin 1912.

Mohrmann, C. "Les origines de la latinité chrétienne à Rome." *VC* 3 (1949): 67–106.

Noll, R. R. "The Search for a Christian Ministerial Priesthood in I Clement." *StPatr* 13. *TU* 116:250–54. Berlin 1975.

Opitz, H. *Ursprünge frühkatholischer Pneumatologie: Ein Beitrag zur Entstehung der Lehre vom Heiligen Geist in der römischen Gemeinde unter Zugrundlegung des I. Clemensbriefes und des „Hirten" des Hermas*. ThA 15. Berlin 1960.

Peterson, E. "Das Praescriptum des 1. Clemens-Briefes." In *Frühkirche, Judentum und Gnosis: Studien und Untersuchungen*, 129–36. Rome 1959.

Pratscher, W. *Der zweite Clemensbrief*. KAV 3. Göttingen 2007.

Pöhlmann, W. *Die heidnische, jüdische und christliche Opposition gegen Domitian: Studien zur Neutestamentlichen Zeitgeschichte*. Diss. Erlangen 1966.

Powell, D. "Clemens von Rom." *TRE* 8 (1981): 113–20.

Quinn, J. D. "'Seven Times He Wore Chains' (1Clem 5.6)." *JBL* 97 (1978): 574–76.

Räisänen, H. "'Werkgerechtichkeit'—eine 'frühkatholische' Lehre? Überlegungen zum 1. Klemensbrief." *ST* 37 (1983): 79–99.

Rohde, J. "Häresie und Schisma im ersten Clemensbrief und in den Ignatiusbriefen." *NT* 10 (1968): 216–33.

Sanders, L. *L'Hellénisme de Saint Clement de Rome et le Paulinisme.* StHell II. Leuven 1943.

Schermann, T. *Griechische Zauberpapyri und das Gemeinde und Dankgebet im 1. Klemens-briefe.* TU 34.2b. Leipzig 1909.

Schmitt, T. *Paroikie und Oikoumene: Sozial- und mentalitätsgeschichtliche Untersuchungen zum 1. Clemensbrief.* BZNW 110. Berlin/New York 2002.

Schneider, G. *Clemens von Rom: Epistola ad Corinthios: Brief an die Korinther.* FC 15. Freiburg i.B. 1994.

Schöllgen, G. "Monepiskopat und monarchischer Episkopat: Eine Bemerkung zur Termi-nologie." *ZNW* 77 (1986): 147–51.

Smith, M. "The Report about Peter in 1 Clement 5:4." *NTS* 7 (1960–1961): 86–88.

Theissen, G. *Untersuchungen zum Hebräerbrief.* StNT 2. Gütersloh 1969.

Ullmann, W. "The Significance of the Epistula Clementis." *JThS.NS* 11 (1960): 295–317.

Van Cauwelaert, R. "L'intervention de l'église de Rome à Corinthe vers l'an 96." *RHE* 31 (1935): 267–306, 765–68.

Van den Broek, R. *The Myth of the Phoenix According to Classical and Early Christian Tradi-tions.* EPRO 24. Leiden 1972.

Van Unnik, W. C. "1 Clement 34 and the 'Sanctus.'" *VC* 5 (1951): 204–48.

———. "Is 1 Clement 20 Purely Stoic?" *VC* 4 (1950): 181–89.

———. *Studies over de zogenaamde Eerste Brief van Clemens I: Het litteraire Genre.* Amster-dam 1970.

———. "'Tiefer Friede' (1. Klemens 2,2)." *VC* 24 (1970): 264–79.

Vielhauer, P. *Geschichte der urchristlichen Literatur: Einleitung in das Neue Testament, die Apokryphen und die Apostolischen Väter.* Berlin/New York 1975.

Vogt, H. J. "Christenverfolgung I." *RAC* II:1167–70.

———. "Frühkirche und Amt—neu in der Diskussion." *ZAC* 8 (2005): 462–84. Weiss, B. "Amt und Eschatologie im 1. Clemensbrief." *ThPh* 50 (1975): 70–83.

Welborn, L. L. "Clement, First Epistle of." *ABD* 1 (1992): 1055–60.

Wickert, U. "Eine Fehlübersetzung zu I. Clem 19.2." *ZNW* 49 (1958): 270–75.

Wong, D. W. F. "Natural and Divine Order in I Clement." *VC* 31 (1977): 81–87.

Wrede, W. *Untersuchungen zum Ersten Klemensbrief.* Göttingen 1891.

Young, F. W. "The Relation of 1 Clement to the Epistle James." *JBL* 67 (1948): 339–45.

Ziegler, A. W. *Neue Studien zum ersten Klemensbrief.* Munich 1958.

Ziegler, A. W., and G. Brunner. "Die Frage nach einer politischen Absicht des Ersten Klemensbriefes." *ANRW* II/27.1:55–76. Berlin/New York 1992.

Zimmermann, C. *Die Namen des Vaters: Studien zu ausgewählten neutestamentlichen Gottesbezichnungen vor ihrem frühjüdischen und paganen Sprachhorizont.* AJEC 69. Leiden 2007.

The Second Epistle of Clement

Wilhelm Pratscher

In the second letter of Clement we have the earliest surviving Christian sermon before us. It is most interesting to learn what the central content of instruction was for eastern Gentile Christians in the mid-second century.[1]

1. Textual Tradition

2Clem is attested in only three manuscripts. The oldest is the fifth-century biblical Codex Alexandrinus (A). The text breaks off at 12.5. The complete Greek text appears in Codex Hierosolymitanus (H) from the year 1056. A Syriac translation exists in a Bible manuscript (S) completed in Edessa in 1170 that offers the text of the Harklensis. H and S come from a text from the fifth or sixth century. In all three manuscripts, 2Clem stands beside 1Clem. Its inclusion in biblical codices shows its high reputation.

In addition, there is a series of allusions and witnesses for an earlier date. The oldest testimony may be offered by Origen, to whom Maximus Confessor (Proleg Op Dionys, PG 4.20D) describes knowledge of four letters by Clement. Orig Comm Jo II 34.207 is very close to 2Clem 1.1 (cf. also Comm Rom VIII 2), and there may be a reference to 2Clem 8.1-2 in his eighteenth homily on Jeremiah. Hippolytus of Rome may also have known 2Clem: a fragment of *Contra gentes de universo* that survives in the *Sacra Parallela* (TU.NF 5.2, pp. 137–43, no. 353) contains an allusion to 17.5 and 19.3-4.

The first explicit reference to a second letter by Clement is Eus HE III 38.4, and another appears in the *Apostolic Canons* of 381 (AposCon VIII 47.85); the latter holds both letters of Clement to be canonical. Jerome's Vir ill 15 (TU 14.1.17) probably depends on Eusebius. The so-called *Praedestinatus* (I 14, PL 53.591 bc), which dates from circa 430, even preserves an awareness of the anti-Gnostic orientation of 2Clem.[2]

---

[1] For details, see Pratscher, *Clemensbrief*, 9–64.

[2] In later times there are quotations as well as testimonies and allusions: A reference to 2Clem 17.5-6 appears in a work falsely attributed to Justin Martyr, *Quaestiones et Responsiones ad Orthodoxos 74 of Theodoret of Kryos* (Otto [3]III/2.108, 110), the author of which may have understood 2Clem to

be part of 1Clem. A quotation of 2Clem 1.1-2 and 9.5a appears in the *Florilegium Edessenum anonymum*, falsely attributed to Timotheus (Aelurus) of Alexandria (+ 477) (SBAW.PH 1933, H 5, pp. 4–5 no. 6 and 7). The text refers to 2Clem with minor differences from the manuscripts. It has a monophysite orientation. The same goes for the quotation

2. Literary Unity

2Clem 19.1–20.4 does not belong to the original sermon 1.1–18.2, 20.5. This fact is attested by a difference in word usage: the salutation in the sermon is always ἀδελφοί (1.1, 4.3, and elsewhere), in the appendix ἀδελφοὶ καὶ ἀδελφαὶ (19.1, 20.2). The sermon refers to itself as συμβουλία (15.1); the appendix understands it as ἔντευξις (19.1). The term ἀντιμισθία, which is central to the sermon (1.3, 5; 9.7; and elsewhere), is missing in the appendix, whereas the terms εὐσέβεια (19.1, 20.4, and elsewhere) and ἀδικία (19.2, 20.1) are absent in the sermon. Different words are used for the same or related topics, such as ἐντολή (3.4, 4.5, and elsewhere) versus πρόσταγμα (19.3).

There are also theological differences. The motif of God's prevenient grace (1.8, 15.3-5) is absent in the appendix. The preacher's strong awareness of sin (16.2-3, 18.2) is weakened by the discussion of the occasional ignorance of evil (19.2).

A final further difference is the congregational situation. While the stress on alms has greater meaning in the sermon and those who are able to give are addressed in particular (16.4), the *anagnose* (or lector, the composer of the appendix) differentiates between unjust wealth and the hard-pressed servant of God (20.1).

All of these facts lead to the conclusion that there were two different authors. The appendix, given that it begins "I read you an exhortation" (19.1), probably does not belong at the end but at the beginning of the sermon as its introduction. The expression "After the God of truth has spoken" (19.1) also does not fit the sermon but must refer to an earlier lection of Scripture. Coming from the spiritual milieu of 1Clem, the *anagnose*[3] would thus have inserted a part between the lection and the sermon in which he introduced the themes of the sermon as in an overture and concentrated on those that were most important to him. Only later, probably when the sermon (1.1–18.2, 20.5) was placed beside 1Clem and lost its

---

from 2Clem 1.1-2 in *Florilegium of Severus of Antioch* (+ 538), *Liber contra impium grammaticum* 3.41 (CSCO 101.283 Syriac, 102.208 Latin translation).—In the second half of the sixth century, Dorotheus Archimandrites, abbot of a monastery in Gaza, quotes freely from 2Clem 7.3 in *Doctr 23* (PG 88.1836b). To the stream of tradition documented in Ps.-Timotheus and Severus belong the seventh-century *Excerpta Patrum* (Lightfoot, *Fathers* I/1, 184–86 Syriac and English translation). Quotations come from 1.1a and 9.1-5. There is little reason to presuppose independent knowledge of 2Clem in these excerpt collections. 2Clem may also be assumed in the *Index of the Six Canonical Books* (7th c.; Preuschen, *Analecta* II², 69). A Greek quotation from 2Clem 20.1, 3 appears in the *Sacra*

Parallela (TU.NF 5.2, p. 2, no. 2). 2Clem is also attested in the *Stichometry* of Nicephorus (ca. 850; Preuschen, *Analecta* II², 64). Allusions to 1.1 and elsewhere appear in Photius *Bibl 126*, and finally a possible citation of 3.2-4a appears in the *Pandects of the Syrian Monk Nikon*, Sermon 18 (around 1088; Cotelier, *Patrum* I, 155).

3 Apparent similarities between the appendix and 1Clem show this fact: e.g., in other early Christian literature, ἔντευξις in the sense of "written exhortation" appears only in 1Clem 63.2. Similarly, apart from Philippians 3:14, σκοπός (19.1) appears only in 1Clem 19.2 and 63.1. The term εὐσέβεια (19.1 and elsewhere) appears among the Apostolic Fathers only in 1Clem 1.2, 11.1, etc.

connection to the lection, would this introduction have been moved to the end of the sermon, with the closing doxology 20.5 forming the conclusion.

3. Structure

The structure of 2Clem is difficult to determine.[4] It lacks an overarching logical thought construction. Rather, the text displays a loose structure of sayings that revolve around the theme of right behavior in view of the coming judgment. However, the salvation event in Christ is emphasized strongly in chapters 1–3. Then follows the eschatological motivation of the exhortation (4–18). Clear divisions exist before 8.1 and 16.1, where the topic turns to timely penance. Chapters 19–20 (minus 20.5) form another unit. From there one can assume the following structure:

1.1–3.5		The primary christological basis of the exhortation
	1.1-8	Description of the salvation event
	2.1-7	Evidence of Scripture
	3.1-5	Confession as consequence of the past deeds of Jesus and as precondition for his eschatological behavior
4.1–18.2		The eschatological basis for the exhortation
	4.1-5	Commanded behavior as a prerequisite for eschatological salvation
	5.1-7	Fear of death and overcoming it by doing the will of Christ
	6.1-9	Conduct appropriate to the future age as precondition for salvation
	7.1-6	Competition for immortality
	8.1–9.6	Timely penance and bodily existence
	9.7–10.5	Timely penance and its eschatological consequences
	11.1-7	Certainty of God's call and the skeptics
	12.1-6	Behavior in view of the coming kingdom of God
	13.1-4	Penance and outsiders

---

[4] A few examples of organizational schemes that run from three to thirteen sections:

3: Gebhardt/Harnack, *Epistulae*, LXVII–LXIX: 1–2 / 3–20.4 / 20.5

4: Lightfoot, *Fathers* I/2, 208–10: 1–8 / 9–12 / 13–14 / 15–20

5: Warns, *Untersuchungen*, 134: 1 / 2–14 / 15–18 / 19.1–20.4 / 20.5

6: Lindemann, *Clemensbriefe*, 197: 1 / 2–7 / 8–14 / 15–18 / 19.1–20.4 / 20.5

7: Knopf, *Clemensbriefe*, 151: 1–2 / 3–4 / 5–6 / 7–8 / 9–12 / 13–18 / 19–20

9: Stegemann, *Herkunft*, 87–90: 1–2 / 3–4 / 5–8.3 / 8.4–13.4 / 14 / 15 / 16–17 / 18 / 19–20

11: Wengst, *Zweiter Klemensbrief*, 209: 1–4 / 5–6 / 7 / 8–9 / 10–12 / 13 / 14 / 15 / 16–18 / 19.1–20.4 / 20.5

13: Baasland, "Rhetorik," 94: 1–2 / 3–4 / 5–6 / 7 / 8 / 9 / 10–12 / 13 /14 / 15 / 16–17 / 18 / 19–20

14.1-5	Participation in the future church
15.1-5	Behavior and forthright prayer

16.1-4	Encouragement to timely penance and to right behavior
17.1–18.2	Penance and judgment
19.1–20.4	Closing exhortation
20.5	Closing doxology

4.   Genre

The traditional designation "letter" comes from the connection to 1Clem first referenced by Eus HE III 38.4 and the evidence of the manuscripts. It obviously does not come from the content. Not only is it missing all characteristic epistolary formulae such as pre- and postscripts, correspondence, and the like, but the document itself never refers to itself as a letter.

The scholarly consensus is that 2Clem, all told, is a sermon. Discussion of it as a homily[5] is plainly mistaken: A sermon that goes verse by verse over a text is not present. However, the character of the sermon or speech is clear from the salutations (1.1; 5.1, 5; and elsewhere) as well as from the references to the present admonition from the presbyter and the process of remembering what was said at home (17.3). According to 19.1 the sermon in 1.1–18.2 and 20.5 was read aloud by the *anagnose*, apparently having been written originally by a presbyter (17.3).

The author refers to the sermon in 15.1 as συμβουλία περὶ ἐγκρατείας; he talks in 17.3 about νουθετεῖσθαι. It is not about sexual abstinence (cf. 4.3, 6.4), but rather generally about distance from worldly ways of behavior, to which the audience is commanded, encouraged, and exhorted. The sermon is thus to be understood as an admonition to penance and to right behavior. It could be characterized as a sermon on penance or as an exhortation. It has an emphatic orientation toward exhortation. Theologically accentuated passages (Christology in chaps. 1–2 and ecclesiology in chap. 14) can be understood on this foundational alignment.

The preceding lection presumed by the *anagnose* in 19.1 in the syntagma θεὸς τῆς ἀληθείας may also have applied to the preacher. A concrete text is impossible to name.[6] 2Clem is not an exegetical sermon, although the author frequently uses quotations from Scripture.

---

5   E.g., Pauli, "Korintherbrief," 329; Frank, *Studien*, 187; Μπονῆς, Συμπόσιον, 5.

6   Zahn, "Kirchengebet," 206, reasoned from the christologically oriented introductory phrase to Acts 10; Knopf, "Anagnose," 272, from the frequent use of Deutero- and Tritoisaiah to Isaiah 54–66; Schüssler, "Klemensbrief," 13, from the juxtaposition of hymns and exhortations in early Christian church services (cf. Plin Ep X 96) to a Christ hymn such as 1 Timothy 3:16.

5. Intertextual Relationships

2Clem offers an inordinate number of quotations from the Old Testament/Jewish and early Christian tradition. The preacher knows himself to be bound by this tradition and understands himself based on it, especially in the debate with his adversaries.

5.1 Quotations from the Old Testament/Jewish Tradition

There are numerous quotations from the Old Testament: 2.1 (Isa 54:1); 3.5 (Isa 29:13); 6.8 (Ezek 14:14-20 in paraphrase[7]); 7.6 and 17.5 (Isa 66:24b); 13.2 (Isa 52:5b); 14.1b (Jer 7:11); 14.2 (Gen 1:27); 15.3 (Isa 58:9); 17.4-5a (Isa 66:18). Except in 2.1 and 17.5, the quotations are all preceded by a citation formula. The decisive verb is λέγειν, which is mostly in the present tense and thus emphasizes the present meaning of the quotation (3.5, 6.8, etc.). The presumed speakers are God (15.3), the *Kyrios* (13.2, 17.4-5a), and the Scriptures (6.8, 14.1b, etc.). By the *Kyrios*, as the New Testament parallels (see below) show, the author probably means Jesus. The citation formulae blur the line between God and Jesus, to the point that in 13.4 God appears as the speaker of a New Testament logion.

There are also quotations from New Testament texts, though ignorance of the contexts there means that they could come from other sources. The possibilities include a manuscript containing the relevant Old Testament texts (Gen, Isa, Jer, and Ezek), an apocryphal gospel, and maybe a collection of quotations. Unique variant formulations could come from oral tradition or from the preacher himself. A few details: 2.1 agrees exactly with Isaiah 54:1 LXX. The quotation appears frequently in early Christian texts (Gal 4:27; Just Apol I 53.5; and elsewhere) and could thus have come from a quotation collection. On the other hand, six of the Old Testament quotations are from Isaiah, so a manuscript of Isaiah is more probable, especially since these quotations are frequently close to the LXX text. The other quotations are sometimes closer to the LXX, sometimes further away. The preacher could have known a collection of quotations. Whether he quoted from it or rather from a manuscript of Isaiah or from an apocryphal gospel must remain an open question, however.

Taken together, the quotations have a general parenetic intention. Only 2.1 and 14.1-2 show additional specific theological (= ecclesiological) implications in this frame of reference.

In addition to the verbatim citations there are a few allusions to the Old Testament: 14.1 is on the theme of creation (Ps 71:5, 17 LXX), 16.3 on judgment (Mal 3:19; Isa 34:4).[8]

---

[7] 6.8 may combine Jeremiah 15:1 with PssSol 2.6.

[8] Warns, *Untersuchungen*, 478–84, sees in 3.1, Psalm 113:25-26 LXX and in 10.2 Psalm 33:15 LXX.

Beyond these quotations, there are a few citations from an unknown (probably) Jewish tradition. Section 11.2-4 (like 1Clem 23.3-4) quotes a logion to dispell doubt about the fulfillment of God's promises. Section 11.7 (like 1 Cor 2:9 and 1Clem 34.8) formulates the greatness of God's deeds for his people. Section 17.7 emphasizes the hope of those who have served God honestly.

5.2 Quotations from the Jesus Tradition

Quotations with Close New Testament Parallels

Seven quotations have close parallels to the New Testament: 2.4 (Matt 9:13; Mark 2:17; Luke 5:32), 3.2 (Matt 10:32; Luke 12:8), 4.2 (Matt 7:21; Luke 6:46), 6.1 (Matt 6:24; Luke 16:13), 6.2 (Matt 16:26; Mark 8:36; Luke 9:25), 9.11 (Matt 12:50; Mark 3:35; Luke 8:21), and 13.4 (Matt 5:44; Luke 6:27, 28, 32). Apart from 6.2 (which is directly after 6.1 and does not need one), all of them are preceded by quotation formulae. The decisive verb is again λέγειν, which is used everywhere except 9.11 (εἶπεν). The written nature of the quotations is also shown in the syntagma ἑτέρα γραφή in 2.4. As speaker Jesus is always referred to by a high title: 3.2, 4.2: Χριστός; 6.1, 9.11: κυριός; 13.4: θεός. The beginning evaluation of the Jesus tradition as Scripture has just as theological a meaning as does the use of these titles, up to θεός, for Jesus.

The source of the quotations is nearly impossible to determine.[9] Apart from the verbatim parallel to Mark in 2.4, no quotation can be definitely attributed to Mark. The literary dependence may be on Matthew, on the apocryphal gospel used in 8.5, or even on a quotation collection. A similar situation holds for the other quotations that in part are closer to Luke than to Matthew (3.2, 4.2, 6.2). Preferences one way or another are possible in the question of the source of the New Testament quotations, but in general there must be a final uncertainty.

The question of intent is another matter entirely. Section 2.4 has a christological orientation. There the preacher sees the unassuming behavior of Christ (or God) formulated. It deals with salvation from heathenism (cf. 1.8), not the coming salvation from judgment. All the other quotations from the Jesus tradition have an emphatically parenetic intent.[10] Of these, only the confession of deeds to Christ has any consequence for the entrance into judgment (3.2). They deal with the fulfillment of justice in contrast to empty lip service (4.2) or with the proper adoration of God in contrast to attachment to the world (6.1-2). The brother of Jesus is only he who does the will of the Father (9.11). The pagans should not be led by the difference between word and deed to blaspheme the name of Christ (13.4). Like the quotations from the Old Testament and Jewish tradition, those from the Jesus tradition also aim at the right ordering of life.

---

[9]   Not least of the reasons for this fact is the open question of orality and written texts in the second century.

[10]   This fact fits the overall parenetic orientation of 2Clem.

There are also possible *allusions* to New Testament texts in a few places, such as 3.4a (Luke 6:46), 3.4b (Mark 12:30; Luke 10:27), 4.4 (Mattt 10:28; Luke 12:4-5), 7.1 (1 Cor 9:24-47), and the like. These are mostly not conscious allusions but excerpts from the common tradition material. The intent is again parenetic.

Apocryphal Quotations

From the apocryphal tradition there are four quotations. Their connection to the New Testament is only marginal or nonexistent: 4.5, 5.2-4, 8.5, 12.2-6a.[11] The citation formulae always speak of the κυριός; only in 5.4 is ὁ Ἰησοῦς named; 12.6a lacks a subject. Κυριός is thus used in the apocryphal tradition more often than in the quotations with meaningful New Testament connections. The relationship is also usually changed from λέγειν (5.2, 8.5) to εἶπεν (4.5, 5.4, 12.2). The originally oral character therefore finds much stronger expression in the apocryphal tradition. Nevertheless, a written example is assumed in 8.5. The preacher thus almost certainly used an apocryphal gospel. Even collected quotations from the Jesus tradition may have come from it.

The question of the origin of the quotations must be undertaken individually because of the uncertainties.[12] 4.5 is developed considerably further than the synoptic tradition (Matt 7:23; Luke 13:27); there is a parallel to the so-called Ἰουδαϊκόν (= probably GosNaz 6, NTApo[6] I, 134). Sections 5.3 and 5.4 are different synoptic texts (Matt 10:16; Luke 10:3 or Matt 10:28; Luke 12:5) arranged into a little scene that has a parallel in Just Apol I 19.7. Section 8.5 does have parallels to Luke 16:10-12 and to Iren Haer II 34.3, but because of the introduction of the quotation, the use of an apocryphal gospel here is the unavoidable conclusion. Finally, a quotation without any New Testament parallels is 12.2-6a, with parallels to the Gospel of the Egyptians via Cl Strom III 92.2 and to the Gospel of Thomas 22; a dependence on one of these texts can be deduced from the minimally developed encratistic attitude. If these quotations do not come from the apocryphal gospel used in 8.5, they may represent a further development of the synoptic tradition and possibly also a collection of quotations.

The intent is, as with (most of) the others, parenetic. The preacher does not go into an explication of the theological thought but constantly impresses on the audience anew the importance of doing right. Nevertheless, a theological profile can be recognized.

6. Theological Profile

6.1 Basic Theological Positions

The goal of a sermon is not to impart theological reflections. Even so they are present, albeit for the most part only assumed or briefly hinted at. In this case they are

---

[11] 5.2-4 and 12.2-6a may be originally independent texts (or pieces thereof).

[12] Thus rightly Gregory and Tuckett, "2 Clement," 278.

always ordered toward the overarching parenetic orientation. They mostly present the standard theology of the second-century church.

Teaching about God

That goes especially for the special theology. God is seen as the God who acts in the past, present, and future. So he is also the *Creator* (15.2). In the frame of eschatological salvation this motif is sensible throughout, such that God's act of new creation is to be seen only in connection with the creative act at the beginning of the cosmos. Thus the discussion of God has above all an emphatic anti-Gnostic direction.[13] This accentuation thus goes beyond the traditional conception of creation, to the point that 14.1 speaks of the creation of the spiritual church (united with the heavenly, preexistent Christ in a syzygy) before the sun and the moon.

Next to the creation is God's *work of salvation*. It includes present (for the Christians: past) and future. God is the one who has called us and, further, accepted us on the condition of repentance. The past of the reception of salvation thus stands beside the present of the assurance of salvation, when one is warned to turn to God as long as we still have him who accepts us (16.1; cf. 10.1). The place of the calling cannot be witnessed. The proof of baptism[14] can be witnessed but should not be exclusively for show. In any case, it is important that God's work precedes the deeds demanded of the sermon's audience, which corresponds objectively to the indicative-imperative relationship seen, for example, in Paul (cf. Gal 5:25, etc.), even when this connection is not reflected more closely. This ordinance is also expressed in the theme of the mission of the Savior (20.5; cf. Gal 4:4, John 8:40, etc.). Moreover, it assumes a series of attributes of God's saving deeds: He is the God who saves (9.7; cf. Isa 6:10, etc.), who cares for his own (e.g., 2.3; cf. Isa 58:9, Matt 6:8, etc.), who is kind (15.5; cf. Ps 30:20 LXX, Rom 2:4, etc.). The connection between promise, prayer, and God's willingness to give (15.3-5) likewise shows the preacher's knowledge of the indicative of salvation.

In addition we find a series of traditional expressions about God that indicate His power: He is the all-knowing (9.9; cf. Wis 6.13, Rom 8:27, etc.), the living (20.2; cf. Judg 8:19, 1 Sam 14:39, etc.), the only (20.5; cf. Isa 37:20, John 5:44, etc.), and the invisible God (20.5; cf. Phil Leg All 3.206, Rom 1:20, etc.). He is the Father and the God of truth (3.1, 19.1, etc.; cf. Exod 34:6, John 17:3, etc.).

Christology and Soteriology

Christology and soteriology also have an important place. The author supports the preexistence and mission Christology that had become dominant in the realm of Gentile Christian tradition (cf. Gal 4:4, Phil 2:5-11, John 1:1-14, etc.). Section 14.1-2 presupposes the heavenly Christ being in a preexistent spiritual syzygy with the church created before the sun and the moon. However, in contrast to

---

[13] See below.   [14] Donfried, *Setting*, 147.

his partner in syzygy, Christ Himself is not assumed to be created. At the end of days he has appeared in order to act as Savior and Leader to immortality, in that he discloses the truth about the heavenly life (20.5). Section 1.4 denotes the salvation event that Christ has brought about in several ways: the giving of light, the recognition of sons, the saving of the lost. The place of the salvation event is the passion, interpreted in the frame of the atonement tradition (1.2): The reason for this act is his mercy (3.1). Section 9.5 speaks explicitly about the incarnation. Since the preacher wants to be thoroughly orthodox, the Incarnation is for him self-evidently framed in an antidocetic direction. The keyword σάρξ is also connected with the earthly church in 14.3. The mission presumes the difference in rank between Christ and God, as does the discussion of "my Father" (9.11, 10.1, etc.; cf. Matt 7:21, John 2:16, etc.).

On the other hand, Christ stands directly beside God. Basic terms are used equally of both: calling (God: 10.1, 16.1; Christ: 1.8, 2.4, etc.), teaching of precepts (God: 17.3; Christ: 4.5, 8.4, etc.), saving (God: 10.1; Christ: 1.4-7, etc.). The nearness between God and Christ is already presented as a theme in 1.1: Christ is to be thought of as God is. He exercises the endtime function of judge (1.1). The logion on loving enemies is also introduced with λέγει ὁ θεός (13.4). To be sure, 2Clem does not offer an explicit identification formula (as in, e.g., John 20:29), but the title of God for Christ is implicitly assumed. In any case, it is indisputable that in his deeds he stands on the same level as God, just as in the placing of faith in him. From an outside perspective, God and Christ are inseparable.

Pneumatology and Ecclesiology

Pneumatological and ecclesiological statements are closely connected. According to 9.5, the original spiritual Christ became σάρξ. However, that does not indicate any loss of spiritual properties (cf. e.g., Mark 1:9-11par). The same is true of the risen Christ.

Only chapter 14 (apart from 20.4)[15] uses the term πνεῦμα, again in a christological context, but especially in an ecclesiological one.[16] The preexistent, spiritual church was united with the heavenly Christ in a syzygy (14.1) and has now appeared as σάρξ Χριστοῦ (14.3) and joined with him (i.e., with the Christ to be once again found in heaven) in a new syzygy. The sarcic church is the incarnation of the heavenly spiritual one—a protest against all docetic ecclesiology. However, the relationship between αὐθεντικόν and ἀντίτυπον (different from the juxtaposition of τὸ ὄν and τὸ γιγνόμενον in Plato, Tim 27d) does not assume any devaluation of the σάρξ-church. The latter is the legitimate earthly recalling of the former. The church also has a future eschatological existence, in which it is again

---

[15] A demonological use of πνεῦμα appears here.
[16] Christology and ecclesiology are also not discussed for their own sake but stand, with regard to their common characteristic appearance, in an ethical context.

imagined as spiritual. In the postexistence we have before us yet a third, once more purely spiritual syzygy between Christ and the church (14.3).

Apart from chapter 14, only 2.1 speaks of the church. Isaiah 54:1 ("Sing, O barren one who did not bear") is applied to the church, which was barren before children were given to it. This reference is clearly an allusion to its strengthening in the fight against Gnosticism. No ecclesiological conclusions are drawn.

In view of the many early Christian statements about the Holy Spirit and the church, the strong restraint on this matter in 2Clem is striking. The connection of the Spirit to the present-day church (and thus with present-day believers) is completely absent. In early Christian texts the working of the Spirit in the various forms of the church's daily life is important, whether in its founding (Acts 1:5 etc.), its growth in the mission (Acts 8:29 etc.), its structure in diverse spiritual gifts (1 Cor 12:28, etc.) and officers (1 Tim 4:14), or its doctrinal orientation (2 Tim 1:14, etc.).

Equally striking is that the connection of the Spirit with the concrete shaping of life is absent. In early Christianity the Spirit's importance in this regard is self-evident, for example, in the frame of a reflected indicative-imperative relationship (Gal 5:25) as well as in the context of the discussion of the indwelling of the Spirit (Jas 4:5) and His operation in love (Col 1:8, 2 Tim 1:7, etc.), sanctification (1 Pet 1:2), or martyrdom (1 Pet 4:14). The absence of this connection between the Spirit and the forming of life is all the more conspicuous because the theme of the Spirit runs through all the texts of the second century (cf. e.g., building the Church: IgnEph 9.1; prophecy: Did 11.7-12; baptism: Did 7.1; testing in life: Barn 4.11, etc.). The reasons for this pneumatological deficit may presumably lie (externally) in the contrast with a Gnostic understanding of the self and (internally) in the high standing of the future-focused eschatology in the parenetic frame.

Eschatology

The future-focused eschatology has an especially great meaning. The discussion of the two ages (6.3, 19.3-4) is as common as that of the day of God's appearing (12.1, 17.4)[17] and that of the kingdom of God (12.1). The early Christian technical term παρουσία (1 Thess 3:13; 1 Cor 15:23; etc.) is absent. Of great importance is the aspect of God's future judgment (16.3, 17.6, etc.). Jesus functions as Judge (1.1). The passing away of the heavens and the earth (16.3) is as significant as the resurrection (9.1, 19.3) and the entering into God's kingdom (6.9, 9.6, etc.).

For the preacher, a major problem is the delay of the second coming: The certainty of the second coming interests him as much as the point in time. With the help of an apocryphal prophetic tradition[18] he attempts in 11.1-5 to deduce the immanence of the second coming from the process of growth in nature. In 9.1

---

[17] This phrase appears only here among early Christian literature.

[18] There is a parallel to 1Clem 23.3-4.

he presumes the continuity of the σάρξ in the resurrection and makes it fruitful for exhortation.

The timing of the second coming is addressed in 12.1-6, again with the help of an apocryphal quotation.[19] The eschatological future will have come when the differentiation of existence in outward/inward, over/under, and male/female has been abolished and the original unity restored. The present-focused interpretation is very interesting from the eschatological standpoint: When the coming of the kingdom is connected to right behavior, which is at least partially already lived, a presence of the kingdom appears (again, at least!) to be in sight. The preacher apparently assumes an implicit present-focused eschatology but neither makes it more explicit nor emphasizes it. Regarding the date he expresses no expectation of its nearness (cf. 1 Thess 4:17, 1 Cor 15:51-52, etc.), but also no nebulous expectation of its distance. He advocates a constant expectation on the basis of the uncertainty of the exact date, but he emphasizes the expectation καθ' ὥραν (12.1; cf. 1 Thess 5:6, Matt 25:13, etc.). The nearness is probably not accentuated any more strongly than IgnEph 11.1 with the reference to the end time or Barn 21.3 with the reference to the day being near. However, he does emphasize timely penance very strongly: as long as we are in the world (8.1-2), as long as we have time for salvation (9.7), as long as we have a kind Father (16.1). However, these statements appear to apply more to the time of the individual's death than to an end of this world as a whole.

6.2 The Praxis of Faith

The main focus of the sermon does not lie, in the genre or in the preacher's intent, on theological reflection. The sermon deals with Christian praxis,[20] but not with ethics as a theoretical reflection of this practice. All theological expressions, however reflective they may be, are oriented toward exhortation.

The Basis of Action

Theological expressions serve as the basis for ethically responsible action. This is true for special theology and Christology as well as for pneumatology/ecclesiology and eschatology.

In the frame of statements about *God* comes a call to do the will of the Father. The goal is eternal life (10.1; cf. 16.1). Statements about creation and calling are only the background for the demand for right behavior. A direct theological basis for the exhortation lies in the referenc to the present God-given opportunity for penance (16.1; cf. 8.1-2, etc.).

The *Christology (including soteriology)* is also parenetically oriented. Section 1.3 already preformulates the consequences of the soteriological statement in 1.4

---

[19] Parallels: GosThom 22 and GosEg (Cl Strom III 92.2).

[20] Parvis, "2 Clement," 41, emphasizes this orientation toward everyday life.

by denoting the commanded behavior as ἀντιμισθία, καρπός, and ὅσια (i.e., ἔργα). Especially characteristic of the preacher's exhortation is ἀντιμισθία (1.5, 9.7, 15.2). The salvation event aims at service in return. Καρπός as a technical term for behavior that shows the new creation is widely used (Matt 3:8par; Rom 6:22; Gal 5:22; etc.). Ὅσια means appropriate behavior toward God (1 Tim 2:8; Titus 1:8; etc.). The basis for exhortation from the saving action of Jesus is quantitatively strong in the background, but it is emphasized at the beginning (1.1, 6; 2.4; 3.1) and thus has a foundational meaning for everything that follows. A christological basis for the exhortation also lies in the emphasis on the working out of Christian existence: 13.1-4 deal with the theme of avoiding outsiders' blaspheming of the name (presumably Christ's) because of believers' inappropriate behavior.

Even *pneumatology* and *ecclesiology*, the areas that most strongly evince the preacher's theological reflection, are parenetically oriented. The three syzygies described earlier in 14.1-3a (preexistent Christ—preexistent spiritual church; resurrected Christ—present sarcic church; resurrected Christ—future spiritual church) are followed in 14.3b with a fourth between πνεῦμα and σάρξ in reference to the believers. The formula τοῦτο λέγει draws a parenetic conclusion from the first three syzygies: Preserve the flesh, that you may receive a share in the Spirit. There is a parallel in 8.6, where the preservation of the flesh and of the seal result in eternal life. The fact that the original spiritual church has taken an incarnate form affects the common physical existence of believers. All this represents not merely an ethical use of ecclesiology, but also a strengthening of anti-Gnostic-oriented ecclesiology through ethics.

Of greater importance is finally the *eschatological* basis of ethically responsible behavior.[21] Arguments deal on one hand with the shortness of the time[22] and the remaining possibility of repentance (5.5, 6.6, etc.) that should be grasped (8.1-2, 9.7, 16.1). On the other hand, the author argues with a reference to the future of the saved and the unsaved. The former is described with a series of traditional technical terms: rescue (4.2, 13.1, etc.), redemption (17.4), mercy (16.2), intercession (3.2-4, 6.9). This salvific future is plainly only for those who can display the corresponding behavior (3.2, 4.2, etc.). Future properties of salvation are the kingdom of God (9.6, 11.7), the future spiritual church (14.3), and the future Spirit (14.3), as well as further metaphorically or directly formulated benefits of salvation, such as the victor's crown (7.2, 20.2), sonship (9.10), justification (11.1), peace (10.2), rest (5.5, 6.7), or eternal life (8.4, 6; 10.1; etc.). At least as important are the references to the future damnation through misbehavior. The theme of judgment appears throughout the sermon (1.1-2, 10.1-3, 17.6, etc.). Punishments include being lost (17.1), being cast out (4.5), or suffering terrible tortures in eternal fire (5.4, 17.7). The preacher's exhortation is thus extremely

---

21 This is a traditional topos; cf. Mark 10:20-21 par, James 2:24, Did 4.13-14, 1Clem 50.5, etc.

22 The view here is less toward a living expectation of immanence and far more toward the physical life expectancy.

anxious (18.2: "I fear the coming judgment"). In an unparalleled forceful effort he seeks to motivate his audience to right behavior, for otherwise they are lost.

Theological Classification of the Exhortation

Thus the question of the theological classification of the ethically oriented exhortation presents itself. In this respect there are always negative judgments of 2Clem: The discussion deals as much with the loss of moral power[23] and a late Jewish trivialized synoptic Christianity[24] as with legalism and moralism.[25] In recent times scholars have rightly been more careful and rate the christological-soteriological assumptions more adequately.[26] For these various attempts at a positive evaluation, it is important not to see the sermon too unhistorically. It is a product of second-century Gentile Christianity with the urgency of the emphasis on responsible behavior in this world. The preacher points to the actions of God and Christ as models for all deeds of believers. He argues within the frame of the indicative-imperative relationship throughout the sermon. The future-focused eschatological basis for the exhortation is admittedly characteristic. The future salvation depends solely on right behavior. The salvation event in the working of Jesus has only the consequence of transferring the pre-Christian into the Christian realm. Everything that follows depends on the current testing. Only good works are recommendations in judgment (6.8-9). The quantity of commandments lead to a qualitative change in the indicative-imperative relationship. A high degree of uncertainty about salvation is the consequence. The corresponding basic attitude of a believer's existence is not joyful, relaxed trust in God but anxiety. In 18.1-2 the preacher formulates it in moving ways and documents thus the overall trend that forms the basis of the exhortation.[27] It is no wonder that the discussion of the πνεῦμα as the all-moving power of Christian existence is completely absent.

Contents of Ethics

The contents of the ethics are traditionally formulated but show important accents. Most of the requirements are of a *universal sort*, such as doing (ποιεῖν) the will of the Father (14.1) or of Christ (6.7), righteousness (4.2), the commandments (4.5), the words of Christ (15.5); striving (σπουδάζειν) for justice (18.2); chasing (διώκειν) after virtue (10.1); striving (ἀσκεῖν) toward service for God (20.4); keeping (τηρεῖν) the Lord's commands (8.4), baptism (6.9), the flesh (8.4), and the like. In a negative forumulation: avoidance (μὴ ποιεῖν) of evil

---

23 Harnack, "Brief," 355.
24 Windisch, "Christentum," 126.
25 Vielhauer, *Geschichte*, 742; Öffner, *Klemensbrief*, 267; Wengst, *Zweiter Klemensbrief*, 235.
26 Powell, "Clemensbrief," 121; Ehrman, *Fathers*, 155; Baasland, "Rhetorik," 127; Lindemann, *Clemensbriefe*, 196; Pratscher, *Clemensbrief*, 47.

27 When Paul speaks of working out one's salvation with fear and trembling in Phil 2:12, he preserves the paradox of the evaluation of works: God accomplishes the desire and the fulfillment in spite of and through all efforts (2:13).

(19.2); abandonment (καταλείπειν) of evil (10.1); flight (φεύγειν) from godlessness (10.1), and the like.

Of greatest importance is the theme of *repentance or penance*. Μετανοεῖν (8.1-3, 9.8, etc.) and μετάνοια (8.2, 16.4) are unusual as demands of the baptized. The preacher does not, like HermVis II 2.5 and others, advocate only a one-time possibility of repentance or deny it completely like Hebrews 6:4-6. To be sure, he does not say with Luther that one's entire life should be a penance,[28] but he is on that road when he sees himself so emphatically as a sinner (18.2) and exhorts himself to timely penance (8.2-3, 9.8, etc.). That penance is required of the baptized assumes its repeatability—otherwise anyone who sins again must indeed be excluded from the possibility of penance. Μετάνοια is thus not a completely new beginning. What it looks like institutionally remains unclear. A development in this regard is apparently at least in the offing.

Concrete exhortation appears in the assignment of *ground principles of Jewish Christian piety*: alms, prayer, and fasting.[29] While Matthew 6:1-18 emphasizes prayer by placing it in the middle, 2Clem 16.4 explicitly presents the series alms—fasting—prayer. The primacy of alms corresponds to the preacher's focus on praxis. In alms, what it means to do justice becomes concrete (albeit still in a qualified way). A more detailed description of works (as in, e.g., Did 1.6) is not given.

The same goes for the ascetic basis of the sermon, abstinence. According to 15.1 the sermon is a counsel of ἐγκράτεια. The term is used in the Greek philosophical tradition (Arist NicEth VII 3.1147b; Xen Mem I 5.1; etc.) self-discipline and control over all emotions. That is also true of early Jewish (Sir 18.30, 4Macc 5:34) and early Christian tradition (Acts 24:25, Gal 5:23, etc.). A specifically sexual connotation (as in 1 Cor 9:5-27, 1Clem 38.2) does not appear in 2Clem, as the assumption of sexual intercourse in marriage (4.3) and the rejection of rape and abortion (6.4) show. The preacher advocates a significantly distinctive distance from the world (5.6-7), but he is very far from a Gnostic denial of the world. His ethical orientation is very catholic, not that of a sect.[30]

The Goal of Action

The goal of ethically demanded action lies in three areas: Mostly and primarily it is the individual's future salvation. Right behavior is the definitive guarantor of passing the final judgment. Despite the universalistic orientation of his apocalyptic eschatology, the preacher has a special interest in the personal future with regard to the resurrection and the judgment.

In addition, right behavior is a requirement for successful missions. The blaspheming of the name of Jesus should be avoided through the agreement between

---

[28] WA 1 (1883), 233.
[29] On the comparable Jewish material cf. Tob 12.7-9; pTaan 2.65b; Billerbeck I:454, IV:533–34.

[30] Cf. Plin Ep 10.96; Baasland, "Rhetorik," 145.

word and deed (13.2-4). Good works should shine and attract others (Matt 5:16, 1 Thess 4:12, 1 Tim 6:1, etc.). The theme of love for enemies that is so important in the Jesus tradition (Matt 5:43-48par) is also central for the preacher (13.4).

Last but not least, right behavior stands in the context of conflict with adversaries. Against the preference for local pleasures among present-focused pneumatics, the preacher emphasizes right behavior as a prerequisite for passing the future judgment (13.1-5). Moreover, the exclusion of the opponents naturally also shows the theological action of the preacher in a positive light.

7.   Opponents

There is a scholarly consensus[31] that the presumed opponents were Gnostics.[32] This likelihood is apparent in all the theological themes, albeit more indirectly than directly because of the sermonic genre.[33]

In reference to *God* it appears insofar as he is known as the Father of truth not only by an elite circle but by the whole congregation (3.1).

The same is true for Christ, whose passion is spoken of as early as 1.2. From the start, Docetism has no place in *Christology*. 9.5 presents the incarnation as self-evident, and it is also taken for granted in 14.2. It is at best questionable to what degree the preacher consciously takes an anti-Gnostic line. The discussion of the κύριος could also have had a specially anti-Valentinian note (cf. Iren Haer I 1.3).

The anti-Gnosticism becomes more apparent in the *ecclesiology*. The motif of the church united with Christ in a preexistent syzygy (14.1-2) has its closest parallels in the Valentinian imagining of the aeons. The highest pneumatic realm consists of four pairs of aeons with λόγος and ζωή in the third rank and ἄνθρωπος and ἐκκλησία in the fourth (Iren Haer I 11.1; ValExp Val NHC XI 29.25-29). The reunification in the pleroma is salvation (Tri TracNHC I 122.12–129.34). The differentiation between the preexistent pneumatic church and the present-day sarcic church (14.3) is certainly anti-Gnostic, especially if one reviews the following argumentation with the term σάρξ in relation to the church, which is to say the individual believers (14.3-5). The sarcic church as ἀντίτυπον of the pneumatic, the αὐθεντικόν, is just as much the church as the other, only in a different situation and in a different way. A differentiation of believers in pneumatics and psychics is thus excluded.

---

[31] The opinion that the adversaries were Ebionites (Lightfoot, *Fathers* I/2, 211) or adherents of mystery religions (Tugwell, *Fathers*, 144) has not found acceptance.

[32] Cf. among others Lütgert, *Amt*, 111–18; Knopf, *Clemensbriefe*, 166; Donfried, *Setting*, 112; Köster, *Einführung*, 672; Wengst, *Zweite Clemensbrief*, 226–27; Powell, "Clemensbrief," 121; Warns, *Untersuchungen*, 76–90; Pratscher, *Clemensbrief*, 50–55.

[33] The sermon does not speak directly to the Gnostic opponents, but to the members of the congregation, especially those susceptible to false teaching, which 9.1-6 in particular shows: In the question of the resurrection of the σάρξ, the author implicitly distances himself from his opponents. He speaks of them in 10.3-5 and elsewhere in the third person. He carries on a pointed debate with them without speaking directly to them.

The *eschatology* also has an anti-Gnostic orientation. The traditional apocalyptic hopes for the future are so strongly emphasized above all in 9.1–12.1 that the present-focused eschatology that is so important for Gnosticism almost completely disappears. So, for example, the σάρξ will be resurrected (9.1-5). Therefore it should also be preserved (9.3; cf. 8.4, 6; 14.3; cf. also the keeping of baptism, 6.9, that is to say of the seal, 7.6, 8.6). Problems with the resurrection of the σάρξ are traditional (1 Cor 15:12-34; 2 Tim 2:18; 1 Clem 23–27; etc.). 2Clem assumes them and takes a definite position. For the author it is about responsibility for life ἐν σαρκί in view of the future. He stands decisively against any docetic or Gnostic denigration of the σάρξ.

Finally, the *ethics*, the foundation of the sermon, also shows an anti-Gnostic orientation. Right living, that is the preservation of the σάρξ, is a prerequisite for receiving the eschatological salvation benefit πνεῦμα (14.3; cf. 8.4, 6, etc.). This outstandingly good valuing of the σάρξ assumes an inadequate understanding of it.[34] A Gnostic context becomes more apparent when one takes into account the purely future-oriented understanding of the πνεῦμα (cf. 14.3) as a countermovement against the Gnostics' emphatically present-focused understanding of the Spirit. It is also shown by the ethical interpretation of a chreia in 12.2-6 about the coming of God's kingdom that was handed down only in the Gnostic tradition (GosThom 22 and GosEg Cl Strom 3.92.2). For all that, the preacher does not advocate a sexual encratism (4.3, 6.4).

As far as a *more precise identification of the adversaries* goes, it must at least include the Valentinians.[35] Not only the technical terms used have Valentinian parallels: for example, ἀνάπαυσις (5.5; cf. Cl Exc 63.1, etc.), πατὴρ τῆς ἀληθείας (3.1, etc.; cf. GosTruth NHC I 16.31-33, etc.); ἐκκλησία πρώτη / πνευματική (14.1; cf. Iren Haer I 11.1, etc.). The same is true of the discussion of whence and whither in 1.2 (cf. Cl Exc 78.2), as well as the description of salvation in 12.2 as the unification of male and female (cf. Cl Exc 21.3).[36] In any case, the preacher assumes Gnostic opponents, among whom are probably also Valentinians. He clearly does not engage them directly, but still purposefully.

---

[34] How that looks concretely, we sadly do not know. Libertinism (so esp. Lütgert, *Amt*, 114; Öffner, *Klemensbrief*, 79; and others) is not particularly close because of the high value placed on asceticism, which the Nag Hammadi texts show. But there is also no specifically antilibertine polemic. The discussion of the ἡδυπάθειαι (16.2, 17.7) opposes only the sensuous involvement with the world in general.

[35] Cf. Donfried, *Setting*, 155–56. This thesis is supported with great certainty by Warns, *Untersuchungen*, 76–90 and passim. Contrary to an all too clear and unilinear classification cf. rightly Markschies, *Valentinus*, 384n349.

[36] Here there may be a polemic against the Valentinian sacrament of the nuptial chamber (Warns, *Untersuchungen*, 448–56). Whether the same holds for the Valentinian theologoumena on confirmation (cf. 2Clem 2) and salvation (cf. 2Clem17) (Warns, 236–44, 409–16) is uncertain.

8.   Authorship

Because the original sermon (1.1–18.2, 20.5) and the appendix (19.1–20.4) are separate, the question of the authorship of both pieces arises. The composer of the sermon was a Gentile Christian. He may have been a presbyter (17.3, 5).[37] We certainly do not know his name. The manuscript tradition assumes that it was Clement of Rome, but he must be ruled out because of the great differences between 1Clem and 2Clem, as Eus HE III 38.4 already recognized. None of the other suggested solutions is convincing, whether it be the Clement responsible for the correspondence of the Roman congregation according to HermVis II 4.3, the Roman bishop Hyginus or Soter, the Corinthian bishop Dionysius, or even Julius Cassian or Clement of Alexandria.[38]

Any identification of the author by name is obviously excluded, especially since the aforementioned possibilities are completely implausible on the basis of geography. He was probably not a well-known personality; otherwise the text would not have fallen into the darkness of anonymity.

Nor can the persona of the epilogist be identified. He may have been a student of the preacher and takes up the preacher's work in order to support and interpret it. He understands himself not as an authoritative preacher, but merely as a lector.

9.   Place of Writing

Four possibilities are always presented, often not exclusively: Rome, Corinth, Syria, and Egypt. The composition in *Rome* is most popular in the oldest literature.[39] It arises from the label "Second Epistle of Clement," but it is not tied to an author named Clement. The Rome thesis does not fit with the genre designation of epistle. Points against Rome include the complete ignorance of the text in the early Western tradition,[40] as well as the differences from 1Clem and Herm.[41]

Corinth is named after Rome.[42] However, the idea of καταπλεῖν = to sail in (7.1) as an allusion to the Isthmian Games is very problematic. The competition metaphor is too common (1 Cor 9:24-27; 1 Tim 6:12; 1Clem 2.4; etc.) to be able to serve as an argument for localization.

---

[37] The idea that he was a bishop (Μπονης, Συμπόσιον, 26) is mere speculation.
[38] Clement: Harnack, "Brief," 363–64. Hyginus: Grand, *Gnosticism*, 216n3. Soter: Hilgenfeld, *Epistulae*, XLV–VI; Harnack, "Ursprung," 69–70; in *Geschichte* II/1, 448, Harnack strongly relativizes this identification. Dionysius: Wocher, *Briefe*, 204. Julius Cassian: Harris, *Authorship*, 200. Clement of Alexandria: Hilgenfeld, *Epistulae*, XLIX, as a further possibility.

[39] More recently: Hausammann, *Kirche*, 41–42 (with caution).
[40] The sermon first appears in the West in Jer Vir Inl 15 (dependent on Eus HE III 38.4).
[41] Cf. to name only two examples, the missing reception of Paul in contrast to 1Clem and the differences from Herm in the conception of penance.
[42] In recent scholarship esp. Donfried, *Setting*, 1, who argues: 2Clem is the sermon of the presbyter restored after the success of 1Clem.

Another possibility is Syria.[43] The decisive argument is the manuscript tradition, in which A and H admittedly have a close relationship with Syria. On the basis of the theological direction, Syria fits at least as well as Rome.

Egypt is also frequently suggested as the place of origin.[44] The struggle against Gnosticism, and especially the traditional connection to the Gospel of the Egyptians (Cl Strom III 92.2) fit well with this location, as do the uninhibited adoption of Gnostic terms, the citation of noncanonical literature, and the possibility that Origen knew it.

Overall, Corinth has the least plausibility. The long absence of Western witnesses speaks against Rome. In the choice between Syria and Egypt, the latter is better given the preference.

10.   Dating

The renunciation of taking up a certain author also means rejecting an exact identification of the time of composition. Leaving out the early association with Clement of Rome and the late association with Clement of Alexandria, there is still a large timeframe, but it can be narrowed significantly on the basis of practical indicators.

A very approximate limit is allowed by the problematizing of the expectation of immanence, the still seldom explicit Christology, the still absent office of bishop, and the development of the understanding of penance. The time around the middle of the second century best comes into consideration in light of all these factors.

Two further indicators can make this assumption somewhat more certain: the use of quotations and the conflict with adversaries. In the first case, the quotations from apocryphal literature are of interest. The preacher has no problem using an apocryphal gospel and is unaware of the canon of four gospels that was in use in catholic Christendom in the second half of the second century. Thus the *terminus ad quem* appears to be the middle of the second century.

For the *terminus ad quo* the conflict with Gnostic adversaries is significant. If it indeed deals with Valentinians as well, only the period after 130 is possible. Thus the time of origin being probably around the middle of the second century[45] comes into consideration.

---

[43] In recent scholarship esp. Stegemann, *Herkunft*, 133. As a possibility beside Egypt, see, e.g., Lindemann, *Clemensbriefe*, 195.

[44] So esp. Warns, *Untersuchungen*, 94; Wengst, *Zweiter Klemensbrief*, 226–27. As a possibility

beside Syria see, e.g., Lindemann, *Clemensbriefe*, 195.

[45] Cf. Köster, *Einführung*, 673. Most authors decide (with admitted deviations) for this conclusion; cf. Pratscher, *Clemensbrief*, 62–63.

11.   Bibliography

Baasland, E. "Der 2. Klemensbrief und frühchristliche Rhetorik: 'Die erste christliche Predigt' im Lichte der neueren Forschung." *ANRW* II 27.1 (1993): 78–157.

Cotelier, J. B. *Sanctorum Patrum, qui temporibus apostolicis floruerunt, Barnabae, Clementis, Hermae, Ignatii, Polycarpi Opera, vera, et suppositicia: Una cum Clementis, Ignatii, Polycarpi Actis atque Martyriis.* Paris 1672.

Donfried, K. P. *The Setting of Second Clement in Early Christianity.* NT.S 38. Leiden 1974.

Ehrman, B. D. *The Apostolic Fathers. I: I Clement, II Clement, Ignatius, Polycarp, Didache, Edited and Translated.* LCL 24. Cambridge, Mass. 2003.

Frank, A. *Studien zur Ekklesiologie des Hirten, II Klemens, der Didache und der Ignatiusbriefe unter besonderer Berücksichtigung der Idee einer präexistenten Kirche.* Diss. München 1975.

Gebhardt, O. de, and A. Harnack. *Clementis Romani ad Corinthios quae dicuntur epistulae: Textum ad fidem codicum et Alexandrini et Constantinopolitani nuper inventi* (Patrum Apostolicorum Opera, ed. O. de Gebhardt, A. Harnack, and T. Zahn, I.1). Leipzig ²1876.

Grant, R. *Gnosticism and Early Christianity.* New York/London ²1966.

Gregory, A. F., and C. M. Tuckett. "2 Clement and the Writings that Later Formed the New Testament." In *The Reception of the New Testament in the Apostolic Fathers*, 251–92. Oxford 2005.

Harnack, A. (von). *Geschichte der altchristlichen Litteratur bis Eusebius.* I: *Die Überlieferung und der Bestand.* Leipzig 1893. II: *Die Chronologie der altchristlichen Litteratur bis Eusebius.* 1. *Die Chronologie der Litteratur bis Irenaeus.* Leipzig 1897. 2: *Die Chronologie der Literatur von Irenaeus bis Eusebius.* Leipzig 1904.

———. "Über den sogenannten zweiten Brief des Clemens an die Korinther." *ZKG* 1 (1877): 264–83, 329–64.

———. "Zum Ursprung des sog. 2. Clemensbriefs." *ZNW* 6 (1905): 67–71.

Harris, R. "The Authorship of the So-Called Second Epistle of Clement." *ZNW* 23 (1924): 193–200.

Hausammann, S. *Alte Kirche: Zur Geschichte und Theologie in den ersten vier Jahrhunderten, I: Frühchristliche Schriftsteller, "Apostolische Väter," Häresien, Apologeten.* Neukirchen-Vluyn 2001.

Hilgenfeld, A. *Clementis Romani Epistulae: Edidit, commentario critic et adnotationibus instruxit; Mosis Assumptionis quat supersunt; Prima edita et illustrata.* Novum Testamentum extra canonem receptum I. Leipzig ²1876.

Knopf, R. "Die Anagnose zum zweiten Clemensbriefe." *ZNW* 3 (1902): 266–79.

———. *Die Lehre der Zwölf Apostel, die zwei Clemensbriefe.* HNT Erg 1. Tübingen 1920.

Köster, H. *Einführung in das Neue Testament im Rahmen der Religionsgeschichte und Kulturgeschichte der hellenistischen und römischen Zeit.* Berlin/New York 1980.

Lightfoot, J. B. *The Apostolic Fathers* I 1.2: *S. Clement of Rome: A Revised Text with Introductions, Notes, Dissertations and Translations.* Hildesheim/New York 1973. (Reprinted from the ²1890 ed.)

Lindemann, A. *Die Clemensbriefe.* Die Apostolischen Väter 1. HNT 17. Tübingen 1992.

Lütgert, W. *Amt und Geist im Kampf: Studien zur Geschichte des Urchristentums.* BFCT 15.4-5. Gütersloh 1911.

Markschies, C. *Valentinus Gnosticus? Untersuchungen zur valentinianischen Gnosis mit einem Kommentar zu den Fragmenten Valentins.* WUNT 65. Tübingen 1992.

Μπονης, Κ. Γ. Συμπόσιον πατέρων: Ἡ καλυμένη Β΄ ἐπιστολὴ Κλήμεντος Ῥώμης Πρὸς Κορινθίους.᾽ Athens 1975.

Öffner, E. *Der zweite Klemensbrief: Moralerziehung und Moralismus in der ältesten christlichen Predigt.* Dess. Erlangen/Nuremburg 1976.

Parvis, P. "2 Clement and the Meaning of the Christian Homily." In *The Writings of the Apostolic Fathers*, edited by P. Foster, 32–41. London/New York 2007.

Pauli, A. di. "Zum sog. 2. Korintherbrief des Clemens Romanus." *ZNW* 4 (1903): 321–29.

Powell, D. "Zweiter Clemensbrief." *TRE* 8 (1981): 121–23.

Pratscher, W. *Der zweite Clemensbrief.* KAV 3. Göttingen 2007.

Schüssler, W. "Ist der zweite Klemensbrief ein einheitliches Ganzes?" *ZKG* 28 (1907): 1–13.

Stegemann, C. *Herkunft und Entstehung des sogennanten zweiten Klemensbriefes.* Diss. Bonn 1974.

Tugwell, S. *The Apostolic Fathers.* Outstanding Christian Thinkers. London 1989.

Vielhauer, P. *Geschicthe der urchristlichen Literatur: Einleitung in das Neue Testament, die Apokryphen und die Apostolischen Väter.* Berlin/New York 1985. (Reprint of the 1975 ed.)

Warns, R. *Untersuchungen zum 2. Clemens-Brief.* Diss. Marburg 1985 (with appendices until 1989).

Wengst, K. *Didache (Apostellehre), Barnabasbrief, Zweiter Clemensbrief, Schrift an Diognet: Eingeleitet, herausgegeben, übertragen und erläutert.* SUC II. Darmstadt 1984.

Windisch, H. "Das Christentum des zweiten Clemensbriefes." In *Harnack-Ehrung: Beiträge zur Kirchengeschichte, ihrem Lehrer A. Von Harnack zu seinem siebzigsten Geburtstage (7. Mai 1921), dargebracht von einer Reihe seiner Schüler*, 119–34. Leipzig 1921.

Wocher, M. J. *Die Briefe der apostolischen Väter Clemens und Polykarpus, neu übersetzt und mit Einleitungen und Commentarien versehen.* Tübingen 1830.

Zahn, T. "Das ältesten Kirchengebet und die älteste christliche Predigt." *ZPK.NF* 72 (1876): 194–209.

The Epistles of Ignatius of Antioch

Hermut Löhr

1. Evidence of Eusebius of Caesarea

The church historian Eusebius of Caesarea gives a report in the third book of his *Ecclesiastical History*, after mentioning Polycarp of Smyrna and Papias of Hierapolis, about Ignatius,[1] "bishop of Antioch, second in succession to Peter"[2] (HE III 36.2):

> Report says that he was sent from Syria to Rome and became food for wild beasts on account of his testimony to Christ. And as he made the journey through Asia under the strictest military surveillance, he fortified the parishes in the various cities where he stopped by oral homilies and exhortations, and warned them above all to be especially on their guard against the heresies that were then beginning to prevail, and exhorted them to hold fast to the tradition of the apostles. Moreover, he thought it necessary to attest that tradition in writing and to give it a fixed form for the sake of greater security.[3]

From Smyrna, as Eusebius further reports, Ignatius also wrote to Ephesus, Magnesia, Tralles, and Rome, then from Troas to the congregations in Philadelphia and Smyrna, as well as to their bishop Polycarp.

Eusebius offers in his report a detailed verbatim quotation from IgnRom (HE III 36.7-9 = IgnRom 5) as well as a shorter passage from IgnSmyrn (HE III 36.11 = IgnSmyrn 3.1-2).

The church historian then gives the testimony of Irenaeus about Ignatius (HE III 36.12; cf. Haer V 28.4, IgnRom 4); further, he quotes from the Epistle of Polycarp to the Philippians (HE III 36.13-14; cf. PolPhil 9, 13 [= IgnPhil 1]), which gives contemporary evidence of Ignatius and his letters. The passage closes with a report on Ignatius' successor as bishop of Antioch, Hero.

So Ignatius appears in Eusebius as one of the greatest personalities of early Christianity in the postapostolic period, who had an especially great effect through his letters. Eusebius' knowledge is clearly limited to the (seven) letters and their

---

[1] On the form of the name—a variation on the common Roman name Egnatius—cf. Fischer, "Ignatius," 113.

[2] According to HE III 22, Evodius was Ignatius' predecessor.

[3] HE III 36.3-4; translated by A. C. McGiffert in Schaff/Wace, 167.

recognizable places of composition. To these facts he adds the information about Ignatius' martyrdom in Rome.[4]

2.   The "Ignatian Question"

In reality late ancient and medieval manuscripts in various languages[5] have been handed down that contain letters of Ignatius, sometimes only fragments, in various numbers and from various sources. This fact raises considerable problems for scholarship to this day, problems which are only referred to as the "Ignatian question."

This Ignatian question unfolds namely in many repects that, however interrelated they are, should be distinguished with methodical clarity. At issue are:

— the manuscript findings of texts handed down under the name of Ignatius;
— the history of the Ignatian tradition based on these manuscripts in antiquity and the Middle Ages before the first printing;
— the authorship of the Ignatian epistles in ther recognizably different stages of tradition;
— the dating and the historical and theological context of the individual texts, the steps of the tradition, and the life of the historical Ignatius.

3.   Textual Tradition and the Three Recensions of the Ignatians

From Polycarp, also quoted by Eusebius (13.2 = IgnPhil 1.2), it emerges that a collection of Ignatius' letters apparently existed quite early. However, the report tells nothing about the origin and content of this collection.[6] Eusebius himself knows a collection of seven letters in the following order: IgnEph, IgnMagn, IgnTrall, IgnRom, IgnPhld, IgnSmyrn, and IgnPol.

If one summarizes the result of the manuscript tradition of the Epistles of Ignatius[7] and excludes the letter from Mary of Cassobola[8] to Ignatius, it appears that three of the Ignatian epistles (IgnPol, IgnEph, IgnRom) have been handed down in three versions that differ significantly from one another, four (IgnSmyrn, IgnMagn, IgnPhld, IgnTrall) in two version and five (IgnMary, IgnTars, IgnAnt, IgnHero, IgnPhil)[9] in only one.

---

4   More or less detailed overviews of the further testimonies of the early church can be found, e.g., in Harnack, *Geschichte*, 79–86; Lightfoot, *Fathers* II/1, 135–232; Fischer, "Ignatius," 113–15.

5   Manuscripts or fragments of the Ignatian epistles exist in Greek, Latin, Armenian, Syriac, Coptic, and Arabic.

6   The reflections presented by Lightfoot, *Fathers* II/1, 423–28, on this subject lead to the conclusion that it included the seven letters.

7   Cf. on this the detailed overviews in Lightfoot, *Fathers* II/1, 70–134; Harnack, *Geschichte*, 76–79.

8   On this place designation cf. Bardenhewer, *Geschichte* I, 151n2.

9   IgnMary = to Mary of Cassobola; IgnTars = to the Tarsians; IgnAnt = to the Antiochenes; IgnHero = to Hero; IgnPhil = to the Philippians.

As a result of these findings, scholarship differentiates between three major "forms" or "recensions" of the letters, one short, one medium, and one long. They are not congruent with the collections in the current manuscripts. The fact that significant text-critical problems exist even with the use of such a really clear categorization and allocation deserves to be noted.

The form of the texts of the Ignatian letters offered in the editions of the "Apostolic Fathers" that are current today rests on one hand on an overwhelming scholarly consensus that is the result of a discussion that has stretched over multiple centuries and has long been shaped by confessional interests. According to this majority opinion, the middle recension is the oldest version that can be reached, compared to which the writings also passed on in the longer version appear to be interpolated, while the Syriac version of IgnEph, IgnRom, and IgnPol presents a significantly shortened form of the texts. The most common selection of seven letters is supported, apart from the results of the textual tradition, by the report of Eusebius as well as by examinations of intratextual and intertextual details.

The preference for the seven letters named by Eusebius in the form of the middle recension admittedly indicates mostly a judgment about the authenticity of the texts. But pseudepigraphy would have been no strange phenomenon at the time of the "Apostolic Fathers" and very compatible with the search for an oldest available text. On this point recent discussion shows anew that the chronological preference for one of the three recensions is not decisive on the question of authenticity and dating.[10]

While the seven letters referred to by Eusebius are available in the middle recension in the critical editions and translations, the letters that this consensus views as "inauthentic" and "interpolated" were included in the edition by Funk and Diekamp[11] and are thus, as well as in the English translation of the *Ante-Nicene Fathers*,[12] still somewhat current today.

4.   The Question of Authenticity

Especially through the work of Theodor Zahn[13] and Joseph Barber Lightfoot[14] in the nineteenth century, the conclusion earlier reached by such scholars as James Ussher, Isaak Voss, and John Pearson—that the seven letters named by Eusebius in the middle recension are the genuine letters of Ignatius—became the majority opinion across confessional boundaries. Fewer of the other theses presented in the course of the history of scholarship have stood the test of time.[15] The assumption

---

[10] On Ignatianist literature cf. also the overview in CPG, 1028–36.
[11] The text of Funk/Diekamp was included in the electronic Thesaurus Linguae Graecae of the Perseus Project of the University of California, Irvine. See http://www.tlg.uci.edu (accessed 17 June 2009).

[12] Roberts/Donaldson/Coxe, *Apostolic Fathers*. The edition is also available online at http://www.ccel.org/fathers.html (accessed 17 June 2009).
[13] Cf. Zahn, *Ignatius*.
[14] Cf. Lightfoot, *Fathers* II/1.
[15] Cf. the overview of the older scholarship in Bardenhewer, *Geschichte* I, 143–50.

of the authenticity of the longer recension, which was to a certain extent the Roman Catholic "standard position" in the sixteenth century, is no longer supported today.[16] But the doubts have never been silenced. The "Ignatian question" remains open to this day, even though the arguments that are once again offered in favor of the inauthenticity do not appear persuasive.

While Robert Joly disputed the authenticity of the seven letters (and the existence of Ignatius) and held them to be a forgery from the years 160–170 C.E., Joseph Rius-Camps pled for the authenticity and early dating of IgnEph, IgnMagn, IgnTrall, and IgnRom, though maintaining that all (apart from IgnRom) were edited and connected to the letters from Troas in the third century. The emphasis on the threefold office in the Ignatian letters supposedly stems from this revision.[17] Reinhard M. Hübner and Thomas Lechner also hold the seven writings in the middle recension (as well as the passages referring to Ignatius in PolPhil) to be forgeries. Their place in theological history is seen as the conflict with the Valentinians, partly (Markus Vinzent) also with Marcionite theology, with the Ignatian position characterized as Monarchianism influenced by Noetus of Smyrna (Hübner).[18]

Yet the authenticity is not without defenders.[19] A very promising new estimation, partly combined with good arguments for the authenticity of the seven letters of the middle recension, was recently accomplished by Philip A. Harland and Allen Brent, who, taking older observations into account, undertake to classify the apparent peculiarities (or anachronisms) of the texts in the linguistic and conceptual context of mystery language and "Second Sophistic."[20]

5.   Dating

There are no direct chronological statements or references to contemporary history in the texts.[21] An approximate *terminus post quem* is given by the apparent references to many New Testament writings,[22] while the use of other texts of the "Apostolic Fathers" cannot be seen as certain.[23] A possible *terminus ante quem* is offered by the Epistle of Polycarp to the Philippians, which mentions a collection of Ignatius' letters in the aforementioned statement in 13.2 (= IgnPhil 1.2).

The witness of Polycarp would certainly be completely worthless for dating the Ignatian letters if the relevant passage were an interpolation that arose in connection with the long recension of the letters. However, this thesis, not recent but

---

[16] Weijenborg, *Lettres*, argues for the dependency of the middle recension on the longer but holds both to be counterfeit—and Eusebius' *Ecclesiastical History* as well!

[17] Cf. Joly, *Le dossier*; Rius-Camps, *Authentic Letters*.

[18] Cf. Hübner, "Thesen"; Lechner, *Ignatius*.

[19] Cf. Barnes, "Date"; Edwards, "Ignatius"; Linde-

mann, "Antwort"; Schöllgen, "Ignatianen"; Vogt, *Bemerkungen*.

[20] Cf. Harland, "Christ-Bearers"; Brent, *Ignatius*; idem, "Enigma"; idem, *Sophistic*.

[21] The one date in the seven texts, 10.3 of the middle recension of IgnRom, does not name a year.

[22] See below.

[23] See below.

reused by scholars who dispute the authenticity of the letters, has been contradicted with good reason.[24]

The satirical novel *De morte Peregrini* may also point to a knowledge of the Ignatian letters. This work by Lucian of Samosata, which was written after 165 and well before 180, shows allusions to the letters that may indicate use.[25]

These witnesses—assuming their authenticity—make it somewhat plain that until around the middle of the second century,[26] a collection of Ignatius' letters existed, but without allowing us to ascertain more precise information about its date and scope.

The context of the mention of Ignatius in Eus HE III 36[27] points to the time of Trajan. Eusebius' *Chronicle*[28] places the bishop's work more exactly in the time between the first year of Vespasian and the tenth year of Trajan.[29]

On the basis of these varying statements, one comes in any case to a time before 117 C.E., the year of Trajan's death; the Ignatian letters were therefore written at the time of the late writings of the New Testament.

As Polycarp's reference to his friend's martyrdom hints, we learn from Irenaeus (Haer V 28.4[30]) and Origen (HomLucam 6[31]) of death by the beasts (which was hinted at multiple times in IgnRom 4–5; further IgnTrall 10, IgnSmyrn 4.2).

To be sure, there have been doubts expressed about this very precise dating to the first two decades of the second century, but they need not be immediately accompanied by assertions of inauthenticity, especially since Eusebius' information about the bishopric of Antioch can hardly be seen as a reliable report.[32] Thus a late date in the time of Hadrian[33] or even later in the second century[34] has also been favored. One is thus relegated to basing the dating of the Ignatian letters essentially on the relationship to PolPhil as well as on the classification in the history of Christian theology in the second century after Christ.

---

[24] Cf. on one side Joly, *Le dossier*, 17–37; Hübner, "Thesen," 48–50; Lechner, *Ignatius*, 6–65; on the other side Brent, *Ignatius*, 144–48.

[25] Cf. the proof in Zahn, *Ignatius*, 517–28; see also the short overview in Lightfoot, *Fathers* II/1, 137–41. Lechner, *Ignatius*, 66–67, is cautious but does not reject the idea. Brent, *Ignatius*, 100, argues against a literary connection.

[26] In his investigation, Lechner, *Ignatius*, summarizing in 116–17, comes to the conclusion that the reference in Irenaeus, *Haer* V 28.4, gives the first certain *terminus ante quem*.

[27] Cf. HE III 33.1 (Pliny the Younger); 34.1 (third year of the reign of Trajan).

[28] Eus Chron; GCS Euseb 7[2], 194.

[29] Jer Vir ill 16 (ed. Bernoulli, 18) dates the martyrdom to the eleventh year of Trajan (109 C.E.).

The so-called Martyrium Colbertinum (also called the Antiochene Martyrdom), the oldest surviving version of the Martyrdom of Ignatius that admittedly comes from the fourth or fifth century, speaks in 2.1 (Lightfoot, *Fathers* II/1, 480) about the ninth year of the same emperor (107 C.E.). A Christian chronicler, Johannes Malalas, places Ignatius' martyrdom around the time of the great earthquake that occurred on 13 December 115 (*Chron.* XI, ed. Dindorf, 276).

[30] SC 153, 360–63.

[31] FC 4/1, 98.

[32] So rightly Hübner, "Thesen," 45–48.

[33] Cf. Harnack, *Zeit*; Munier, "A propos."

[34] Cf. Heussi, *Petrustradition*, 34–35; most recently Barnes, "Date."

6.   Place and Situation of Writing

All the texts are to be classified as prison letters. They repeatedly describe Ignatius' situation, a prisoner (IgnEph 1.2, 11.2; IgnMagn 1.2, 12; IgnTrall 1.1, 12.2; IgnRom 1.1, 4.3; IgnSmyrn 4.2) condemned to death (IgnTrall 3.3; IgnRom 4.3; IgnSmyrn 4.2) who finds himself on a journey from Syrian Antioch to Rome (IgnEph 1.2, 21.2; IgnRom 5.1) and expects to die there fighting beasts (IgnEph 1.2; IgnRom 5.2-3), and he visits various fellowships in Asia Minor along the way. The seven texts of the middle recension purport to have been written in different places: While IgnEph gives no explicit information about its place of writing, Ign-Magn, IgnTrall, and IgnRom come from Smyrna. IgnPhld and IgnSmyrn are sent from Troas, while IgnPol refers in 8.1 to the sea journey from Troas to Neapolis (near Philippi).[35]

The journey, the route of which has been reconstructed only in fragments based on these references, travels from east to west[36] through a region that is both known as the region of Paul's missionary journeys and referred to in Revelation (cf. the letters to the churches in Rev 2–3). Western Asia Minor is also connected with early church traditions about the Gospel of John.[37]

In Antioch, the place of departure for the journey, Christians were first given that name (according to Acts 11:26) and by it became recognizably distinguished for the outside world from the Diaspora Judaism of the time. There are other references, both in Acts and in the Pauline Epistles (cf. Gal 2:11-14), to the importance of the Antiochene church as well.

The letters show a network of churches, their representatives, and emissaries. Burrus and Crocus appear as companions of Ignatius on his way to Rome (IgnEph 2.1; IgnRom 10.1; IgnPhld 11.2; IgnSmyrn 12.1),[38] as do Philo and Rheus Agathopus above all in the later letters (IgnPhld 11.1;[39] IgnSmyrn 13.1; also IgnPhil 15.1; IgnTars 10.1; IgnAnt 13.2). There is a special connection to Polycarp of Smyrna (cf. IgnEph 21.1; IgnPol).

One sees more clearly from the Epistle of Polycarp than from Ignatius' own writings that the bishop was not transported to Rome alone, but together with other Christians (cf. PolPhil 1.1, 9.1, 13.2 [= IgnPhil 1.2]). The transport was

---

[35] IgnTars, IgnAnt, and IgnHero purport to come from Philippi; IgnPhil may perhaps have been written in Italy (the place given in 15.2, Rhegium, is not text-critically certain). IgnMaria does not contain an explicit mention of place; the fact that Cassian is named as his host (as in IgnAnt 13.1; IgnHero 9.1) gives no information about the place of writing.

[36] On the staged character of the journey, which does not necessarily contradict its historicity, see Brent, *Ignatius*, 44–70.

[37] Cf. Hengel, *Frage*, 9–95. According to Jerome's chronicle, Ignatius was a disciple of John (GCS 24, 194); cf. also MartIgn Colbertinum 1.1, 3.1 (Lightfoot, *Fathers* II/2, 477, 485).

[38] IgnRom 10.2 refers to someone who travels ahead of Ignatius to Rome. Schoedel, *Ignatius*, 191 believes it to be Crocus.

[39] The passage may indicate that Rheus Agathopus, like Ignatius, was awaiting death; contra Schoedel, *Ignatius*, 214n14.

undertaken under heavy guard, which is described particularly impressively in the passage IgnRom 5.1.

At the same time, however—and this report among others has raised doubts in scholarship about its historicity—these prisoners were allowed to visit the Christian churches along the way.

So Ignatius speaks in Philadelphia at the congregational meeting there (IgnPhld 6.3–8.2), is received warmly in Smyrna by Polycarp and the fellowship (IgnEph 21.1; IgnMagn 15; IgnTrall 12.1) and received delegations from Ephesus, Magnesia, and Tralles (IgnEph 21.1; IgnMagn 15; IgnTrall 1.1). The bishop writes to all three churches and to Rome;[40] the letter to Rome may have been carried by Crocus (IgnRom 10.1).

In Troas, where Ignatius was apparently even allowed to preach (IgnPhld 11.1), the news of peace in Antioch reached him through Philo and Rheus Agathopus, who followed him. That probably means the end of the persecution that caused Ignatius himself to be imprisoned and sent to Rome (IgnPhld 10.1; IgnSmyrn 11.2; IgnPol 7.1), but related conflicts within the congregation are also possible.[41] In the letters dictated to Burrus (IgnPhld 11.2; IgnSmyrn 12.1), Ignatius thanks the churches in Philadelphia and Smyrna, as well as their bishop at the time, for their offer of hospitality. Deacons of the fellowships should, according to the will of the bishop, go to Antioch and bring greetings to the congregation (IgnPhld 10; IgnSmyrn 11.2-3; IgnPol 7.2). Because of a surprise order, Ignatius himself must go on to Neapolis in Macedonia and, contrary to his intention, cannot write to the congregations along the rest of the route; he asks Polycarp to take over this task for him (IgnPol 8.1).

Polycarp then proves the friendly reception of Ignatius and other prisoners in Philippi (IgnPhil 1.1, 9.1, 13.1). Here the further letters of the long recension concur.

The intent of the writings goes beyond the organization of the trip and the building and maintaining of contacts with the individual churches, however. Far more recognizable are conflicts of a fundamentally theological nature that, assuming the authenticity of the Ignatian letters, provide useful insights into the organization and thought of Christian fellowships at the beginning of the second century.

7. Structure of the Seven Writings of the Middle Recension

An overview of the structure of the seven letters of the middle recension is not easy to construct. Nevertheless, I will attempt to do so in what follows.[42]

---

[40] A second letter to Ephesus is reported (IgnEph 20.1) but has not survived.

[41] Cf. Brent, *Ignatius*, 14–43.

[42] Cf. the information on structure in Fischer, "Ignatius," 115–18. A short summary of the content of the further texts of the long recension appears in Bardenhewer, *Geschichte* I, 151–52.

To the Ephesians

Prescript	
1.1–2.2	Praise for the church and its delegation, led by the bishop
3	Request for attention to an admonition
4.1–6.2	Admonition to submission to the bishop and presbyters in the life of the community
7.1–9.2	Warning about false teachers; praise for steadfastness against heretics
10	Request for prayer
11.1	Announcement of the end times
11.2–12.2	Belonging to Christ and connection to the audience
13	Exhortation to the congregational meetings
14	Request for faith and love
15	On proper silence and reading
16	Warning about defilement by sin and false teaching
17.1–19.3	Warning about the Prince of this world and the mysteries of salvation
20.1	Reference to another letter
20.2	Holding together in faith
21	Request for intercession for Ignatius and the church in Syria

To the Magnesians

Prescript	
1	The wish for unity of the churches
2	The delegation from Magnesia
3–4	Admonition to submission to the bishop and warning against schismatics
5	Two Ways
6–7	Request for unity under the bishop
8–11	Warning against false teaching
12	Praise for the fellowship
13	Admonitions, including submission
14	Exhortation to intercession
15	Closing greetings

To the Trallians

Prescript	
1	Joy over the news from Tralles
2–3	Strengthening of the fellowship under the bishop, the presbyter, and the deacons
4–5	Reference to his own imperfections
6–7	Warning against false teaching

8	Admonition to virtuous living
9–11	Warning against false teaching
12–13	Closing greetings and exhortations, request for intercession

To the Romans

Prescript	
1–8	Request not to interfere with martyrdom
9–10	Request for intercession, greetings, closing remarks

To the Philadelphians

Prescript	
1	Praiseworthiness of the bishop of Philadelphia
2–4	Exhortation to obedience to the bishop
5	Hope of the goal
6–9	Conflict with heresy; review of his own appearance
10	Request for a delegation to Antioch
11	Closing admonitions, greetings

To the Smyrnaeans

Prescript	
1–3	Praiseworthiness of the fellowship and description of right belief
4–7	Polemic against heretics
8.1–9.1	Admonition to stand by the bishop
9.2–10.2	Thanks for proven hospitality
11	Request for an emissary to be sent to Syria to congratulate the church there on the restoration of peace
12–13	Closing greetings

To Polycarp

Prescript	
1.1	Praise of Polycarp
1.2–3.2	Exhortation to Polycarp to do justice to his position
4–5	Further exhortations
6.1	Admonitions addressed to the congregation to submit to the officials of the church
6.2	Further exhortations
7	Request to send an emissary to Antioch
8.1	Request to Polycarp to write to the churches in Ignatius' place
8.2-3	Closing greetings and wishes

8.   Intertextual Relationships, Traditional and Religious History

8.1 Old Testament and Early Jewish Writings

The Old Testament Scriptures are seldom mentioned expressly in the letters, but that does not indicate a general rejection or denigration of them. The letters make plain (IgnMagn 8.2, 9.2; IgnPhld 5.2, 9.2; or IgnSmyrn 7.2) that the "prophets" are valued positively as witnesses of Christ, indeed as "disciples in the Spirit." Their preaching was "directed toward the Gospel"; their salvation is proven (Ign-Phld 5.2). IgnPhld 9.1 refers to the patriarchs Abraham, Isaac, and Jacob together with the apostles and the church among those that enter into unity with God.[43]

In IgnEph 5.3 (Prov 3:34; cf. Jas 4:6, 1 Pet 5:5); IgnMagn 12 (Prov 18:17), and possibly in IgnTrall 8.2 (Isa 52:5; cf. Rom 2:24) there are three recognizable quotations from the Old Testament, the first two introduced by a quotation formula, the last not.[44] The quotations are used in parenetic contexts and do not carry the bulk of the argument. Other allusions to Old Testament passages[45] and extracanonical early Jewish texts are evident; the author may have had 4Macc particularly in mind.[46]

8.2 Early Christian Tradition and Texts

The Ignatian letters' acquaintance with the "Gospel story" is plain in impressive passages that sum it up in a form that from a distance recalls the later creeds:

> Stop your ears, therefore, when any one speaks to you at variance with Jesus Christ, who was descended from David and was also of Mary; who was truly born and ate and drank. He was truly persecuted under Pontius Pilate; He was truly crucified, and [truly] died, in the sight of beings in heaven and on earth and under the earth. He was also truly raised from the dead, His Father quickening Him [. . .]. (IgnTrall 9.1-2)[47]

To what extent Ignatius reaches back here to preexisting material cannot be deduced with certainty. On the whole, the possibility of the reconstruction of preliterary formulas and creeds is judged more skeptically at present in the exegesis of early Christian texts than it was in the heyday of classic form criticism in the twentieth century. That said, the possibility that Ignatius repeatedly uses such preliterary traditions (shorter and longer creedal formulas, hymns, etc.) cannot be ruled out.

---

[43] For discussion of the expression ἐν τοῖς ἀρχείοις in IgnPhil 8.2 (OT? Early Christian documents or archive?), see Munier, "Question," 389n64; Schoedel, "Archives."

[44] Paulsen, *Ign*, 63, assumes the use of a dominical saying.

[45] Cf. IgnEph 15.1; IgnMagn 10.3, 13.1; and Fischer, "Ignatius," Apparatus *loc. cit.*

[46] Cf. Perler, *Makkabäerbuch.*

[47] Cf. IgnEph 18.2–19.1; IgnSmyrn 1. [English translations are from Roberts/Donaldson/Coxe unless otherwise noted.]

The use of texts on the person and work of Paul is beyond question.[48] The Apostle to the Nations is referred to explicitly in IgnRom 4.3 and especially in IgnEph 12.2:

> You are the persons through whom those pass that are cut off for the sake of God. You are initiated into the mysteries of the Gospel with Paul, the holy, the martyred, the deservedly most happy, at whose feet may I be found when I shall attain to God; who in all his Epistles makes mention of you in Christ Jesus.

The connection between Paul and Ephesus is assumed here just as much as the knowledge of a collection of Pauline Epistles. Futhermore, one can speak literally of Ignatius following Paul; his path appears analogous to Paul's missionary travels and to his route to martyrdom.

Beyond such general references to early Christian traditions and forms, there may also be a use of early Christian texts. Thus Ignatius' use of 1 Corinthians appears very likely,[49] as does his knowledge of Ephesians (IgnEph *praescr.*, 1.1, 12.2, 20.1; IgnMagn 7.1; IgnSmyrn 1.2; IgnPol 1.2, 5.1, 6.2). Less certain is the use of Romans[50] (IgnEph 18.2, 20.2; IgnTrall 9.1; IgnRom 7.3; IgnSmyrn 1.1), Galatians (IgnMagn 8.1-2, 10.2-3;[51] IgnRom 2.1; IgnPhld 1.1), Colossians (IgnEph 2.1, 10.2; IgnMagn 2; IgnTrall 5.2; IgnRom 5.3; IgnSmyrn 6.1), Philippians (IgnMagn 10.3; IgnPhld 10.1; IgnTrall 9.1; IgnSmyrn 4.2, 11.3), perhaps also 1 Thessalonians, Philemon, 1 Timothy, and Titus. Against this background it is striking that the terminology of the justification theology that is central for Paul[52] is scarcely used.

Evidence of references to concrete gospel texts is harder to find.[53] A similarity between IgnSmyrn 1.1 and Matthew 3:15 shows knowledge of the first gospel.[54] IgnPol 1.3 may be considered a use of Matthew 8:17 (cf. also Isa 53:4). IgnEph 17.1 shows knowledge of the story of the anointing in Bethany, presumably in the Matthean version.[55] IgnEph 14.2 (cf. Matt 12:33/Luke 6:44) may indicate the use of oral tradition. A use of Mark or Luke/Acts is hardly provable.

Various references to the fourth gospel in the Ignatian letters have also been considered. They may appear especially in IgnEph 5.2 (John 6:33), 7.2 (John

---

[48] Cf. Lindemann, *Paulus*, 199–221; Reis, *Following*. AposCon 7.46 maintains that Ignatius was ordained bishop by Paul. That is a pious fantasy.

[49] Cf. IgnEph 16.1 (1 Cor 6:9-10), 18.1 (1 Cor 4:13; 1:18, 23; 1:19-20); IgnRom 5.1 (1 Cor 4:4), 9.2 (1 Cor 15:8); IgnPhld 3.3 (1 Cor 6:9-10). Cf. also Foster, "Epistles."

[50] Cf. Rom 1:3(-4), but also John 7:42; 2 Timothy 2:8.

[51] Cf. Niebuhr, "Judentum," 230 with n39.

[52] δικαιοῦν appears only in IgnRom 5.1 and IgnPhld 8.2; δικαιοσύνη only in IgnSmyrn 1.1; νόμος in IgnMagn 2.1, 8.1 v. l., IgnSmyrn 5.1.

[53] εὐαγγέλιον can hardly already mean the written gospels for Ignatius; contra Goulder, "Docetists," 16 with n3; Hill, "Ignatius."

[54] Köster, *Überlieferung*, 59, argues against this idea in favor of common tradition.

[55] Cf. Schoedel, *Ignatius*, 82.

1:14), IgnMagn 7.1 (John 5:19, 30; 8:28; 10:30; cf. 12:49), IgnMagn 8.2 (John 1:1–3:14, 8:29), IgnRom 7.2 (John 4:10, 7:38), IgnRom 7.3 (John 6:27, 33, 51–56), IgnPhld 7.1 (John 3:8, 8:14), and IgnPhld 9.1 (John 10:7, 9).[56] In this context the ancient church tradition of Ignatius' acquaintance with the Apostle John should be remembered.[57]

The use of other texts of the "Apostolic Fathers" in the Ignatian letters is very uncertain; suspects include primarily 1Clem (cf. esp. IgnRom 3.1 and 4.3), 2Clem, Herm, and OdesSol.[58]

The quotation in IgnSmyrn 3.2 cannot be identified; even Eusebius[59] did not know its source. Jerome[60] suspects the Gospel of the Hebrews, Origen[61] a *Doctrina Petri*.[62]

8.3 Other Influences

The religious-historical work on the Ignatian letters has entered a new phase. If the older research influenced by the school of religious history of the early twentieth century (e.g., Heinrich Schlier, Hans-Werner Bartsch[63]) sought to prove Gnostic influences in various thematic areas and later turned to the Nag Hammadi texts as well,[64] the present scholarship, in connection with the debate over authenticity, considers more strongly the anti-Gnostic position of the letters, perhaps in conflict with Valentinians, with Marcus and the Marcosians, with Marcion, or with Ptolemy.[65] Special attention is devoted to the so-called "Star Hymn" in IgnEph 19.2-3.[66] Yet one still suspects, without reference to Gnosticism, other conceptual and linguistic influences of pagan religion, philosophy, and politics.[67]

9.   Genre, Diction, and Style

The Ignatian epistles are, according to their form, genuine *letteres*. They are, except for the majority of IgnPol, addressed to congregations in general.

The prescripts, which are formulated differently in detail and in extent (IgnRom *praescr.* is especially detailed), contain the following constant elements:[68]

---

[56] Cf. Nagel, *Rezeption*, 207–51; see further Mauer, *Ignatius*.

[57] See above.

[58] Cf. Munier, "Question," 397.

[59] HE III 36.11; Schwartz, *ed. min.*, 116.

[60] Vir ill 2; ed. Bernoulli, 8.

[61] Princ *praef.* 8; SC 252, 86.

[62] Vinzent, "Verhältnis," traces the quotation to the *Kerygma Petri*, an important argument for the theological-historical placement he assumes for the Ignatian letters.

[63] Cf. Bartsch, *Gut*; Schlier, *Untersuchungen*.

[64] Cf. Paulsen, *Studien*; Schoedel, *Ignatius, passim*.

[65] See above.

[66] Cf. Lechner, *Ignatius, passim*; Stander, *Starhymn*.

[67] See above.

[68] This strict formality is lost in the further letters of the long recension.

superscripto	"Ignatius, also called Theophoros"
adscripto	Detailed naming of the ἐκκλησία being addressed, which can also include the theme of the letter
salutatio	Giving the circumstances and the greeting formula πλεῖστα χαίρειν[69]

In addition, there are repeated declarations of thanksgiving and praise for the addressees, sometimes already in the prescript, but also in the actual introduction to the letter. Allusions to the Pauline epistolary formula are plain; the mention of the "apostolic style" in IgnTrall *praescr.* could recall such a reference. But in the essentials, the Ignatian letters adhere to the Greek epistolary formulae, with a special similarity to the diplomatic letters of Hellenistic kings.[70] The closing of the letter with personal information, exhortations, greetings, and instructions to greet others is always significantly set off from the body of the letter.[71]

The texts are of varying lengths. Their disposition is differently developed and generally relaxed. This fact may be due partly to the circumstances of the composition. Anacolutha appear repeatedly (e.g., IgnEph 1.3; IgnMagn 2, 5.1-2; IgnRom 1.1; IgnPhld 7.2). But there are also numerous recognizable elements of style like proverbial formulas (IgnEph 15.1; IgnRom 3.3; IgnPol 1.3, 7.3), head rhymes and anaphoras (IgnSmyrn 4.2), similes, word pictures, and metaphors (IgnPhld 6.1; IgnPol 2.1, 3; 3.1; 6.2), parallelisms and antitheses (IgnEph 7.2, 8.2, 12.1; IgnMagn 13.1), rhythmic forms and end rhymes (IgnEph 11.1, 12.2; IgnRom 3.2, 4.3, 6.1; IgnPhld 3.3, 7.2, etc.). Many of the figures of speech do not succeed (e.g., IgnEph 9.1; IgnRom 7.2-3; IgnPhld 2.2; IgnPol 1.3). An overall assessment of the letters with regard to rhetorical analysis has not yet occurred.

In the letters there are frequent neologisms, combinations of words, and new semantic coinages for traditional concepts.[72] In addition, we find lexemic influences from Jewish and early Christian literature, but also from pagan religion and philosophy, as well as technical expressions from architecture, handwork, sports, the military, music, medicine, and the like.[73] Loan words from Latin (IgnEph 2.1; IgnTrall 3.2; IgnSmyrn 12.1: ἐξεμπλάριον; IgnPol 6.2: δεσέρτωρ, δεπόσιτα, ἄκκεπτα) occur, as do Semitisms.[74]

---

[69] Different from Paul's greeting, the greeting formula lacks the reference to χάρις, but the phrase still plays an important role in the epistolary formulae (in the *adscription*: IgnEph praescr. v. l.; IgnMagn praescr.; IgnRom praescr.; in the conclusion: IgnSmyrn 12.2, 13.2; IgnPol 8.2) and elsewhere (IgnEph 11.1, 20.2; IgnMagn 2, 8.1-2; etc.).

[70] Cf. Munier, "Question," 380–85; Sieben, *Briefe.*

[71] There are no "in my own hand" remarks (as, e.g., in 1 Cor 16:21; Gal 6:11; 2 Thess 3:17) in these letters, which may be a sign that they were dictated.

[72] Cf. Bartelink, *Studie.*

[73] Cf. Munier, "Question," 387.

[74] The oft-cited trademarks of the Ignatian style are also referred to here by Eduard Norden; see his *Kunstprosa* II, 510–11.

10. Theological Profile

The Ignatian letters come to speak of various theological and ethical themes in an unsystematic way, in which a special detailedness and redundancy can be observed in those cases where actual requests, problems, or questions about theological fundamentals appear to be touched upon. The details allow their author to be recognized as an original theological thinker of early Christianity with regard to care for souls and church leadership.

One can describe the Ignatian theology in general as a theology of unity. A programmatic statement appears in IgnMagn 1.2:

> For as one who has been thought worthy of the most honourable of all names, in those bonds which I bear about, I commend the Churches, in which I pray for a union both of the flesh and spirit of Jesus Christ, the constant source of our life, and of faith and love, to which nothing is to be preferred, but especially of Jesus and the Father [. . .].

The keyword ἕνωσις ("unification") used here, which has ecclesiological, ethical, and theological connotations, appears frequently; it refers to the fellowship (IgnMagn 13.2; IgnPhld 7.2), God (IgnTrall 11.2),[75] the Eucharist (IgnPhld 4), and the works of Ignatius and Polycarp (IgnPhld 8.1; IgnPol 1.2), as well as to marriage (IgnPol 5.2).

The lexemes from the same root, ἑνότης ("unity"; IgnEph 4.2, 5.1, 14.1; IgnPhld 2.2, 3.2, 5.2, 8.1) and ἑνοῦν ("unite"; IgnEph *praescr.*; IgnMagn 6.2, 14.1; IgnRom *praescr.*; IgnSmyrn 3.3) are always used in an ecclesiological, ethical, and theological sense.

Repeatedly the letters also plead for "harmony" with a political catchphrase[76] (ὁμόνοια, IgnEph 4.1-2, 13.1; IgnMagn 6.1, 15; IgnTrall 12.2; IgnPhld *praescr.*, 11.2). Antonyms are "faction" (αἵρεσις; IgnEph 6.2; IgnTrall 6.1) and "division" (μερισμός; IgnPhld 2.1, 3.1, 7.2, 8.1; IgnSmyrn 7.2; cf. IgnPhld 3.3: σχίζειν). The effort for unity of congregations and the church is understood in the texts as a decidedly theological task, since the unity of the ἐκκλησία is theologically and christologically grounded. Thus the letters can also speak of the ὁμόνοια θεοῦ (IgnMagn 6.1, 15.1; IgnPhld *praescr.*) or the ἑνότης θεοῦ (IgnPhld 8.1, 9.1; IgnSmyrn 12.2; IgnPol 8.3) or Χριστοῦ (IgnPhld 5.2); verbal IgnMagn 7.1.

10.1 The Unity of the ἐκκλησία

From numerous passages it becomes clear that the ἐκκλησία can be understood as the fellowship or church of a city or a region (cf. in addition to the prescripts IgnMagn 1.2, 15; IgnTrall 13.1; IgnRom 4.1; IgnPhld 10.1-2; IgnSmyrn 11.1;

---

[75] Cf. Schoedel, *Ignatius*, 157–58, who rejects Gnostic backgrounds for the imagery.

[76] On the background cf. Brent, *Sophistic*, 231–311; Maier, "Politics."

IgnPol 7.1, 8.1). If the Antiochene fellowship is called "the church in Syria" (IgnEph 21.2; IgnMagn 14.1; IgnTrall 13.1; IgnRom 9.1; cf. IgnRom 2.2: τὸν ἐπίσκοπον Συρίας), it presents a somewhat exaggerated metonymy (more precise and Antioch-focused in formulation are IgnPhld 10.1; IgnSmyrn 11.1; IgnPol 7.1) and not a reference to an already developed diocesan structure. There is even a hint in IgnSmyrn 13.1-2 to the organization of the addressed fellowship in houses.

More significant than the more-than-regional concept of the one church is the ecclesiological metaphoric language, which includes the images of building and temple (IgnEph 9.1)[77] as well as of the body of Christ and its members (IgnEph 4.2; IgnTrall 11.2; IgnSmyrn 1.2). The expression of the "all-embracing" church (καθολικὴ ἐκκλησία) appears for the first time in Ignatius (IgnSmyrn 8.2). The church is immortal (IgnEph 17.1) and her bishops are established to the ends of the earth (IgnEph 3.2). The unity of the church finds its image in the unity of Christ with the Father (IgnMagn 1.2).

Whether the prescript of IgnRom contains the concept of a more-than-regional primate of the Roman church is disputed. The ceremonial expressions may indicate a special position of honor without meaning already special institutionalized or legalized authority.

The pragmatism of all these statements is significant: The actual request of Ignatian ecclesiology is the effort for harmony even within the individual city churches, which is expressed in numerous exhortations and examples (e.g., IgnEph 4.2; IgnMagn 1.2). The grounds for this accentuation are attempts and practices that lead to heretical teachings, which in the view of the texts considerably endanger the unity of the ἐκκλησία.

The most important practical expressions of unity are the meeting of the congregation and its liturgical celebration (IgnMagn 7), which Ignatius repeatedly exhorts his audience to fulfill (IgnEph 5.3, 13.1; IgnPhld 6.2; IgnPol 4.2). Apparently this is not an indirect reference to a lax practice of faith but to the existence of smaller congregational groups that more easily escape the bishop's control (IgnMagn 4, 7.1; cf. IgnSmyrn 8).

10.2 The Offices of Unity

The most striking essential feature of the Ignatian letters is the emphasis on the ordering of the church offices of bishop, presbyters or the presbytry, and deacons. The author appears to assume such a structure in all the churches of Asia Minor that he writes to; it was clearly not uncontroversial.[78] IgnRom does not appear to assume the monepiscopate, and it is not noticeably present in PolPhil either.

---

[77] The discussion of the "temples" in IgnEph 15.3 seems to be an individual ethical application of the image.

[78] The idea that the implied opponents were enthusiasts (so Trevett, "Prophecy") is not recognizable from the texts, however.

The main office-holders are the bishop ("overseer," ἐπίσκοπος), the presbyter ("elder," πρεσβύτεροι) or council of elders (πρεσβυτέριον), and the deacons ("servant," διάκονοι). These offices are often referred to together (IgnMagn 6.1, 13.1; IgnTrall 2.2-3, 3.1; IgnPhld *praescr.*, 7.1). In other passages the duality of bishop and presbyter is presented (IgnEph 2.2, 4.1, 20.2; IgnMagn 7.1).

The function of the bishop is especially accentuated, particularly in the mode of the exhortation. He is the leader and representative of the whole fellowship (IgnTrall 1.1) and can be compared to a property manager (IgnEph 6.1). The idea of apostolic succession does not appear to be developed;[79] what is said is that the bishops are (founded?) "in the mind" of Jesus Christ (ἐν γνώμῃ), just as Jesus is the mind of the Father (IgnEph 3.2; cf. IgnPhld *praescr.*).

Obedience to the bishop is necessary in order to defend the integrity of one's relationship with God (IgnEph 5.3); he is to be seen like the "Lord"[80] Himself (IgnEph 6.1). Whoever submits to him submits to Jesus Christ (IgnTrall 2.1); whoever betrays the bishop betrays God (IgnMagn 3.2). Repeatedly the audience is exhorted not to do anything without the bishop (IgnTrall 2.2; IgnPhld 7.2;[81] IgnSmyrn 8.1–9.1)—an admonition that can also be extended to the functions of the other officers (IgnMagn 6.1, 7.1; IgnTrall 7.2). Obedience to the presbyter as well as the bishop is the ideal (IgnMagn 3.1) to which the audience is exhorted (IgnEph 4.1; IgnTrall 12.2). In addition to the comparison of the bishop with God (the Father) and Jesus Christ, there is also one with the "instruction" (ἐντολή) in IgnTrall 13.2. IgnPhld 2.1 makes use of the image of shepherd and flock for the relationship between the bishop and the congregation. Prayer led by the bishop (IgnEph 5.2) is emphasized as much as the celebration of the Eucharist, with the bishop's participation if at all possible (IgnSmyrn 8.1). Neither baptism nor the love feast should proceed without him (IgnSmyrn 8.2). There is one reference to the bishop's preaching (ὁμιλία; IgnPol 5.1).

While Ignatius refers to himself only once as the "bishop of Syria" and states that after his departure from Antioch there was no serving bishop (IgnRom 9.1), other bishops are named personally: Onesimus (IgnEph 1.3), Damas (IgnMagn 2), Polycarp (IgnMagn 15), Polybius (IgnTrall 1.1), as well as the nameless bishop in IgnPhld 1. IgnPol as a whole is addressed to a bishop.

The presbytery is equated with the circle or "council" (συνέδριον) of the apostles[82] (IgnMagn 6.1, 7.1; IgnTrall 2.2; IgnSmyrn 8.1; cf. IgnPhld 5.1) and also referred to as "God's council" (συνέδριον θεοῦ; IgnTrall 3.1). As the presbyters must follow the bishop (IgnEph 4.1; IgnMagn 3.1; IgnTrall 12.2), so they

---

79 On the orientation toward the apostles, see IgnMagn 6.1, 7.1, 13.1-2; IgnTrall 7.1, 12.2.

80 This probably means Christ.

81 Behind IgnPhld 7.1-2 may lie contentious events in the fellowship gatherings in Philadelphia; cf. Speigl, "Philadelphia."

82 The apostles are imagined significantly as the form of the (past) early days of Christianity; cf. IgnEph 11.2. They have high authority for the present (IgnMagn 13.1; IgnTrall 3.3, 7.1). Nevertheless, the author never speaks of the "twelve" apostles and accordingly views Paul as an apostle equal to Peter (IgnRom 4.3).

themselves are owed obedience (IgnEph 2.2, 20.2; IgnMagn 7.1; IgnTrall 7.2, 13.2; IgnPol 6.1). They are equated with the "law of Jesus Christ" (IgnMagn 2). Presbyters whose names are given are Bassus and Apollonius (IgnMagn 2).

The tasks of the deacons are expressly not (only?) applied to the church service (IgnTrall 2.3); apparently they also regularly functioned as emissaries of the congregation (IgnPhld 10.1; but see also 10.2). The deacons ought also to be heeded like God's commands (IgnSmyrn 8.1); they are owed reverence (IgnTrall 3.1; cf. 7.2). IgnTrall 3.3 shows that something in this regard was especially causing turmoil in Tralles. Deacons, in turn, are urged to obedience toward the bishop and presbyters (IgnMagn 2). Deacons mentioned by name are Zotion (IgnMagn 2) and Philo (IgnPhld 11.1).

If these three offices stand prominently in the foreground, it is also apparent from individual remarks that other services and tasks belonged to the lives of the congregations addressed in the letters. Primary among these are the emissaries, who safeguard the communication between the author and the churches above all. These emissaries could have been, but did not have to be, drawn from the circle of the other office-holders (IgnPhld 10.1, 11.1; IgnSmyrn 11.3). From this circle also come the companions placed at Ignatius' disposal (IgnSmyrn 12.1, 13.1). Their meaning and worth can be expressed by the references to them as "God's messengers" (θεοπρεσβευτής; IgnSmyrn 11.2) or "God's runners" (θεοδρόμος; IgnPhld 2.2; IgnPol 7.2).

The texts mention the others who pass through (IgnEph 9.1; IgnSmyrn 4.1) and warn against them; the references are clearly to wandering teachers. There is also a reference to "superiors" (IgnMagn 6.2, προκαθημένοι).[83] In IgnSmyrn 13.1 and IgnPol 4.1[84] widows are presented as a fixed group within the congregation.[85] They are beneficiaries of the church's care.

With the verb χειροτονεῖν Ignatius gives a fixed limit to the appointment of officials with the exception of the bishop (IgnEph 3.2: ὁρίζειν), cf. with reference to a deacon chosen as an emissary IgnPhld 10.1; also with reverence to the emissary function in IgnSmyrn 11.2; IgnPol 7.2.[86]

Central to Ignatius' self-understanding is the concept of "disciples" (or "students," μαθητής). Discipleship is not an office, nor an interchangeable term for being Christian, but rather a not yet fully reached (IgnTrall 5.2) ideal that begins its path in suffering and reaches fulfillment only in martyrdom (IgnEph 1.2, 3.1; IgnTrall 5.2; IgnRom 5.1, 3). Here elements of an early Christian idea of martyrdom that come from the example of Christ's passion can be seen.

---

[83] On the background of this expression cf. Brent, *Sophistic*, 43–66.
[84] Cf. IgnSmyrn 6.2.

[85] In the NT cf. Acts 6:1 (in connection with the ordination of deacons); 1 Timothy 5:3-16.
[86] The verb is also used in the NT, cf. Acts 14:23 and 2 Corinthians 8:19.

Distinctive is the reference Ignatius regularly makes to himself in the pre-scripts as "God-bearer" (θεοφόρος), which has no direct exemplar known to us.[87] It is also applied to the audience in IgnEph 9.2 amid a series of other expressions (e.g., χριστοφόρος).

10.3 The One Eucharist

The Ignatian letters show a concept of the Christian meal celebration called "Thanksgiving" (εὐχαριστία) developed beyond that of the New Testament writings.[88] The term (as in Did 9.1, 5) is to be understood as a metonym for the entire celebration. The letters also speak of "bread-breaking" (IgnEph 20.2)[89] or simply of "God's bread" (IgnEph 5.2; IgnRom 7.3).

One frequently cited passage is the discussion of the "medicine of immortality" (φάρμακον ἀθανασίας) in IgnEph 20.2; the addressees should come together

> so that you obey the bishop and the presbytery with an undivided mind, breaking one and the same bread, which is the medicine of immortality and the antidote to prevent us from dying, but [which causes] that we should live for ever in Jesus Christ.

The term seems to ascribe saving power to the use of the sacramental elements. It belongs in the context of the graphic ecclesiological language of the author and can hardly be understood in the sense of an actual sacramental soteriology or magic.[90]

The Eucharist is not understood as a sacrifice, but passages like IgnEph 5.2, IgnMagn 7.2, IgnTrall 7.2, or IgnPhld 4 come close to such an understanding in their pictorial language. A clear identification of the Eucharist with the flesh of Christ appears only in IgnSmyrn 7.1; the discussion of the flesh and blood of Christ (IgnTrall 8.1; IgnRom 7.3; IgnSmyrn 12.2; cf. IgnPhld 5.1) is indeed influenced by the imagery of the Eucharist but proves to have primarily strong ethical connotations. The exhortation to come together more often[91] to "God's Eucharist" and to "praise" can be a hint that a regular celebration of the meal (on Sundays) is not yet firmly established. The Eucharist can itself be brought into the image-giving realm in the argumentation, such as in IgnRom 4.1 and 7.3 as a metaphor for Ignatius' self-perception leading up to his martyrdom.

The letters speak of baptism less often than of the Eucharist. Its effectiveness is expressed in metaphors of purification (IgnEph 18.2) or in the frame of the image of weaponry (IgnPol 6.2).[92] There may be a special consideration of the

---

[87] On possible backgrounds of the term cf. Brent, *Sophistic*, 140–80.

[88] For details, see Wehr, *Arznei*, 37–181.

[89] Other early Christian uses include Acts 2:42, 46; 20:7, 11; Did 14; cf. Luke 24:35.

[90] Cf. also John 6:53, 58; Did 10.2-3.

[91] This understanding of πυκνότερον is more probable than the alternative, according to which the exhortation points to a greater number of participants in the Eucharist; cf. Lightfoot, *Fathers* II/1, 66; Schoedel, *Ignatius*, 74n1.

[92] In the NT, cf. on this Ephesians 6:11-17.

baptismal water behind IgnEph 18.2.[93] There is one reference to the anointing (IgnEph 17.1), which may have been completed in connection with baptism.[94]

The special importance of the bishop is also emphasized in connection with the sacraments; it is not permitted to baptize or hold the love feast (ἀγάπη[95]) without the bishop (IgnSmyrn 8.1-2). Marriage must also proceed with his consent (IgnPol 5.2). The texts do not give any information regarding a regulated institution of penance or firm rules for excommunication and readmittance. The interaction with opponents moves on the level of publicity, admonition, and threat.[96]

10.4 God and Spirit

The theological thought of the author in a stricter sense is fundamentally Trinitarian (IgnEph 9.1; IgnMagn 13.1-2), with the accent falling on the "unity" of God (IgnTrall 11.2).

Though the first Person of the Trinity does not stand in the foreground of the actual theological efforts of the letters, the personal conception of the understanding of God is important, which comes to expression in a wealth of statements about God's plans, his actions, and both his individual attention and believer's attention to God as a personal relationship.[97] God is the Creator (IgnEph 15.1; IgnRom *praescr*.), the Father of Jesus Christ (IgnEph 2.1; IgnMagn 3.1; etc.) and the Father in an absolute sense (IgnEph *praescr*., 9.1; IgnMagn 3.1; etc.).

The relationship to God is often expressed as existence "in God" (ἐν θεῷ; IgnEph 1.1, 6.2; IgnMagn 3.1, 14; IgnTrall 4.1, 8.2; IgnPol 1.1, 6.1; cf. IgnEph 21.2; IgnMagn *praescr*.). Ignatius also uses the term κατά θεόν (IgnEph 2.1, 8.1; IgnMagn 1.1, 13.1; IgnTrall 1.2; IgnPhld 4.1; IgnSmyrn 11.3) and combinations with the genitive [τοῦ] θεοῦ (IgnEph 8.1; IgnMagn 5.2, 10.1; IgnRom 6.2; IgnPhld 3.2), which are overwhelmingly intended ethically and express the correspondence to God in action. Having a part in God is discussed in various formulations (IgnEph 4.2, 8.1; IgnMagn 14; IgnRom 6.3): One should also recall Ignatius' self-designation as "God-bearer."

Individual statements of a negative theology appear (IgnPol 3.2; cf. IgnEph 7.2); IgnEph 19.1 speaks of God's "silence" (cf. IgnEph 15.2 of Jesus).[98] There are also phrases that speak of God's fullness and greatness (IgnEph *inscr*.).

Less defined is the discussion of the Holy Spirit. He appears as the Third Person of the Trinity, as well as an expression of divinity in humanity and in the church with its officials (IgnEph 18.2; IgnMagn 9.2; IgnPhld *praescr*., 7.1-2; IgnPol 1.3). According to IgnEph 9.1, he is the medium of the salvation achieved in

[93] Cf. Lightfoot, *Fathers* II/2, 75–76.

[94] On this cf. Schoedel, *Ignatius*, 82.

[95] Apparently this refers to the celebration otherwise called "Eucharist" and not to a special love feast; cf. Wehr, *Arznei*, 137–41, 167–68.

[96] Cf. von Campenhausen, *Amt*, 155–58.

[97] Cf. the listing in Schoedel, *Ignatius*, 18.

[98] Whether or not IgnMagn 8.2 (cf. IgnEph 6.1 on the bishop, IgnPhld 1.1 on Christ) identifies God with "silence" is debated among textual critics; the manuscript evidence indicates not (cf. Barnes, "Date," 125; Hübner, "Thesen," 51–52).

Christ. There is also the possibility of personal inspiration (IgnPhld 7.1-2). The Spirit works in the deeds of the believers (IgnEph 8.2; IgnPhld 7.2; IgnPol 1.3).

10.5 Antidocetic Christology

Jesus Christ appears most prominently of the three persons of the Godhead. Securing the right understanding of Jesus Christ as very God and very Man is one of the chief tasks of the texts.

The letters know a whole series of christological terms and titles. Jesus Christ is repeatedly referred to as "God" (IgnSmyrn 1.1; IgnTrall 7.1) or "our God" (IgnEph 15.3, 18.2; IgnRom *praescr.*, 3.3; IgnPol 8.3) and "Lord" (IgnEph 15.3, 19.1; IgnMagn 7.1, 13.1; IngTrall 8.1, 10; IgnPhld *praescr.*, 1.1, 4; etc.), as well as "the Son of God" (IgnEph 20.2; IgnRom *praescr.*), "Son of Man" (IgnEph 20.2) or "new Man" (IgnEph 20.1), "Word of God" (IgnMagn 8.2), plus "Savior" (σωτήρ; IgnMagn *praescr.*), "Physician" (IgnEph 7.2), and "Teacher" (IgnEph 15.1; IgnMagn 9.1-2). He is the high priest and door to the Father (IgnPhld 9.1), the "mind of the Father" (IgnEph 3.2), his "mouth" (IgnRom 8.2), hope (IgnEph 21.2; IgnMagn 11.1; Ign Phld 11.2; etc.), the knowledge of God (IgnEph 17.2), and unshakeable or true life (IgnEph 3.2; IgnSmyrn 4.1).

Yet the christological profile and its actual use are not to be read only from the use of titles. The texts emphasize on one hand the unity of the Son with the Father and his true divinity (IgnRom 3.3; IgnMagn 1.2). So the Son is preexistent (IgnMagn 6.1) and Creator of the world (IgnEph 15.1), and he remains united with the Father despite his incarnation (IgnMagn 1.2, 7.1-2; IgnRom 3.3; IgnSmyrn 3.3). Subordinationist-sounding christological formulas (IgnEph 3.2; IgnMagn 2; IgnTrall 3.1; IgnPhld 7.2; IgnSmyrn 8.1) fit within the theological historical context of the early second century.

On the other hand, Ignatius time and again brings up the full incarnation up to the suffering, death, and bodily resurrection (IgnMagn 1.2; IgnTrall 10; IgnRom 6.1; IgnSmyrn 4.2). In this perspective the Son of God is also the Son of David (IgnEph 18.2, 20.2) and of Mary (IgnEph 7.2, 18.2, 19.1; IgnTrall 9.1). The consequently conceived unity of Father and Son allows one to speak of the blood, flesh, and sufferings of God (IgnEph 1.1, 7.2; IgnRom 6.3; IgnPol 3.2). Even the powers of heaven, if they do not believe on the "blood of Christ," will face judgment (IgnSmyrn 6.1).

In particular, passages from IgnEph and IgnTrall make it advisable to speak of an antidocetic point to the Christology of the Ignatian letters. IgnEph 7.2 formulates it in the context of a polemic against adversaries:

> There is one Physician who is possessed both of flesh and spirit, both made and not made, God existing in flesh, true life in death, both of Mary and of God, first passible and then impassible—even Jesus Christ our Lord.

The duality of "flesh" and "spirit" expressed here also forms the framework for the christological statement in IgnSmyrn 3.2-3.[99]

Also in the above quotation from IgnTrall 9.1,[100] which emphasizes *vere homo*, we see the contemporary reason, and it becomes clearer in the continuation in chapter 10:

> But if, as some that are without God, that is, the unbelieving, say that He only seemed to suffer (they themselves only seeming to exist),[101] then why am I in bonds? Why do I long to be exposed to the wild beasts? Do I therefore die in vain? Am I not then guilty of falsehood against [the cross of] the Lord?

Ignatius clearly fights in at least a few of his letters against teachers who advance a docetic Christology. Whether this theological position is connected with the propagation of "Judaism"[102] is less clear. There may also be differences here between the individual congregations.[103]

10.6 The Defense against Judaism

Ignatius knows of the unity in the church of Jews and Gentiles (IgnSmyrn 1.2). Yet it is clear, especially in IgnMagn and Phil, that Ignatius is against the "Judaism" (ἰουδαϊσμός) that is understood as a way of life (cf. the use of the verb ἰουδαΐζειν in IgnMagn 10.3). It appears primarily in the letters to Magnesia and Philadelphia: "For if we still live according to the Jewish law, we acknowledge that we have not received grace" (IgnMagn 8.1).[104] The right relationship between "Christianity" (χριστιανισμός—here for the first time in Christian literature![105]) and Judaism is to observe and protect (IgnMagn 10.3). The knowledge of Christ and the Jewish lifestyle are mutually exclusive (IgnMagn 8.1, 10.3). Concretely, the observation of the Sabbath is rejected (IgnMagn 9.1). The position combated here may have its own origins in Gentile Christianity: "But if any one preach the Jewish law unto you, listen not to him. For it is better to hearken to Christian doctrine from a man who has been circumcised, than to Judaism from one uncircumcised" (IgnPhld 6.1). Events in Philadelphia especially seem to be decisive for Ignatius' position.[106]

10.7 Ethics and Eschatology

The implicit ethics of the Ignatian letters is oriented toward virtue on one hand and teleologically structured on the other.

---

[99] For other statement connections cf. Schoedel, *Ignatius*, 23–24, anthropological in, e.g., IgnTrall 12.1; IgnPol 1.2, 5.1; but ethical in IgnPol 2.2.

[100] See above under "Early Christian Tradition and Texts."

[101] Cf. the same phrase in IgnSmyrn 2.

[102] See below.

[103] Goulder, "Docetists," sees the Ignatian letters as arguing against Judaizing Docetism, more specifically Ebiontes.

[104] On the textual criticism cf. Fischer, "Ignatius," 166 Apparatus *loc. cit.*

[105] Cf. on this Lightfoot, *Fathers* II/1, 415–19.

[106] Cf. Schoedel, *Ignatius*, 214; Speigl, "Philadelphia."

Faith (πίστις, πιστεύειν) and love (ἀγάπη, ἀγαπᾶν) are repeatedly referred to together[107] and are the central Christian virtues (IgnSmyrn 6.1), beginning and end of the Christian life (IgnEph 14.1) that is oriented toward the passion of the Lord (IgnSmyrn 1.1). From them come the other virtues (IgnEph 14.1). They become concrete in orthodoxy (IgnEph 10.2), unity of the fellowship (IgnEph 14.2; IgnMagn 1.1-2, 5.2, 7.1; etc.), and obedience to the officials of the church (IgnEph 2.1-2; IgnMagn 6.1; IgnTrall 3.2; etc.). The absence of love will overthrow the adversaries (IgnSmyrn 6.2). While faith unfolds as "belief on . . ." (IgnEph 16.2; IgnPhld 8.2) and as steadfastness (IgnEph 3.1, 8.2, 14.2), love is shown toward fellow Christians (IgnMagn 6.2; IgnTrall 13.2; etc.) and officeholders (IgnEph 1.3; IgnMagn 6.1; IgnTrall 3.2; etc.), as well as to God and Christ (IgnEph 9.2, 15.3; IgnPol 5.1). Faith and love lead to God (IgnEph 9.1; cf. IgnTrall 12.3); indeed, love is itself a transcendent phenomenon (IgnEph 1.3; IgnRom 7.3).

The highest realization of Christian morality is martyrdom.[108] It is understood as suffering with the Lord (IgnSmyrn 4.2) and as an imitation of Christ (IgnRom 6.3). So it is understandable that Ignatius can describe his own death in eucharistic language (IgnRom 2.2, 4.1-2). The martyr is a complete disciple of Christ (IgnEph 1.2; IgnRom 4.2), a complete Christian and believer (IgnRom 3.2), and a fulfilled person (IgnRom 6.1-2; cf. 9.2). Ignatius' hope rests on meeting Jesus Christ (IgnRom 5.3) or God in death (IgnEph 12.2; IgnMagn 14; IgnTrall 12.2; etc.). The author can also connect the expectation of the resurrection to the death of the individual (IgnEph 11.2; IgnRom 4.3; cf. generalized IgnSmyrn 5.3).[109] He thus emphasizes, beyond the personal hope of the future martyr, the physicality of the resurrection (IgnSmyrn 2, 7.1).

To his own death Ignatius ascribes a soteriological function for others (ransom: IgnEph 21.1; IgnSmyrn 10.2; IgnPol 2.3, 6.1; sin offering: IgnEph 8.1; cf. IgnTrall 13.3). Indeed, the author even wants to understand his way as a sin offering for the cross of the Lord (IgnEph 18.1). Here aspects of the *imitatio Christi* are worked out and connected to martyrdom that already appear in the New Testament in Colossians 1:24.

Apart from the application to his own person and situation, the texts present a very conventional eschatology that functions mostly parenetically: Fundamentally decisive is the knowledge of living in the last times (IgnEph 11.1; cf. IgnSmyrn 9.1), which began with the appearance of Christ (IgnMagn 6.1). Ignatius hints at the outstanding Last Judgment (IgnEph 11.1; IgnSmyrn 6.1). Resurrection is promised to the believers (IgnTrall 9.2; cf. IgnTrall *praescr.*); immortality and

---

[107] In contrast, the triad of faith, hope (ἐλπίς), and love familiar from the NT does not appear in Ignatius. The combination with ἀγάπη is in Ign-Magn 7.1.

[108] The term μαρτύριον is in IgnTrall 12.3; Ign-Phld 6.3 does not use it technically; elsewhere in the Greek manuscripts in IgnEph 1.2; cf. Scho-edel, *Ignatius*, 42n13; critical of the *textus receptus* Hüebner, *Thesen*, 50–51; cf. also Barnes, "Date," 128–30.

[109] According to IgnMagn 9.2, the prophets have already risen from the dead.

eternal life are presented to Polycarp as well (IgnPol 2.3). The schismatic and heretical adversaries are condemned to "unquenchable fire" (IgnEph 16.2) and destruction (IgnPol 5.2; cf. also IgnSmyrn 2). Ignatius also speaks of the "Kingdom of God" (IgnEph 16.1; IgnPhld 3.3) in connection with the exclusion of the schismatics.[110]

11. Bibliography

Bardenhewer, O. *Geschichte der Altkirchlichen Literatur, I: Vom Ausgang des apostolischen Zeitalters bis zum Ende des zweiten Jahrhunderts*. Darmstadt ²2007 (reprint of the 1913 ed.).

Barnes, T. D. "The Date of Ignatius." *ET* 120 (2008): 119–30.

Bartelink, G. J. M. *Lexicologisch-semantische Studie over de Taal van de apostolische Vaders: Bijdrage tot de studie van de groeptaal der Griekse christenen*. Utrecht 1952.

Bartsch, H.-W. *Gnostisches Gut und Gemeindetradition bei Ignatius von Antiochien*. Gütersloh 1940.

Brent, A. *Ignatius of Antioch and the Second Sophistic: A Study of an Early Chrsitian Transformation of Pagan Culture*. STAC 36. Tübingen 2006.

———. *Ignatius of Antioch: A Martyr Bishop and the Origin of Episcopacy*. London/New York 2007.

———. "The Enigma of Ignatius of Antioch." *JEH* 57 (2006): 429–57.

Campenhausen, H. von. *Kirchliches Amt und geistliche Vollmacht in den ersten drei Jahrhunderten*. BHT 14. Tübingen ²1963.

Edwards, M. J. "Ignatius and the Second Century: An Answer to R. Hübner." *ZAC* 1 (1997): 214–26.

Fischer, J. A. "Die sieben Ignatius-Briefe." In *Die apostolischen Väter*, 109–225. SUC I. Darmstadt 1981.

Foster, P. "The Epistles of Ignatius of Antioch and the Writings That Later Formed the New Testament." In *The Reception of the New Testament in the Apostolic Fathers*, edited by A. F. Gregory and C. M. Tuckett, 159–86. Oxford 2007 (reprint).

Funk, F. X., and F. Diekamp, eds. *Patres Apostolici* I–II. Tübingen ³1913.

Goulder, M. D. "Ignatius' 'Docetists.'" *VC* 53 (1999): 16–30.

Harland, P. A. "Christ-Bearers and Fellow-Initiates: Local Cultural Life and Christian Identity in Ignatius' Letters." *JECS* 11 (2003): 481–99.

Harnack, A. von. *Die Zeit des Ignatius und die Chronologie der antiochenischen Bischöfe bis Tyrannus nach Julius Africanus und den späteren Historikern: Nebst einer Untersuchung über die Verbreitung der Passio S. Polycarpi im Abendlande. Leipzig 1878.*

———. *Geschichte der altchristliche Literatur bis Eusebius: I.1: Die überlieferung und der Bestand*. Leipzig ²1958.

Hengel, M. *Die johanneische Frage: Ein Lösungversuch: Mit einem Beitrag zur Apokalypse von Jörg Frey*. WUNT 67. Tübingen 1993.

---

[110] For numerous further references I thank Mr. David C. Bienert of Münster.

Heussi, K. *Die römische Petrustradition in kritischer Sicht.* Tübingen 1955.

Hill, C. E. "Ignatius, the 'Gospel,' and the Gospels." In *Trajectories through the New Testament and the Apostolic Fathers*, edited by A. F. Gregory and C. M. Tuckett, 267–85. Oxford 2007 (reprint).

Hübner, R. M. *Der paradox Eine: Antignostischer Monarchianismus im zweiten Jahrhundert: Mit einem Beitrag von Markus Vinzent.* VC.S 50. Leiden 1999.

———. "Thesen zur Echtheit und Datierung der sieben Briefe des Ignatius von Antiochen." *ZAC* 1 (1997): 44–72.

Joly, R. *Le dossier d'Ignace d'Antioche.* Brussels 1979.

Köster, H. *Synoptische Überlieferung bei den Apostolischen Vätern.* TU 65. Berlin 1957.

Kraft, H., ed. *Eusebius von Caesarea: Kirchengeschichte.* Translated by P. Haeuser and H. A. Gärtner. Munich 1967.

Lechner, T. *Ignatius Adversus Valentinianos? Chronologische und theologiegeschichtliche Studien zu den Briefen des Ignatius von Antiochien.* VC.S 47. Leiden 1999.

Lightfoot J. B. *The Apostolic Fathers, II.1–2: S. Ignatius, S. Polycarp: A Revised Text with Introductions, Notes Dissertations, and Translations.* Hildesheim 1973 (reprint of the 2nd ed. 1889).

Lindemann, A. "Antwort auf die 'Thesen zur Echtheit und Datierung der sieben Briefe des Ignatius von Antiochen.'" *ZAC* 1 (1997): 185–94.

———. *Paulus im ältesten Christentum: Das Bild des Apostels und die Rezeption der paulinischen Theologie in der frühchristlichen Literatur bis Marcion.* BHT 58. Tübingen 1979.

Maier, H. O. "The Politics and Rhetoric of Discord and Concord in Paul and Ignatius." In *Trajectories through the New Testament and the Apostolic Fathers*, edited by A. F. Gregory and C. M. Tuckett, 308–24. Oxford 2007 (reprint).

Maurer, C. *Ignatius von Antiochien und das Johannesevangelium.* Zurich 1949.

Munier, C. "A propos d'Ignace d'Antioche: Observations sur la liste épiscopale d'Antioche." *RSR* 55 (1981): 126–31.

———. "Où en est la question d'Ignace d'Antioche? Bilan d'un siècle de recherches 1870–1988." *ANRW* II 27.1 (1993): 359–484.

Nagel, T. *Die Rezeption des Johannesevangeliums im 2. Jahrhundert: Studien zur vorirenäischen Aneignung und Auslegung des vierten Evangeliums in christlicher und christlich-gnostischer Literatur.* Arbeiten zur Bibel und ihrer Geschichte 2. Leipzig 2000.

Niebuhr, K.-W. "'Judentum' und 'Christentum' bei Paulus und Ignatius von Antiochien." *ZNW* 85 (1994): 218–33.

Norden, E. *Die antike Kunstprosa: Vom VI. Jahrhundert v. Chr. bis in die Zeit der Renaissance* II. Darmstadt ²1958.

Paulsen, H. *Die Briefe des Ignatius von Antiochia und der Brief des Polykarp von Smyrna: Zweite, neubearbeitete Aufl. der Auslegung von Walter Bauer.* HNT 18. Tübingen 1985.

———. *Studien zur Theologie des Ignatius von Antiochien.* FKDG 29. Göttingen 1978.

Perler, O. "Das vierte Makkabäerbuch, Ignatius von Antiochien und die ältesten Märtyrerberichte." *RivAC* 25 (1949): 47–72.

Reis, D. M. "Following in Paul's Footsteps: *Mimêsis* and Power in Ignatius of Antioch." In *Trajectories through the New Testament and the Apostolic Fathers*, edited by A. F. Gregory and C. M. Tuckett, 288–305. Oxford 2007 (reprint).

Rius-Camps, J. *The Four Authentic Letters of Ignatius, the Martyr.* OCA 213. Rome 1980.

Roberts, A., and J. Donaldson. *The Apostolic Fathers—Justin Martyr—Irenaeus: American Reprint of the Edinburgh Edition: Revised etc. by A. C. Coxe.* ANF 1. Grand Rapids 1973 (reprint).

Schlier, H. *Religionsgechichtliche Untersuchungen zu den Ignatiusbriefen.* BZNW 8. Gießen 1929.

Schoedel, W. R. Ignatius and the Archives." *HTR* 71 (1978): 97–106.

———. *Ignatius of Antioch: A Commentary on the Letters of Ignatius of Antioch.* Hermeneia. Philadelphia 1985.

———. "Polycarp of Smyrna and Ignatius of Antioch." *ANRW* II 27.1 (1993): 272–358.

———. "Polycarp's Witness to Ignatius of Antioch." *VC* 41 (1987): 1–10.

Schöllgen, G. "Die Ignatianen als pseudepigraphisches Briefcorpus." *ZAC* 2 (1998): 16–25.

Speigl, J. "Ignatius in Philadelphia: Ereignisse und Anliegen in den Ignatiusbriefen." *VC* 41 (1987): 360–76.

Stander, H. F. "The Starhymn in the Epistle of Ignatius to the Ephesians (19:2-3)." *VC* 43 (1989): 209–14.

Trevett, C. "Prophecy and Anti-Episcopal Activity: A Third Error Combatted by Ignatius?" *JEH* 34 (1983): 1–18.

Vinzent, M. "'Ich bin kein körperloses Geistwesen': Zum Verhältnis von Κήρυγμα Πέτρου, 'Doctrina Petri,' Διδασκαλία Πέτρου und IgnSm 3." In Hübner, *Der paradox Eine*, 241–86.

Vogt, H. J. "Bemerkungen zur Echtheit der Ignatiusbriefe." *ZAC* 3 (1999): 50–63.

Wehr, L. *Arznei der Unsterblichkeit: Die Eucharistie bei Ignatius von Antiochien und im Johannesevangelium.* NTA.NF 18. Münster 1987.

Weijenborg, R. *Les lettres d'Ignace d'Antioche: Étude de critique litteraire et de théologie.* Leiden 1969.

Zahn, T. *Ignatius von Antiochien.* Gotha 1873.

The Epistle of Polycarp

Boudewijn Dehandschutter

1. Authorship

We know Polycarp of Smyrna relatively well. Both the story of his martyrdom (MartPol, ca. 156 C.E.[1]) and the early evidence of Irenaeus are important. The bishop of Lyon makes Polycarp a direct student of the apostles, ordained by them as bishop of Smyrna (Haer III 3.4). The birth year deduced from the words of the *Martyrdom*, around 70 C.E.,[2] makes Polycarp's eventual contact with Ignatius possible, but the doubt about the authenticity of the epistles of Ignatius forbids any statement about a relationship between the two.[3] In any case, at the time of Anicetus of Rome (ca. 155–ca. 166), Polycarp was the most important defender of the practice of Quartodecimianism from Asia Minor in Rome.[4] His stay in Rome must have taken place shortly before his martyrdom (ca. 156). For Irenaeus,

---

[1] See Buschmann, *Martyrium*, 39; Dehandschutter, *Polycarpiana, passim.* Not a few scholars prefer the dating based on Eusebius, i.e., 167 C.E. But cf. recently Parvis, *Martyrdom*, 127–32.

[2] Polycarp tells the proconsul that he has served his Lord for eighty-six years (MartPol 9.3). On the one hand, this statement could point to his having been baptized as a child; on the other hand, these words could refer to his entire lifetime (cf. Buschmann, *Martyrium*, 192). The "Harris Fragments" make Polycarp over 100 years old! Cf. Weidmann, *Polycarp, passim.*

[3] Ignatius speaks of Polycarp several times (IgnEph 21.1; IgnPol) and always with reference to his bishopric. This stands in contrast to the beginning of PolPhil, in which Polycarp does not refer to himself as a bishop. One can interpret this fact to mean that Polycarp understood himself as a "co-presbyter," a sort of *primus inter pares* (Bauer/Paulsen, *Polykarpbrief*, 113). Even if the formulation of the address gives no cause for it, one can still agree with J. B. Bauer, *Polykarpbriefe*, 33–35, that the development of the monarchical episcopacy in Smyrna (and in Philippi!) had not yet advanced that far. The antithesis to the Ignatian letters in this regard can be explained by a later

dating of the Ignatiana (in the 2nd half of the 2nd c.), when the monarchical episcopacy had developed more strongly. In any respect one can conclude that the letters of Ignatius should not be used to reconstruct the historical context of Polycarp, however much the connection was also suggested by Eusebius (HE III 36)! The fact that Polycarp himself refers to Ignatius' letters (PolPhil 13) does not mean that he refers to any letter that resembles what we know as the (middle recension of the) letters of Ignatius (see below).

[4] Irenaeus via Eus HE V 24.14-17. Among Christians in Asia Minor, Easter, following Jewish use, was always celebrated on 14 Nisan (quartadecima). Although Anicetus could not agree with Polycarp in this matter, the ecclesiastical peace was maintained (HE V 24.16), which would no longer be the case later under Victor of Rome. Eusebius brings up a letter by Irenaeus to Victor of Rome that contains a long passage on the Easter controversy (V 23–25), which also cites a letter by Polycrates that refers to Polycarp among others as one of the illustrious examples of those who kept the Asian practice (alongside the Apostles Phillip and John!); for the whole story: Brox, *Tendenzen*, 291–324.

Polycarp was also someone who opposed every form of heresy with all his might.[5] That problems with "orthodoxy" had undermined Polycarp's authority in his own fellowship and even made him the proponent of a minority is apparent to some from the opening words of PolPhil.[6] In this letter Polycarp does not actually call himself a bishop but places himself, in a noteworthy formulation, alongside the "presbyters who are with him."[7] However, the hypothesis that Polycarp's words point to a problem of authority fueled by theological conflicts is not very convincing,[8] though some have accepted it.[9]

The reasons for the persecution experienced by the church in Smyrna around 156 are not clear. Much of the evidence points to it stemming from an arbitrary act approved by the masses. Polycarp also fell victim to this persecution, as the twelfth martyr, but "his memory is greater than that of the other" (MartPol 19.1). As a bishop he appeared to the pagans as a "teacher of impiety,"[10] the father of Christians, the destroyer of our gods, he who incited many to refuse to bring them sacrifice and show them reverence (MartPol 12.2). His death marked the end of the persecution (MartPol 1.1). The earliest known "Harris Fragments," which contain a unique version of the death of Polycarp, appear to place emphasis on the role of the Jews in Polycarp's arrest,[11] though this fact is not absent from MartPol (12.2, 13.1, 17.2, 18.1). The later[12] *Vita Polycarpi* is not directed toward the martyrdom but places more emphasis on Polycarp's blameless ascetic life, his suitability for his office, and his running of the "*cursus honorum*": deacon, presbyter, bishop. It is significant that for the author of the *Vita*, Polycarp completely fulfilled a picture of the ideal bishop as described primarily in the Pastoral Epistles. Even if one does not accept this idealistic picture, there is still the question of whether Irenaeus' presentation of Polycarp also corresponds to an ideal image of the bishop—as a link in the apostolic succession.[13]

---

5 Iren Flor via Eus HE V 20.6-7 and Haer III 3.4: during his stay in Rome Polycarp supposedly converted several heretics, Valentinians, and Marcionites. In the letter to Florinus, Irenaeus remembers Polycarp and speaks especially of his loyalty to the teaching of the apostles. See now on Irenaeus as a source for Eusebius and his reception of Polycarp: Willing, *Eusebius*, 30–34.

6 Bauer, "Rechtgläubigkeit," 73–74.

7 "Πολύκαρπος καὶ οἱ σὺν αὐτῷ πρεσβύτεροι."

8 Irenaeus himself names Polycarp "the blessed and apostolic *presbyter*" (Eus HE v 20.7; emphasis added).

9 E.g., Vielhauer, *Geschichte*, 561–62.

10 Our reading. Many follow the reading "teacher of Asia."

11 See Weidmann, *Polycarp*, 94–96.

12 According to A. Stuart-Sykes, *Polycarp*, 4–16, this *Vita* still dates to the third century and provides an important witness to the conversion from the model of the "philosophical *Vita*" to a more hagiographical conception. By contrast, many others hold the *Vita* to be a worthless hagiographical text from the fourth century.

13 Cf. Dehandschutter, "Images of Polycarp," 271–77; idem, *Heresy*, 7–22. Some skepticism over the worth of Irenaeus' information, especially the direct connection between the Apostle John and Polycarp, appears in Hartog, *Polycarp*, 35–41. By contrast, the "Harris Fragments" make Polycarp a student of John's without regard.

2.   Textual Tradition

The textual tradition of PolPhil is "fairly mangled."[14] The eight (or nine[15]) long-recognized Greek manuscripts all have the same problem: that the text breaks off in 9.2 with the words καὶ δι' ἡμᾶς ὑπό and switches to Barn 5.7 τὸν λαὸν τὸν καινόν and so forth. Even the "archetype" of the Greek codices, Vaticanus Graecus 859 (11th c.), contains this error. The editors have thus attempted to resolve this deficiency by using on the one hand the letters in Eus HE III 36.13-15, which quote chapter 9 in its entirety and almost all of chapter 13, and on the other with completions from the Latin translation of the letter, which is indeed relatively old but is fairly free and partly untrustworthy. Nevertheless, the weight of this translation is heavily emphasized by some; J. B. Bauer has just published a new edition of it.[16] New information about the manuscript material offers no enlightenment.[17] It may be noted as well that the author of the *Martyrium Ignatii* (Martyrium Romanum) adds Polycarp's testimony about Ignatius to the end of his text, and that based on the text in Eusebius, who still brings in a further tradition of the Greek text for chapters 9 and 13, to which in turn the Coptic and Armenian versions can be traced.[18] Editions of PolPhil have long ignored this information from the tradition of the *Martyrium Ignatii*. Irenaeus already knew the "letters" of Polycarp (so in *Ad Florinum*, quoted in Eus HE V 20.8[19]), of which he actually knew only one, a "very educational letter" to the Philippians (Haer III 3.4 = Eus HE IV 14.8). Eusebius, who includes the greatest possible amount of material on Polycarp,[20] knows the letter as well and quotes it as previously mentioned (HE III 36.13). The author of the *Vita Polycarpi* (ch. 12) refers to the existence of a letter to the Philippians among other witnesses[21] that were "lost during the persecution." Jerome also refers to the letter (Vir ill 17) and the circumstance that it was read among the Asian churches even in his day.[22] Elsewhere, quotations from PolPhil appear in the Syriac translation of the work of Timotheus Ailurus and of Severus of Antioch.[23]

---

[14]   Bihlmeyer, *Väter*, XXXIX.

[15]   Bihlmeyer, *Väter*, XL; now really nine or ten manuscripts, cf. n. 17. Enumeration of manuscripts, e.g., in J. B. Bauer, *Polykarpbriefe*, 14–15.

[16]   J. B. Bauer, *Polykarpbriefe*, 15–18, 88–93 (edition following Funk). Bauer still speaks of an Armenian translation that has not come down to us without being more specific about it (14); cf. Thomson, *Bibliography, passim*.

[17]   Neither the manuscript Vaticanus Graecus 1655 referred to by Prostmeier, "Überlieferung," nor the manuscript in the Bibliotheca Vallicellana we described (Dehandschutter, *Text*, 29–33) offers any conclusion.

[18]   See the Greek text in Lightfoot II/2, 538–40; both Coptic versions in Lefort, *Les Pères apostoliques*, 102–4; the Armenian in Petermann, *Epistulae, passim*.

[19]   Letters that Polycarp wrote to "the neighboring churches or to many of the brothers."

[20]   Eus HE IV 15 includes almost the full text of the *Martyrdom of Polycarp*, though situated under Marcus Aurelius on the basis of an imprecise chronology.

[21]   It is possible, though not certain, that the *Vita* borrows these sources from Eusebius.

[22]   "Scripsit ad Philippenses epistolam valde utilem, quae usque hodie in Asiae conventu legitur."

[23]   See on this Lightfoot, *Fathers* II/1, 563–65; also Phot Bibl 126 is acquainted with the one letter of Polycarp.

3.   Literary Unity and Integrity

Scholars still cannot agree on this question.[24] There is a known contradiction between the text of chapter 9 and that of chapter 13: in the first there is a reference to the example of Ignatius and his companions who like others "have gone to their eternal place with the Lord," in other words, have suffered martyrdom. In chapter 13 one plainly reads that, on the basis of his sending his "collection" of Ignatius' letters at the Philippians' request, Polycarp inquires how Ignatius and his companions are faring; in other words, he believes them to be still alive. The latter text receives especially great attention because of its early proof of a collection of Ignatius' letters. The criticism of the nineteenth and twentieth centuries, which denied the authenticity of the Ignatian epistles, thus saw in chapter 13 a later interpolation to make a falsehood—that there were letters by Ignatius—believable: Even Polycarp knew Ignatius' letters![25] Editors like Zahn, Lightfoot, and Funk rejected this interpolation hypothesis and brought up the fact that Polycarp speaks about Ignatius and his martyrdom in chapter 9 only in general terms, which does not require there to be a chronological conflict with chapter 13.

In any case, P. N. Harrison presented a different, influential hypothesis in 1936: Chapters 13 and 14 should be separated from the rest of the letter and treated as a kind of "covering note" for the sending of the letters by Ignatius that the Philippians had requested. This exchange took place before Ignatius' martyrdom. Chapters 1–12 are a second, later letter to the Philippians, clearly written around the time of Ignatius' martyrdom (ca. 135 C.E.). This suggested solution had great success. Editors, translators, and scholars followed the hypothesis of the two letters, bearing in mind that Irenaeus stated that Polycarp wrote multiple letters. However, chapter 14 is generally connected to the later second letter as a conclusion and the date of this letter set about ten years earlier (ca. 120).[26] The "division hypothesis" has not been accepted across the board, however, and constantly meets with skepticism, for example in P. Hartog, who has most recently restated the pros and cons of the idea.[27] He comes to the conclusion that the literary unity still remains the best hypothesis. One must remember that when authors like Irenaeus and Eusebius speak concretely about PolPhil, they speak of *one* letter. The "division hypothesis" also goes too far on the assumption that the

---

[24] Reviews of scholarship in, among others, Schoedel, "Polycarp," 276–85; Lechner, *Ignatius,* 6–65.

[25] The radical critics even held that PolPhil is itself a fraud with the goal of obscuring the pseudepigraphical character of the Ignatian epistles (thus still Grégoire, *Persécutions,* 105–6).

[26] See Kleist, *Didache, passim;* Meinhold, "Polykarpos," 1662–93; Camelot, *Polycarpe de Smyrne,* 197–209; Fischer, *Väter,* 233–45; Köster, *Überlieferung,* 122; Barnard, *Problem,* 31–39; Lindemann,

Paulus, 87–91; J. B. Bauer, *Polykarpbriefe,* 18–21; Berding, "Polycarp and Paul," 17–24. Ritter, "De Polycarpe," 151–72, and Ehrman, *Fathers,* 328, also accept this assumption. The literary activity of Polycarp in a further sense has, however, recently been asserted by Hill, "Teaching," *passim,* who turns back to the hypothesis that Diogn, among others, could be a work by Polycarp; cf. Beatrice, *Presbyter,* 179–202.

[27] Hartog, "Polycarp," 148–69.

style of gospel citation in PolPhil cannot be situated as early in the second century as the "unity hypothesis" implies. Above all the interpretation of the thirteenth chapter must be revised: The closing words *et de ipso Ignatiu et de his qui cum eo sunt, quod certius agnoveritis, significate,* which are missing from the Greek, can be read as an unfortunate translation that implies the present tense (*sunt*), even though this is not expressed in the Greek; the time perspective must thus not be changed with respect to chapter 9; in other words, chapter 13 does not assume Ignatius to still be living after all. There are also hints that the Latin passage cited above could just as easily come from the pen of the editor of the long recension of the Ignatian letters (in Latin) and thus does not belong to the original text.[28] The following passages presuppose both the literary unity and the authenticity of the letter.[29]

4. Dating

The dating of PolPhil is closely connected with the *unity* of the text. If one follows Harrison, one comes to a "late" date, for example, 135 C.E., which is primarily based on Harrison's conviction that the "second letter" (1–12) is inspired by anti-Marcionite sentiments. Here the statements in 7.1 are important, especially the climax, "Whoever twists the words of the Lord [. . .] is the firstborn of Satan."[30] Many scholars, however, including some who support Harrison's two-letters hypothesis, have reconsidered his idea of the relationship to Marcion.[31] Most authors find no evidence in chapter 7 of a significant Marcionite theologumenon, only a relatively general warning about the danger of a docetic Christology (see below). Moreover, 7.1 is formulated in traditional language (similar to 1 John) that has no affinity with the Marcionite standpoint. Others have spoken for a

---

[28] See primarily Brent, *Ignatius of Antioch,* 144–58; the fact that Eusebius in his quotation "omits" the last words could also be explained if they were absent from his example.

[29] I must mention, however, that the unity and authenticity are not a convincing argument for the authenticity of the Ignatian epistles (in the middle recension). The fact that Polycarp knew the martyr Ignatius and some of his letters does not mean that what he knew were the letters we know in the reconstruction of the middle recension. PolPhil as a whole hardly allows any information about these letters. Brent, *Ignatius of Antioch,* must also concede this fact. It is also not necessary, as Völter, *Polykarp,* and many who follow him do, to strike out the references to Ignatius in PolPhil 1, 9, and 13 to maintain literary unity; see on this Dehandschutter, "Polycarps Epistle," 154–55; cf. in any case Holmes, "Polycarp," 108–25. However,

Lechner, *Ignatius, passim* (also Hübner, "Thesen," 44–72) returns impressively to the interpolation hypothesis: In the authentic PolPhil some passages (1 and 13) that refer to Ignatius were interpolated with the goal of making the fiction of the Ignatian epistles believable. Lechner also dismisses our view out of hand! Earlier Pilhofer had already expressly thrown out our interpretation, but only to support the hypothesis of *two* letters of Polycarp: Pilhofer, "Philippi," 206–9.

[30] Iren Haer III 3.4; the same anecdote also appears in the appendices of MartPol, see the Epilogus Mosquensis, and now the detailed appendix in Codex Kosinitza (Dehandschutter, *Polycarp,* 14–26).

[31] This view is still defended by, among others, Meinhold, "Polykarpos," 1662–93; Nielsen, "Polycarp and Marcion," 297–99; Aono, "Entwicklung," 384–97.

"late" dating because of the fact that the reception of the matter of the dominical sayings shows an influence from the (already known, later canonized) Gospels.[32] But this argument is not decisive either: Such an influence already in the early second century cannot be excluded. Usually PolPhil is dated not long after the death of Ignatius, although this latter fact is far less certain to determine than was long believed. We lean toward a dating of the "one" PolPhil around 120 C.E., though its contents permit a greater margin of error.[33]

5.   Structure and Content

The general letter structure of PolPhil is as follows:

Inscriptio

1	Praise for the Philippians
2.1–4.1	Request for faith and just living
4.2–6.2	Duties of members of the fellowship: *Haustafel*
6.3–7.2	Warning against heretics
8.1–9.2	Admonition to persistence in difficulties and in times of oppression
10	Closing consolation
11–12.1	The fall of Valens
12.2–14	End of the letter: Closing recommendations and personal correspondence

On the basis of this outline, *one* aspect of unity of the text comes to light without a doubt: Polycarp wants to write about "justice," and that at the request of his audience itself (3.1). This theme is then referred to throughout.

Immediately after the praise in the introduction follows a parenetic turn regarding the relationship between faith and living justly (2). This concept is repeated with the reference to Paul's teaching, which is then attached to the "*Haustafel*," which occasionally speaks individually to the various groups within the community (4–6.1). The warning against the heretics follows a further time in a parenetic context (6.2–7.2), in this case a conflict over the hope, followed by examples of Christian perseverance (8–9). The admonition to follow the Lord's example is conversely concluded with an incentive, while the example of the presbyter Valens, who fell through greed, forms a negative contrast (10–11). According to the final exhortations, the letters of Ignatius are also described as having the same content ("they treat of faith and patience, and all things that tend to

---

[32] So already Harrison, *Letters, passim*; later Köster, *Überlieferung*, 122, etc.

[33] That is, a margin with Polycarp's death as the *terminus ante quem*.

edification in our Lord"), while the recommendation of Crecens, the letter carrier, not without a reference to his excellent behavior, closes the text (12–14).[34]

This thematic unity does not mean, however, that the content of the letter completely agrees with it; in other words, PolPhil is not only a parenesis on "justice," any more than it is simply a collection of recommendations on reference to the concrete case of Valens (see below).

6.   Genre

PolPhil can be seen without hesitation as a letter. The epistolary opening with sender, addressee, and greeting corresponds closely to the letter form used in early Christianity, as we know from Paul. The end of the letter is also formally in order: transmission, recommendation, and greeting are the normal components of an early Christian letter.[35] Above all the *situation of the letter* is clear: Polycarp answers a request of the Philippian church (3.1) and thus follows Paul who, after his departure from the fellowship, uprightly maintained contact with them by letter (3.2). It is no wonder that the content of this letter works very parenetically in the first place: The Philippians' request calls for it, but so does the example of 1 Clem, which the author clearly has in view. PolPhil contains no elements that are merely incidental or artistic.[36] The theme of "justice" treated here is accompanied by the specific case of Valens that the Philippians set forth in their letter. Thus the content of the letter goes further, even to such things as deal with the working out of Christian life and are applicable to all Christians.

As a rule one describes the style of the letter as minimally original. "The originality is les than the good will of the letter writer."[37] This negative judgment is mostly accompanied by the reference to Polycarp's close adherence to the formulations in the early Christian sources that precede him (a "cento" according to Harnack[38]), but the use of parenetic themes is naturally not unusual in this context. It is all the more important to pay more detailed attention to Polycarp's reception of early Christian literature.

---

[34] One can read the passage about Crecens in such a way that it implies that Polycarp had been to Philippi; see Oakes, "Leadership," 353–73, especially his interpretation of the "in praesenti" in ch. 14. [English quotations from PolPhil are from Roberts/Donaldson/Coxe.]

[35] For more, see Hertog, *Polycarp*, 109–20.

[36] Therefore, and also because of its parenetic character, PolPhil is more often called an "epistle" than a "letter"; the encouraging statements go beyond the strict situation of the letter, without making it secondary.

[37] Jordan, *Geschichte*, 137–38; see further comparable judgments in J. B. Bauer, *Polykarpbriefe*, 12; Dibelius, *Geschichte*, 118–20 (though Dibelius still sees PolPhil as a genuine letter, different from, e.g., 1 Pet or 1 Clem).

[38] Harnack, *Polycarp*, 86–93, cf. 87.

7. Intertextual Relationships

Even Eusebius observed that Polycarp must have known 1 Peter.[39] Other early Christian literary sources clearly resonate with the text as well. So the influence of 1Clem on the formulation of PolPhil has been overwhelmingly recognized.[40] The bishop of Smyrna also knows most of the Pauline Epistles. He refers explicitly to Paul's teaching, to his stay in Philippi, and to his letter to this church (PolPhil 11.2-3). On the basis of this information from PolPhil, a scholarly consensus has been formed with regard to Polycarp's knowledge of some of Paul's letters. Nor has the correspondence with the Pastoral Epistles gone unnoticed,[41] although it remains difficult to speak of exact borrowing. On this point the hypothesis of H. von Campenhausen that Polycarp wrote the Pastoral Epistles remains noteworthy but unsuccessful: Common language and common context do not mean a common author.[42]

The new editions by Berding, Hartog, and Holmes should be expressly referenced on this point. Berding, who researches above all the relationship between Paul and Polycarp, studies the problematic in detail with regard to the grades of certainty to be expected in a "quotation." In a review of all the books of the Bible, he believes he can determine with *certainty* borrowings in PolPhil from Psalms, Matthew, Romans, 1–2 Corinthians, Galatians, Ephesians, Philippians, 1–2 Timothy, 1 Peter, and 1 John; with *probability* from Proverbs, Isaiah, Jeremiah, Tobit, Luke, Acts, and 2 Thessalonians; and *possibly* from Ezekiel, Sirach, Mark, John, Colossians, 1 Thessalonians, and Hebrews. Berding wants above all to look into the influence of Pauline theology and hints that half of all the quotations and allusions are taken from the Pauline Epistles. On the basis of this fact alone, Polycarp *must* have known most of the apostle's letters (and he even expects his audience to know these letters!). The influence of Paul on PolPhil points to a form of *imitatio*, which emerges from an accumulation of quotations and reminiscence that highlights the importance of the Pastoral Epistles. In any case, Polycarp's use of Paul contradicts the assumption that there was no knowledge of Paul's letters at the beginning of the second century.

Also striking is the minimal interest in the Old Testament, which neither Berding nor Hartog attempt to explain. For Hartog it appears certain that Polycarp knew Romans, 1 Corinthians, Galatians, Ephesians, Philippians, 1 Timothy, and 1 Peter; he holds it to be possible that Polycarp knew Matthew, 2 Corinthians,

---

[39] HE IV 14.9: "But Polycarp, in his above-mentioned epistle to the Philippians, which is still extant, has made use of certain testimonies drawn from the First Epistle of Peter" (translation from Schaff/Wace). On early Christian reception of 1 Peter, see Merkt, *1 Petrus, passim*.

[40] See the list of parallels in J. B. Bauer, *Polykarp-briefe*, 28–30; for more, see Berding, "Polycarp and

Paul," *passim*; Hartog, *Polycarp*, 176.

[41] All in all only small letters like Philemon and Titus could be left out of the list of Pauline letters; cf. further Berding, "Polycarp and Paul," *passim*; Hartog, *Polycarp*, 170–94; Holmes, "Polycarp's Letter," 187–227.

[42] Cf. on this Merz, *Selbstauslegung*, 114–40.

2 Timothy, and 1 John. Hartog cautiously suggests the possible knowledge of the books Jeremiah and Tobit. He is conspicuously reserved regarding the "Gospel" quotations and refers to the difficulties in PolPhil itself caused by the method of quotation: A reference to the words of the Lord does not necessarily require knowledge of one or more gospels. On the other hand, Hartog also sees the direct literary influence of some of Paul's letters as unmistakable.

One could rate this reception of Paul in PolPhil as a subtle rewriting of the Pauline texts. However, this "rewriting" would be very difficult to explain solely on the basis of memory (so Berding). If it is true that Paul has authority for Polycarp equal to that of the Old Testament of the sayings of the Lord, and if this authority was also assumed by his readers, then we can presume a written, definitive—if not (yet) "canonical"—text. It is thus superfluous to speculate about Polycarp having a *Corpus Paulinum* (or its equivalent) in the strictest sense: "Paul and his letters" have authority (PolPhil 3.2; 11.2: "sicut Paulus docet") equal to other Scriptures (12.1).[43] In summary one can say with Lindemann that PolPhil "wants to be understood as standing in the Pauline tradition."[44] This fact is not unimportant for the theology of the letter.

The same is more difficult to recognize for the gospel quotations. The references in PolPhil present essential sayings of Jesus and can just as easily be explained as coming from the oral synoptic tradition as from the use of current collections of saying (comparable to 1Clem 13) or the text of any one gospel (especially Matt and Luke), sometimes on the basis of the influence of the liturgical tradition, for example, the Lord's Prayer (7.2).

Based on the work of Harrison and Köster, an influence from the Gospels has become ever more widely accepted (also as a result of a later dating), but for others it is still in question, because of the citation style in PolPhil among other reasons. The letter explicitly refers to that which the Lord "said": 2.3: "being mindful of what the Lord said in His teaching" ("Judge not, that you be not judged," etc.); 7.2: "'not to lead us into temptation,' as the Lord has said"; and 7.1 warns of those who twist "the words of the Lord." In no way does Polycarp indicate that he quotes a text, but that does not preclude the knowledge of the Gospels in the aforementioned cases: The references are used in an ethical-parenetic discourse and are embedded together in it. So the second half of the "quotation" in 2.3 consists of a combination of two macarisms that one cannot

---

[43] Cf. Lindemann, *Paulus*, 87–91, 220–32; an opinion like that of Nielsen, according to which Polycarp viewed the Pauline corpus as "Scripture" and consequently can serve as a first witness to the growing New Testament canon, is not convincing (Nielsen, "Polycarp, Paul, and the Scriptures," 199–216). Cf. recently the skepticism of Holmes, "Polycarp's Letter," 226–27, among others. Holmes, however, remains critical of the possibility

of determining exact Scripture references: He sees no problem with 1 Corinthians, Ephesians, and 1 Peter, allows a high degree of probability for 1 Timothy, 2 Timothy, 1 John, Romans, and Galatians, but Philippians must be satisfied with a lower degree of possibility (226). Holmes' judgment is thus far more strict than that of Berding and Hartog.

[44] Lindemann, *Paulus*, 223. The author of the

find again in the text of Matthew, which still does not mean that the passage does not borrow from Matthew.

One can speak of a methodical dilemma: Should one prefer the norm of a strict citation style and textual agreement (in which above all the redactional elements of a quotation play a role) to be able to speak of the use of Mathew, Luke, etc.? Or should one allow the bishop of Smyrna his own use of the Scripture that can be described more as interpretive and directed toward the parenetic situation? The limits of the first choice should be kept in view: To reject a direct use on the grounds of differences from the (modern) standard text of a gospel makes little sense because we do not know the exact original text of the gospel(s) available to Polycarp.[45] Therefore, one cannot reject the use of one or more gospels solely on the grounds of a mangled word-for-word agreement.

These points taken together allow the following conclusion: Although PolPhil allows us to recognize a sense of "sacrae litterae" (12.1), the knowledge of which was not lacking in the audience (!), and although one cannot conclude too much from that kind of formulas of courtesy or modesty,[46] both the author of the letter and its audience view the words of the Lord, above all as they appear in the Gospels (especially Matthew), as "law." They are, in other words, to be taken as γραφή, even in the *form* of a "reception," which is directed more strongly toward the reformulation of these sources than toward "quotation" in the formal sense. What Polycarp wants is to build an argument on the basis of the reflection on the Christian tradition he received, clearly a tradition that was already written down, such as the Pauline tradition that can be decisive for one and all.[47]

John's gospel remains strikingly absent. If one overwhelmingly assumes the influence of 1 John on the passage in 7.1 (see above),[48] the presence of the Johannine tradition as such is limited in PolPhil and a meaningful recollection of the fourth gospel all but evident. One finds such an allusion in passages like PolPhil 5.2 on the resurrection (cf. John 5:21, 6:44), which for C. E. Hill, among others, suffices as proof of the knowledge of this gospel.[49] In any case there are few other elements in PolPhil that point in this direction. We must therefore conclude that Polycarp's reception of early Christian tradition should not be judged in the light of a canonical education.

Vita has referred to it in exactly that way.

[45] So it also makes little sense to want to derive a direct knowledge of Luke from an isolated element, e.g., from ἀντιμετρηθήσεται in 2.3, that differs from Matthew (contra Bellinzoni, "Gospel," 59–60; but see Gregory, "The Reception of Luke," 132–34).

[46] See the summary of the discussion in J. B. Bauer, *Polykarpbriefe*, 69–71; Bauer/Paulsen, *Polykarpbrief*, 125.

[47] Dehandschutter, "Polycarp's Epistle," 153–71; to a certain degree this explains the lack of

references to the Old Testament. They do exist, however, most inconspicuously in 12.1 (Ps 4:5), 10.2 (Tob 4:11, 12:9), 10.3 (Isa 52:5). In any case the prophets, "who proclaimed beforehand the coming of the Lord" (6.3), are referred to next to Christ and the apostles as authorities.

[48] Although one could also speak hear of the "Johannine tradition," cf. Holmes, "Polycarp's Letter," 223–25. That is to say, the formulation of 7.1 is very common and not a direct allusion to 1 John.

[49] Hill, "The Johannine Corpus," 416–20; but this is very questionable, cf. Holmes, "Polycarp's

8. Opponents

Without exaggerating the adversarial aspect in 6.3–7.1, one can see in this section a warning against the kind of opinion that threaten the Christian fellowship, both in Philippi and elsewhere. It is very unlikely that it deals with Marcion: The general christological formulae in PolPhil, for example, Christ as the Son of God (the Father), speak against it—among other objections.[50] But against whom is the polemic directed, then? One can see very faintly sketched docetic opinions: Anyone who denies the reality of the incarnation (the coming ἐν σαρκί) will also doubt the meaning of the passion (the witness of the cross) and the resurrection. One can extend the "heresiological spectrum" of PolPhil 7.1 to this idea and thence refer to the fact that each of the three statements can have another negative meaning in view at the same time: not only Docetism as such (first statement), but more precisely those who deny the soteriological meaning of the crucifixion (second statement), which can lead one to think of the early Gnostics; the twisting of the words of the Lord (third statement) could then refer to a libertinism ("according to their own desires") rejected by Christian asceticism and likewise not mindful of the perspective of the resurrection and the judgment. This would be denoted as the opinion of "the many," a false teaching, already warned against in 2.1, where a traditionally formulated summary of the contents of the faith is presented (2.1-2a). Although 7.1 mentions no names, one can deduce far more tendencies that threatened to be assimilated into Christian belief[51] and required a reaction from Polycarp.

9. Theological Profile and Parenesis

Polycarp already appears to Irenaeus as a guarantor of orthodoxy. The bishop of Lyon especially emphasizes the confrontation between Polycarp and Marcion (Haer III 3.4 = Eus HE IV 14.7). Even so, there is hardly any explicit antiheretical polemic to be found in PolPhil (see above). PolPhil is a short letter, written in a specific circumstance, and cannot serve as a summary of important theological themes that were current in the first half of the second century. It thus makes little sense to classify such a text in the development of so-called "early Catholicism."[52] The letter actually provides an early Christian ecclesiological understanding. The discussion, borrowing from 1Clem, sees the ἐκκλησία in Philippi as

---

Letter," 197–99.

[50] See Schoedel, "Polycarp," 279–85; Hartog, *Polycarp*, 95–101; Berding, "Polycarp and Paul," *passim*.

[51] One can compare the situation with that of the Pastoral Epistles (cf. von Campenhausen, *Polykarp, passim*), but there some names are named

that do not enlighten us at all; see also Dehandschutter, *History*, 211–21. See also 2Clem. Van Eijk, "Résurrection," 127–34, is mainly concerned about the crisis regarding the eschatology, which is caused by the absence of the Parousia.

[52] As Ritter, "De Polycarpe," 151–72, actually wants to do.

παροικοῦσα[53] and thus assumes the mode of thought present in Hebrews. This congregation is still led by presbyters, and the question deals with submission to the presbyters (5.3).[54] Furthermore, the congregation is not yet perfect, we are all guilty of sin (6.1), and there are differences of opinion regarding the content of the faith. The letter is specific on the points where he warns against anyone who treats the words of the Lord hypocritically (6.3). There are those who do not recognize Christ's appearance ἐν σαρκί and so do not accept the witness of the cross. In every respect the antidocetic attitude of the author is very close to that of 1 John in terms of motive and terminology, but there is no word-for-word quotation (see above).

The *christological* statements in PolPhil can thus also be summarized especially as salvation-historical and soteriological:[55] Christ has truly come to us as a man and died on the cross, but just as truly rose again; and he will come to judge (7.1; cf. 2.1, 6.2). His suffering and death occurred for the sake of our sins (1.2; 8.1; 9.2). He is therefore our hope and the pledge of our righteousness (8.1). Here the author speaks in traditional formulas about Christ as the Son of God the Father, the eternal high priest (Heb), the one who was awakened from the dead (12.2). Faith in him requires following him (10.1), which can be described for the Christian as δικαιοσύνη. The soteriology is thus "ethicized": We have been saved, but this salvation means "for our part" following in the love of our brothers, mutual love, and not shirking good works (10.1-2).[56]

The *Christian life as a life in* δικαιοσύνη is the decisive theme that is drawn through PolPhil and that the author summarizes as the "word of righteousness" (9.1). The fact that the theme is thus more ethical than theological-eschatological[57] arises from the situation of the letter (3.1):[58] The Philippians request details about this topic. Polycarp begins with praise for the Christian behavior of the Philippians: They have received the martyrs with all due care and sent them on their way. It is easy to imagine that such action was not without risks in an environment in which Christians formed not seldom a weakened minority. Polycarp continues with a call to the Philippians to defend the faith that they have received of old and to observe the instructions, which implies faith in Christ; this immediately gives rise to a traditionally formulated "catalogue of vices," followed by recommendations of Christian morality (1 Pet 3:9) and the words of the Lord himself (2). They

---

[53] Camelot, *Polycarpe de Smyrne*, 176–77; J. B. Bauer, *Polykarpbriefe*, 35–36; this view is also recognizable in the epistolary address of MartPol, cf. Buschmann, *Martyrium*, 68–69.

[54] The recommendations to the presbyters are always formulated in the plural (6.1). The common leadership of the congregation may have caused the other presbyters not to know what to do with the fall of Valens and to seek advice from a personality with authority, like Polycarp (Pilhofer, *Philippi*, 222–23).

[55] Cf. Holmes, "Polycarp," 116–20.

[56] Cf. on all this 2Clem 1.3, 5, etc.

[57] Steinmetz, *Polykarp*, 63–75; Bovon-Thurneysen, *Ethik*, 241–56; J. B. Bauer, *Polykarpbriefe*, 24–25; Hartog, *Polycarp*, 135–47.

[58] The eschatology has not disappeared, however: Christ will come as judge (2.1); we will all "appear at the judgment-seat of Christ, and must every one give an account of himself" (6.2). It is "of the devil" to deny the judgment (7.1); cf. 2Clem 1.1, etc.

deal with love of God, of Christ, and of the neighbor (3.3; 10.1), which in action is shown by a Matthean interpretation of the expression δικαιοσύνη.

It is no accident that Polycarp specifically directs the parenesis toward various groups within the Christian community. (Married) women and widows are not only explicitly vulnerable groups but also those that are conspicuous in a non-Christian setting: Their behavior is not without consequences. The same goes for deacons, youth, virgins, and presbyters. They bring the Christian existence "to expression." The fall of Valens is thus alarming. This presbyter and his wife have apparently fallen victim to greed[59] but threaten to bring the rest of the congregation into disrepute with outsiders. Polycarp's strict recommendation to imitate the example of the Lord in loving one another (10.1) is followed by the request that they under no circumstances draw the misfortunes of the outside world upon themselves: *conversationen vestram irreprehensibilem habentes in gentibus* (10.2), so that they will earn praise and the name of the Lord will not be slandered. The warnings against greed (2.2; 4.1, 3; 5.2; 6.1; 11.1-2), the traditional catalogues of vices and virtues (2.2; 4.3; 5.2; 6.1; 12.2), and the *Haustafel* (4.2–6.2) serve to lend stability to the situation in Philippi; this is possible when everyone lives in righteousness, keeps the Lord's commandments, and follows the directions of the apostles. All of this serves the ὑπομονή, the perseverance, which the Christian community needs in hard times. Even here Christ went ahead as an example (8.1-2), as did the martyrs, Paul, and the apostles (9.1).[60] A general interpretation of PolPhil thus leads us to the recognition that Polycarp wanted to protect the congregation from persecution. There are persecutors and haters, enemies of the cross. Christians can at least pray for them, as they do for the authorities (12.3). Polycarp writes in a time in which Christians as a group are threatened. They want to be good citizens (cf. 1 Pet; 1 Clem; also MartPol) and pray for the authorities, but the conflict with the imperial cult increases. Suffering "for the sake of the Name" (cf. 1 Pet) is a not too distant possibility. Polycarp answers with a call for a life in δικαιοσύνη. This end both summarizes the Christian identity and reaches further to the specific Philippian problem.

10. Bibliography

Aono, T. *Die Entwicklung des paulinischen Gerichtsgedanken bei den Apostolischen Vätern.* EHS.T 137. Bern 1979.

Barnard, L. W. "The Problem of St. Polycarp's Epistle to the Philippians." In *Studies in the Apostolic Fathers and their Background*, 31–39. Oxford 1966.

---

[59] To be sure, this is not stated in so many words, but it can be assumed from 11.1 and the references to the reprehensibility of the love of money elsewhere in the letter. Pilhofer, *Philippi*, 218–24 has come closer with a description of the financial obligations of the cultic and community functionaries, a responsibility that Valens may have taken on and that led to abuse.

[60] Cf. Baumeister, "Anfänge," 289–91.

Bauer, J. B. *Die Polykarpbriefe.* KAV 5. Göttingen 1995.

Bauer, W. *Die Briefe des Ignatius von Antiochien und der Polykarpbrief.* HNT.Erg.Bd. Tübingen 1920.

———. *Rechtgläubigkeit und Ketzerei im ältesten Christentum.* BHT 10. Tübingen ²1964.

Bauer, W., and H. Paulsen. *Die Briefe des Ignatius von Antiochien und der Polykarpbrief.* HNT. Tübingen 1985.

Baumeister, T. *Die Anfänge der Theologie des Martyriums.* MBTh 45. Münster 1980.

Beatrice, P. "Der Presbyter des Irenäus, Polykarp von Smyrna und der Brief an Diognet." In *Pleroma: Salus carnis: Homenaje a Antonio Orbe,* edited by E. Romero-Pose, 179–202. Santiago de Compostela 1990.

Bellinzoni, A. J. "The Gospel of Luke in the Apostolic Fathers: An Overview." In *Trajectories through the New Testament and the Apostolic Fathers,* edited by A. F. Gregory and C. M. Tuckett, 45–68. Oxford 2005.

Berding, K. *Polycarp and Paul. An Analysis of Their Literary and Theological Relationship in the Light of Polycarp's Use of Biblical and Extra-Biblical Literature.* VC.S 47. Leiden 1999.

Bihlmeyer, K. *Die Apostolischen Väter: Neubearbeitung der Funkschen Ausgabe, hg. von W. Schneemelcher.* Tübingen ³1970.

Bovon-Thurneysen, A. "Ethik und Eschatologie im Philipperbrief des Polykarp von Smyrna." *ThZ* 29 (1973): 241–56.

Brent, A. *Ignatius of Antioch and the Second Sophistic: A Study of an Early Christian Transformation of Pagan Culture.* STAC 36. Tübingen 2006.

Brox, N. "Tendenzen und Parteilichkeiten im Osterfeststreit des zweiten Jahrhunderts." *ZKG* 83 (1972): 291–324.

Buschmann, G. *Das Martyrium des Polykarp.* KAV 6. Göttingen 1998.

Camelot, P. T. *Ignace d'Antioche, Polycarpe de Smyrne, Lettres, Martyre de Polycarpe.* SC 10. Paris ⁴1969.

Campenhausen, H. von. "Polykarp von Smyrna und die Pastoralbriefe." In *Aus der Frühzeit des Christentums: Studien zur Kirchengeschichte des ersten und zweiten Jahrhunderts,* 197–252. Tübingen 1963.

Committee of the Oxford Society of Historical Theology, ed. *The New Testament in the Apostolic Fathers.* Oxford 1905.

Dehandschutter, B. "Heresy and the Early Christian Notion of Tradition." In *Heretics and Heresies in the Ancient Church and in Eastern Christianity: Studies in Honor of Adelbert David,* edited by J. Verheyden and H. Teule. Special issue. *JEastCS* 60 (2008): 7–22.

———. "The History of Religious Background of 1 Timothy 4:4." In *The Creation of Heaven and Earth: Re-interpretation of Genesis 1 in the Context of Judaism, Ancient Philosophy, Christianity, and Modern Physics,* edited by G. Van Kooten, 211–21. Leiden 2005.

———. "Ignatiusbriefe." RGG⁴ (2001): 34–36.

———. "Images of Polycarp: Bibliography and Hagiography about the Bishop of Smyrna." In *Polycarpiana,* 271–77.

———. *Polycarpiana: Studies on Martyrdom and Persecution in Early Christiantiy: Collected Essays.* BETL 205. Leuven 2007.

————. "Polycarp of Smyrna: Some Notes on the Hagiography and Homiletics of a Smyrneasn Martyr." In *Volksglaube im antiken Christentum: Festschrift Theofried Baumeister*, edited by A. Merkt and H. Grieser, 14–26. Darmstadt 2009.

————. "Polycarp's Epistle to the Philippians: An Early Example of 'Reception.'" In *Polycarpiana*, 153–71.

————. "The Text of the Martyrdom of Polycarp Again (with a Note on the Greek Text of Polycarp, AD PHIL.)." In *Polycarpiana*, 29–33.

Dibelius, M. *Geschichte der urchristlichen Literatur*. Reprint edited by F. Hahn. Munich 1975.

Ehrman, B. D. *The Apostolic Fathers I: 1 Clement, 2 Clement, Ignatius, Polycarp, Didache, Edited and Translated*. LCL 24. Cambridge, Mass. 2003.

Fischer, J. A. *Die Apostolischen Väter*. Munich 1956.

Foster, P., ed. *The Writings of the Apostolic Fathers*. London 2007.

Garrison, R. "The Love of Money in Polycarp's Letters to the Philippians." In *The Graeco-Roman Context of Early Christian Literature*, 74–79. JSNT.SS 137. Sheffield 1997.

Grégoire, H. *Les persecutions dans l'empire romain*. Brussels 1964.

Gregory, A. *The Reception of Luke and Acts in the Period before Irenaeus: Looking for Luke in the Second Century*. WUNT II/169. Tübingen 2003.

Harnack, A. von. "Zu Polycarp ad Philipp. 11." In *Patristische Miszellen*, 86–93. TU 20. Leipzig 1900.

Harrison, P. N. *Polycarp's Two Letters to the Philippians*. Cambridge 1936.

Hartog, P. "The Opponents of Polycarp, Philippians, and 1 John." In *Trajectories through the New Testament and the Apostolic Fathers*, edited by A. F. Gregory and C. M. Tuckett, 375–91. Oxford 2005.

————. *Polycarp and the New Testament: The Occasion, Rhetoric, Theme, and Unity of the Epistle to the Philippians and its Allusions to New Testament Literature*. WUNT II/134. Tübingen 2002.Hill, C. E. *From the Lost Teaching of Polycarp: Identifying Irenaeus' Apostolic Presbyter and His Impact on Church History*. WUNT 186. Tübingen 2006.

————. *The Johannine Corpus in the Early Church*. Oxford 2004.

————. "Polycarp contra Marcion: Irenaeus' Presbyterial Source in AH 4.27-32." *StPatr* 40:399–412. Leuven 2006.

Holmes, M. W. "A Note on the Text of Polycarp Philippians 11.3." *VC* 51 (1997): 207–10.

————. "Polycarp, Epistle to the Philippians." In *The Writings of the Apostolic Fathers*, edited by P. Foster, 108–25. London 2007.

————. "Polycarp's Letter to the Philippians and the Writings That Later Formed the New Testament." In *The Reception of the New Testament in the Apostolic Fathers*, edited by A. F. Gregory and C. M. Tuckett, 187–227. Oxford 2005.

Hübner, R. M. "Thesen zur Echtheit und Datierung der sieben Briefe des Ignatius von Antiochen." *ZAC* 1 (1997): 44–72.

Jordan, H. *Geschichte der altchristlichen Literatur*. Leipzig 1911.

Kleist, J. A. *The Didache, The Epistle of Barnabas, The Epistles and the Martyrdom of Polycarp, The Fragments of Papias, The Epistle to Diognetus*. ACW 6. Westminster, Md. 1948.

Köhler, W.-D. *Die Rezeption des Matthäusevangeliums in der Zeit vor Irenäus.* WUNT 24. Tübingen 1987.

Köster, H. *Synoptische Überlieferung bei den Apostolischen Vätern.* TU 65. Berlin 1957.

Lechner, T. *Ignatius adversus Valentinianos? Chronologische und theologiegeschichtliche Studien zu den Briefen des Ignatius von Antiochien.* VC.S 47. Leiden 1999.

Lefort, T. *Les Pères apostoliques en copte.* CSCO.C 17–18, CSCO 135–36. Louvain 1952.

Liebaert, J. *Les enseignements moraux des Pères apostoliques.* Gembloux 1970.

Lightfoot, J. B. *The Apostolic Fathers I-II: A Revised Text with Introductions, Notes, Dissertations and Translations.* London ²1889–1890.

Lindemann, A. *Paulus im ältesten Christentum: Das Bild des Apostels und die Rezeption der paulinischen Theologie in der frühchristlichen Literatur bis Marcion.* BHT 58. Tübingen 1979.

Maier, H. O. "Purity and Danger in Polycarp's Epistle to the Philippians: The Sin of Valens in Social Perspective." *JECS* 1 (1993): 229–47.

Massaux, E. *Influence de l'Evangile de saint Matthieu sur la littérature chrétienne avant saint Irénée.* Louvain 1950 (BETL 75, Louvain 1986).

Meinhold, P. "Polykarpos 1." RECA 21 (1952): 1662–93.

Merkt, A. *1 Petrus.* NTP 21. Göttingen 2008.

Merz, A. *Die fiktive Selbstauslegung des Paulus: Intertextuelle Studien zur Intention und Rezeption der Pastoralbriefe.* NTOA 52. Göttingen/Fribourg 2004.

Nielsen, C. M. "Polycarp and Marcion: A Note." *TS* 47 (1986): 297–99.

———. "Polycarp, Paul and the Scriptures." *ATR* 47 (1965): 199–216.

Norris, F. W. "Ignatius, Polycarp and 1 Clement: Walter Bauer Reconsidered." *VC* 30 (1976): 23–44.

Oakes, P. "Leadership and Suffering in the Letters of Polycarp and Paul to the Philippians." In *Trajectories through the New Testament and the Apostolic Fathers,* edited by A. F. Gregory and C. M. Tuckett, 353–73. Oxford 2005.

Parvis, S. "The Martyrdom of Polycarp." In Foster, 126–46.

Petermann, J. H. S. *Ignatii Patris apostolici quae feruntur Epistulae una cum eiusdem Martyrio.* Leipzig 1849.

Pilhofer, P. *Philippi, I: Die erste christliche Gemeinde Europas.* WUNT 87. Tübingen 1995.

Prostmeier, F. R. "Zur handschriftlichen Überlieferung des Polykarp- und Barnabasbriefes: Zwei nicht beachtete Deszendenten des Cod. Vat. Gr. 859." *VC* 48 (1994): 48–64.

Ritter, A. M. "De Polycarpe à Clément: Aux origins d'Alexandrie chrétienne." In *Aleksandrina: Mélanges C. Mondésert,* 151–72. Paris 1987.

Roberts, A., and J. Donaldson. *The Apostolic Fathers, Justin Martyr, Irenaeus: American Reprint of the Edinburgh Edition: Revised etc. by A. C. Coxe.* ANF 1. Grand Rapids 1973 (reprint).

Schaff, P., and H. Wace. *Eusebius of Pamphilius: Church History, Life of Constantine, Oration in Praise of Constantine.* NPNF II/1. Buffalo 1890.

Schoedel, W. R. "Polycarp of Smyrna and Ignatius of Antioch." *ANRW* II 27.1 (1993): 272–358.

Steinmetz, P. "Polykarp von Smyrna über die Gerechtigkeit." *Hermes* 100 (1972): 63–75.

Steward-Sykes, A. *The Life of Polycarp: An Anonymous Vita from Third-Century Smyrna.* Sydney 2002.

Thomson, R. W. *A Bibliography of Classical Armenian Literature to 1500 AD.* Turnhout 1995.

Van Damme, D. "Polycarpe." *DSp* 12 (1986): 1902–8.

Van Eijk, T. H. C. *La résurrection des morts chez les Pères Apostoliques.* ThH 25. Paris 1974.

Vielhauer, P. *Geschichte der urchristlichen Literatur: Einleitung in das Neue Testament, die Apokryphen und die Apostolischen Väter.* Berlin 1975.

Völter, D. *Polykarp und Ignatius und die ihnen zugeschriebenen Briefe neu untersucht.* Leiden 1910.

Weidmann, F. W. *Polycarp and John: The Harris Fragments and Their Challenge to the Literary Traditions.* Notre Dame 1999.

Willing, M. *Eusebius von Cäsarea als Häreseograph.* PTS 63. Berlin 2008.

The Martyrdom of Polycarp

Gerd Buschmann

The Martyrdom of Polycarp presents us the oldest martyrdom handed down as an independent text from the middle of the second century, which influenced the form of later martyrdom literature and is influenced by Jewish martryrdom texts from the intertestamental period; it is also interesting for the form-historical connections to the passion narratives in the Gospels. Bishop Polycarp of Smyrna, student of Ignatius of Antioch, is one of the most important church fathers of the second century. Irenaeus of Lyon presents himself as a student of Polycarp (Eus HE V 20.5-6). One of the key problems of the text is the question of whether the presentation deals with an authentically recorded report that makes use of procedural acts or whether—as the author intends—it is essentially a kerygmatic text that was written for the edification and exhortation of the early Christian fellowships and propagates a "by the gospel" theology of martyrdom (κατὰ τὸ εὐαγγέλιον). Connected to this question is the scholarly historical controversy over whether the shorter text handed down in Eus HE IV 15 is more original than the text handed down independently. MartPol enjoyed great popularity in the early church. In the view of those within the church, MartPol emphasizes the parallels between the suffering of the Lord and of the martyrs in order to defend an enthusiastic longing for martyrdom and to practice an appropriate veneration of the martyrs. Formally MartPol is not simply presented as a "report" of the event; in terms of content, Polycarp's deeds are presented as "in accordance with the gospel"—in contrast to the enthusiasts' urge to be martyred (MartPol 4). Likewise, the liturgically celebrated veneration of the martyrs in the early church begins with this text, but still as a modest, appropriate, Christ-centered cult of the martyrs.

1. Textual Tradition

1.1 Greek Manuscripts[1]

The modern editions of MartPol have been based since Lightfoot's edition[2] on five, since Bihlmeyer's edition[3] on six, Greek manuscripts that all contain

---

[1] Cf. Lightfoot, *Fathers* II/3, 355–57; Dehand-schutter, *Martyrium Polycarpi*, 27–34; Dehand-schutter, "Research," 486–87—For a more precise presentation cf. Buschmann, *Martyrium*, 13.

[2] In the 2nd ed., 1889.

[3] *Die Apostolischen Väter*, Tübingen 1924.

menologies for the month of February[4] and come from the tenth to the thirteenth centuries:

B Baroccianus 238, Oxford / P Parisinus graecus 1452, Paris / V Vindobonensis historicus graecus 3, Vienna / H Hierosolymitanus S. Sepulchri 1, Jerusalem / C Chalcensis 95, Istanbul / M Mosquensis 390, Moscow, differs from the BCHPV group, is close to Eus HE IV 15, and offers the *epilogus Mosquensis* with the continuations to Polycarp and Irenaeus, missing MartPol 22.1.

1.2 Eusebius, HE IV.15[5]

Eusebius offers here the text of MartPol; he quotes the beginning verbatim up to 1.1 (διωγμόν), summarizes the contents of 2.2–7.3, and quotes again verbatim from 8.1–19.1 (λαλεῖσθαι), where he ends. A comparison of the Greek manuscripts with Eusebius' version gives the following conclusion: "Eusebius not only quotes but 'rewrites' the text [. . .] that means that where Eusebius differs from MPol, he does not necessarily follow a different textual tradition."[6]

1.3 Indirect Greek Textual Witnesses[7]

Indirect Greek textual witnesses are comprised of various Greek manuscripts of MartPol, including a panegyric on Polycarp by Ps.-Chrysostom and a *Vita Polycarpi*[8] by Ps.-Pionius, from which derives the theory of a Corpus Polycarpianum,[9] *Chronicon Paschale*, *Martyrium Sabae* and *Martyrium Olbiani*, which points to a complex textual tradition for MartPol.

1.4 Early Translations[10]

In the early Middle Ages a Latin *Passio Polycarpi* was common, but its meaning for text criticism is questionable on the basis of its paraphrastic character. Armenian, Syriac, Coptic,[11] and Old Slavic translations "were finally recognized as adaptations of the text of Eusebius."[12]

---

4   On this liturgical form of tradition cf. Dehandschutter, *Martyrium Polycarpi*, 27n1.

5   Cf. Dehandschutter, *Martyrium Polycarpi*, 34–38; idem, "Research," 487–88; Lightfoot, *Fathers* II/3, 357–58.

6   Dehandschutter, "Research," 488. Cf. idem, *Martyrium Polycarpi*, 38.

7   Cf. Dehandschutter, *Martyrium Polycarpi*, 38–48; Dehandschutter, "Research," 488–89.

8   Cf. also Reuning, *Erklärung*, 6ff.

9   It includes the Epistle of Polycarp, the Martyrdom of Polycarp, and *Vita Polycarpi*. —Cf. Grégoire, "Date," 4ff.; Lightfoot, *Fathers* II/1, 638–45; II/2, 423–31. Dehandschutter, *Martyrim*

Polycarpi, 63–71; idem, "Research," 491–92, doubts Lightfoot's hypothesis of a Corpus Polycarpianum on text-critical grounds: the parallels between MartPol 22 and *Vita Polycarpi* do not suffice for such a hypothesis. It is only certain that the *Vita Polycarpi* and *Epilogus Mosquensis* are both based on Irenaeus' comments about Polycarp.

10   Cf. Dehandschutter, *Martyrium Polycarpi*, 48–55; Dehandschutter, "Research," 489–90; Lightfoot, *Fathers* II/3, 358–61.

11   New, long-unpublished Coptic fragments are reviewed in Weidmann, *Martyrdom*.

12   Dehandschutter, "Research," 490.

2. Editions and Synopsis of MartPol in Eus HE IV 15

Until the discovery of the manuscripts M and H, most editors were convinced of the importance of the textual tradition of Eusebius.[13] The value of M has been debated from the beginning, since its defects were named early on,[14] but Schwartz[15] valued it, and his opinion strongly influenced the "classic" edition of MartPol by Bihlmeyer.[16] The agreement between M and Eusebius serves as the central textual criterion: "With regard to the production of the text, we can assume that the meeting of m and E, especially if b and p also concur, may serve as sufficient criterion for the originality of a reading."[17] Bihlmeyer's edition has become a widely used tool and forms the foundation of most anthologies of martyrdom texts or new editions of the Apostolic Fathers by Camelot,[18] Ruhbach,[19] Lazzati,[20] Baumeister,[21] and Lindemann/Paulsen.[22] Stand-alone editions of MartPol have been produced recently only by Musurillo,[23] Dehandschutter,[24] and Orbán.[25] Orbán's edition differs in only three places from Bihlmeyer. Musurillo's edition requires a careful critical handling with regard to text edition and translation; the criteria for the construction of the text are unclear,[26] and at times significant secondary readings from M are preferred arbitrarily. Only the edition by Dehandschutter remains to be emphasized; it counters Bihlmeyer's edition of the text and its heavy reliance on M and Eusebius with thirty-five suggested changes.[27] The fact that the value of Dehandschutter's textual and literary-critical analysis lies less in the content preparation—many of the textual variants are relatively unimportant in terms of content—and far more in the evaluation of the textual history and tradition and the new weighting of the Greek manuscripts against Eusebius—which is also important for the evaluation of literary-critical interpolation hypotheses!—can be traced to the easily approachable Bihlmeyer text. Yet the synopses of MartPol and Eus HE IV 15 in the Dehandschutter edition, including the list of changes from Bihlmeyer, should be considered for comparison and improvement.[28]

---

[13] E.g., Lightfoot, *Fathers* II/3, 358.

[14] Zahn, *Fragmenta*, LV; Funk, *Opera*, XCIX; Hilgenfeld, *Epistulae*, XXI.

[15] Schwartz, "Pionio et Polycarpo," 4.

[16] Bihlmeyer, *Väter*, XLIII–IV.

[17] Bihlmeyer, *Väter*, XLIII. Cf. Schoedel, *Fathers*, 49.

[18] Camelot, *Martyre*.

[19] Ruhbach, *Märtyrerakten*.

[20] Lazzati, *Martiri*.

[21] Baumeister, *Genese*.

[22] Lindemann/Paulsen, *Väter*.

[23] Musurillo, *Acts*.

[24] Dehandschutter, *Martyrium Polycarpi*.

[25] Orbán, *Atti*.

[26] Cf. among others the critical review by Millar, "Rez. Musurillo," 240: "without any clear statement of his criteria."

[27] Cf. Dehandschutter, *Martyrium Polycarpi*, 72–109.

[28] Cf. Dehandschutter, *Martyrium Polycarpi*, 109 and 110–29. This synopsis of MartPol and Eus HE IV.15 is reproduced in Buschmann, *Martyrium*, 17–36, and is in this respect easily approachable. A synopsis also appears in Campenhausen, "Bearbeitungen," 293–301.

3.   Authenticity and Integrity[29]

Doubts about the integrity of MartPol have arisen especially first from the parallels κατὰ τὸ εὐαγγέλιον, second through the so-called wonder elements, and third with regard to the chronological appendix MartPol 21–22 Keim[30] and Lipsius[31] have disputed the authenticity of MartPol fundamentally. Primarily because of the supposed anachronistic warnings against an exaggerated cult of the martyrs (MartPol 17–18), they date MartPol to the third century. However, Lightfoot[32] already recognized that 1) the comparison with the passion of Christ is normal in early martyrdom texts, 2) other early martyrdom texts also include "wonderous" elements, and 3) the chronological appendix in MartPol 21 is plausible when compared to other contemporary sources. With the help of interpolation theories, some scholars wanted to rescue MartPol from Keim and others as a "historical" early source, for example, Müller,[33] against whom Baden,[34] Sepp,[35] and Reuning[36] argue successfully. In 1957 Campenhausen[37] very influentially[38] revived the interpolation hypothesis[39] already upheld by Schwartz.[40] According to this hypothesis, a gospel-editor who did not yet know the text in Eusebius went to work; second came an anti-Montanist, pre-Eusebian interpolation of the anti-Montanism in MartPol 4 and the polemic against the veneration of the martyrs in 17.2-3 and 18.3; third came a pre-Eusebian miracle redaction (MartPol 5.2, 9.1, 15.2); and finally a post-Eusebian continuation in MartPol 21 and 22.2-3.

More recent scholarship has thoroughly vanquished the interpolation hypotheses[41] with the following arguments:

— The deficient credibility of Eusebius with regard to the textual tradition and his apologetic, not "historical," understanding of martyrdom[42]
— Unnecessary destruction of the internally clearly outlined and coherent MartPol

---

[29] Cf. the following reviews of scholarship: Dehandschutter, "Research," 492–97; Schoedel, "Polycarp of Smyrna," 353; Saxer, "Authenticité"; Buschmann, *Studie*, 15–70.

[30] Keim, *Urchristenthum, passim*.

[31] Lipsius, *Märtyrtod*, 188–214.

[32] Lightfoot, *Fathers* II, *passim*.

[33] Müller, "Martyrium Polycarpi," 1–16.

[34] Baden, *Nachahmungsgedanke*, 115–22.

[35] Sepp, *Martyrium Polycarpi, passim*.

[36] Reuning, *Erklärung, passim*.

[37] Campenhausen, "Bearbeitungen," 253–301.

[38] Cf. Dehandschutter, "Research," 494.

[39] Renewed in 1978 by Conzelmann, "Bemerkungen," strengthened with easy continuations, according to which more on the twelve martyrs was secondarily removed from the text to benefit the hero Polycarp.

[40] Schwartz, "Pionio," *passim*.

[41] Despite the fact that the interpolation hypotheses are still included in some publications even in recent days, e.g., in Jensen, "Töchter," 295; Butterwick, *Martyriumssucht*, 113–14—Cf. also the comprehensive critiques of the interpolation hypotheses in Barnard, "Defence," 192–204; Barnes, "Pre-Decian Acta," 509–31; Beyschlag, *Clemens*, 246n2, 312n2; Buschmann, *Studie*, 15–70; Dehandschutter, *Martyrium Polycarpi*, 131–55; Rordorf, *Martyre*, 381–403; Saxe, "Authenticité," 979–1001.

[42] Cf. on this Buschmann, *Studie*, 39–48; Dehandschutter, *Martyrium Polycarpi*, 144–50, 214–15.

— The great age and not secondary nature of the motif of the imitation of Christ

— Internal contradictions within the interpolation hypotheses, for example, some of the supposedly interpolated texts showing up in Eusebius

— The beginnings of the Christian martyr cult already in the second century: MartPol 17–18 is authentic

— Liturgical positioning of the prayer in MartPol 14 in the second century

— MartPol as literature in the kerygmatic-parenetic trend, not a "historical" report of facts: an assumed prototype from *bruta facta* proves form-critically to be inappropriate[43]

— However, the assumption of authenticity and integrity of MartPol ends with MartPol 20, which marks the end of the letter. MartPol 21–22 forms a secondary continuation.[44]

4.   Dating

The dating[45] of MartPol is dependent on the approximate date of Polycarp's death. According to MartPol 18.3 the anniversary of the martyrdom is not yet celebrated, so MartPol must have been written within a year after Polycarp's death. The debate over the date of Polycarp's death has lead to three basic suggested dates over the course of scholarly history:

1. Circa 155–156 C.E.: no later than 160 because of the known proconsuls of Asia Minor and the chronological statements in MartPol 21 (Waddington, Turner, Corssen, Schwartz, Schoedel, Barnes, Dehandschutter, et al.)

2. 167 C.E.: since Eusebius dates MartPol to the seventh year of the reign of Marcus Aurelius (HE IV 14.10–15.1; cf. also his *Chronicle*) (Telfer, Marrou, Campenhausen, Brind'Amour, et al.)

3. 177 C.E.: according to Grégoire/Orgels, the phrase "seventh year" in Eusebius' *Chronicle* is miswritten and means the "seventeenth year" of Marcus Aurelius.

The discussion of the dating experienced a new beginning in 1867 with Waddington's study of the Greek rhetorician Aelius Aristides, who also refers to the proconsul Statius Quadratus who appears in MartPol (Ἱεροὶ Λόγοι 47, 22.41). Up to that point Quadratus' proconsulate had been dated to the 160s on the basis of Eusebius' *Chronicle*. Waddington, however, starts from the chronology of the proconsulate of Asia Minor and dates Quadratus earlier: to 154–155 C.E. Since this dating matches with the chronological statements in MartPol 21, according to which 2 Xanthicos was a Sabbath, which was true in 155 or 156, the early date was established from that point on. Independent of the difficult question of the

---

43   Cf. Schoedel, "Polycarp," 353–54.
44   Cf. Buschmann, *Studie*, 16–19.

45   Cf. for the relevant literature: Buschmann, *Martyrium*, 39n53.

"Great Sabbath" (MartPol 8.1, 21.1),[46] which as an allusion to the Gospels (cf. John 19:31) should not be overrated for the question of dating, Lightfoot[47] set forth the early dating connected with the following arguments:

1. Eusebius' chronology is often imprecise.
2. The chronological statements in MartPol 21 are believable.
3. Irenaeus' report that Polycarp was a student of the Apostle John fits better with an early dating.
4. Polycarp's meeting and discussion with Bishop Anicetus of Rome on the Easter question fits well in the year 154.
5. Quadratus' proconsolate is attested in 142, and a distance of thirteen years between consulate and proconsulate was the norm.

This early dating, acknowledged by the majority of scholars, was first doubted in 1951 by Grégoire and Orgels under a reconsideration of the Eusebian tradition with the following argument for a late date of circa 177 (or 167):

1. Preeminence of the Eusebian text and its chronology
2. Unreliability of MartPol 21, presumably composed late by Ps.-Pionius in the frame of a Corpus Polycarpianum
3. Anti-Montanist orientation of MartPol and MartLugd and the dating of the beginning of Montanism to circa 170 C.E.

Although Grégoire's late dating was generally contradicted[48] and found little following in scholarship, from that point on a number of scholars began once more to date MartPol (appealing to Eusebius) to the 160s (167). More recent works—apart from the improbable ultralate date of Ronchey[49]—return to the early dating. Buschmann, to be sure, takes up the anti-Montanist direction of MartPol emphasized by Grégoire[50] and therefore dates the beginnings of Montanism earlier.

5.   Structure

An outline of MartPol seldom appears in scholarly literature,[51] which is a methodological error, especially for the proponents of the literary-critical interpolation hypothesis that MartPol is one conception complete in itself, not directed only toward the bare facts but comments on and interprets them, as in MartPol 6.2, 7.1, 9.1, 12.3, 15, 16, and 17.2—passages that Campenhausen and others view with critical suspicion. Such interpretive, commentative readings of events appear throughout the text and are often introduced with the particles ἵνα or γάρ or

---

[46] Cf., among others, Rordorf, "Problem," 245–49; Devos, "ΜΕΓΑ ΣΑΒΒΑΤΟΝ," 293–306.
[47] Lightfoot, *Fathers* II/1, 646–722.
[48] Cf., among others, Griffe, "A propos," 107–17; Meinhold, "Polykarpos," 1662–93.

[49] Ronchey, *Indagine, passim.*—For criticism: Boeft/Bremmer, "Notiunculae V," 146–51.
[50] Cf. especially Buschmann, *Martyrium Polycarpi* 4, 105–45.
[51] Cf. only Schoedel, *Martyrdom,* 50 and Dehandschutter, *Martyrium Polycarpi,* 151.

something similar: MartPol 1.1b–2.1b: ἵνα / γάρ; MartPol 4c: διὰ τοῦτο / οὖν; MartPol 6.2, 7.1: γάρ / ἵνα; MartPol 12.3b: γάρ; MartPol 15.2: γάρ; MartPol 17.3: γάρ.[52]

MartPol presents a sensible and self-contained structure:

Inscr		Inscriptio of the letter—expanded to "Diaspora circular"
1.1-2		Theme of the letter—Polycarp as example of a martyr's deeds in line with the gospel
2–4		The example of the noble martyrs of Christ
	2.1-4	Praise for the example of the noble martyrs of Christ
	3.1-2	The one way: the positive example of the steadfastness of Germanicus
	4	The other way: the negative example of the Phrygian Quintus—The urge for martryrdom
5.1–18.3		The admirable example of the by-the-gospel martyrdom of Polycarp
	5.1-2	Polycarp's flight from martyrdom and the prediction of his death
	6.1-2	Polycarp's arrest: The causes
	7.1-3	Polycarp's arrest: The capture
	8.1-3	Polycarp's temptation and steadfastness on the way to martyrdom
	9.1–11.2	Polycarp's trial
	9.1	Polycarp's strengthening through the wondrous voice from heaven
	9.2-3	Beginning of the trial: Question of identity, temptation to recant, order to swear, steadfastness
	10.1-2	Middle of the trial: Acknowledgment of being Christian
	11.1-2	End of the trial: Threats and steadfastness
	12.1–14.3	Preparation for the execution of Polycarp
	12.1-3	Reactions to the trial and the instigation of the Jews and Gentiles
	13.1-3	Polycarp's behavior in the face of the stake
	14.1-3	Polycarp's prayer at the stake
	15.1–16.2	Polycarp's execution: Burning, dying, and wonder (admiration)
	15.1-2	The burning: The fire of the stake and its miraculous behavior
	16.1-2	Wonder and admiration at the burning

---

[52] Cf. Dehandschutter, *Martyrium Polycarpi*, 155.

Rhetorically, then, MartPol is structured as follows:

	MartPol
0. Epistolary frame	Inscr
1. Proem / προοίμιον	–
2. Story / narratio / διήγησις	1.1a
3. Propositio / πρόθεσις	1.1b–2.4
4. Argumentative section / probatio / πίστις	3–4 and 5–18
5. Closing / conclusio / peroratio	19
0. Epistolary frame	postscr 20

The form-critical[53] work on martyrdom texts also supports this outline. It is only insufficiently pursued. "Martyrdom text" is broadly defined here:[54]

> In a martyrdom text, the death of a martyr and its reasons are described. Genre markings like details of the trial, philosopher martyrdom, scolding of tyrants, or the martryrdom being in letter form correspond to only a part of the texts that are understood by scholars to be martyrdom narratives.

---

[53] Cf. on this Buschmann, *Martyrium*, 43–45.

[54] With Van Henten, "Selbstverständnis," 128–29, through the following quotation.

In the establishment of a martyrdom, scholars often refer to literary motifs that appear to be characteristic. These motifs include the complete surrender to God's will; the steadfast behavior in suffering; the scorn of the torments; the obedience to the Torah; the attempt of the prince to lead the martyr to fall away with promises of gifts or a courtly career; the martyrdom as a sporting competition or the joy in suffering.

A systematic survey of the topic and elements of content, form, and genre exists only to a certain extent. Only Kellermann[55] has collected material corresponding to 2Macc 7, which he understands as the "original model of martyrdom stories." Kellerman places typical martyrdom motifs together,[56] taken from Jewish, New Testament, and early church martyrdoms, as well as from salvation stories and philosopher martyrdoms. In addition to fifty-one different individual motifs, he names eight structural requirements and fundamental motifs of Jewish martyrdom narratives that, with differences, can be translated to the early Christian martyrdom texts:

> 1. The militant conflict with Hellenism as a threat within Palestinian Judaism; 2. the presentation of foreign political powers as religious force against the devout; 3. the readiness of the faithful man to die for the Torah and πάτριοι νόμοι, especially in the first three commandments of the Decalogue; 4. the use of torture that nevertheless serves to test the faithful man and helps bring his victory over his opponents to expression; 5. the interpretation of the death by the martyrs themselves; 6. the dialogue between the martyr and his oppressor; 7. the death of the martyr; and 8. his special acceptance by God after death.[57]

Without naming parallel texts, both Fishel[58] and Leclerq[59] are concerned with presenting the typical structure, especially of the trial, of a martyrdom. Hoffmann[60] lists the "components of the Christian martyrdom report." Van Henten[61] points to a common structural schema with Jewish martyrdom stories. The structural relationship with Jewish martyrdom narratives does not diminish the unique literary form and the specific content of MartPol. There are numerous possibilities for form-critical comparison of MartPol with earlier martyrdom texts.[62]

6.   Form, Genre, and *Sitz im Leben*

Based on the form, the *proprium* of MartPol lies in the connection of narrative elements of the martyrdom story (epidictic) with argumentative and commentative elements of early Christian theology and parenesis (symbouleutic) through

---

[55] Kellermann, *Auferstanden*, 35–58.
[56] Kellermann, "Danielbuch," 71–75.
[57] Kellermann, "Danielbuch," 54–55.
[58] Fishel, "Martyr," 383–84.
[59] Leclerq, *Actes*, 381.
[60] Hoffmann, "Dialog," 46–49.
[61] Van Henten, "Einfluß," 714–15.
[62] Cf. on this the table in Buschmann, *Martyrium*, 453.

an epistolary form. A theological and parenetic application of the exemplar story of the martyr κατὰ τὸ εὐαγγέλιον to the recipients succeeds through this connection. Form-critically, elements of a martyrdom report[63] and symbouleutic argumentation[64] predominate in MartPol, supported and linked by epistolary features.[65] The epidictic martyrdom story is thus placed entirely in the service of symbouleutic argumentation.[66] "This document [. . .] is [. . .] often regarded as the first 'Acts of the Martyrs.' Judged by its literary form it does not, however, belong to this category but to early Christian epistolography."[67]

Thus MartPol as a letter forms an original Christian mixed genre *sui generis* with a meaningful and self-contained structure. In content, too, MartPol offers something new; for the first time, the description of a martyrdom forms the content of an entire Christian writing.[68] MartPol proves itself to be a text of unusual formal influence; it cannot be classified as coming directly from either Jewish or Hellenistic literature. MartPol develops its *proprium* in its very amalgamation of differing form elements, motifs, and thoughts on martyrdom. It has influenced the martyrdom literature that came after it, even when these developed into new forms (such as apologetic).

MartPol is a true letter.[69] The Diaspora letter warns, exhorts, and comforts in a situation of suffering. The connection between letter and martyrdom explains itself from the parenetic intent, for which both elements are originally suited. MartPol is not a historical report nor an act of the martyrs, which first developed later as a separate genre in an apologetic context. It is intended far more as a Diaspora letter[70] shortly after the date of Polycarp's death to be read in various churches (MartPol inscr; 20.1). Here the place of reading may have been the worship service; the liturgical influence on MartPol 14 points in that direction.[71] The letter pursues the intention to celebrate the anniversary of Polycarp's death ritually in the future (MartPol 18.3). For such a purpose MartPol 14 proves to be a fitting eucharistic prayer that was accepted through redactional insertions for the theme of martyrdom. The reference to incense in connection with the pleasing fragrance of the dying martyr also suggests a liturgical use of MartPol (cf. MartPol 15.2). Through the memory of the examples of the martyrs and Χριστοῦ κοινωνός (MartPol 6.2) in the performance of the liturgy, the church should defend itself

---

63 Cf. Berger, *Formgeschichte*, §97.

64 Cf. Berger, *Formgeschichte*, §30.

65 Cf. Berger, *Formgeschichte*, §61.

66 Cf. Berger, *Formgeschichte*, §45: Martyrium-sparänese.

67 Quasten, *Patrology*, 77.

68 Cf. Surkau, *Martyrien*, 126: "Here, with the Martyrdom of Polycarp, for the first time a martyrdom gives rise to an independent text that is written and circulated for the edification of the church."

69 Cf. Dehandschutter, *Martyrium Polycarpi*, 157–90.

70 Cf. Andresen, "Formular," 247–59.

71 Cf. Andresen, *Geschichte* I, 13: "The letters were probably read in the church service. This was also the *Sitz im Leben* for the text with which the church of Smyrna later reported the martyrdom of its bishop Polycarp [. . .]."

against the influence of heretical currents and strengthen the christological orientation of martyrdom. Thus martyrdom texts like MartPol are products of the veneration of saints, not the writing of history, and are therefore literature for edification that serve as readings for the feast days of the martyrs.

Because of its form as a mixed genre piece, the influence of MartPol could also reach beyond the concrete situation that gave rise to the letter. The kerygmatic-tending κατὰ τὸ εὐαγγέλιον-styling of MartPol is taken further by Eusebius. He places MartPol in a historical context from the outset for the sake of apologetic goals (HE IV 15.1-2). The martyrdom no longer holds the function of a parenetic example for him but serves as a historical recollection with apologetic interest: The heroic courage of the martyrs clarifies the superiority of Christianity. The questioning of the martyrdom story, which serves (in MartPol) second only to the proof of the steadfastness of the martyr with the climax of the acknowledgment Χριστιανός εἰμι (MartPol 10.1), later develops increasingly widely into an apologetic speech by the martyr. So the form *sui generis* that MartPol first achieved becomes varied and used for different goals.

7. Intertextual Relationships

While the question of New Testament influence on MartPol assumed under the perspective of the synoptic or Johannine tradition in relation to the quartodecimian question, as well as questions about the authenticity of the gospel parallels overall (Lipsius),[72] were raised in the nineteenth century, today *all* New Testament allusions are under review.[73] Within a blueprint that relies on Jewish martyrdom stories

> traditions of various origin are reworked. Striking are [. . .] the parallels to the narratives of Jesus' passion. The author has probably reached back to all four gospels and possibly also to traditions outside the New Testament. Some parallels are explicit: between Polycarp and Jesus Christ (betrayal and arrest, MartPol 1.2, 6.2); between the servants of the country estate, who are household companions of Polycarp, and Judas (6.2); and between the police officer of Herod, who brings Polycarp to the stadium, and Herod Antipas (6.2; 8; Luke 23:6-12). There are yet other parallels that are indeed shown by agreements in terminology but are primarily a matter of content. However, they are never completely identical, so that the suitable distance between Polycarp and Jesus Christ is maintained. This action is so obvious that we can assume that it was deliberately chosen by the author.[74]

---

[72] Lipsius, "Märtyrertod," 188–214.
[73] Cf. the summarized list in Dehandschutter, *Martyrium Polycarpi*, 241–54, as well as Van Henten, "Einfluß," 715–16.

[74] Van Henten, "Einfluß," 715.

The discussion at the beginning of the twentieth century presented a false dichotomy: Either the parallels to the Gospels are authentic and guarantors of the factuality of the reports (Lightfoot),[75] or they are not original and must have been inserted secondarily in order to reach back to a historical-factual original form of MartPol (Müller;[76] later: Campenhausen[77]). And in order to save the authenticity and historicity of MartPol, Reuning[78] and Sepp[79] (later: Schoedel[80]) attempt to minimize every allusion to the Gospels. This dichotomy is false because all of the participants are laboring under a historical misapprehension: The one side tries to save the historical factuality of MartPol, including the gospel parallels, while the other side excludes them as later interpolations.

This historical literary-critical perspective must give way to a theological form-critical one. A theological understanding of the parallels κατὰ τὸ εὐαγγέλιον already appears early in Egli.[81] The early Campenhausen[82] from 1936 also goes further than his later interpolation hypothesis (1957) would lead one to believe: Stephen and James serve in the early church, like Polycarp, as examples to be imitated because they imitate the passion of Christ. According to this view, the gospel parallels show a church-normative interest with regard to martyrdom. The imitation theme κατὰ τὸ εὐαγγέλιον is not secondary but central for the theology of MartPol: The martyrdom of Polycarp appears to be a church-normative guiding principle of a perfect, gospel-following martyrdom.[83] Surkau's[84] and Baumeister's[85] form-critical works also show MartPol to be the point of departure for a theology of martyrdom in which the martyr is understood as an imitator of Christ.

Buschmann's form-critical study[86] stands in this tradition of a theological understanding of the gospel parallels and sees in the phrase κατὰ τὸ εὐαγγέλιον the central statement of MartPol. We should become imitators of the gospel-following martyrdom of Polycarp—set in negative contrast are μὴ μόνον σκοποῦντες τὸ καθ᾽ ἑαυτούς (MartPol 1.2) and the example of Quintus (MartPol 4).

> Overall the same church-normative interest appears that the introduction to the letter explicitly promises. Euarestos does not want simply to provide a historical account of the end of Polycarp. He writes an instructional text that in emphatic ways pursues the intent to present to the church the right behavior in times of persecution.[87]

Polycarp thus becomes Χριστοῦ κοινωνός (MartPol 6.2). The point[88] of MartPol proves to be its κατὰ τὸ εὐαγγέλιον-styling. It contradicts first the freely willed

---

75 Cf. Lightfoot, *Fathers* II/1, 610–14.
76 Müller, "Martyrium Polycarpi," 1–16.
77 Campenhausen, "Bearbeitungen," 253–301.
78 Reuning, *Erklärung*, 10–20.
79 Sepp, "Martyrium Polycarpi," 5–14.
80 Schoedel, *Fathers*, 51–52.
81 Egli, *Altchristliche Studien*, 72–74.

82 Campenhausen, *Idee*, 82–85.
83 Cf. also Saxer, *Bible*, 27–35.
84 Surkau, *Martyrien, passim.*
85 Baumeister, *Anfänge, passim.*
86 Buschmann, *Studie, passim.*
87 Campenhausen, *Idee*, 83.
88 Cf. Berger, "Gegner," 380.

craving for martyrdom (προσελθεῖν ἑκόντας) (MartPol 4) against God's will (τὸ θέλημα τοῦ θεοῦ) (MartPol 2.1, 7.1), second the will to save oneself and do it alone (μόνον ἑαυτὸν θέλειν σῴζεσθαι) (MartPol 1.2), third the falling away in the face of martyrdom (ἰδὼν τὰ θηρία ἐδελίασεν / saw the beasts and became a coward) (MartPol 4). A similar point, that here there is a conflict with other conceptions of martyrdom, can be discerned concretely from MartPol 4: "Antithetical formulations are understood as disputing of opposing positions."[89] The explicitly censured Quintus and his followers are juxtaposed antithetically with Germanus, who is praised as most noble of spirit. Quintus is held to last as the negative example of the presentation of the by-the-gospel martyrdom of Polycarp. Finally "the thesis of the opponents [. . .] is confronted by their own contradictory behavior":[90] Quintus' craving for martyrdom and his ἰδὼν τὰ θηρία ἐδελίασεν.

Buschmann interprets the κατὰ τὸ εὐαγγέλιον intention of MartPol as catholically normative and antienthusiastic: for one thing, because the fellowship of suffering of the martyrs with Christ is emphasized, for another, because every (Montanist) urge toward martyrdom is spoken against (MartPol 4)[91] and the point of reference of martyrdom is seen not in new revelations ("nova fidei exempla," MartPerp 1) but in references back to τὸ εὐαγγέλιον.[92]

> Insofar as Polycarp did not crave martyrdom of his own free will [. . .] the theme of the gospel-following martyrdom also serves as the basis for the rejection of the craving for a martyr's death.[93] The phrases ὡς καὶ ὁ κύριος (MartPol 1.2) and κατὰ τὸ εὐαγγέλιον (MartPol 1.1; cf. 4, 19.1) are common in Hegesippus and Polycrates of Ephesus (Eus HE IV 22.4, V 24.6) as ecclesiastical standards.[94]

With the basis of the censure of the freely willed urge toward martyrdom through the Phrygian Quintus, MartPol reaches back to a central category that characteristically runs throughout MartPol and cannot be excluded as a secondary εὐαγγέλιον-redaction.[95] The gospel styling of MartPol draws weight rather from the conflict with Montanism; yet the confrontation with Montanism with regard to the building of firm tradition as opposed to constant new revelations ranks with the canon question.[96] Therefore an element of the κατὰ τὸ εὐαγγέλιον appears to be central to the conflict. Even the literary-critical statements of Campenhausen and Conzelmann that break MartPol to bits see this fact correctly: "With the tendency against the craving for martyrdom, this episode (= MartPol 4/Quintus) fits with the εὐαγγέλιον-redaction in 2.1."[97]

---

[89] Berger, "Gegner," 375.

[90] Berger, "Gegner," 375.

[91] Cf. Buschmann, "Martyrium Polycarpi 4," 105–45; idem, *Studie*, 153–60.

[92] Cf. Buschmann, *Studie*, 294–307: comparison between MartPol and MartPerp.

[93] Baumeister, *Anfänge*, 302.

[94] Beyschlag, *Clemens*, 312n2.

[95] Cf. Buschmann, *Studie*, 42–60, against Campenhausen, Conzelmann, et al.

[96] Cf., e.g., Paulsen, "Bedeutung," 19–52.

[97] Conzelmann, "Bemerkungen," 14. Cf. similarly Campenhausen, "Bearbeitungen," 274. On the anti-Montanist tendency of MartPol, cf. Buschmann, *Martyrium*, 51–58, and Buschmann, "Martyrium Polycarpi 4," 105–45.

8.   Theological Profile

MartPol plays a decisive role in the development of a theology of martyrdom. The modern research into martyrdom theology appears in 1859–1860 to be connected with the research by Gaß,[98] who describes MartPol as an example of testimony as discipleship and imitation of the Lord. Heinrici[99] sees the substance of Christian martyrdom in the new valuing of death in the act of following Jesus. In the early systematic description of martyrdom theology, the witness of blood is always connected to μίμεσις/emulation and *imitatio Christi*: The completion of the testimony through death in the imitation of Christ makes the witness a martyr (μάρτυς).[100] Thus Jewish (the martyr in place of the prophet[101]), Hellenistic (the martyr as stoic hero[102]), or autonomous Christian influence (*imitatio Christi*[103]) played the decisive role. With MartPol the technical term "witness of blood" (= martyr) asserts itself against the New Testament witness terminology.[104] According to Campenhausen,[105] the center point is no longer the living acknowledgement (= testimony) of Jesus before the Gentiles or Jews, but "the establishment of the 'evangelical' norm of martyrdom" (= blood witness). The Christians should imitate Polycarp as he imitated Christ. According to Surkau,[106] MartPol begins a new literary genre.

More recent scholarship also emphasizes the idea of imitation in the theology of MartPol.[107] MartPol appears as a narrative working out of Ignatian[108] martyrdom theology (IgnRom 6.3: "Permit me to be an imitator of the passion of my God.")—at least with specific corrections to Ignatian theology; for example, the "Vita" of Christ plays no role in Ignatius and MartPol 17–18 preserves a meaningful distinction between the martyr and Christ.[109] "MPol is clearly directed against a misunderstanding of martyrdom [. . .]. The careful distinction in MartPol 17:3 between the worship of Christ and the veneration of martyrs [. . .] also shows that MPol was taking account of an incipient tendency to honor the martyrs too highly."[110] Dehandschutter thinks here of the Gnostic conceptions of martyrdom,[111] Buschmann of the Montanist understanding.[112]

---

98 Gaß, "Das christliche Märtyrererthum," 337.
99 Henrici, "Das altchristliche Märtyrertum," *passim*.
100 Cf. Corssen, "Begriff," 498ff.; Reitzenstein, "Bemerkungen," 459–62.
101 Cf. Holl, "Vorstellung," 68–102; Schlatter, *Märtyrer, passim*; later: Surkau, *Martyrien, passim*; Fischel, *Martyr and Prophet*, 265–80, 363–86; Klauser, "Christlicher Märtyrerkult," 27–38; Kretschmar, "Christliches Passa," 287–323 interprets less from the prophets than from the Jewish concept of Passover and the bound ram (MartPol 14.1).
102 Reitzenstein, "Bemerkungen," 417–67.
103 Campenhausen, *Idee, passim*.
104 Cf. on the development of the μάρτυς-term,

among others: Günther, "Zeuge und Märtyrer," *passim*; Strathmann, "μάρτυς," 477–514; Brox, "Zeuge," *passim*; Rordorf, "Martyre," *passim*.
105 Campenhausen, *Idee*, 87.
106 Surkau, "Martyrien," 132.
107 Delehaye, *Passions*, 19. Cf. similarly: Camelot, *Ignace*, 220ff.; Schoedel, *Fathers*, 53–54.
108 Cf. on this Baumeister, *Anfänge*, 270–89; Bommes, *Weizen Gottes, passim*.
109 Cf. Dehandschutter, "Research," 514n148.
110 Schoedel, "Polycarp," 358.
111 Dehandschutter, "Martyre," 665–67.
112 Buschmann, "Martyrium Polycarpi 4," 105–45; idem, "Χριστοῦ κοινωνός," 243–64; idem, *Studie*, 153–60.

The theology of MartPol is characterized by an example Christology κατὰ τὸ εὐαγγέλιον in which the martyrdom exhortation is grounded. Germanicus, Polycarp, and Christ serve this theme alike: ἵνα μιμηταὶ καὶ ἡμεῖς αὐτοῦ γενώμεθα (MartPol 1.2). MartPol has carried the notion of the *imitatio Christi* to its logical conclusion for the first time.[113] It thus uses the old title παῖς christologically and emphasizes the communion of suffering that the martyrs have with Christ with an anti-enthusiastic purpose (MartPol 14.2). As παῖς Christ orders the following and imitation (μιμητής) to the point of martyrdom. Above all in the conflict with Montanist self-promotion, Christ as παῖς becomes in his lowliness the example of selflessness (Phil 2:4; MartPol 1.2) and of the innocent, humble victim (MartPol 14). MartPol is dominated theologically by a devotion to Christ in the form of an emerging passion mysticism κατὰ τὸ εὐαγγέλιον that grasps martyrdom as the highest form of following Christ (Χριστοῦ κοινωνός). This notion is served by the adulatory presentation of the martyr's fate of Polycarp, who with God's help enables the moral testing of the suffering. Wonder elements in MartPol 15–16 seek to encourage such belief. The imitation concept ὡς καὶ ὁ κύριος / like the Lord (MartPol 1.2) / κατὰ τὸ εὐαγγέλιον (MartPol 1.1) also applies to the martyrdom of Stephen and James and is a common early Christian image. The Christology is not treated in the sense of an atonement theory.[114] Salvation is mediated by the imitation of the Lord in martyrdom; in addition, MartPol knows a sacramental mediation of salvation (MartPol 14), in which eucharistic terminology is deliberately limited with martyrdom terminology: ἐν ἀριθμῷ τῶν μαρτύρων (MartPol 14.2).

Eschatology plays only a subordinate role in MartPol; the traditional reflection on the Christian being a foreigner in the world serves as preparation for taking leave of this world (MartPol *inscr*). The eschatological aspect of the resurrection is seldom emphasized and used traditionally (MartPol 2.3). MartPol emphasizes the aspect of the fellowship of suffering rather than the fellowship of resurrection, while in Macc, for example, the belief in the resurrection forms the basis for the security of the martyr. The hope of resurrection in MartPol remains tied to the communion of suffering with the Lord in a gospel-following martyrdom.

The exhorting and comforting character of MartPol corresponds to a certain authoritative relationship to the addressees (cf. MartPol 4 and *Paideutikon* in the conclusion of the letter). It is a chain of tradition mediated in the sense of "as Christ, so the martyrs, so also we." Christ is the διδάσκαλος for the martyr; the martyr is διδάσκαλος for the Christians (cf. MartPol 16.2, 17.3). "Every new μιμητής / imitator is in his turn an example as Christ was for him."[115] Christ is not only the Savior of our souls and captain of our bodies, but also the shepherd of the catholic church (MartPol 19.2). Polycarp appears in the early church as

---

[113] Cf. Surkau, *Martyrien*, 133.
[114] Cf. on this Lohse, *Märtyrer und Gottesknecht*, *passim*.

[115] Reitzenstein, " Martyrienliteratur," 462.

churchman (cf. the emphasis on ἐκκλησία in MartPol) and heresy fighter *par excellence*. He fought docetic Christology and rigorist asceticism. MartPol also stands in such an adversarial position with reference to the testimony of the gospel and the suffering presentation of the catholic bishop and heresy fighter Polycarp. The κατὰ τὸ εὐαγγέλιον-styling of MartPol corresponds to the Pastoral Epistles: In the fight against the heretics, the fixed apostolic teaching tradition is decisive (cf. MartPol 4: οὐχ οὕτως διδάσκει τὸ εὐαγγέλιον).

With respect to ecclesiology, the first striking element in MartPol is the exclusion of other Christian groups (e.g., Montanism, MartPol 4). Thus the "antiheretical" polemic is legitimated theologically from the tradition κατὰ τὸ εὐαγγέλιον and based on the office of the exemplar-martyr Polycarp, who is depicted as ἐπίσκοπος τῆς ἐν Σμύρνῃ καθολικῆς ἐκκλησίας (MartPol 16.2). To this extent the office plays a fundamental role in MartPol—especially in comparison to a martyrdom like MartPerp, which refers back to new revelations.

In terms of tradition history with respect to the theology of martyrdom in MartPol, the relationship of MartPol to the martyrdom theology of Ignatius of Antioch on one hand and to the Jewish martyrdom tradition on the other is especially worth consideration. Ignatius of Antioch[116] had a lasting impact on the thought of the students and imitators of the unparalleled teacher (IgnMagn 9.1-2; IgnEph 1.2; IgnRom 4.2-3, 6.3; IgnTrall 1.2). MartPol is to be understood in a milieu shaped by Ignatius. Μιμητής Χριστοῦ theology appears more often in the Apostolic Fathers than in the New Testament. Already in Ignatius "imitator" (μιμητής) belongs to the special terminology of the idea of martyrdom.[117]

> Thus Ignatius writes to the Romans (6.3): "Permit me to be an imitator of the passion of my God!" And to the Ephesians (10.3) he writes: "Let us strive to be imitators of the Lord." Whoever suffers for the sake of his name, enduring martyrdom, glorifies him (1Pet 4:16; cf. 3:14). "All who once suffered for the name of the Lord are honorable before God," states the ninth similitude of Hermas (Sim IX 28.3).[118]

The (misattributed) Ignatian longing for martyrdom is criticized in MartPol. The concept of martyrdom as sacrifice seen in MartPol 14 can also be traced to Ignatius. The παῖς θεοῦ should—mediated by the Eucharist—encourage one to imitation in the face of all danger. Humility and grateful following in suffering contradict (Montanist) self-promotion. MartPol also shares with Ignatius the christological and suffering-parenetic orientation of martyrdom as joining the martyr to his Lord (cf. also PolPhil 1.1-2, 8.2, 9-10), though with terminology that explicitly differs from Ignatius: πάθος and ἀνάστασις do not appear; the "Vita" of Jesus plays no role; the technical title μάρτυς does not yet appear in

---

116 On Ignatius' concept of martyrdom, cf. among others: Campenhausen, *Idee*, 65–78; Bommes, *Weizen Gottes*, passim; Baumeister, *Anfänge*, 257–89; Schoedel, *Ignatius of Antioch*, 28–31, 178–91,
231–35, 264–65; Bauer/Paulsen, *Briefe*, 73–74; Van Henten, "Einfluß," 711ff.
117 Cf. Brox, *Zeuge*, 204–7.
118 Bauer, *Polykarpbriefe*, 61.

Ignatius. The relationships between Ignatius and Polycarp are direct; they knew one another personally. A decisive borderline appears to run between "desiring and provoking martyrdom."[119] Ignatius apparently finds himself in exactly this border area when he can, for example, state in IgnRom 4.1: ἐγὼ ἑκὼν (cf. Mart-Pol 4) ὑπὲρ θεοῦ ἀποθνήσκω, ἐάνπερ ὑμεῖς μὴ κωλύσητε / "I shall willingly die for God, unless you hinder me." Such a desire is at least open to Montanist eagerness for martyrdom:

If Ignatius carried his desire for death in martyrdom so far as to intentionally cause it, however, he finds himself in opposition to the convictions of the majority of the church. Outstanding Christians have either withdrawn themselves from martyrdom through flight or approved of such an escape.[120]

Ignatius, however, still appears to stand on this side of the line; for "it remains unknown whether we are to read from the ἑκὼν / 'willingly' that Ign intentionally pressed himself toward martyrdom and sought out the conflict with the authorities. Otherwise the ἑκὼν has the connotation of 'gladly.'"[121] Ignatius' student Polycarp can also state his longing (MartPol 14.2) to embrace his martyrdom like Ignatius as a sacrifice that is pleasing to God (MartPol 14; IgnRom 4.1-2) and interpret it christologically,[122] as well as expressing his steadfastness (MartPol 10.1, 12.1-2).

Next to the commonalities between MartPol and Ignatian theology,[123] however, the differences from Ignatius' understanding of martyrdom should not be overlooked:

1. The ἑκὼν used positively by Ignatius[124] is judged negatively in MartPol 4 and condemned as willful pushing toward martyrdom.
2. Ignatius' individual statemens about martyrdom with respect to his impending death, which isolate him from the church[125] and are open to the egoism of enthusiasts, are altruistically relativized in MartPol (MartPol 1.2). The

---

[119] Tabbernee, "Voluntary Martyrdom," 37.

[120] Bauer/Paulsen, *Briefe*, 74. Supporting evidence is available there.—Cf. Wendebroug, "Martyrium," 307: "In the great majority of opinions that speak out against (the craving for martyrdom), it is striking how disunited and uncertain the arguments are with which one does so [. . .]. That one refuses the urge toward martyrdom is overwhelmingly true; but one has no theological and ethical argument for doing so, one has used them all for the elevation of martyrdom."

[121] Bauer/Paulsen, *Briefe*, 73.

[122] MartPol 1.1, etc.: κατὰ τὸ εὐαγγέλιον; 1.2: ὡς καὶ ὁ κύριος; 2.2: οἱ [. . .] μάρτυρες τοῦ Χριστοῦ; 6.2: Χριστοῦ κοινωνός. In Ignatius cf. the keyword: θεοφόρος, cf. Bauer/Paulsen, *Briefe*,

22–23, 26; Paulsen, *Studien*, 183–87.

[123] a. Imitation concept and christological orientation of martyrdom: MartPol 1.2, 17.3, 19.1; IgnEph 1.2, 15.1; IgnMagn 9.1; IgnTrall 5.2. b. Antidocetic martyriological conception: MartPol 2.2, 14.2, 17.3; IgnSmyrn 4.2, 5.1; IgnTrall 10. c. Connection of martyrdom to Eucharist: MartPol 14; IgnRom 2.2, 4.1-2; IgnSmyrn 7.1. d. Day of commemoration of a martyr as ἡμέρα γενέθλιος: MartPol 18.3; IgnRom 6.1. e. κατὰ-statements: MartPol 1.1, 4, 19.1 (κατὰ τὸ εὐαγγέλιον); IgnEph 8.1 (κατὰ Θεόν); IgnMagn 1.1; IgnPhld 8.2 (κατὰ Χριστομαθίαν / according to the teaching of Christ), etc.

[124] IgnRom 4.1; cf. Bauer/Paulsen, *Briefe*, 73–74.

[125] Cf. Paulsen, *Studien*, 183–87.

mystical union (ἕνωσις) with the suffering of Jesus Christ in Ignatius gives way to the parenetic orientation of a μιμεῖσθαι κατὰ εὐαγγέλιον Χριστοῦ in MartPol (19.1).

3. The Ignatian equality with Christ (IgnRom 2.1, 4.1-2, etc.),[126] which does not expressly preserve a inferiority of the martyr with regard to the person of Christ, meets with criticism in MartPol 17.3, where the distinction between God's Son and the martyrs is explicitly upheld.

4. The anxiousness of Ignatius (IgnTrall 4.1-2; IgnRom 7.1; etc.) stands in contrast to the calm resignation of Polycarp (MartPol 7.1-2, etc.).

The connections of MartPol to Jewish martyrdom tradition have been researched especially by van Henten:[127] MartPol shows no literary dependency on 2/4Macc, for example, but stands in the same martyrological tradition:

1. Common structural scheme, especially in MartPol 5–16
2. Common motifs (e.g., age of the martyr, contempt for torture, victor's crown, joy in suffering)
3. Last prayer of the martyr (Dan 3:39-40 LXX/Th—MartPol 14, specifically Christianized)
4. Miracle of fire (Dan 3:46-50 LXX/Th—MartPol 15)

Traits that are specific to MartPol as against the Jewish martyrdom tradition are:

— A martyrdom written as a letter
— Parenetic orientation addressed to other Christians
— Conflict with other conceptions of martyrdom
— The question of veneration of the martyrs
— Parallels to the narratives of the passion of Jesus κατὰ τὸ εὐαγγέλιον

As a catholic Diaspora letter,[128] MartPol is also directed against Montanism, although its effect exceeds the specific occasion. MartPol serves in a persecution situation as an exhortation to right behavior in martyrdom and thus warns against the rash Montanist drive toward martyrdom. MartPol encourages its audience to steadfast perseverance of a martyrdom once begun while it pursues edifying christological preaching.

> In fact the conclusion is inevitable—if one studies the persecution sayings of the Gospels in light of the later persecution literature—that the goal of every saying and the literature itself was [. . .] namely to prepare the adherents of the cult of Christ for

---

[126] Cf. Campenhausen, *Idee*, 78: "A fundamental difference between teachers and students who have arrived at perfection is no longer recognizable." Cf. also Paulsen, *Studien*, 183–84; Brox, *Zeuge*, 221–22.

[127] "Einfluß," 714–23. Cf. also Surkau, *Martyrien*, 9–82; Baumeister, *Anfänge*, 6–65, 295–98.
[128] Cf. Holl, "Vorstellung," 76: "In the epistolary tale the epistle is not just couching."

persecution [. . .]. So it was their immediate goal to encourage those being persecuted to "confession" of their loyalty or, negatively, to prevent "disavowal."[129]

Consequently, the claim of MartPol lies not in the apologetic (as is the case with the Acts of the Martyrs) or missionary aspect but in intra-Christian conflicts.[130] Polycarp is presented as an orthodox example for catholic Christians as opposed to heretics—not as an argumentative speaker against pagans. MartPol is concerned with a conflict with Montanism (cf. MartPol 4).[131] The behavior of Montanist martyrs is disapproved of in an almost official tone; in MartPol the martyrdom thematic is usurped by the catholic-orthodox, in that the proper martyrdom behavior is ascribed to the bishop and heretic fighter Polycarp as opposed to an urge to martyrdom; for Polycarp flees at first (MartPol 5–8). MartPol has the purpose of advocating to the churches the right behavior in the form of an evangelical norm of martyrdom:Ἴσχυε, Πολύκαρπε, καὶ ἀνδρίζου / "Be strong, and show yourself a man, O Polycarp!" (MartPol 9.1). Thus the relationship of MartPol to its audience, differently from MartLugd, can be viewed as tense because of the missing *laudatio*. MartPol has an example-recommending (cf. the terms μαθητής and μιμητής), censuring/rebuking, and comforting/edifying intent. The gospel-following martyrdom serves the rationale for rejecting the urge to martyrdom. Montanist charismatics should be exhorted to sobriety and sluggish Christians encouraged to a steadfast martyrdom. Thus different antithetical forms of martyrs' behavior are presented (MartPol 3–4). Polycarp appears as the paradigmatic overcomer of suffering; miracles (MartPol 15–16) praise and affirm his behavior.

9.   Bibliography

Aland, K. "Bemerkungen zum Montanismus und zur frühchristlichen Eschatologie." In *Kirchengeschichtliche Entwürfe*, 105–48. Gütersloh 1960.

Andresen, C. *Geschichte des Christentums, I: Von den Anfängen bis zur Hochscholastik*. ThW 6. Stuttgart 1975.

———. "Zum Formular frühchristlicher Gemeindebriefe." *ZNW* 56 (1965): 233–59.

Baden, H. "Das Polykarpmartyrium." *PastB* 24 (1911): 705–13 and *PastB* 25 (1912): 71–81, 136–51.

———. "Der Nachahmungsgedanke im Polykarpmartyrium." *TGl* 3 (1911): 115–22.

[129] Riddle, "Verfolgungslogien," 286–87. Cf. Barnes, "Pre-Decian Acta," 528: "The Marytrdom of Polycarp and the Martyrs of Lugdunum are both letters written in the first instance to definite recipients by Christian communities which had suffered persecution."

[130] Cf. Campenhausen, "Mission," 76, which speaks of a "two-sidedness" of martyrdom, which has an intra-Christian and a missionary goal orientation.

[131] Dehandschutter, "Martyre," 666, has a different opinion: "Il nous semble très invraisemblable que l'auteur du M.Pol, réagisse déjà contre une conception montaniste [. . .]. Nous sommes assez tentés [. . .] à chercher une solution dans une autre direction, notamment, la polémique avec certains conceptions gnostiques [. . .] du martyre."

Barnard, L. W. "In Defence of Pseudo-Pionius' Account of Saint Polycarp's Martyrdom." In *Kyriakon: FS J. Quasten*, vol. 1, edited by P. Granfield, 192–204. Münster 1970.

Barnes, T. D. "Pre-Decian Acta Martyrum." *JThS* 19 (1968): 509–31.

Bauer, J. B. *Die Polykarpbriefe*. KAV 5. Göttingen 1995.

Bauer, W., and H. Paulsen. *Die Apostolischen Väter, II: Die Briefe des Ignatius von Antiochia und der Polykarpbrief.* HNT 18. Tübingen ²1985.

Baumeister, T. *Die Anfänge der Theologie des Martyriums.* MBTh 45. Münster 1980.

———, ed. *Genese und Entfaltung der altkirchlichen Theologie des Martyriums.* Traditio Christiana 8. Bern 1991.

Berger, K. "Die impliziten Gegner: Zur Methodik des Erschliessens von 'Gegnern' in neutestamentlichen Texten." In *Kirche: FS G. Bornkamm*, edited by D. Lührmann and G. Strecker, 373–400. Tübingen 1980.

———. *Formgeschichte des Neuen Testaments.* Heidelberg 1984.

Beyschlag, K. *Clemens Romanus und der Frühkatholizismus: Untersuchungen zu I. Clemens 7.* BHT 35. Tübingen 1966.

Bihlmeyer, K., ed. *Die Apostolischen Väter.* SAQ 2.1.1. Tübingen ³1970.

Boeft, J., and J. Bremmer. "Notiunculae Martyrologicae 1–5." *VC* 35 (1981): 43–56; *VC* 36 (1982): 383–402; *VC* 39 (1985): 110–30; *VC* 45 (1991): 105–22; *VC* 49 (1995): 146–64.

Bommes, K. *Weizen Gottes: Untersuchungen zur Theologie des Martyriums bei Ignatius von Antiochien*, Theophan. 27. Cologne 1976.

Brox, N. *Zeuge und Märtyrer: Untersuchungen zur frühchristlichen Zeugnis-Terminologie.* SANT 5. Munich 1961.

Buschmann, G. *Das Martyrium des Polykarp.* KAV 6. Göttingen 1998.

———. *Martyrium Polycarpi—eine formkritische Studie: Ein Beitrag zur Frage nach der Entstehung der Gattung Märtyrakte.* BZNW 70. Berlin 1994.

———. "Martyrium Polycarpi 4 und der Montanismus." *VC* 46 (1995): 105–45.

———. "Polycarp von Smyrna." RGG⁴ 6 (2003): 1479–80.

———. "Χριστοῦ κοινωνός (MartPol 6,2), das Martyrium und der ungeklärte κοινωνός-Titel der Montanisten." *ZNW* 86 (1995): 243–64.

Butterweck, C. *"Martyriumssucht" in der Alten Kirche? Studien zur Darstellung und Deutung frühchristlicher Martyrien.* BHT 87. Tübingen 1995.

Camelot, P. T. *Ignace d'Antioche, Polycarpe de Smyrne, Lettres, Martyre de Polycarpe.* SC 10. Paris ⁴1969.

Campenhausen, H. von. "Bearbeitungen und Interpolationen des Polykarpmartyriums." In *Aus der Frühzeit des Christentums: Studien zur Kirchengeschichte des ersten und zweiten Jahrhunderts*, 253–301. Tübingen 1963.

———. "Das Martyrium in der Mission." In *Kirchengeschichte als Missionsgeschichte, I: Die Alte Kirche*, edited by H. G. Frohnes and U. W. Knorr, 71–85. Munich 1974.

———. *Die Idee des Martyriums in der Alten Kirche.* Göttingen ²1964.

Conzelmann, H. "Bemerkungen zum Martyrium Polycarps." *NAWG* (1978): 3–20.

Corssen, P. "Begriff und Wesen des Märtyrers in der Alten Kirche." *NJahrA* 18 (1915): 481–501.

Dehandschutter, B. "Le Martyre de Polycarpe et le développement de la conception du martyre au deuxième siècle." *StPatr* 17.2 (1982): 659–68.

———. "The Martyrium Polycarpi: A Century of Research." *ANRW* 2.27.1:485–522. Berlin 1993.

———. *Martyrium Polycarpi: Een literair-kritische studie.* BETL 52. Leuven 1979.

Delehaye, H. *Les passions des martyres et les genres littéraires.* SHG 13.2. Brussels ²1966.

Devos, P. "'ΜΕΓΑ ΣΑΒΒΑΤΟΝ' chez Saint Epiphane." *AnBoll* 108 (1990): 293–306.

Egli, E. *Altchristlichen Studien: Martyrien und Martyrologien ältester Zeit: Mit Textausgaben im Anhang.* Zurich 1887.

Fischel, H. A. "Martyr and Prophet—a Study in Jewish Literature." *JQR* 37 (1946–1947): 265–80, 363–86.

Frend, W. H. C. *Martyrdom and Persecution in the Early Church: A Study of a Conflict from the Maccabees to Donatus.* Oxford 1965.

Funk, F. X. *Opera patrum apostolicorum, I–II.* Tübingen ²1878–1881.

Gass, F. W. "Das christlichen Märtyrerthum in den ersten Jahrhunderten, und dessen Idee." *ZHTh* 29 (1859): 323–92/30 (1860): 315–81.

Grégoire, H., and P. Orgels. "La veritable date du martyre de S. Polycarpe (23. février 177) et le 'Corpus Polycarpianum.'" *AnBoll* 69 (1951): 1–38.

Griffe, E. "A propos de la date du martyre de Saint Polycarpe." *BLE* 52 (1951): 170–77.

Günther, E. "Zeuge und Märtyrer." *ZNW* 47 (1956): 145–61.

Heine, R. E. *The Montanist Oracles and Testimonia.* PatMS 14. Macon 1989.

———. "The Role of the Gospel of John in the Montanist Controversy." *SecCent* 6 (1987–1988): 1–19.

Heinrici, D. "Das altchristliche Märtyrtum." *Jahrbuch der sächsischen Missionskonferenz 1904*, 14–42.

Hilgenfeld, A. *Ignatii Antiocheni et Polycarpi Smyrnaei epistulae et martyria.* Berlin 1902.

Hill, C. E. *From the Lost Teaching of Polycarp: Identifying Irenaeus' Apostolic Presbyter and the Author of Ad Diognetum.* WUNT 186. Tübingen 2006.

Hoffmann, M. *Der Dialog bei den christlichen Schriftstellern der ersten vier Jahrhunderte.* TU 96. Berlin 1966.

Holl, K. "Die Vorstellung vom Märtyrer und die Martyrerakte in ihrer geschichtlichen Entwicklung." In *Gesammelte Aufsätze zur Kirchengeschichte 2*, 68–102. Tübingen 1928 (reprint Darmstadt 1964).

Jensen, A. *Gottes selbstbewußte Töchter: Frauenemanzipation im frühen Christentum?* Freiburg/Basel/Vienna 1992.

Karpinski, P. *Annua dies dormitionis: Untersuchungen zum christlichen Jahrgedächtnis der Toren auf dem Hintergrund antiken Brauchtums.* EHS.T 300. Frankfurt/Bern/New York 1987.

Keim, T. *Aus dem Urchristenthum: Geschichtliche Untersuchungen in zwangloser Folge, I.* Zurich 1878.

Kellermann, U. *Auferstanden in den Himmel: 2. Makkabäer 7 und die Auferstehung der Märtyrer.* SBS 95. Stuttgart 1979.

———. "Das Danielbuch und die Märtyrertheologie der Auferstehung." In *Die Entstehung der jüdischen Martyrologie*, edited by J. W. van Henten et al., 51–75. StPB 38. Leiden 1989.

Klauser, T. "Christlicher Märtyrerkult, heidnischer Heroenkult und spätjüdische Heiligenverehrung: Neue Einsichten und neue Probleme." In *Arbeitsgemeinschaft für Forschung des Landes Nordrhein-Westfalen: Geisteswissenschaften: Heft 91*, 27–38. Cologne 1960.

Kretschmar, G. "Christliches Pass im 2. Jahrhundert und die Ausbildung der christlichen Theologie." *RSR* 60 (1972): 287–323.

Lazzati, G., ed. *Gli sviluppi della letteratura sui martiri nei primi quattro secoli.* Turin 1956.

Leclerq, H. "Actes des martyres." *DACL* 1:373–446.

Lightfoot, J. B. *The Apostolic Fathers, Part II: S. Ignatius, S. Polycarp: Revised Texts with Introductions, Notes, Dissertations, and Translations.* Vol. 1–3. London ²1889 (reprint Hildesheim 1973).

Lindemann, A., and H. Paulsen, eds. *Die Apostolischen Väter: Griechisch-deutsche Parallelausgabe auf der Grundlage der Ausgaben von F. X. Funk/K. Bihlmeyer/M. Whittaker: Mit Übersetzungen von M. Dibelius und D.-A. Koch neu übersetzt und herausgegeben.* Tübingen 1992.

Lipsius, R. A. "Der Märtyrertod Polykarps." *ZWTh* 17 (1874): 188–214.

Lohse, E. *Märtyrer und Gottesknecht: Untersuchungen zur urchristlichen Verkündigung com Sühntod Jesu Christi.* FRLANT 64. Göttingen ²1963.

Meinhold, P. *Polykarpos.* PW 21. 1662–1693.

Millar, F. "Rez. H. Musurillo, *The Acts of the Christian Martyrs*, 1972." *JTS* 24 (1973): 239–43.

Müller, H. "Das Martyrium Polycarpi: Ein Beitrag zur altchristlichen Heiligengeschichte." *RQ* 22 (1908): 1–16.

Musurillo, H. A., ed. *The Acts of the Christian Martyrs.* OECT. Oxford ²1979.

Orbán, A. P. *Atti e passioni dei martiri: Introduzione di A. A. R. Bastiaensen: Testo critico e commentato a cura di A. A. R. Bastiaensen, A. Hilhorst, G. A. A. Kortekaas, A. P. Orbán, M. M. Assendelft: Traduzioni di G. Chiarini, G. A. A. Kortekaas, G. Lanata, S. Roncey, Scrittori greci e latini.* Fonazione Lorenzo Valla 1987. 3–45: *Martyrim Polycarpi* Testo critico a cura di A. P. Orbán, Traduzione di Silvia Ronchey; 371–81: Commento al "Martyrium Polycarpi" a cura di A. P. Orban.

Paulsen, H. "Die Bedeutung des Montanismus für die Herausbildung des Kanons." *VC* 32 (1978): 19–52.

———. *Studien zur Theologie des Ignatius von Antiochien.* FKDG 29. Göttingen 1978.

Quasten, J. *Patrology I: The Beginnings of Patristic Literature.* Utrecht/Brussels 1950.

Reitzenstein, R. "Bemerkungen zur Martyrienliteratur, I: Die Bezeichnung Märtyrer." *NGWG.PH*, 417–67. Berlin 1916.

Reuning, W. *Zur Erklärung des Polykarpsmartyriums.* Darmstadt 1917.

Riddle, D. W. "Die Verfolgungslogien in formgeschichtlicher und soziologischer Beleuchtung." *ZNW* 33 (1934): 271–89.

Ronchey, S. *Indagine sul Matirio di San Policarpo: Critica storica e fortuna agiografica di un caso giudiziario in Asia Minor.* Istituto storico italiano per il medio evo. Nuovi Studi Storici 6. Rome 1990.

Rordorf, W. "Martyre et 'Témoignage': Essai de réponse à une question difficile." In *Liturgie, Foi et Vie des Premiers Chrétiens: Etudes Patristiques*, 381–403. ThH 75. Paris 1986.

———. "Zum Problem des 'großen Sabbats' im Polykarp- und Pioniusmartyrium." In *PIETAS: FS B. Kötting*, edited by E. Dassmann and K. S. Frank, 245–49. JAC.E 8. Münster 1980.Ruhbach, G., ed. *Ausgewählte Märtyreakten: Neubearbeitung der Knopf'schen Ausgabe von Gustav Krüger, mit einem Nachtrag von Gerhard Ruhbach.* SAQ.NF 3. Tübingen [4]1965.

———. "Martyre." *DSp* 10:718–32. Paris 1980.

Saxer, F. *Bible et Hagiographie: Textes et thèmes bibliques dans les actes des martyres authentiques des premiers siècles.* Bern 1986.

———. "L'Authenticité du 'Martyre de Polycarpe': Bilan de 25 ans de critique." *MAH* 94 (1982): 979–1001.

Schlatter, A. *Der Märtyrer in den Anfängen der Kirche.* BFCT 19.3. Gütersloh 1915.

Schoedel, W. R. *The Apostolic Fathers: A New Translation and Commentary, V: Polycarp, Martyrdom of Polycarp, Fragments of Papias.* Camden, N.Y. 1967.

———. "Polycarp of Smyrna and Ignatius of Antioch." *ANRW* II 27.1:272–358. Berlin 1993.

Schwartz, E. *De Pionio et Polycarpo.* Göttingen 1905.

Sepp, B. *Das Martyrium Polycarpi nebst Anhang über die Afralegende.* Regensburg 1911.

Slusser, M. "Martyrium III/1: Neues Testament/Alte Kirche." *TRE* 22 (1992): 207–12.

Strathmann, M. "μάρτυς κτλ." *ThWNT* 4 (1942): 477–520.

Surkau, H. W. *Martyrien in jüdischer und frühchristlicher Zeit.* FRLANT 54. Göttingen 1938.

Tabbernee, W. "Early Montanism and Voluntary Martyrdom." *Colloquium: The Australian and New Zealand Theological Review* 17 (1985): 33–44.

Van Damme, D. "Polycarp von Smyrna." *TRE* 27 (1997): 25–28.

Van Henten, J. W. "Das jüdische Selbstverständnis in den ältesten Martyrien." In *Die Entstehung der jüdische Martyrologie*, edited by J. W. van Henten et al., 127–61. StPB 38. Leiden 1989.

Weidmann, F. W. *The Martyrdom of Polycarp, Bishop of Smyrna in Early Christian Literature: A Re-evaluation in Light of Previously Unpublished Coptic Fragments.* Ph.D. Yale University 1993.

Wendebourg, D. "Das Martyrium in der Alten Kirche als ethisches Problem." *ZKG* 98 (1987): 295–320.

Wischmeyer, W. "Märtyrer II: Alte Kirche." *RGG*[4] 5 (2002): 862–65.

———. "Märtyrerakten." *RGG*[4] 5 (2002): 873–75.

Zahn, T. "Ignatii et Polycarpi epistulae, martyria, fragmenta." In *Patrum Apostolicorum Opera II*, edited by O. Gebhardt, A. Harnack, and T. Zahn. Leipzig 1876.

The Papias Fragments

Ulrich H. J. Körtner

The λογίων κυριακῶν ἐξηγήσεως συγγράμματα πέντε of Papias of Hierapolis are one of the numerous texts of early Christianity that have gone missing. The existence of the work is attested by multiple reports that are admittedly partly dependent on one another. The tradition reports little about its contents. Nothing is known about other works of Papias.

1. Textual Tradition

1.1 State and Location of the Papias Fragments

Since the seventeenth century, the accessible reports and quotations have been systematically collected. Today they number over twenty texts.[1] Their designation as Papias fragments is misunderstood, however, since only a few of the texts are presumably *word-for-word quotations* from the work of Papias. The inclusion of most of the fragments in the Papias tradition is disputed. At least one of them is most likely not ascribable to Papias from Hierapolis, but rather a lexicographer from the Middle Ages by the same name. The Hierapolitan wrote his works in Greek. A portion of the scattered reports or quotations appear in Latin and Armenian texts, however.

The oldest references to the work of Papias come from Irenaeus of Lyon (ca. 180 C.E.),[2] who in Haer V 33.3-4 quotes a supposed saying of Christ on the fruitfulness of the millennium from the fourth book of Papias and remarks of the author himself that he was a student of the Apostle John and a contemporary of Polycarp of Smyrna. This biographical note on a text that otherwise survives only in Latin was quoted in Greek by Eusebius in HE III 39.1. The most comprehensive fragments (Chronicon II [anni Abrahae 2114]; HE II 15, III 36.1-2, 39) also appear in Eusebius (ca. 300 C.E.), including remarks on the origin of Mark and Matthew. From the fourth book of Papias Apollinaris of Laodicea (ca. 310–390) has handed down a legendary report of the end of Judas Iscariot. The

---

[1] On the locations of the fragments and suggested historical-critical editions of the church fathers in which they appear, see Körtner, *Papiasfragmente*, 9–22.

[2] On the dating of the works of the church fathers treated below, cf. Altaner/Stuiber, *Patrologie*, *passim*.

text appears in three versions.[3] Three other Papias fragments appear around the end of the fourth century in Jerome (Vir ill 18; Epist 71.5, 75.3), who freely admits to not having read the writing of the Hierapolitan himself. A short summary of Papias' work appears in the surviving fragments of the church history of Philippus Sidetes, a friend of John Chrysostom, written between 434 and 439. The excerpt partly recalls Eus HE III 39 but also includes a report by Papias in the second book of his exegesis on the deaths of both of the sons of Zebedee. Andrew of Caesarea includes Papias in the prologue of his commentary on Acts (between 563 and 614) as a witness of the divine inspiration of Acts. Also, in the thirty-fourth chapter of his commentary in the frame of his interpretation of Acts 12:7-8, he quotes a comment of Papias on the temporary angelic rule that existed in primeval times. To Maximus Confessor (d. 662) are widely ascribed the *Scholia* of Dionysius the Areopagite that refer in two places to statements in the first and in the fifth books of Papias (Scholion in DionysAreop Lib Coel Hier 2, 7). As H. U. von Balthasar has shown,[4] however, the overwhelming majority of the portion of the *Scholia* ascribed to Maximus actually come from John of Scythopolis (after 532), including both of the Papias fragments. Two other references to the work of the Hierapolitan appear in Anastasius Sinaita (d. shortly after 700). He reports in his *Anagogicarum Contemplationum in Hexameron* I and VII, without exact information on the location, that Papias interpreted the six days of creation as referring to Christ and the church and also interpreted the story of paradise spiritually and connected it to the church. Very uncertain is the tradition of a Papias fragment from the second book of his exegesis, on the martyrdom of the Apostle John in the time of Nerva, that appears in an excerpt from the chronicle of Georgius Monachus with the epithet Hamartolus (9th c.). This text excerpt, which recalls the *Epitome* of Philippus Sidetes and may depend on it, appears only in Cod. Coislin. 305, from which H. Nolte published the text in 1862.[5] One stumbles on a further reference to the work of Papias in the *Myriobiblon* of Photius (9th c.), which is also known under the name *Bibliotheca*. In codex 232 of this report on 280 mostly lost works of pagan and Christian authors we read that the Monophysite Stephanus Gobarus (2nd half of the 6th c.) rejected both Papias and Irenaeus of Lyon because of their chiliastic views, a judgment that Photius endorses in Ep I 24.21. According to a dark tradition, in five "exoteric" (= exegetical?) books Papias supposedly proves the authorship of the Apostle John for John and maintained in this regard that he was himself the amanuensis for the son of Zebedee. At issue is the "Argumentum secundum Iohannem," an old gospel prologue, that was already published in the eighteenth century and was newly edited with a text-critical apparatus in 1928 by D. de Bruyne in light of

---

3   On the groups of texts and attempts at reconstruction cf. Körtner, *Papiasfragmente*, 10.

4   Balthasar, *Kosmische Liturgie*, 644–72; cf. also Altaner/Stuiber, *Patrologie*, 508–9.

5   Nolte, "Exzerpt," 464–68.

all available manuscripts.[6] A. von Harnack dates the text, according to the report that Papias took action against Marcion, which he suspects to be a historical recollection, to the second half of the second century.[7] To the Papias tradition can also be attributed a Latin note on the four Marian forms of the New Testament, published in 1700 by Grabe from the Cod. Bodleiane 2397.[8] There is no support in the text for the repeatedly remarked-upon suspicion that the marginal reference to "Papia" actually refers to the medieval lexicographer. However, the Papias quotation in question does fall under suspicion as a pseudonymous quotation that originated in the Latin West.

Other texts that have been discussed as possibly belonging to the Papias tradition are excluded on closer examination. Eusebius claims in HE III 39.17 to have read the story of a very sinful woman in Papias. However, this story, as J. B. Lightfoot suspects, cannot be identified with John 7:53–8:11.[9] Eusebius' detailed report of the content can just as easily match the Jesus story passed on by Didymus of Alexandria in Eccl. theol. IV 223.6-13, which according to the analysis of D. Lührmann very probably comes from the GosHeb.[10] But whether Papias himself quoted from the place in GosHeb in question or knew the story of the sinful woman, which was only secondarily inserted in John, in another version cannot be determined. In various places in Haer Irenaeus reworked traditions that appealed to a circle of known πρεσβύτεροι or to an individual *senior*. A. von Harnack and F. Loofs suspect Papias as the main source for the presbyter tradition in Irenaeus of Lyon.[11] Neither Loofs nor Harnack provides proof for their hypothesis, however. Haer V 33.3-4, where Papias is quoted by name, is a far better starting point for concluding that this quotation is offered by Irenaeus as a second source apart from the presbyter tradition on the end-times fruitfulness of creation that probably came to Irenaeus by word of mouth. Apart from this place, there is no evidence that the work of Papias was a written predecessor for Haer. F. Siegert relates Papias to more texts from Armenian sources.[12] However, sometimes the identity of the author being referred to is questionable, and sometimes the source makes a secondary reference to notes about Papias known elsewhere. Thus the source base is also not broadened by Siegert.

Reports on Papias of Hierapolis appear through the Middle Ages into the early Renaissance.[13] Yet the survival of reports that do not depend on one another, but above all of verbatim quotations of the work of the Hierapolitan, remains

---

6   Bruyne, "Prologues," 198–99.
7   Harnack, "Evangelien-Prologe," 14–16.
8   Cf. Hilgenfeld, *Papias*, 268.
9   Lightfoot, *Essays*, 203ff.
10 Lührmann, "Geschichte," 304–16.
11 Harnack, *Geschichte* II/1, 333–40; Loofs, "Theophilus," 310–38.
12 Siegert, "Papiaszitate," 605–14.

13 Papias is referred to, e.g., in the world chronicle of the doctor and humanist Hartmann Schedel (1440–1514) (folio CVIIv; facsimile reproduction Dortmund 1978), but Schedel's source is probably Jerome's Vir ill 18. The immediate decisive reference to Quadratus in Schedel can be explained by the fact that Vir ill 19 deals with Quadratus, though without maintaining a relationship between him and Papias.

minimal. There is also nothing reliable known about Latin translations of his five books. A thirteenth-century fragment ascribed to the Hierapolitan in 1927 by J. Sykutris that deals with the Janus cult in Philadelphia[14] more likely comes from the medieval lexicographer of the same name.[15] To be sure, Papias is still referred to in convent library catalogues in Stams[16] and Canterbury,[17] but no manuscripts are known from either convent.

1.2 Textual Form and Classification of the Fragments

In view of the difficult source situation, it comes as no surprise that the various editions and translations of the Papias fragmens sometimes differ significantly from one another in the content and order of the text. One of the chief editiorial difficulties comes from the differentiation between fragments of the work in the strictest sense of the word and statements from secondary reports on the author and his writing. Because most editions include both quotations or excerpts and biographical reports on Papias in varying stages of completeness, K. Bihlmeyer included in his revision of F. X. Funk's edition "only those pieces that somehow include statements by Papias himself, not counting the bare statements of the ancients about him."[18] This limitation cannot be denied its objective right. It cannot be followed through to its logical end, however, which would require one to break up coherent texts like Eus HE III 39 or Iren Haer V 33.3-4 in order to separate the biographical notes and the theological marginalia of the authors. In this case the context of the fragments in question would remain unaccounted for, and without this knowledge, critical research on the actual Papias quotations is not possible. On the contrary, the fragmentary nature of the texts requires one to publish the results in as much detail and as unabridged as possible. The fact that in this way even mere reports appear in the edition of the text must indeed be acknowledged for the sake of methodological clarity, but they must be deliberately accepted in order to compile the most complete picture possible of the Papias tradition.

The ordering of the fragments can succeed on two different criteria. Either one orders the texts according to their actual known or suspected locations in the work of Papias itself or else chronologically according to the age of the secondary sources to which we owe the reports and excerpts. Since for many reports an exact ordering within the lost work of Papias cannot be carried out, a chronological ordering recommends itself. It allows the inclusion of all the texts and also takes into account both the embedding of the individual reports in various literary contexts and the dependency of more recent sources on older texts. These factors in turn play a role in the question of authenticity. Newer editions

---

14 Sykutris, "Papiaszitat," 210–12.
15 Cf. Goetz, "Papias," 348.
16 Bickell, "Papiashandschrift," 799–803.

17 Donaldson, *Fathers*, 401–2.
18 Funk/Bihlmeyer, *Väter* I, XLVI.

quote the fragments according to the particular historical-critical editions of the various church fathers. The most important German-language editions (texts and translations) are those by Hübner/Kürzinger (1983), Lindemann/Paulsen (1992, based on the edition by Funk/Bihlmeyer [1924, reprinted 1970]), and Körtner (1983/1998). The latter includes the following fragments in chronological order:

1 Irenaeus, *Adversus Haereses* V 33.3-4
2 Eusebius, *Chronicon* II, anni Abrahae 2114
3 Eusebius, *Historia Ecclesiastica* II 15
4 Eusebius, *Historia Ecclesiastica* III 36.1-2
5 Eusebius, *Historia Ecclesiastica* III 39
6 Apollinaris of Laodicea, reconstruction from catenas
7 Jerome, *De viris inlustribus* 18
8 Jerome, *Epistula* 71.5
9 Jerome, *Epistula* 75.3
10 Philippus Sidetes, *Historia Ecclesiastica*, fragment in Cod. Baroccianus 142
11 Andrew of Caesarea, *Commentarius in Apocalypsin, praefatio*
12 Andrew of Caesarea, *Commentarius in Apocalypsin*, ch. 34
13 Maximus Confessor (John of Scythopolis), *Scholia in Dionys.Areop. Liber de coelesti hierarchia* 2
14 Maximus Confessor (John of Scythopolis), *Scholia in Dionys.Areop. Liber de coelesti hierarchia* 7
15 Anastasius Sinaita, *Anagogicarum Contemplationum in Hexameron* I
16 Anastasius Sinaita, *Anagogicarum Contemplationum in Hexameron* VII
17 George the Monk (Hamartolos), *Chronicon*, after Cod. Coislin. 305
18 Stephen Gobarus after Photius, *Bibliotheca* Cod. 232
19 Photius, *Epistolarum Liber I*, XXIV 21
20 *Argumentum secundum Iohannem*
21 *Catena Patrum Graecorum in S. Iohannem*, Prooemium
22 Fragment from Cod. MS 2397, Bibliotheca Bodleianae, fol. 286, col. 2

2.   Questions of Authenticity and Methodological Problems

In discussions of the diversity of quotations, paraphrases, and biographical reports, the question of the authenticity of the individual traditions must be stated differently. The question of authenticity is essentially twofold:

a) Are we dealing with genuine quotations or believable reports about the work of Papias and the person of the author? b) Is the information that Papias himself collected in his work historically reliable or legendary? The second question applies, for example, to the details he reports regarding the history of the origins of Mark and Matthew. The following remarks primarily discuss the first question of the authenticity of the individual fragments.

Verbatim quotations appear in fragments 1, 5, 7, 12, and 22, possibly also in fragment 9. The authenticity of the quotations in 1 and 5 is beyond doubt, even though the exact phrasing of the specific original text is no longer exactly checkable in the absence of possibilities for comparison. The quotation from the prologue of Papias' work in Jerome is only a page reference that relies on Eusebius. The authenticity of fragments 6 and 12 is also beyond question. By contrast, the authenticity of fragment 10 is doubtful, which is discussed in detail in the secondary literature. The text in Philippus Sidetes, which is mainly dependent on Eus HE III 39, contains a previously unknown note about the sons of Zebedee that supposedly appeared in the second book of Papias. The age of Sidetes' work could speak for the plausibility of the report. However, although the early death of James was known in the early church from Acts 12:2, it is difficult to imagine that a report on the supposed martyrdom of John son of Zebedee would remain unnoticed until the beginning of the fifth century, especially since martyrdom enjoyed great esteem.[19] Various conjectural suggestions[20] are not convincing. Provided that the tradition in Sidetes is not without any basis in the work of the Hierapolitan, the note about the Zebedees can be explained only as an irreparable distortion of a note by Papias.[21] Fragment 22, the Latin excerpt on the four New Testament Marian forms, is not genuine. Its author probably comes from the Latin West.

We find *paraphrased excerpts* in fragments 1, 3, 5, 7, 10, 11, 13–17, and 20. The greatest reliability can be ascribed to the paraphrases by Eusebius, which admittedly do not rely directly on Papias for many singularities, including the origin of Mark, but on Clement of Alexandria. Uncertain are the reports of Philppus Sidetes in fragment 10 on a raising from the dead and more on those raised from the dead by Christ who had supposedly lived until the time of Hadrian. Although the possibility that Papias spoke of someone being raised from the dead is not to be excluded, but the second report lies under the suspicion that Sidetes depends here on the Quadratus fragment (Eus HE IV 3.2).[22] By contrast, the details of Papias regarding the testimonies for the divine inspiration of Revelation in fragment 11 are not suspicious. The reliability of fragments 13 and 14 is also beyond doubt. On the other hand, fragments 15 and 16 are truly dark and not very trustworthy. The reports in 17 and 20 are not genuine.[23]

Reports about Papias are not limited to biographical information but are partly interspersed with theological judgments about Papias and his work, directed primarily against the chiliasm of Papias (Eus HE III 39.11-13; Jerome Vir ill 18;

---

[19] Thus quite rightly Harnack, *Geschichte* II/1, 665–66. By contrast, Oberweis, "Papias-Zeugnis," 227–84, holds the report by Philippus Sidetes in the present phrasing to be genuine.

[20] Zahn, *Forschungen* VI, 147–51; Harnack, *Geschichte* II/1, 666; Lightfoot, *Essays*, 212.

[21] Contra Schwartz, *Tod, passim*.

[22] Cf. Chapman, *John the Presbyter*, 95–101; Schwartz, *Tod*, 15; contra Vielhauer, *Geschichte*, 758–59, et al.

[23] Cf. Steitz, "Papias," 94; Hilgenfeld, "Papias," 268; Overbeck, "Ansichten," 63ff.

Stephen Gobarus [fragment 18] and Photius [fragment 19]). Especially contentious and already doubted by Eusebius (HE III 39.1-2, 5-7) is the claim that
Papias was a student of the Apostle John. This point is discussed separately below
in the section on authorship. In any case, however, the claim of fragment 21, that
in times of terrible heresy the Apostle John dictated his gospel to Papias himself,
belongs to the realm of legend.

3. Structure and Content

The exceptionally small basis of genuine quotations and excerpts, as well as the
trustworthy reports about Papias, makes it impossible to draw a seamless por-
trait of his lost work and the person of the author. Any analysis of the fragments, however fundamental, supplies only an incomplete sketch of limited
meaningfulness. Only with great reservations are conclusions about the content
and structure, exegetical methods, and theological profile of the five books of
the Hierapolitan possible.

3.1 Structure

The title of the work, λογίων κυριακῶν ἐξηγήσεως συγγράμματα πέντε, raises
questions rather than serving as a satisfactory answer to the question of genre and
content, method and goal of the work. A review of the surviving reports, however,
allows some foundations of the lost work to be reconstructed with a certain degree
of likelihood.

A division of the work of Papias into five books is attested. However, the
literary nature connected with this structure can no longer be reconstructed. Conjectures that it was a counterpart to a division of Matthew into five parts or a commentary on a five-part source of sayings for which Matthew in turn served as an
example[24] have no foundation. Besides, there are genuine five-part works known
from Judaism and early Christianity, beginning with the Pentateuch and the Psalter.[25] Whether Papias was influenced by that kind of example can no longer be
determined, however.

3.2 Content

Since Schleiermacher's study "Ueber die Zeugnisse des Papias von unsern beiden
ersten Evangelien" (1832),[26] the λόγια that Papias collected and found in Matthew, among other sources (HE III 39.16), have been interpreted as sayings or
discourses of Jesus.[27] But neither an Aramaic sayings source nor a collection of
Old Testament testimonies on which Papias may have commented[28] is at issue.

---

24 Hawkins, *Horae synopticae*, 132, et al.
25 Cf. Nestle, "Fünfteilung," 252–54.
26 Schleiermacher, "Zeugnisse," 361–92.

27 So, e.g., Hilgenfeld, "Papias," 238ff.; Campenhausen, *Entstehung*, 153–59.
28 So Harris, "Testimonies," *passim*.

The sense of what Papias meant by λόγια κυριακά appears with some certainty from the Mark note in HE III 39.15-16. According to that statement, they were Jesus stories that Peter, among others, related in his teachings. In any case, it would be rash to equate the λόγια κυριακά of Papias with the material in the later canonized Gospels. For example, neither the discussion between Jesus and his disciples regarding the fruitfulness of the end times related in fragment 1 nor (originally) the story of the sinful woman (HE III 39.17) appears in the canonical Gospels. The λόγια of Papias deal far more with traditional material, some of which appears in the New Testament Gospels, but which was just as common in oral form at the time of composition of Papias' work.

Form history suggests the classification of the λόγια κυριακά as apophthegmata. However, HE III 39.15 shows that they included miracle stories as well. For Papias a λόγιον κυριακόν meant very generally a short story about Jesus.[29] However, as a genre designation, λόγιον is difficult to connect with modern genre names. The expression is thus similar to the ancient genre designation ἀπομνημονεύματα, which according to modern understanding is completely undifferentiated.[30] The observation that Papias speaks of μνημονεύειν and ἀπομνημονεύειν in connection with the activity of Mark (HE III 39.15) fits here. This genre-historical classification is confirmed by the references to the Gospels as apomnemoneumata in the apologetics of the second century.[31]

According to the title of the work, Papias offers in five books a ἐξήγησις of the λόγια κυριακά that he assembled. The meaning of the term ἐξήγησις is difficult to determine, since neither the substantive nor the related verb ἐξηγέομαι appear in other places in the Papias fragments. In addition to ἐξήγησις, Papias uses the term ἑρμηνεῖαι (HE III 39.3), while Eusebius in his presentation also uses the term διήγησις (HE III 39.9, 12, 14), which at the time was synonymous with the expression ἐξήγησις. From this context it becomes clear that Eusebius speaks of διηγήσεις in the sense of tales or stories (cf. Luke 1:1!) and thus means the same thing with this term as with the designation παραδόσεις.

The character of the ἑρμηνεῖαι of Papias can best be seen from a comparison of the proem with the notes on Mark and Matthew.[32] As the comparison in detail shows, Papias thinks of the compositional and tradition-historical relationships primarily of Mark as being very similar to those of his own text, except that Papias

---

[29] Contra Baum, "Papias," 257–76, who updates the translation of λόγια κυριακά with "Sayings of the Lord" that Papias finally found in the modern canonical Gospels. Conceptually, the λόγια κυριακά of Papias must be differentiated from the λόγοι κυρίου but also from the λόγια τοῦ κυρίου in PolPhil 7.1, which in contrast to the λόγια of Papias have Jesus not as their subject but as their object.
[30] Cf. Schmid/Stählin, *Geschichte*, 54. J. Kürzinger

sees in HE III 39.15 a comparison between the teaching activity of Jesus and the ancient Χρεία literature. Cf. Kürzinger, "Papiaszeugnis," 24–35; idem, "Aussage," 248–64. However, Χρεία is not used as a rhetorical term in the place mentioned, since its rhetorical meaning was no longer current in the time of Papias.
[31] Cf. Tat Or 21; Just Apol I 33; Or Cels 7.54. See also Heard, "Quotations," 123–29.
[32] So Heard, "Quotations," 122–23, judges.

by his own understanding represents the next generation after Mark. While Papias finds fault with Mark for his mangled τάξις of the material, he is obviously concerned with a clear ordering of his own material (συγκατατάξαι ταῖς ἑρμηνείαις). Thus the work of Papias can hardly be a commentary on a single text. No more likely is the ἑρμηνείαι of the presbyter that Papias collected by his own admission to be a commentary on written sources in the strictest sense, but rather such traditions as Eusebius very generally refers to as παραδόσεις. Papias' ἑρμηνείαι are traditions that came to him orally or were set before him in written form and could be understood partly as commentaries on Jesus stories or sayings of Jesus. Papias' ἐξήγησις thus clearly consisted of the presentation of such stories with explanatory character, also admittedly a commentary insofar as he not only made reference to his written sources of λόγια κυριακά that are known to use from Mark and Matthew, and further details his oral and written sources and judges them critically in his prologue, but also in that according to Eusebius he often named the current source of a story. However, in the main, Papias apparently presented the λόγια κυριακά as a result of his having simply retold or completed them through relevant stories and sayings. The ἑρμηνείαι are a commentary in story form, which is already a form of interpretation in the means of presentation. Therefore, one should best translate the title of the work of Papias as "Interpretive Account of Jesus Stories."

4.   Genre

In terms of genre history, the work of Papias is in no sense a commentary on the Gospels. The text shows far more commonalities with the early Christian gospel literature itself.[33] In contrast to the Gospels known to us, however, Papias, according to everything we know, has not written a continuous narrative of Jesus stories. In the presentation of sources his work is more comparable to a commentary, but Papias uses "neither the interpretive method of the later patristic exegesis nor the contemporary Jewish or even Greco-Roman interpretation literature."[34] The work of Papias is a unique specimen in genre history, comparable to the Ὑπομνήματα of Hegesippus (ca. 180 C.E.).

The five books of the Hierapolitan are also important for canon history for two reasons, for one because of the author's attitude toward writing down the tradition, for another because of the place of the work in the history of early Christian literature and of the New Testament canon. According to Eus HE III 39.4, Papias treasured the oral tradition overall more than written texts. The appeal to the *viva vox* is an ancient topos.[35] Even in Clement of Alexandria we

---

33 Cf. Zyro, *Beleuchtung*, 15; Kürzinger, "Titel," 185–86. One should note that even the NT gospel literature is shot through with commentative remarks and interpretations.

34 Vielhauer, *Geschichte*, 761.

35 Cf. Karpp, "*Viva vox*," 190–98.

find a similar critical attitude toward writing down Christian tradition. Irenaeus also saw in a written canon only something makeshift (cf. Haer I 10.2, III 4.2). Papias is in any case "a long way from seeing the final or canonical form of the Jesus tradition in the Gospels, but rather confesses with pathos to the priority of the oral tradition."[36]

Admittedly Papias sees himself presented with the task of distinguishing between true and false, orthodox and heretical traditions and guarding against forgetfulness. He therefore collects and writes down the traditions in the forms presented by early Christian fathers whose time was drawing to an end, and he does not spurn even written sources. From this fact we can conclude that Papias' negative judgment about books is relative, since the very fact that someone who appeals with such pathos to the *viva vox* is himself writing a book is a performative contradiction.

In terms of canon history, Papias' work finds a certain parallel in the double work of Luke. Without already assuming a New Testament canon or even presenting even the idea of a written canon, the five books of Papias are still to be valued as a developmental step on the way toward such a canon. Put more exactly, they are the prototype of a form, later not preserved, of the canonization of the matter of the Gospels, a forerunner of the later four-gospel canon.[37]

5.   Intertextual Relationships

5.1 Written Sources

As written sources, the fragments explicitly name only Mark and Matthew (Eus HE III 39.15-15), 1 Peter and 1 John (HE III 39.17), and Revelation (in fragment 11). Since these statements may contain an accidentally retained selection of reports, there has been intense debate over Papias' possible knowledge of other early Christian texts, especially the later canonized books. Through conclusions from isolated indications, especially with the help of the argument from silence, scholars have sought to prove that Papias knew Luke–Acts and John, as well as the Pauline Epistles or the GosHeb.

The GosHeb is referred to in HE III 39.17, though apparently not by Papias himself, but merely by Eusebius in commenting on Papias. It is erroneous to identify the text of Matthew named in HE III 39.16 with the GosHeb. In any case, Papias could have seen in GosHeb, GosEb, or GosNaz a translation of Matthew, which he believed to have been written in Hebrew. But this assumption is also doubtful.

---

[36] Campenhausen, *Entstehung*, 154.
[37] Interestingly, instead of the four gospels, the original Syriac canon used Tatian's *Diatessaron* (ca. 172 C.E.), a gospel harmony that may have used a source written by Justin (ca. 165). In this fact we can see a side piece of the place of Papias' work in canon history.

In contrast, we cannot exclude from the outset the possibility that Eusebius suppressed negative judgments by the Hierapolitan about Paul, Luke, Acts, or John. However, in the surviving fragments neither an especially anti-Marcionite[38] nor an anti-Pauline[39] tendency can be seen in Papias. We can well assume that he knew Pauline letters, but they do not appear to have played any special role for his work and his theology. Nor can an antiheretical polemic regarding John be proven for Papias. The idea that Eusebius did not pass on reports from the Hierapolitan only because they contained nothing new is thus highly improbable, since Eusebius relied heavily on reports of the early use of the homologumena (HE III 25), among which he counted not only the Pauline Epistles but also 1 John and 1 Peter, the mere use of which by Papias earns a note from him in HE III 39.17. This especially applies to the four-gospel canon (HE III 25.1). On the other hand, Iren Haer III 1.1 cannot be taken as evidence for Papias' knowledge of all four gospels, since Irenaeus does not appeal solely to Papias for his examples. Further indications for the knowledge of Luke, Acts, and John raised in discussion likewise do not withstand closer scrutiny. The use of other written sources cannot be excluded, but the extant excerpts and paraphrases give no evidence of them.

5.2 The πρεσβύτεροι

According to the proem (HE III 39.3-4), a special group that Papias calls πρεσβύτεροι takes a special place among his sources for the oral tradition. Next to the "presbyters" there is also a reference to the daughters of Philip the Evangelist as guarantors (HE III 39.8-10), which shows that the presbyter tradition was not the only oral source Papias used.

The πρεσβύτεροι apparently refers to a group of people well known in Papias' day but whose identity is admittedly disputed between Eusebius and Irenaeus. While Irenaeus imagines the circle of people in question to be students of the apostles (cf. Haer V 33.3-4, etc.), Eusebius equates the πρεσβύτεροι of Papias in HE III 39.7 with the apostles named in HE III 39.4. That is grammatically possible, but it does not withstand examination of the history of terminology. Neither the πρεσβύτεροι are interchangeable with the apostles, nor does Papias use πρεσβύτερος as merely a sign of age or the title of an office. The πρεσβύτεροι belong far more to some circle of tradents of early Christian tradition, the dignified name of which is best translated, as G. Bornkamm has suggested, as "fathers."[40] Such forms of fathers meet us in the presbyter traditions in Irenaeus, but also in Clement of Alexandria, Origen, and Hippolytus of Rome. As such an early Christian "father" one can think of the πρεσβύτερος in 2 and 3 John. Common to the circle of people in question is the belonging to the apostolic teaching

---

38 Cf. Bauer, *Rechtgläubigkeit*, 187, 189–90, 217–18.

39 So already F. C. Baur. Cf. also Nielsen, "Papias," 529–35.

40 Bornkamm, "πρέσβυς," 676–80.

succession. More often we otherwise meet the phenomenon that an outstanding teacher figure is honored simply as πρεσβύτερος. For the presbyters of Papias we can determine that they were apparently wandering teachers, as their students are also described as travelers. As such Papias' presbyters and their students belong to the broad spectrum of early Christian itinerant preachers, for whom in other contexts terms like ἀπόστολοι,[41] προφῆται,[42] or εὐαγγελισταί[43] are common.

Like Irenaeus, Justin, or Clement of Alexandria, Papias also holds up one teacher figure in particular: ὁ πρεσβύτερος (HE III 39.15), who may be identified with the presbyter John referred to in HE III 39.4. He is referred to as κυρίου μαθητής like Aristion, another guarantor of Papias (HE III 39.7, 14). Therein apparently consists the preference for both of the named persons over the other presbyters. The notation κυρίου μαθηταί can be explained most naturally by the assumption that Papias believed John and Aristion to be personal disciples of Jesus, probably because they came from Palestine. The term μαθητής is actually applied to individual Jewish Christians; though admittedly it does not have to indicate a direct discipleship. Papias could have misunderstood such a title as proof of eyewitness status, but neither John nor Aristion is known to us further. The identification of John with the son of Zebedee and the insistence on his authorship for John, the Johannine epistles, and even Revelation have no basis in the Papias fragments that withstands closer scrutiny.[44]

To the aforementioned fathers, especially Aristion and the presbyter John, Papias owes not only an important potrion of his traditions but also especially the apocalyptic-chiliastic tradition material. The chiliasm criticized by Eusebius goes back, as research on the relevant fragments shows, to the influence of the πρεσβύτεροι. Written parallels to Iren Haer V 33.3-4 appear in the realm of Jewish apocalyptic literature. Again, there are connections between Papias and the circle supposed to stand behind Revelation. One has to think with the πρεσβύτεροι as with the environment surrounding Revelation of groups to which Palestinian Christians belonged that may have moved to Asia Minor after 70 C.E. Aristion and the presbyter John may also have belonged to them.

5.3 The Selection Criteria of Papias with Regard to His Sources

Papias emphasizes in the proem of his work that to him falls the differentiation of trustworthy traditions from heretical traditions. Admittedly, neither canonicity nor apostolicity, that is, the ability to trace individual reports back to the testimony of one of the apostles equated with the Twelve, is the rule for his exegetical work. Papias knows a circle of disciples that goes beyond that of the twelve apostles, and the early church fathers legitimate themselves not only by their relationship

---

[41] Cf. Revelation 2:2, possibly also Revelation 18:20; Romans 1:1; 1 Corinthians 1:1; Acts 14:4; Galatians 1:19; Romans 16:7; Did 11.3-6.
[42] Did 13.1-7.

[43] Cf., e.g., Acts 21:8; 2 Timothy 4:5; Ephesians 4:11.
[44] Cf. on this Körtner, *Papias*, 125, 127–28.

as students of the Twelve, but also through their relationships to other personal disciples of Jesus. Papias' criterion for believable tradition and orthodox ἑρμηνείαι is the possibility of their ability to be traced to disciples of the Lord through the presbyters. Even in the case of Mark the mere appeal to the Mark–Peter tradition does not suffice, but only its attestation by a presbyter proves Mark to be a trustworthy source. As a historically contingent quantity, the presbyters clearly could not continue to function as guarantors of orthodox tradition and teaching. That is precisely why Papias composed his work, to secure the inheritance of the fathers.

6.   Theological Profile

6.1 Preliminary Remark

The recent interest in the work of Papias as limited itself, as is the case with interest in Eusebius, primarily to introductory questions. Since F. Schleiermacher's research in 1832, HE III 39.15 and HE III 39.16 stand at the center of interest. Papias' notes on Mark and Matthew served constantly as evidence for or against the apostolic authorship of Matthew and the origin of Mark from the circle around Peter, but also for the various ur-Mark and ur-Matthew theories as well as support for the modern two-source theory. Beyond these questions, the Papias fragments also play a role in the so-called Johannine question. So one sees to this day drawn from the Papias fragments not only the apostolicity of John, but also attempts to prove the authorship of John, son of Zebedee, for the Johannine letters as well as for Revelation and Papias described as the guarantor of the tradition from long years of residence with the Apostle John in Ephesus.[45]

In light of these introductory discussions, the interest in the work of Papias himself and his theology have long stood in the background. Important impulses toward Papias scholarship independent of questions about New Testament introductions have come primarily from W. Bauer,[46] whose program of a regionally differentiated theological history has been continued by H. Köster and J. M. Robinson.[47] Their study opens the perspective to evaluate the work of Papias in terms of literary and theological history within the spectrum of early Christian lines of development. In this context interest in the apocalyptic traditions in Papias has grown, since here the relationships of his thought to contemporary strains of early Christianity in Asia Minor can be most clearly grasped.[48]

In its details, the picture that we can form of the Hierapolitan's theology on the basis of the surviving reports remains sketchy of necessity. We find, for example, nothing about his Christology, his soteriology, or his teaching about

---

[45] Cf. Iren Haer III 11.1; ClemAl *Hypotyposeis* 6 (with Eus HE VI 14.7); Canon Muratori 9–34; Theoph Autol II 22.
[46] Cf. Bauer, *Rechtgläubigkeit*, 81–98, 187–91, etc.

[47] Köster/Robinson, *Entwicklungslinien, passim.*
[48] Cf., among others, de Jonge, "ΒΟΤΡΥΣ ΒΟΗΣΕΙ," 37–49; Dubois, "Remarques," 3–10.

God. At least we have rudimentary information about his eschatology and about one detail from the realm of cosmology.

6.2 Cosmology and Eschatology

Fragment 12 leads us with hints into the area of the doctrine of creation and cosmology. On Revelation 12:7 Andrew of Caesarea quotes two statements by Papias that tell of an earthly rule of the godly angels and their fall. A parallel to this quotation appears in Justin, Apology II 5. It consists of a reference to the Old Testament story of creation and to the report on the marriage of angels in Genesis 6:2-4. While, according to Justin, Christ was the first to cast out demons, Papias thinks of the stripping of power from the angels as a prehistoric event. Papias may have encountered the image of the overthrow of the angels, similarly to other church fathers, independently from Revelation 12:7. It thus belongs plainly not with the eschatology, but with the cosmology.

For the eschatology of Papias, too, the surviving material is too meager to reconstruct a complete picture of his conception. In Haer V 33.3-4 Papias assumes from the presbyter tradition a word about the fruitfulness of the millennium, the substantial meaning of which is beyond doubt. To be sure, the Millennial Reign itself is not discussed in this quotation from Papias, but we have no reason to doubt the statement of Irenaeus, according to which the statement refers to the millennium. Papias probably expected a messianic intermediate kingdom in the sense of Revelation 20:1-6. For this time a ten-thousand-fold fruitfulness is promised, of which Revelation admittedly knows nothing. This image, like that of the eschatological interregnum, has parallels in Judaism. The hope of the millennium encountered in Revelation and supported by Papias can be understood as an independent further development of a Jewish concept in a Christian context that sometimes runs parallel to the development of Jewish eschatology. What other eschatological ideas Papias may have embraced can no longer be determined.

6.3 The Work of Papias in the Spectrum of Early Christian Lines of Development

His eschatology, for which Papias relies on the presbyter tradition, shows him to be a late supporter of the apocalypticism that flourished in Asia Minor after 70 C.E. It is very likely that Papias stood in relationship to the circle in which Revelation was composed. Hierapolis, where Papias was bishop, lies on the road between Philadelphia and Laodicea, to whose churches the author of Revelation wrote two of his letters one or two decades before the composition of Papias' work. Montanism brought about a revival of the Asia Minor apocalyptic, the developmental line of which includes Papias. At the beginning people called Montanism "new prophecy"; later after its place of origin, in which Hierapolis also lies, it was called the "Phrygian heresy." Influences of the five books of Papias on this movement, which later spread to Africa, Rome, and Gaul, are not known to us. The question remains open as to whether the work of the Hierapolitan is one of the links between Revelation and the Revelator's circle at the beginning of the second century and Montanism. Since Papias wrote his work at the beginning of the second century (see below), its belonging to Montanist circles can in any case be excluded.

The chiliasm attested by Papias spread far throughout Asia Minor and found adherents in numerous varieties throughout all of church history. To be sure, Eusebius deliberately goes out of order and definitely too far when he makes Papias out to be the originator of chiliasm. In the history of apocalypticism in Asia Minor, Papias does not function as the keystone but plays rather a supporting role, at best that of a middle link.

On the basis of the identification of the presbyter John in HE III 39.4 with the son of Zebedee, as well as under the appeal to the legends of the Apostle John's long residence in Ephesus, scholars have constantly attempted to establish a special connection between Papias and the Johannine circle. However, as the examination of his sources shows, Papias appears to have known only 1 John. A special link to the Johannine circle cannot be concluded from that fact.

By contrast, many texts show evidence of the influence of Jewish Christian tradition. Apart from the Jewish Christian background of the presbyter tradition, this fact is indicated by the reports—to be classified as legendary—by Papias on Matthew and Mark. There is limitless discussion about the wording and interpretation of HE III 39.15-16. Most probable is still the understanding of HE III 39.16 in the normal meanings of the words. Papias reports as follows: Matthew— evidently meaning the apostle named in 39.4—assembled a collection of sayings of the Lord, that is, Jesus stories, in the Hebrew language that was later translated into various languages. Apparently Papias meant the later canonized Matthew, the Semitic origins of which were also assumed by Irenaeus and Origen.[49] According to this view, the Greek text of Matthew appears to be a translation, with the help of which, combined with the oral presbyter tradition, Papias believed he advanced directly to the Palestinian origins of the Jesus tradition.[50]

According to Papias, Mark also has Palestinian origins. The report in HE III 15 assumes that Peter's Greek was not (sufficiently) strong and that he therefore needed an interpreter on his missionary journeys. Consequently, in the eyes of Papias, Mark is indeed the work written in Greek of an author who was not himself an apostle or an eyewitness but rests on the Hebrew or Aramaic presentations of the Apostle Peter, so that this gospel—despite the mangled τάξις of the material—does not stand behind Matthew in terms of dignity and authority. Even though Papias' note on Mark hardly corresponds to the historical facts, it is

---

[49] Cf. Iren Haer III.1.1; Origen in Eus HE VI 25.4.
[50] A contrary opinion is held by Baum, "Urmatthäus," 257–72, who applies the statements of Papias to an actually existing Aramaic early form of Matthew that was supposedly translated targumically by the churches that spoke Greek in worship.

informative insofar as it ascribes Mark to an author who appears in 1 Peter 5:13 as a co-laborer with Peter, though in other contexts he is referred to in connection with Paul.[51] Apparently the figure of Mark, at first—though only poorly—anchored in the Pauline tradition, entered the Petrine tradition around the end of the first century. Behind 1 Peter as behind the orientation of Mark in the Petrine tradition we find groups in Asia Minor who appealed not to Paul, but to Peter as the figure with whom they identified.[52] A distinctive Petrine theology or even school is not recognizable, however. One also does not meet in the aforementioned circles any explicit anti-Paulinism. 1 Peter even shows an affinity for Paulinism. Beyond decided Paulinism, pointed Jewish Christianity, or even Johannine theology, Petrine Christianity in Asia Minor represented a theological-historical conglomerate.

7.   Opponents

The quotation from the prologue in HE III 39.3-4 shows that Papias pursues a polemical intent with his work. Apparently he has specific opponents in view when he turns against those who thresh straw (οἱ τὰ πολλὰ λέγοντες) or uphold false commandments (τὰς ἀλλοτρίας ἐντολάς). Paul or Paulinism can hardly be meant by these phrases. Gnostics are sometimes suspected as the opponents, and the chiliasm in Papias could have an anti-Gnostic direction.[53] An anti-Marcionite tendency is also suspected. Both hypotheses, however, work only with a late dating of the work. Another possibility often discussed is an anti-Montanist position, which for Papias would be directed specifically against the Johannine texts,[54] but that is clearly improbable because otherwise the so-called Alogians, who rejected both John and the Revelation that Papias treasured, would have appealed to the Hierapolitan.

Under the assumption that Papias wrote his five books around 110 C.E., we must think of other opponents. Groups that, for example, are condemned as false teachers in Revelation come into question: for one, wandering preachers not identified more specifically (Rev 2:2); for another, the adherents of the so-called teaching of Balaam (Rev 2:14); a prophetess defamed as Jezebel (Rev 2:20-24); and finally the Nicolaitans (Rev 2:6, 15), who may have carried out their mission through wandering apostles. To be sure, nothing certain about the named circle can be discovered. Whether the groups in question were Gnostics, as old church tradition would have it, can no longer be satisfactorily determined.

---

[51] Colossians 4:10; 2 Timothy 4:11; Philemon 24; Acts 12:12; etc.

[52] Cf. also the Peter party already in 1 Corinthians 1:12.

[53] Cf. Lightfoot, *Essays*, 169–70; Schwartz, "Tod," 10ff.

[54] Cf. Bauer, *Rechtgläubigkeit*, 189, 210n4.

8. Authorship

The surviving sources report that Papias was bishop of the Christian community in the Phrygian town of Hierapolis. We know nothing more about his origins, but his name points to Phrygia or to the neighboring provinces Caria, Isauria, and Lycaonia. According to inscriptions many men in these areas had names derived from familiar forms ἄπα, ἄπτα, ἄπφα, or τάτα.[55] The name Παπίας (written in fragment 2 and some manuscripts of fragments 11 and 12: Παππίας) appears often in inscriptions from Hierapolis. Papias could thus have been born in Hierapolis, but the dates of his life and more particulars about his biography are not known to us. Corresponding conjectures belong to the realm of speculation.

Irenaeus describes Papias as Polycarp's ἑταῖρος and as ἀρχαῖος ἀνήρ (Haer V 33.4). Both phrases are admittedly far too indeterminate to establish a more exact historical classification for Papias. Further, Irenaeus holds the Hierapolitan to be a student of the Apostle John. The evaluation of this report hangs on the interpretation of the proem passed on by Eusebius, in which the name John is used twice. The core question is whether the πρεσβύτερος Ἰωάννης is identical with the apostle of the same name or not. The latter is the interpretation that Eusebius already supports in HE III 39.5-7. Even though Eusebius' interpretation is not convincing in every detail, his grammatical argument is still valid, according to which Papias speaks of Aristion and the presbyter John in a new part of the sentence from that in which he earlier spoke of the category of apostles. Actually Papias not only refers to the name John twice but parallel to those references portrays two groups of the Lord's disciples who are distinguished not only by a change of tense but also by the fact that Papias uses the definite article for one (οἱ τοῦ κυρίου μαθηταί) and not for the other (τοῦ κυρίου μαθηταί). Papias was therefore not a student of the apostles, but rather a man of the third Christian generation and certainly a student of one or more πρεσβύτεροι who are not identical with the apostles. However, more precise details about this discipleship cannot be determined from the surviving fragments.

9. Place of Writing

Hierapolis, the modern Pamukkale, lies in the Lycus Valley, a river that neighbors the Meander.[56] Some ten kilometers south of Hierapolis one reached Laodicea in Papias' day; some twenty kilometers southeast was Colosse. Hierapolis was an especially important city during the Attalid period and in antiquity was famous as much for its thermal springs as for a cave containing carbonite. Among

---

[55] Details in Lightfoot, *Essays*, 153; Hatch, "Papias," 83.

[56] On Hierapolis cf. Humann et al., *Altertümer*, *passim*; Ramsay, *Cities*, 84–121; Jones, *Cities*, 54–55, 73–74.

others, the town possessed great regional influence because of its wool production through both the Roman and the Byzantine periods. The residents mostly
spoke Greek. Aside from some Roman citizens, the city also contained numerous
Jews whose relocation went back to the time of Antiochus III. The city's best-
known son is Epictetus.

Hierapolis was the city of Cybele and thus a center for Phrygian mystery
cults. Apparently, however, an Apollo Archegetes cult suppressed that of Cybele
in the second half of the first century C.E. Archaeologically, little is known about
the beginnings of Christianity there. The existence of Christians in Hierapolis is
first referred to in Colossians 4:13. In the sixth century the city was elevated to an
independent metropolitan and thereby reached its high point in church history.

10. Dating

The most certain *terminus ad quem* for the five books of Papias is Irenaeus'
text *Adversus haereses*, which is dated to around 180 and uses the work of the Hierapolitan. The reports in Irenaeus admittedly do not allow an exact conclusion
about the age of the text. With various arguments, most of which are strongly
hypothetical, scholars have tried to date the work of Papias between 80 and 160.
The majority of scholarship points to the date of writing as 125/130.[57]

Clues toward the date come primarily from three fragments: Philippus Sidetes reports in fragment 10 that Papias tells of people raised from the dead who
lived into the time of Hadrian (117–138). This report places the date around 125.
The Sidetes fragment is admittedly heavily dependent on Eus HE III 39 on the
one hand and on the other proves to be historically unreliable on the question of
the death of the sons of Zebedee. The information that Papias wrote about people
raised from the dead in the reign of Hadrian probably rests on a confusion of the
Hierapolitan with Quadratus (cf. Eus HE IV 3.2). The Sidetes fragment thus
offers no convincing basis for the dating of Papias' work.

By contrast, little attention has been paid to Eusebius' note in Liber Chro-
nicorum II (frag. 2), according to which Papias and Polycarp became acquainted
after the death of the Apostle John, who lived until the time of Trajan. Eusebius
makes this notation for the year 2114 after Abraham, the year 100 C.E. Granted,
this statement could have been influenced by Iren Haer V 33.4, but Eusebius held
fast to the early dating for the work of Papias, even when he took it upon himself
to dispute his apostolic discipleship. In HE III 36.1-2 Eusebius reports that in
the reign of Trajan Polycarp worked beside not only Papias, but also Ignatius of
Antioch. This note is largely not observed and is passed over in older editions of
the Papias fragments. But since Ignatius probably suffered martyrdom around

---

[57] For a discussion of the various suggested dates,
see in detail Körtner, *Papias*, 88–94, 225–26.

110 C.E., Eusebius' statements lead to the conclusion that Papias' work was written around 110. Also in favor of this suggested date are observations regarding the structure of Eusebius' *Ecclesiastical History*, namely that Eusebius never goes beyond the time of Trajan in HE III.[58] Besides, the dating of the five books of Papias fits with the image of the content, genre, and theological-historical place of the author that arise from the fragments.

11. Bibliography

Altaner, B., and A. Stuiber. *Patrologie: Leben, Schriften und Lehre der Kirchenväter.* Special ed. Freiburg 1993.

Balthasar, H. U. von. *Kosmische Liturgie: Das Weltbild Maximus' des Bekenners.* Einsiedeln ²1961.

Bartlet, V. "Papias's 'Exposition': Its Date and Contents." In *Amicitiae Corolla* (FS James Rendel Harris), edited by Herbert G. Wood, 15–44. London 1933.

Bauer, W. *Rechtgläubigkeit und Ketzerei im ältesten Christentum.* Edited by G. Strecker. BHT 10. Tübingen ²1964.

Baum, A. D. "Ein aramäischer Urmatthäus im kleinasiatischen Gottesdienst: Das Papiaszeugnis zur Entstehung des Matthäusevangeliums." *ZNW* 92 (2001): 257–72.

———. "Papias als Kommentator evangelischer Aussprüche Jesu: Erwägungen zur Art seines Werkes." *NT* 38 (1996): 257–76.

Bickell, G. "Ein Papiashandschrift in Tirol." *ZKT* 3 (1897): 799–803.

Bornkamm, G. "πρέσβυς, πρεσβύτερος κτλ." *ThWNT* VI:651–83. Stuttgart 1965.

Bruyne, D. de. "Les plus anciens prologues latins des Evangiles." *RBen* 40 (1928): 193–214.

Campenhausen, H. von. *Die Entstehung der christlichen Bibel.* BHT 39. Tübingen 1968.

Chapman, J. *John the Presbyter and the Fourth Gospel.* Oxford 1911.

de Jonge, H. J. "*ΒΟΤΡΥΣ ΒΟΗΣΕΙ*: The Age of Kronos and the Millennium in Papias of Hierapolis." In *Studies in Hellenistic Religions*, edited by M. J. Vermaseren, 37–49. EPRO 78. Leiden 1979.

Donaldson, J. *The Apostolic Fathers: A Critical Account of Their Genuine Writings and of Their Doctrines.* London 1874.

Dubois, J.-D. "Remarques sur le fragment de Papias cité par Irénée." *RHPhR* 71 (1991): 3–10.

Funk, F.-X., and K. Bihlmeyer. *Die Apostolischen Väter I: Mit einem Nachtrag von Wilhelm Schneemelcher.* SAQ II.1.1. Tübingen ²1956.

Goetz, G. "Papias von Hierapolis oder der Glottograph?" *ZNW* 27 (1928): 348.

Günther, M. *Die Frühgeschichte des Christentums in Ephesus.* ARGU 1. Frankfurt/Main ²1998.

———. *Einleitung in die Apostolischen Väter.* ARGU 4. Frankfurt/Main 1997.

---

[58] On the consequences for the dating of the work of Papias cf. also Bartlet, "Exposition," 22.

Harnack, A. von. "Die ältesten Evangelien-Prologe und die Bildung des Neuen Testaments." *SPAW.PH* XXIV: 322–41. Berlin 1928.

———. *Geschichte der altchristlichen Litteratur bis Eusebius.* Vol. II.1. Leipzig ²1958.

Harris, J. R. *Testimonies* I–II. Cambridge 1916/1920.

Hatch, W. H. P. "Über den Namen Papias." *ZNW* 12 (1911): 83.

Hawkins, J. C. *Horae synopticae.* Oxford 1897.

Heard, R. (A) "The ΑΠΟΜΝΗΜΟΝΕΥΜΑΤΑ in Papias, Justin, and Irenaeus." (B) "Papias' Quotations from the New Testament." *NTS* 1 (1954–1955): 122–29, 130–34.

Hilgenfeld, A. "Papias von Hierapolis." *ZWT* 18 (1875): 231–70.

Humann, C., C. Chicorius, W. Judeich, and F. Winter. *Altertümer von Hierapolis.* Berlin 1898.

Jones, A. H. M. *The Cities of the Eastern Roman Provinces.* Oxford ²1971.

Karpp, H. "*Viva vox.*" In *Mullus* (FS Theodor Klauser), edited by A. Stuiber et al., 190–98. JAC.E1. Münster 1964.

Körtner, U. H. J. "Papiasfragmente." In *Papiasfragmente, Hirt des Hermas* by U. H. J. Körtner and M. Leutzsch, 1–103. SUC III. Darmstadt 1998.

———. *Papias von Hierapolis: Ein Beitrag zur Geschichte des frühen Christentums.* FRLANT 133. Göttingen 1983

Köster, H., and J. M. Robinson. *Entwicklungslinien durch die Welt des frühen Christentums.* Tübingen 1971.

Kürzinger, J. "Das Papieaszeugnis und die Erstgestalt des Matthäusevangeliums." *BZ.NF* 4 (1960): 19–38.

———. "Die Aussage des Papias von Hierapolis zur literarischen Form des Markusevangeliums." *BZ.NF* 21 (1977): 245–64.

———. *Papias von Hierapolis und die Evangelien des Neuen Testaments.* Eichstätter Materialen 4, Abt. Philosophie u. Theologie. Regensburg 1983.

———. "Papias von Hierapolis: Zu Titel und Art seines Werkes." *BZ.NF* 23 (1979): 172–86.

Lightfoot, J. B. *Essays on the Work Entitled Supernatural Religion.* London 1889.

Lindemann, A., and H. Paulsen, eds. *Die Apostolischen Väter: Griechisch-deutsche Parallelausgabe auf der Grundlage der Ausgaben von Franz Xaver Funk, Karl Bihlmeyer und Molly Whittaker.* Tübingen 1992.

Loofs, F. *Theophilus von Antiochien adversus Marionem und die anderen theologischen Quellen bei Irenäus.* TU 46.2. Leipzig 1930.

Lührmann, D. "Die Geschichte von der Sünderin und andere apokryphe Jesusüberlieferungen bei Didymos von Alexandrien." *NT* 32 (1990): 289–316.

Nestle, E. "Die Fünfteilung im Werk des Papias und im ersten Evangelium." *ZNW* 1 (1900): 252–54.

Nielsen, C. M. "Papias: Polemicist against Whom?" *TS* 1974:529–35.

Nolte, J. H. "Ein Exzerpt aus dem zum größten Teil noch ungedruckten Chronicon des Georgius Hamarolus." *ThQ* 44 (1862): 464–68.

Oberweis, M. "Das Papias-Zeugnis vom Tode des Johannes Zebedäi." *NT* 38 (1996): 277–95.

Overbeck, F. "Ueber zwei neue Ansichten von Zeugnissen des Papias für die Apostelgeschichte und das vierte Evangelium." *ZWT* 10 (1867): 35–74.

Ramsay, W. M. *The Cities and Bishoprics of Phrygia* I. Oxford 1895.

Schleiermacher, F. "Ueber die Zeugnisse des Papias von unsern beiden ersten Evangelien." *TSK* 1832:735–68. Now in *Saemmtliche Werke* I/2, 361–92. Berlin 1836.

Schmid, W., and O. Stählin, eds. *Wilhelm von Christs Geschichte der Griechischen Literatur* II/1. Reprinted 1954.

Schwartz, E. *Ueber den Tod der Sohne Zebedaei: Ein Beitrag zur Geschichte des Johannesevangeliums.* 1904. Reprinted Nendeln/Göttingen 1970.

Siegert, F. "Unbeachtete Papiaszitate bei armenischen Schriftstellern." *NTS* 27 (1981): 605–14.

Steitz, G. E. "Des Papias von Hierapolis 'Auslegung der Reden des Herrn' nach ihren Quellen und ihrem mutmaßlichen Charakter." *TSK* 41 (1868): 63–95.

Sykutris, J. "Ein neues Papiaszitat." *ZNW* 26 (1927): 210–12.

Vielhauer, P. *Geschichte der urchristlichen Literatur: Einleitung in das Neue Testament, die Apokryphen und die Apostolischen Väter.* Berlin 1975.

Zahn, T. *Forschungen zur Geschichte des neutestamentlichen Kanons und der altkirchlichen Literatur* VI. Leipzig 1900.

Zyro, F. F. *Neue Beleuchtung der Papiasstelle in der Kirchengeschichte des Eusebius III, 39.* Darmstadt 1869.

Quadratus

Wilhelm Pratscher

The shortest fragment of an apology from early Christianity comes from Quadratus. Its importance arises solely from its age.

1. Textual Tradition and Authorship

1.1 Textual Tradition

The fragment of the apology is attested only in Eusebius, HE IV 3.2. The text reads:

> But the works of our Saviour were always present, for they were genuine:—those that were healed and those that were raised from the dead, who were seen not only when they were healed and when they were raised, but were also always present; and not merely while the Saviour was on earth, but also after his death, they were alive for quite a while, so that some of them lived even to our day.[1]

In the introduction to the quotation, Eusebius speaks of the dedication and transmission of the apology to the emperor Hadrian. The reason for the writing supposedly arose from the pestering of Christians by certain evil people. Moreover, the text offers shining evidence of the spiritual potency and the apostolic orthodoxy of the author. The text is also still in current use in Eusebius' day (HE IV 3.1).[2] In conclusion (HE IV 3.2) Eusebius refers again to the apology, likewise addressed to Hadrian and still extant, of the equally orthodox Aristides.

---

[1] τοῦ δὲ σωτῆρος ἡμῶν τὰ ἔργα ἀεὶ παρῆν ἀληθῆ γὰρ ἦν, οἱ θεραπευθέντες, οἱ ἀναστάντες ἐκ νεκρῶν, οἳ οὐκ ὤφθησαν μόνον θεραπευόμενοι καὶ ἀνιστάμενοι, ἀλλὰ καὶ ἀεὶ παρόντες, οὐδὲ ἐπιδημοῦντος μόνον τοῦ σωτῆρος, ἀλλὰ καὶ ἀπαλλαγέντος ἦσαν ἐπὶ χρόνον ἱκανόν, ὥστε καὶ εἰς τοὺς ἡμετέρους χρόνους τινὲς αὐτῶν ἀφίκοντο, (GCS Eus II 1: 302, 304). The textual tradition of this portion of Eusebius is unproblematic. Whether Eusebius also exactly reproduced the fragment must admittedly remain uncertain but can be safely assumed. A knowledge of Quadratus by Papias is assumed by Harnack, *Chronologie*, 270–71: Papias reports (Philip of Side, HE = Fragment 10 in Körtner,

Papias, 62) that people whom Jesus raised from the dead lived until the time of Hadrian. That recalls the statement of Quadratus that such people lived until his (Quadratus') day. The idea that this mention leads to the conclusion that Papias actually knew Quadratus is more than questionable. Likewise, the opinion of Zahn, *Forschungen*, 110–11, that Papias spoke only of the long lifetimes of the people raised from the dead and the reference to Hadrian comes from Philip of Side, is pure conjecture. [English quotations from HE taken from Schaff/Wace unless otherwise noted.]

[2] Conclusions about the actual dispersal of the text are difficult to draw from this statement. In any case, no independent manuscript has survived.

In the *Chronicle* handed down in Armenian, Eusebius remarks after the chronological report (*Ad Ann Abr* 2141; parallel notation: ninth year of Hadrian): "Kodratos, hearer of the Apostles, and Aristides, philosopher from our movement, the Athenian, addressed to Hadrian petitions to account for the 'religion' statutes."[3] Apart from the chronological statement we find nothing new about what is said in HE IV 3.1-3. The question is whether we know anything more detailed about Quadratus. After all, the name comes up frequently.

1.2 Authorship

In two places Eusebius refers to a *prophet* Quadratus: in HE III 36 he refers to the apostolic disciple Polycarp and his contemporaries Papias and Ignatius (with sometimes detailed quotations). This passage concludes in III 37.1 with the note that among other outstanding men who lived at that time was Quadratus, who was remarkable for having the gift of prophecy just like the daughters of Philip. At the same time yet others made a name for themselves who took the first place in the succession of the apostles and who worked as shepherds (bishops?) or evangelists (missionaries) (HE III 37.4). Quadratus is thus understood here as an outstanding member of the first postapostolic generation.

Eusebius refers to the prophet Quadratus a further time in HE V 17.2-4. He quotes from an anonymous anti-Montanist work: Among the prophets of the new covenant were a certain Amnia and Quadratus (2). The Montanists would appeal unjustly to Agabus, Judas, Silas, the daughters of Philip, Amnia of Philadelphia, Quadratus, or anyone else (3), and another special reference is made to Quadratus and Amnia (4).

Finally, Eusebius refers (HE IV 23.3) to a *bishop* Quadratus. The Corinthian bishop Dionysius (ca. 170) reminisces in a letter to the church of Athens about their bishop Quadratus, who after the martyrdom of Publius gathered the fellowship again and led them to new zeal for the faith.

The question remains as to whether and what identifications can be made between the apologist, the prophet, and the bishop Quadratus. Jerome writes to the rhetor Magnus (Ep 70.4) that the disciple of the apostles and Athenian bishop Quadratus wrote a treatise defending our religion to the prince Hadrian as he was initiated into the Eleusinian mysteries and that Hadrian was so impressed that he ended the persecution.[4] He knows yet more extensively to report in Vir ill 19 that after the martyrdom of the Athenian bishop Publius, the apostles' disciple Quadratus was appointed to his place and gathered again the congregation scattered by the persecution by virtue of his zeal for the faith. When Hadrian spent the winter in Athens and was to be initiated in the Eleusinian mysteries as well as

---

3 From the translation by Karst, GCS Eus V, 220.

4 Quadratus, apostolorum discipulus et Atheniensis ecclesiae pontifex, none Adriano principi Eleusinae sacra inuisenti librum pro nostra religione tradidit et tantae admirationi omnium fuit, ut persecutionem grauissimam illius excellens sedaret ingenium? (CSEL 54, 704–5).

nearly all the holy traditions of Greece, Quadratus took the opportunity to write him a book defending the Christian religion that was overall usefull, full of the Spirit and of faith and worthy of the apostolic teaching. In it he—proving his great age—said that he had himself seen people who had been healed and raised from the dead by the Lord.[5] In the *Chronicle* (226th Olympiad, Hadrian IX[6]) he reports that the apostolic disciple Quadratus and the Athenian philosopher Aristides had sent Hadrian apologies. He does not make an identification with the bishop Quadratus here, but he does refer to the fact that Hadrian concluded from the apologies that only criminal acts were to be punished.

The identification between the apologist and the bishop[7] is usually questioned,[8] if not rejected outright.[9] Jerome here combines the reports by Eusebius without considering the problems thus caused for the timeline. If Quadratus still knew a great number of those who belonged to the first generation of Christians, his birthdate must be set around the middle of the first century. By the time of the writing of the apology in the 120s, he would already have been an old man. The Athenian bishop, however, cannot have worked before the middle of the second century. One can thus safely exclude the identification on chronological grounds.

The situation is different with the question of the identification of the apologist with the prophet Quadratus. To be sure, Eusebius nowhere states that the two are identical. But the relative nearness of the references (apologist: HE IV 3.1-3; prophet: III 37.1) speaks in favor of the connection,[10] as does the fact that Eusebius never indicates that these references deal with two people with the same name.[11] There is no chronological problem with this identification. It is true that the combination with the daughters of Philip (HE III 37.1) and the inclusion in the series of prophets begun by Agabus, Judas, and Silas through the daughters of Philip and Amnia of Philadelphia does not give an exact chronological ordering, but it is

---

[5] Quadratus, apostolorum discipulus, Publio, Athenarum episcopo, ob Christi fidem martyrio coronato, in locum eius substituitur et ecclesiam grandi terrore dispersam fide et industria sua congregat. Cumque Hadrianus Athenis exegisset hiemem, inuisens Eleusinam et omnibus paene Graeciae sacris initiatus dedisset occasionem his qui Chrisitanos oderant absque praecepto imperatoris vexare credentes, porrexit ei librum pro religione nostra compositum, valde utilem plenumque rationis et fide et apostolica doctrina dignum. In quo, et antiquitatem suae aetatis ostendens, ait plurimos a se visos qui sub Domino variis in Iudaea oppressi calamitatibus sanati fuerant, et qui a mortuis resurrexerant. (TU 14.1, 19–20).

[6] GCS Eusebius [3]VII, 199.

[7] So, e.g., Zedler, "Quadratus," 25; Dorner, *Entwicklungsgeschichte*, 177; Roberts/Donaldson, *Fathers*, 749; Andriessen, "Kodratos," 366; Marrou, *Diognète*, 257n1; n.n., "Quadratus," 1354.

[8] Barnard, "Apologetik," 383; Ehrman, *Fathers*, 89.

[9] So already Harnack, *Überlieferung*, 102–3; Zahn, "Apologet," 284; Bardenhewer, "Quadratus," 646; more recently: Bardy, "Quadratus," 81; Grégoire/Orgels, "Date," 36; Quasten, *Patrology* I, 191; Altaner/Stuiber, *Patrologie*, 61; Lindemann/Paulsen, *Väter*, 287; Prostmeier, "Quadratus," 1852. For the older literature cf. already Otto, "Quadratus," 337.

[10] So already Otto, "Quadratus," 333–34; Zahn, "Apologet," 283, contra Harnack, *Überlieferung*, 102n10 (in *Chronologie*, 271, Harnack leaves the question open); in more recent times: Kraft, *Eusebius: Kirchengeschichte*, 196n3; Fischer, *Väter*, 269; Lindemann/Paulsen, *Väter*, 286.

[11] Admittedly, the same applies to the reference to the bishop Quadratus in HE IV 23.3, but in this case the aforementioned chronological problem remains.

chronologically conceivable. In HE IV 3.1-3 Eusebius does not explicitly call the apologist Quadratus a student of the apostles, but he does emphasize his great age and praises his being anchored in the apostolic tradition. In HE III 37.1 he states after the reference to Quadratus and the daughters of Philip that at the same time several others made a name for themselves who took the first place in the apostolic succession. Thus, in both places the apostolic categorization of Quadratus is maintained. An identification can be assumed with the greatest probability.

The following facts about the person of Quadratus are thus important: He belonged to the first postapostolic generation and appears to have been a prophet and apologetic writer whom Eusebius praises for his intelligence (διάνοια, HE IV 3.1). Whether he belonged to the circle of shepherds (bishops) or evangelists can be considered on the basis of Eus HE III 37.4.[12] After the reference to Quadratus and the daughters of Philip in HE III 37.1-3, Eusebius speaks very generally of the missionary and church-organizational work of the disciples of the apostles. He concludes in 37.4 by saying that, with regard to the great number of those who were active as shepherds or evangelists, listing them all by name would be impossible. He therefore limits himself to naming those whose apostolic teachings were handed down in texts to his own day.[13]

An unusual thesis appeared in a series of publications in the mid-twentieth century, supported primarily by P. Andriessen.[14] According to this view, the apology of Quadratus is identical with the letter to Diognetus. Dorner had already believed in the mid-nineteenth century[15] that Quadratus could be thought of as the author of the letter to Diognetus. Andriessen suspects that the Quadratus should be placed in the existing gap between Diogn 7.6 and 7.7. The thesis has occasionally been called an interesting supposition[16] with noteworthy arguments,[17] but on the whole it is so hypothetical that it could not survive.[18] The

---

12 Zahn, *Forschungen*, 44n2.

13 Quadratus is named only minimally in the later literature, which does not give us more information about the person or his work (cf. below under "Theological Meaning"). It is self-evident that Quadratus had nothing to do with the bishop Quadratus of Utica, who was martyred in 259. The fact that there are many combinations in the later menaea, menologia, and martyrologies (cf. on this Harnack, *Überlieferung*, 105–6; Zahn, *Forschungen*, 43n2) is understandable, but the statements have no value for reconstructing the life and work of the apologist and prophet Quadratus.

14 Andriessen, "Apologie," 5–39, 125–49, 237–60; idem, "Authorship," 129–36; idem, "Epilogue," 121–56; idem, "Quadratus," 44–54; idem, "Prophète," 140–50; idem, "Kodratos," 336. Cf. Ruiz Bueno, "Padres," 820–44.

15 Dorner, *Entwicklungsgeschichte*, 178n32. The

reason Dorner sees in a remark in the *Martyrologium* of the Venerable Bede (see below on this) that after Quadratus no intellectual and humanist food was turned away by the Christians; the same draws on Diogn 4. In the same place he also points to the philosophical and rhetorical training as well as his universal orientation and his ethics, which would all fit with Quadratus. Conclusion: "One could thus think of Quadratus as the author."

16 Jefford/Harder/Amezaga, *Fathers*, 161.

17 Altaner/Stuiber, *Patrologie*, 62.

18 Cf., to name only a few, Peterson, "Quadrato," 363: "non esce dal campo delle ipotesi"; Andresen, "Quadratus," 728: "has no reason"; Marrou, *Diognète*, 257n3: "ne peuvent convaincre"; Grant, "Quadratus," 178: "highly improbable"; Barnard, "Epistle," 136: "goes beyond the evidence"; idem, "Apologetik," 375: "pure speculation"; Foster, "Quadratus," 60: "speculative proposal."

missing direct link between 7.6 and 7 speaks against it in the first place.[19] Without knowledge of the Quadratus fragment one would be hard-pressed to come to the idea that any such text has gone missing from the letter to Diognetus at all, since we do not know the length of the lost text and, stylistic aspects aside, the shortness of the Quadratus fragment could not be shown to its best advantage. Secondly, the fact that the addressee is given as Diognetus is problematic. Hadrian did not call himself Διόγνητος (= Zeus-born), but rather "Imperator Caesar Traianus Hadrianus Augustus."[20] Nor does Eusebius say anything about such an unusual way of speaking to Hadrian in the apology of Quadratus. Third but not least, the presumed late date of the letter to Diognetus[21] does not fit with an apology addressed to Hadrian.

2.   Occasion, Audience, Genre

Understandably, the question of what circumstances surrounded the origin of this text cannot be answered with certainty from the short fragment in Eus HE IV 3.2. The emphasis on the reality and believability of the miracles of Jesus could point to very different contexts. However, when the fragment is taken together with the context of IV 3.1-3, important discoveries are still possible.

2.1 Occasion

The occasion for the writing and sending of a text to Emperor Hadrian lies, according to HE IV 3.1, in the circumstance that "certain wicked men had attempted to trouble the Christians" (ὅτι δή τινες πονηροὶ ἄνδρες τοὺς ἡμετέρους ἐνοχλεῖν ἐπειρῶντο). It is rather improbable that Eusebius relies on a phrase in Quadratus for this description of the occasion.[22] What he (or if necessary Quadratus) has more specifically in mind can be only vaguely described. Fischer thinks of Christians being pestered by pagan circles, especially provincial officials.[23] An appeal to the emperor makes sense only if one can expect him to use his influence as a result. Such a case is surely far less likely to be denigration by private citizens than squabbles with the authorities. Intervention in the latter is clearly demanded since the correspondence between Pliny the Younger and Trajan (Plin Ep X 96–97) about reports[24] and accuracy in the avowal of Christians. The matter must thus

---

19 The theme of the Quadratus fragment fits only directly with the letter to Diognetus (cf. Grant, "Future," 114): In the previous context the discussion deals with the sending of Jesus, i.e., the second coming, in the following with the value of steadfastness in persecution as evidence of his presence. The discussion of Jesus' miracles could thus indeed find a place thematically, but one would also have to postulate a further connection that is not directly shown in any case.

20 Eck, "Hadrianus," 60.

21 Lona, *Diognet*, 68–69.

22 The verb ἐνοχλεῖν and related nouns appear often in debates in Eusebius (HE IV 13.6, VII 13, IX 1.5, etc.); cf. Grant, "Quadratus," 178.

23 Fischer, *Väter*, 270.

24 Anonymous reports will not be considered (Plin Ep X 97).

have been forms of action against Christians that did not conform to the law and that the emperor was willing and able to stop.

In this context belongs a rescript by Hadrian to the proconsul of the province of Asia, Minucius Fundanus,[25] that Justin, Apol I 68 (and dependent thereon Eus HE IV 9.1-3) hands down. In it, Hadrian requires minute investigation of complaints. A judgment must be realized in conformity with the law. Slanderers are to be punished. Here an action analogous to that of Trajan is demanded: Christans are not to be sought out and are to be judged only because of illegal behavior, not solely because of their confession in itself.[26] Whether the exact phrasing is preserved here is questionable,[27] but Hadrian still appears in this case to have maintained the precedent set by Trajan. The goal of writing the apology is thus to refute the political and social reservations against Christians.

2.2 Audience

Eus HE IV 3.1 gives the addressee of the apology as Aelius Hadrian. To him Quadratus dedicated and sent an apology for the Christian faith (λόγον προσφωνήσας ἀναδίδωσιν, ἀπολογίαν συντάξας ὑπὲρ τῆς καθ᾽ ἡμᾶς θεοσεβείας). There follows in 3.3 a note that Aristides also left behind an apology dedicated to Hadrian (ἀπολογίαν ἐπιφωνήσας Ἀδριανῷ καταλέλοιπεν). But Aristides—according to the Syriac translation—sent his apology to Antoninus Pius.[28] If that is correct, then Eusebius erred in this classification of the apology of Aristides. That does not mean, however, that Quadratus' apology was also addressed to Antoninus Pius.[29] In 3.2 he presumes to have possession of the latter; by contrast, he does not give evidence of owning the apology of Aristides. There is thus no reason to doubt the statement of Eusebius in this regard.

The dedication and report of the sending to Hadrian still does not necessarily require that the text actually made it into the ruler's hands, never mind that he read it and reflected on its arguments.[30] It is certainly not impossible, however, and given Hadrian's interest in religion, there is a very good chance that he did read it. By contrast, the idea that he was deeply influenced by it and therefore stopped the persecution, as Jer Ep 70.4 (see above) reports, is plainly pious exaggeration. Eusebius reports nothing of the kind.

---

25 An assumption of the rescript of Hadrian is the inquiry that the predecessor of Minucius Fudanus, Licinius Serenius Granianus (proconsul 123–124 C.E.), sent to Hadrian regarding the handling of complaints against Christians.

26 Cf. Birley, *Hadrian*, 127.

27 In the case of a complaint, however, a refusal of the alleged victim is illegal.

28 Harris, *Aristides*, 10ff.

29 Contra Harris, *Aristides*, *loc. cit.* Cf. already Görres, "Quadratus," 355; Bardenhewer, "Quadratus," 646–47.

30 Lietzmann, *Geschichte*, 17,5 holds it to be "more than questionable" that any of the apologetic pamphlets ever came before the emperor's eyes.

2.3 Genre

The traditional classification as an apology is accordingly correct, even though that cannot be concluded from the fragment itself but only appears in Eusebius' remarks. In addition, the description as the oldest,[31] or more accurately the oldest known,[32] apology can also be retained. Whether Quadratus was in fact the first to write an apology, however, must remain uncertain in the absence of more precise reports. Perhaps one could cautiously understand him as a representative of the first generation of apologists.[33]

3. Dating

Eusebius speaks of the sending of the apology to Hadrian in HE IV 3.1 without mentioning the date. He gives a more accurate report in the *Chronicle* (GCS. Eusebius V 220). In the frame of the 226th Olympiad he tells of the sending of the apologies of Quadratus and Aristides in the 2141st year of Abraham and the ninth year of Hadrian. With Hadrian's reign beginning in 117, this report would correspond roughly to the year 125.[34] Taken strictly that would mean that both apologies were sent in the seame year. Thus Jerome maintains the same thing in Vir ill 20 ("eodem tempore quo et Quadratus Hadriano prinicpi dedit"), but in Ep 70.4 he offers no such time association. If the apology of Aristides actually, as it appears, was sent to Antoninus Pius, at least the chronological connection of both apologies cannot be maintained. The report about the transmission of the apology of Quadratus is not disturbed by this fact, however. An earlier dating to the year 123/124 (on the assumption of Asia Minor as the destination)[35] does not recommend itself. It has at least no direct documentary support behind it. The same goes for the suggestion of a dating to 128/129[36] or 129/130.[37]

Admittedly, the report in Eusebius' *Chronicle* is not undoubtedly certain.[38] He also notes in the same place the letter of Licinius Serenus Graianus to Hadrian and Hadrian's reply to Licinius' successor Minucius Fundanus. These documents

---

[31] Cf., to name a few, Görres, "Quadratus," 354; Bardenhewer, *Geschichte*, 183; Bihlmeyer, *Väter*, XLVI; Barnard, "Apologetik," 375; Voss, "Quadratus," 1284.

[32] Cf., to name a few, Lebreton, "Apologétique," 423; Soden, "Quadratus," 1661; Stark, "Quadratus," 753; Prostmeier, "Quadratus," 1852; Drobner, *Fathers*, 73.

[33] So Foster, "Quadratus," 59.

[34] Seen as a possibility by Hilgenfeld, "Überlieferung," 1; Harnack, *Überlieferung*, 95; Scheel, "Quadratus," 1997; Lother, *Geschichte*, 98; Bardy, "Apologetik," 539; Marrou, *Diognète*, 257; Barnard, "Apologetik," 375; Goodspeed, *Apologeten*, 1; Ehrman, *Fathers*, 89.

[35] So at most, at least as an alternative, cf., to name a few: Bardenhewer, *Geschichte*,184; Bihlmeyer, *Väter*, XLVII; Andresen, "Quadratus," 727; Quasten, *Patrology*, 191; Lindemann/Paulsen, *Väter*, 286; Prostmeier, "Quadratus," 1851; Drobner, *Fathers*, 73.

[36] Goodspeed, *Apologeten*, 1; Prostmeier, "Quadratus," 1851; Drobner, *Fathers*, 73 (with a view to Athens) and Andresen, "Quadratus," 727; Bihlmeyer, *Väter*, XLVII; Altaner/Stuiber, *Patrologie*, 61; Lindemann/Paulsen, *Väter*, 286; Drobner, *Fathers*, 73 (with a view to Asia Minor).

[37] Harnack, *Überlieferung*, 95.

[38] Fischer, *Väter*, 269.

cannot be dated exactly, but they may both have originated before 125/126. That still does not appear to touch the correctness of the report on the composition of the apology. Eusebius only connects the two here and thus can show a great success for both of the named apologies. Looking back two centuries later, that idea may be understandable. In my opinion, the most probable solution remains the composition and transmission of the apology in the year 125/126 C.E.[39]

4. Place of Writing

This conclusion also brings us closer to a solution to the question of the place. Should the aforementioned date be correct, the determination of the place automatically appears at once, or at least with greater probability than that of the time of writing—that is, if by place we mean only the place of transmission, since the place of origin is not necessarily identical.

At the time in question, circa 125 C.E., Hadrian was in Athens. After his initiation in the Eleusinian mysteries in 124, he spent the following winter (124–125) in this city.[40] Even if one follows the older chronological detail, namely placing Hadrian's stay in Athens in 125–126,[41] this localization does not change. Should the report in the *Chronicle* of Eusebius be false, Athens would still be a possible place of transmission, namely in 128–129 or 131–132.[42]

What cannot serve as a point in favor of Athens, however, is the connection of the apology of Quadratus with that of the Athenian Aristides (so Eusebius, see above), as Jerome tries to make it do in Ep 70.4, and especially not Jerome's identification of the apologist with the Athenian bishop Quadratus (Ep 70.4; Vir ill 19).[43] However, the rejection of this argument in no way requires the rejection of Athens as the probable destination of the apology.

Asia Minor is often assumed as the possible home of Quadratus and destination of his apology.[44] If the apologist and the prophet Quadratus are identical,

---

[39] Foster, "Quadratus," 55, also suggests on the basis of Eus HE IV (end of the reign of Trajan and beginning of the reign of Hadrian) a date between 117 and 120. He believes this date range to be just as likely as that of 124/125. But the latter has an explicit reference by Eusebius behind it that would have to be proven to be arbitrary, while the former only presents a supposition.

[40] Kienast, *Kaisertabelle*, 128.

[41] Dürr, *Reisen*, 43 (as a further alternative even 126–27); Rohden, *Hadrianus*, 507.

[42] Kienast, *Kaisertabelle*, 129.

[43] Against this already Zahn, *Forschungen*, 71n2: this argument is "a pure swindle." Foster, "Quadratus," 56, points to the fact that Jerome assumes the following sequence of events: installation in the bishopric—writing and sending of the apology. But

that would date the apology to the second half of the second century, which is not Jerome's intent. Vir ill 19 does not follow a linear chronological report but speaks first of the installation in the Athenian bishopric and then looks back to the time of Hadrian. Jerome's certainty with regard to the transmission of the apology in Athens is not to be shared (and definitely not the identification of the apologist and the bishop Quadratus). However, he may be on the right track with the reference to Athens.

[44] Cf., to name a few: Bardenhewer, *Geschichte*, 184; idem, "Quadratus," 646; Funk, *Väter*, XXX; Zahn, *Forschungen*, 49; Bihlmeyer, *Väter*, XLVII; more recently Quasten, *Patrology*, 191; Altaner/Stuiber, *Patrologie*, 61; Klijn, *Vaders*, 122; Lindemann/Paulsen, *Väter*, 286; Frank, *Geschichte*, 183; Drobner, *Fathers*, 73.

one can see this location as at least a good possibility, since the daughters of Philip (Eus HE III 37.1, V 17.3) as well as Amnia of Philadelphia (Eus HE V 17.3) are likewise to be found there and the appeal by the Montanists to all of these and several others (Eus HE V 17.3-4) also fits well with such a localization. Aside from these points, one recalls Papias, Fragment 10 (in Philip of Side, HE; Körtner, "Papiasfragmente" 63), where as in the Quadratus fragment (see below) people raised from the dead by Jesus and lived a long time afterward are named.[45] Hadrian stayed in Asia Minor in 123–124 as well as in 129 and 131.[46] The problem lies in the report of Eusebius regarding the ninth year of Hadrian. Thus it is readily conceivable that Quadratus sent the apology from Asia Minor to Athens.

Questions remain with both solutions. Still, the detailed report by Eusebius speaks for the greatest probability of the localization in Athens.

5.   Historical and Theological Profile

5.1 The Later Tradition

The theological meaning of a text surely also comes to expression in its reception. However, one must beware of rash conclusions, since too many unknown aspects could play a role. In terms of evaluating the reception history of Quadratus, one must observe on the one hand the absence of manuscript sources. Granted, many texts were lost in antiquity (at least according to our current knowledge), but the absence of manuscripts is still a sign of faulty reception, though the apology of Quadratus was never suppressed by the church.

A single verbatim fragment in Eusebius is certainly not much, but it does allow (together with the introduction by Eusebius) some conclusions. Also worth considering is the reception by Jerome, who admittedly does not offer any independent information on Quadratus and his apology but does document their high esteem.

The same is true for the further late ancient and early medieval tradition about Quadratus that sometimes repeats what we already know and sometimes offers pieces of information that cannot be verified:

First is the apocryphal *Letter of the Lord's Brother James to Quadratus*.[47] James praises Quadratus' good name and his faith in the Lord (1) and emphasizes his zeal for preaching the gospel, his hospitality for Christians, and his commitment against Jews and pagans (2).[48] Old historical knowledge is not to be presumed; the references to faith, preaching, hospitality and apologetics for Christianity are already known or can be "re"constructed without difficulty.

---

[45] To be sure, Papias states that these people lived until the time of Hadrian, while Quadratus (Eus HE IV 3.2) says only that some were still alive in his day; cf. Fischer, *Väter* 273n4.

[46] Kienast, *Kaisertabelle*, 128–29.

[47] Now in: Van den Broek, "Brief," 56–65; German translation of the letter 57–58 (= translation by P. Vetter, "Rezension," 259–60).

[48] Currently van den Broek, "Brief," 57.

A reference to Quadratus also appears in a tractate by the Armenian mathematician and philosopher *Ananias of Shirak* about Easter (600–650).[49] The combination with Aristides in the presentation of Quadratus, attested since Eusebius, is here phrased such that Aristides appears as companion and student of the apostle Quadratus. The title of apostle is not yet used by Eusebius and Jerome and shows impressively the growth of the tradition. The apostolic discipleship has become apostolicity.

The *Venerable Bede*, in his *Martyrologium* (ca. 725–731),[50] in which he "expanded the relatively scanty reports of a calendar of saints with historical-hagiographical notes,"[51] ascribes to Quadratus the opinion that there are no forbidden foods for Christians. It is questionable whether Bede had the apology of Quadratus in front of him. The reports of Eusebius give no hint toward the theme of food regulations. The possibility that Bede preserved a piece of old knowledge cannot be excluded, but it appears more likely that he presents a later embellishment.

Georgius Cyncellus (d. after 810) also knew of Quadratus; he refers to him in his *Ecloga chronographica* as one who heard the Apostles[52] and quotes Eus HE IV 3.2 practically verbatim. There is no information about Quadratus that goes beyond Eusebius.

Finally, *Photius* (ca. 810–893/894[53]) also knew Quadratus. In his *Bibliothek* (Bibl 162, Henry II 132) he reports that Eusebius of Thessalonica (end of the 6th c.) had appealed to Quadratus along with the Fathers of the fourth and fifth centuries in his debate with the Aphthartodocetic monk Andrew. This statement assumes Quadratus' designation as an orthodox theologian (Eus HE IV 3.1).[54]

In general, these later texts affirm the details of Eusebius. Statements that go beyond his reports are derived from them or are fanciful new creations.[55]

5.2 The Theological Position

Eus HE IV 3.1 calls Quadratus the ἀποστολικὴ ὀρθοτομία. Ὀρθοτομία = "the straight cut" and corresponds here to ὀρθοδοξία.[56] Quadratus carries out the right apostolic cut, as it were, in the frame of the theological explication of the Christian faith. The question is whether conclusions about the direction of the apology can be drawn from that statement.

---

[49] Conybeare, "Ananias," 578: "Aristides [. . .] a companion and pupil of Kodratus the apostle."

[50] PL 94.729; on the period classification cf. Schneider, "Beda Venerabilis," 122.

[51] Schneider, *loc. cit.*

[52] Mosshammer, *Ecloga*, 425 ll. 23–24: Κοδρᾶτος ὁ ἱερὸς τῶν ἀποστόλων ἀκούστης Αἰλίῳ Ἀδριανῷ τῷ αὐτοκράτορι λόγους ἀπολογίας ὑπὲρ Χριστιανῶν ἐπέδωκεν.

[53] Meier, "Photius," 579.

[54] On references in late Byzantine menaea or

by later medieval authors cf. Otto, "Quadratus," 337–38; Harnack, *Überlieferung*, 105; etc.

[55] The thesis of Harris, which finds traces of Quadratus' apology in the *Acts of Catherine of Sinai*, the chronicle of John Malalas, and the romance "Barlaam and Joasaph" ("Apology," 355–83) has rightly been rejected because of its speculative character; cf. already Krüger, "Mitteilung," 431–32; Klostermann/Seeberg, *Apologie, passim*; Rauschen, *Patrologie*, 70.

[56] Pape, *Handwörterbuch*, 376.

Grant believes that Quadratus belongs to the conflict between orthodoxy and heresy[57] and attacks heretics; his text had nothing to do with external conflicts. He reaches this conclusion from the fragment, which reports on the long life of those healed and raised from the dead by Jesus. No pagan savior figure is distanced here, but Christian heretics, more specifically Gnostics. In contrast to them, Quadratus (so Grant argues) emphasizes the physical reality of the historical Jesus through the reference to the reality of the miracles (recognizable from the long life of those healed and raised from the dead). From the reality of the miracles, the meaning of the miracle-worker becomes apparent.[58]

Such an intrachurch orientation of the section on miracles is not the principle conclusion.[59] One might be able to see an implicit orientation of this kind, but explicitly it is not in view either in the fragment or in the context of Eusebius' introduction. Eusebius believes, as he states in the introduction to the fragment (HE IV 3.1), that Quadratus belongs in the early days of Christianity because he personally knew people who had been healed and resurrected by Jesus. Thus there is no talk of orthodoxy or heterodoxy. The fact that he holds Quadratus to be orthodox is another matter. He says so himself by way of introduction with the remark about the ἀποστολικὴ ὀρθοτομία. However, he has not thereby described Quadratus primarily as a warrior for orthodoxy. The matter at hand is not a conflict with adversaries but an apology. The former is implicitly given, however, and should not be denied.

Grant also assumes yet another "setting":[60] Quadratus could stand in the context of pagan religions in which miracles serve as proof of deified sons of gods. Jesus is, like Heracles, Asclepius or the Dioscuri, one who did good deeds and was called a god after his death. The believability of the wonder-worker Jesus shows itself through the reality of the wonders, recognizable from the long further life of those healed and raised from the dead. Thus the same argument used against the Gnostics is made to serve against pagan critics of Jesus' miracles.

For the general understanding of Quadratus' apology, the miracle theme must not be emphasized too strongly.[61] For a polemic on pagan miraculous healings presented as the center of the text would be counterproductive in the frame

---

[57] Grant, "Quadratus," 181–82. The fact that the differentiation between "orthodoxy" and "heresy" in the period in question is not yet significantly constructed and many transitions exist must not be forgotten; the classification was already covered at the time by Otto, "Quadratus," 333–41.

[58] Fischer, *Väter*, 270: The goal of the reference to the miracles is "the proof of the real divinity and all-powerful goodness of the Savior."

[59] Think about just the conflict with the wonders of the Carpocratians and the Simonians, Iren Haer II 32.3; cf. Otto, "Quadratus," 333–41; against this thesis Foster, "Quadratus," 58 rightly points

out that intrachurch polemic would be unusual in an apology, that apart from that the "wicked men" (Eus HE IV 3.1) would just as likely be found outside the church, and that finally no opponent can be named.

[60] Grant, *Apologists*, 26: This "setting may be equally important"; cf. Ehrman, *Fathers*, 90.

[61] But cf. also Just Apol I 56; Dial 69. The miracle theme nevertheless plays a certain role in later apologetic contexts (Tert Apol 21; Min Fel Oct 26; Ps-Clem H I 6, II 34, R I 58; Or Cels I 68, II 44, etc.; cf already Baur, *Vorlesungen*, 352–55; Bauer, *Leben*, 366–67).

of an apology that is intent on the understanding and goodwill of the audience.[62] Moreover, the reproduction of just these few lines is determined by Eusebius' interest in the central arrangement of Quadratus and does not show Quadratus' fundamental orientation. Eusebius speaks only of the straightforward orthodox position of Quadratus, according to the standard of the church, in the frame of his classification in the tradition of the disciples of the apostles. A more precise determination of the theological position is not possible. The fact that Quadratus supports the demands of the developing catholic church as an apologist says nothing about his theology as a whole.

6.   Evaluation

The meaning of the apology of Quadratus is difficult to evaluate. The reference to the long-lived people who were healed or resurrected has naturally become meaningless in the interim. The same cannot be said for the emphasis on the miracle-worker and thus for the Christology, regardless of the point Quadratus was making. His classification in the apostolic tradition is important, even though we do not know how it was made explicit in his work. For Eusebius it was plainly important. However, Quadratus appears to have been especially important for the development of the "apologetic" genre. One should not overdraw his place in the frame of early Christian social and theological history (the minimal reception of his text shows that), but it also should not be undervalued. In any case, in his situation he cast a brave and convincing vote for the Christian faith.

7.   Bibliography

Altaner, B., and A. Stuiber. *Patrologie: Leben, Schriften und Lehre der Kirchenväter*. Freiburg [9]1980.

Amann, É. "Quadratus." *DTC* 13 (1937): 1429–31.

Andresen, C. "Quadratus." *RGG*[3] IV (1961): 727–28.

Andriessen, P. "The Authorship of the Epistula ad Diognetum." *VC* 1 (1947): 129–36.

———. "Kodratos." *LTK*[2] VI (1961): 366.

———. "L'Apologie de Quadratus conservée sous le titre d'Épître à Diognète." *RTAM* 13 (1946): 5–39, 125–49, 237–60.

———. "L'Épilogue de l'Épître à Diognète." *RTAM* 14 (1947): 121–56.

———. "Quadratus a-t-il été en Asie Mineure." *SE* 2 (1949): 44–54.

———. "Un prophète du Nouveau Testament." *BPTF* 11 (1950): 140–50.

Bardenhewer, O. *Geschichte der altchristlichen Literatur I: Vom Ausgang des apostolischen Zeitalters bis zum Ende des zweiten Jahrhunderts*. Darmstadt 1962 (reprint of the 1913 ed.).

---

[62] A "criticizing [of] the Eleusinian savior" (Grant, "Chronology," 25) hardly lies in Quadratus' best interest.

————. "Quadratus." *KL*² X (1897): 645–47.

Bardy, G. "Apologetik." *RAC* I (1950): 533–43.

————. "Sur l'apologiste Quadratus." *AIPHOS* 9 (1949): 75–86.

Barnard, L. W. "Apologetik I: Alte Kirche," *TRE* III (1978): 371–411.

————. "The Epistle ad Diognetum: Two Units from One Author?" *ZNW* 56 (1965): 130–37

Bauer, W. *Das Leben Jesu im Zeitalter der neutestamentlichen Apokryphen.* Tübingen 1909.

Baur, F. C. *Vorlesungen über die christliche Dogmengeschichte, I: Das Dogma der Alten Kirche, 1: Von der Apostolischen Zeit bis zur Synode von Nicäa.* Leipzig 1865.

Baus, K. *Von der Urgemeinde zur frühchristlichen Großkirche.* Handbuch zur KG 1. Freiburg 1999 (reprint of the 1985 ed.).

Beck, M. "Quadratus." In *Lexicon der antiken christlichen Literatur,* edited by S. Döpp and W. Geerlings, 605. Freiburg ³2002.

Bihlmeyer, K. *Die Apostolischen Väter: Neubearbeitung der Funkschen Ausgabe, Unveränderter Nachdruck der mit einem Nachtrag von W. Schneemelcher versehenen 2. Aufl., I: Didache, Barnabas, Klemens I und II, Ignatius, Polykarp, Papias, Quadratus, Diognetbrief.* SAQ 2.1.1. Tübingen ³1970.

Birley, A. R. *Hadrian: The Restless Emperor.* London 1997.

Conybeare, F. C. "Ananias of Shirak (A.D. 600–650c.)." *ByzZ* 6 (1897): 572–84.

Dorner, I. A. *Entwicklungsgeschichte der Lehre von der Person Christi von den ältesten Zeiten bis auf die neueste dargestellt, I: Die Lehre von der Person Christi in den ersten fier Jahrhunderten.* Berlin ²1851.

Drobner, H. R. *The Fathers of the Church: A Comprehensive Introduction.* Peabody, Mass., 2007 (German: 1994).

————. "Quadratus." *BBKL* VII (1994): 1081–84.

Dürr, I. *Die Reisen des Kaisers Hadrian.* AAES 2. Vienna 1881.

Eck, W. "Hadrianus." *DNP* V (1998): 59–64.

Ehrman, B. D. *The Apostolic Fathers: Epistle of Barnabas, Papias and Quadratus, Epistle to Diognetus, The Shepherd of Hermas, Edited and translated.* LCL 25. Cambridge, Mass. 2003.

Fischer, J. A. *Die Apostolischen Väter: Eingeleitet, herausgegeben, übertragen und erläutert.* SUC I. Darmstadt 2004 (reprint of the 1993 ed.).

Foster, P. "The Apology of Quadratus." In *The Writings of the Apostolic Fathers,* 52–62. London 2007.

Frank, K. S. *Lehrbuch der Geschichte der Alten Kirche.* Paderborn 1996.

Funk, F. X. *Die Apostolischen Väter.* Tübingen ²1906.

Georgii Syncelli. *Ecloga Chronographica.* Edited by A. A. Mosshammer. BSGRT. Leipzig 1984.

Goodspeed, E. J. *Die ältesten Apologeten: Texte mit kurzen Einleitungen.* Göttingen 1984 (reprint of the 1914 ed.).

Görres, F. "Quadratus." *RE*³ XVI (1905): 354–56.

Grant, R. "The Chronology of the Greek Apologists." *VC* 9 (1955): 25–33.

————. *Greek Apologists of the Second Century.* Philadelphia 1988.

————. *"Quadratus, the First Christian Apologist."* In *A Tribute to Arthur Vööbus: Studies in Early Christian Literature and Its Environment, Primarily in the Syrian East*, edited by R. H. Fischer, 177–83. Chicago 1977.

Grégoire, H., and P. Orgels. "La véritable date du martyre de S. Polycarpe (23 février 177) et le 'Corpus Polycarpianum.'" *AnBoll* 69 (1951): 138.

Harnack, A. von. *Die Überlieferung der griechischen Apologeten des zweiten Jahrhunderts in der Alten Kirche und im Mittelalter*. TU 1. Berlin 1991 (reprint of the 1882–1883 ed.).

————. *Geschichte der altchristlichen Litteratur bis Eusebius: II: Die Chronologie der altchristlichen Litteratur bis Eusebius: 1: Die Chronologie der Litteratur bis Irenäus*. Leipzig 1897.

Harris, J. R. *The Apology of Aristides*. 1893.

————. "A New Christian Apology." *BJRL* 7 (1922–1923): 355–83.

Hausammann, S. *Alte Kirche: Zur Geschichte und Theologie in den ersten vier Jahrhunderten: I: Frühchristliche Schriftsteller, "Apostolische Väter," Häresien, Apologeten*. Neukirchen 2001.

Hilgenfeld A. "Die Überlieferung über die griechischen Apologeten des Christenthums im zweiten Jahrhundert und ihr neuester Censor." *ZWT* 26 (1883): 145.

Jefford, C. N., K. J. Harder, and L. D. Amezaga. *Reading the Apostolic Fathers: An Introduction*. Peabody, Mass. 1996.

Kienast, D. *Römische Kaisertabelle: Grundzüge einer römischen Kaiserchronologie*. Darmstadt 1996.

Klijn, A. F. J. *Apostolische Vaders: 2: Brief van Barnabas, Fragmenten van Papias, Brief aan Diognetus (met fragmenten mit de prediking van Petrus), Apologie van Quadratus, Pastor van Hermas: Vertaald, ingeleid en toegelicht*. Kampen 1983.

Klostermann, E., and R. Seeberg. *Die Apologie der heiligen Katharina*. SKG.G 1.2. Berlin 1924.

Körtner, U. H. J., and M. Leutzsch. *Papiasfragmente, Hirt des Hermas: Eingeleitet, herausgegeben, übertragen und erläutert*. SUC III. Darmstadt 1998.

Krüger, G. *Geschichte der altchristlichen Litteratur in den ersten drei Jahrhunderten*. GThW II/3. Freiburg ³1898.

————. "Mitteilung." *TLZ* 48 (1923): 431–32.

Lebreton, J. "L'Apologétique chrétienne au IIᵉ siècle." In *L'Église primitive*, by J. Lebreton and J. J. Zeiller, 419–64. HE 1. Paris 1946.

Lietzmann, H. *Geschichte der Alten Kirche: II: Ecclesia catholica*. Berlin ³1961.

Lindemann, A., and H. Paulsen, eds. *Die Apostolischen Väter: Griechisch-deutsche Parallelausgabe auf der Grundlage der Ausgaben von Franz-Xaver Funk/Karl Bihlmeyer and Molly Whittaker, mit Übersetzungen von M. Dibelius und D.-A. Koch, neu übers. und hg*. Tübingen 1992.

Lona, H. E. *An Diognet: Übersetzt und erklärt*. KfA 8. Freiburg 2001.

Lother, H. *Geschichte des Christentums: I: Das Christentum in der griechisch-römischen Welt*. Leipzig 1939.

Marrou, H. K. *A Diognète: Introduction, Édition critique, Traduction et Commentaire*. SC 33. Paris ²1965.

Meier, M. "Photius." In *Lexicon der antiken christlichen Literatur*, edited by S. Döpp and W. Geerlings, 579–81. Freiburg ³2002.

Murphy, F. X. "Quadratus, St." *NCE*² XI (2003): 848.

N.n. "Quadratus." *ODCC*³ (1997): 1354.

Otto, C. T. "Quadratus." *Corp Ap* IX (1872): 333–41.

Peterson, E. "Quadrato." *EC* X (1953): 362–63.

Prostmeier, F. "Quadratus." *RGG*⁴ VI (2003): 1851–52.

Quasten, J. *Patrology I: The Beginnings of Patristic Literature*. Utrecht 1975.

Rauschen, G. *Patrologie: Die Schriften der Kirchenväter und ihr Lehrgehalt*. Freiburg 1931.

Roberts, A., and J. Donaldson. *The Ante-Nicene Fathers: Translations of the Writings of the Fathers Down to A.D. 325, Revised and Chronologically Arranged, with Brief Prefaces and Occasional Notes by A. C. Coxe, VIII: The Twelve Patriarchs, Excerpts and Epistles, The Clementina, Apocrypha, Decretals, Memoirs of Edessa and Syriac Documents, Remains of the First Ages*. Grand Rapids 1989 (reprint).

Rosenbaum, H.-U. "Kodratos." *BBKL* IV (1992): 226–28.

Ruiz Bueno, D. *Padres Apostólicos: Edicion Bilingüe Completa: Introducciones, Notas y Versión Española*. BAC 65. Madrid ⁵1985.

Scheel, O. "Quadratus." *RGG*¹ IV (1913): 1997.

Schmid, W., and O. Stählin. *Wilhelm von Christ's Geschichte der griechischen Literatur: II: Die nachklassische Period der griechischen Literatur: 2: Von 100 bis 530 nach Christus*. Munich 1924.

Schneider, H. "Beda Venerabilis." In *Lexicon der antiken christlichen Literatur*, edited by S. Döpp and W. Geerlings, 120–24. Freiburg ³2002.

Schuster, M. "Quadratus 1." *RECA*² 24 (1963): 677.

Soden, H. von. "Quadratus." *RGG*² IV (1930): 1661.

Stark, M. "Quadratus (Kodratos), Apologet." *LTK*³ VIII (1999): 753.

Sychowski, S. von. *Hieronymus als Litteraturhistoriker: Eine quellenkritische Untersuchung der Schrift des H. Hieronymus "De viris illustribus."* Münster 1894.

Van den Broek, R. "Der Brief des Jakobus an Quadratus und das Problem der judenchristlichen Bischöfe von Jerusalem (Eusebius, HE IV, 5, 1-3)." In *Text and Testimony: Essays on New Testament and Apocryphal Literature in Honour of A. F. J. Klijn*, edited by T. Baarda et al., 56–65. Kampen 1988.

van Rohden, P. "Aelius Hadrianus." *RECA*² I/1 (1893): 493–520.

Vetter, P. "Rezension von. J. Daschean, *Die Lehre der Apostel, das apokryphe Buch der Kanones, der Brief des Jakobus an Quadratus und die Kanones*." *LitRdsch* 22 (1896): 259–60.

Voss, B. "Quadratus." *KlPauly* 4 (1979): 1284.

Zahn, T. "Der älteste Apologet des Christentums." *NKZ* 2 (1891): 281–87.

———. *Forschungen zur Geschichte des neutestamentlichen Kanons: VI: 1: Apostel und Apostelschüler in der Provinz Asien; 2: Brüder und Vettern Jesu*. Leipzig 1900.

Zedler, J. H. "Quadratus." In *GVUL* XXX, 25. Second reprinting of the 1741 ed. Graz 1996.

Diognetus

Horacio E. Lona

J. M. Sailer calls the text "To Diognetus" "a pearl of Christian literature." As befits a priceless pearl, it is valuable and attractive but hard to reach.

1.   Textual Tradition

The history of the textual tradition of *Ad Diognetum* is unusual.[1] Before the text was accidentally discovered in Constantinople around 1436,[2] both the title and the content of the text were completely unknown. In the period thereafter the manuscript past through many hands—John of Ragusa, the Dominican monastery in Basel, Johannes Reuchlin, the University Church of St. Michael in Pforzheim, the margrave's residence in Durlach—until, in 1580 in Durlach, Bernard Haus finished a clear transcript of the original for his teacher Martin Crusius, which was then preserved in Tübingen. A second copy was written by Henricus Stephanus (Henri Estienne), who published the *editio princeps* in 1592 in Paris. A third transcript, which unfortunately has not survived, occupied Johannes Beurer between 1587 and 1591 in Freiburg. In the period between 1793 and 1795 the Straßburg city library took over the manuscript from the Abbey of Maursmünster, which was dissolved in 1790. The manuscript belonged to Codex Argentoratensis (A), which included among other texts several attributed to the philosopher Justin as well as *Ad Diognetum*. The text remained in Straßburg until 1870, when it fell victim to the fires caused by bombardment of the city on August 24. Thus, whoever studies *An Diognetum* now has no original in front of him but is dependent on the transcripts of Haus and Stephanus, on their references to the copy of Beurer and on his *editio princeps*. Apparently the codex was difficult to read, since the transcripts do not always agree. After 7.6 and 10.8 the scribe who copied A refers to a lacuna in the manuscript. The extent of the lost text cannot be determined exactly. This truly small manuscript basis forms the only foundation for the scholarship on *Ad Diognetum*.

---

[1]   On the following cf. Lona, *Diognet*, 11–69. The translation of the text and the division into verses are taken from the commentary. In the thematic treatment, too, the fundamental statements can be traced to it.

[2]   The bizarre story of the discovery is well documented and can be reconstructed to a considerable degree.

2.   Content and Structure

The first chapter contains a proem fashioned in accordance with the rules of ancient rhetoric, in which the author takes the role of teacher and as such formulates the questions that his supposed student Diognetus put to him (Diogn 1.1): First, the question of the God of Christian belief, of the behavior of Christians in the world and regarding death, of the basis of their rejection of both the Greek gods and the Jewish religion; second, the question of Christian love; and, third, the question of the reason for the late appearance of Christianity. The questions are not handled systematically, but they do not go unanswered.

The following chapters can be divided into two secions. The *first section* (Diogn 2–4) is purely polemical-apologetical, directed first against the gods of the pagans (2.1-10), then against the Jewish religion (3.1–4.6). At the end of each section (2.10; 4.6) the author presents the Christians' rejection of both phenomena as the logical consequence of their evident deficiencies. The *second part* (Diogn 5–12) offers a positive presentation of Christianity that consists of small, clearly delineated thematic units. First: Christians in the world between integration, threat, and superior distance (Diogn 5–6); second: the revelation of the mysteries of God through the Son (Diogn 7–8) and their realization in the saving work of the Father through the Son (Diogn 9); third: tasks and prospects: imitation of God and readiness for martyrdom (Diogn 10); fourth: life in the church under the leadership of the Logos (Diogn 11–12).

Both sections are marked by a consistently maintained "blocky" disposition of the material that distinguishes itself in the thematic sequence and the corresponding concepts. The author thus shows great linguistic competence in composing his independent work with different stylistic "registers." In any case, "blocky" here does not mean "disjointed." It is far more the case that every content step "leaves its predecessor behind" because the progression of thought constantly moves forward and at the same time assumes what has gone before. The meaning of this remark will become clear in the next section.

3.   Literary Form and Genre

Often the text is called the "Epistle to Diognetus." The title goes back to the first editor, but it has no basis in the tradition. Codex A has only the reference to Justin as the author and the name of the addressee of the work: "The same *Ad Diognetum*" (τοῦ αὐτοῦ πρὸς Διόγνητον). Beyond this note there is no sign that can justify the classification of the text among the epistolary literature. On the basis of content, it is a *discourse* in the form of a *treatise*.

However, two genre markers appear in the content: The sharp polemic against the gods of the pagans (Diogn 2) and against aspects of the Jewish religion (Diogn 3–4) belong to the Christian *apologetic*, which supports and legitimates the faith by ruthlessly exposing the errors of adversaries—apart from the soundness of the argumentation. The thematically broadly intended presentation of Christianity (Diogn 5–12) speaks for the reality of the faith in the assumption that the reader, like Diognetus, becomes a "hearer of a new doctrine" (Diogn 2.1) and is receptive to the offer directed toward him: the superiority of Christians to the world (Diogn 5–6), the grace of the revelation with the p through the Son (7–9), the tasks of the Christian in the world (Diogn 10) and his home in the church of the Logos (Diogn 11–12). The presentation belongs in the *protreptic* literature, which is devoted to the art of persuasion. Apologetic polemic and protreptic goal-setting are not to be seen as separate matters, however. Both complete each other and actually belong together, as the *Protrepticus* of Clement of Alexandria and the apologetic literature of Christianity show.

Independent of these considerations, whether one sees Diognetus as historical or only as a fictional character, the text directs itself toward a readership of pagan origin open-minded about the Christian offer to open the way of faith to them.[3]

4. Literary Unity

The discussion of the literary unity of the work begins with the opinion of the first editor, Stephanus, that the last two chapters are insertions. Since Diogn 10.8 breaks off in the middle of a sentence, Stephanus believes that Justin—whom he holds to be the author of the text—closed the discussion with a different remark, not with Diogn 11–12, which do not correspond to Diogn and are different from the other works of Justin. The opinion of Stephanus, later supported by Otto in his *Corpus Apologetarum*, established itself as the scholarly consensus, even if the question did not remain undisputed. In some versions of the text the last two chapters were not even printed—so confident were the editors of the point.[4] Three arguments are often brought forward to justify the literary-critical decision to view Diogn 11–12 as an element foreign to Diogn 1–10: variations in vocabulary, linguistic-stylistic differences, and contradictions in content.[5]

However, there is also no shortage of authors who insist on the literary unity of the work.[6] If one examines the aforementioned reasons for the separation between Diogn 1–10 and Diogn 11–12 in more detail, their cogency becomes questionable.

---

[3] The fact that an essay on *Ad Diognetum* appears in a handbook on the so-called "Apostolic Fathers" comes from a pragmatic criterion that is not disturbed by the opinion just given. *Ad Diognetum* appears in the majority of editions of the "Apostolic Fathers." The self-presentation of the author as a "disciple of the Apostles" (Diogn 11.1) gives rise to this state. But if one considers the audience of the text, who do not belong to the Christian community, the inclusion of the text among the "Apostolic Fathers" becomes questionable.

[4] Wilamowitz, Geffcken, and Blackeney.

[5] Representative of these critics are Meecham, Norelli, Wengst, et al.

[6] In the last decade these include Marrou, Barnard, Lorenz, Rizzi, and Lona.

Vocabulary: The different thematic units in the two sections often show a very differentiated vocabulary. Diogn 1–10 does not contain a unified vocabulary that one could draw upon as a basis for comparison with Diogn 11–12. Compared to Diogn 2–4, Diogn 9–10 also appears to be a foreign body.

Style: The assertion that Diogn 11–12 are shaped by the so-called "Asianish" rhetoric is correct, but 7.2, 9.2, and 10.2 also show similar stylisitic peculiarities. It must be remarked that the author possesses the authorial competence of the "Second Sophistic," which is displayed not least in stylistic breadth.

Content: The difficulty, already observed by Stephanus, that a pagan like Diognetus in Diogn 11–12 will listen to a discourse with biblical quotations and deep theological reflections misjudges the character of a prophetic text, which seeks to take the reader on an *iternerarium mentis in fi*dem and already shows him the goal of the journey. A comparison with the

Protrepticus of Clement of Alexandria shows the argumentative richness contained in such texts, which not only proclaim the faith but also attempt to move the audience to take up this faith. Accordingly, such texts include passages that direct themselves to the audience in such a form as if they had long ago decided for the faith. This characteristic style does not appear first in 11–12, however, but already marks 8–10.

Certainly, the final word on the question of the literary unity of *Ad Diognetum* has not thus been said, but the scholarship will have to engage the arguments presented to reach a reasonable judgment.

5.   Intellectual Milieu

5.1 The Biblical and Early Christian Tradition

The Old Testament

The Old Testament is not expressly cited, and there are very few places influenced by Old Testament concepts.[7] Compare Diogn 5.17 and 1 Samuel 13:5, 17:2, and elsewhere (Christians as "a foreign tribe"); Diogn 10.2 and Genesis 1:26, 2.7 (the making of humans in the image of God); Diogn 12.1-3 and Genesis 2:8-9 (the paradise of delight; the tree of life in the center of paradise). On the basis of the scant evidence, it would be unjustified to suspect only a superficial knowledge of the Hebrew Scriptures or to assume deeper knowledge that was not used. Neither position can be verified. The reason for the sparing use of the Old Testament probably lies in the negative judgment of Judaism.[8]

---

[7]   In this section only selected examples will be cited without striving for completeness of the presentation. [English translations will be quoted from Roberts/Donaldson/Coxe unless otherwise marked.]

[8]   See below, "Christianity as a '*Tertium Genus.*'"

The New Testament

Although the New Testament is expressly quoted only once (1 Cor 8:1 in Diogn 12.5) and word-for-word agreements, apart from the "peristasis catalogue" in Diogn 5.12-16, appear fairly seldom, numerous hints of Pauline and Johannine theology can be drawn from the second part of the work (5–12): 4.5a and Galatians 4:10 (the observation of days and months); 5.8 and 2 Corinthians 10:3 (the existence in the flesh but not according to the flesh); 6.3 and John 17:11, 14 (being in the world but not of the world); 6.6 and Matthew 5:44 (love for enemies); 8.5 and John 1:18 (no one has seen God); 9.1b and Titus 3:4 (God's goodness and friendliness toward humanity); 9.2c and 1 Peter 3:18 (the righteous for the unrighteous); 10.2 and 1 John 4:9 (the sending of the only Son of God); 11.1a and 1 Timothy 2:7 ("the teacher of the nations"); 12.6a and 1 Corinthians 8.2 ("if one thinks he knows something").

There are two themes that show a special affinity toward Paulinism: first, the revelation of mysteries (7–8) and its realization in the saving work of God through the Son in the frame of a revelation scheme (9); second, the salvation of humans from their lostness through the love and kindness of God by means of the gift of the Son (9).

An echo of Johannine theology can be heard especially significantly in Diogn 10.2-3: The singular love of God for humanity, to whom he gave his only Son, is greater than human love. The sending of the mediator of creation as a sign of love and not of judgment (7.5) belongs to the same traditional context. It is self-evident that the reception of Pauline and Johannine motifs completes itself in the framework of another theological concept that integrates them in the characteristic stated intention.

Early Christian Apologetic Tradition

The influence of the early Christian apologetic tradition is most noticeable in Diogn 1–4 but appears elsewhere as well. The emptiness of the gods is shown on the basis of the worthlessness and transience of the materials from which the idols are made. Where the text touches on the sacrificial nature of the Jews, it emphasizes that God does not require sacrifice. The reality of the revelation places the many opinions of the philosophers in question and discloses the error of the pagans. The themes follow the argumentation of earlier apologists without showing originality.

The commonalities with the *Alexandrian Christianity* advanced by Clement are remarkable. They correspond not only to the *Protrepticus*, but also to the other works of the Alexandrian: the *Paedagogus*, the *Stromata*, and the little text *Quis dives salvetur*. Similar-sounding phrases and related expressions and motifs[9] point

---

9   For individual proof cf. Alfonsi, "Protrettico," 101–8; Lona, *Diognet*, 57–58.

to a common cultural background. This observation gives rise to important consequences for the questions of the place of origin and the dating of *Ad Diognetum*.[10]

Gnosticism

The relationship to Gnosticism is often discussed in scholarship. The most important recent attempt was undertaken by S. Pétrement. She lists eleven themes that can be explained if Valentinus were the author of *Ad Diognetum*.[11] Close examination of the argument shows its cogency to be unconvincing, even though many of the points of contact are not to be denied. The author of *Ad Diognetum* does not turn against Gnosticism in his polemic, though some statements can be understood in this sens (cf. Diogn 8.7-8). The Gnostic coloring of many phrases and images is far more likely to have come from the cultural environment, which was oriented toward learning and cultural openness. A comparison with Clement of Alexandria is recommended here as well.

5.2 Greek Philosophy

Only Diogn 8.2 makes special reference to the philosophers, who with their "vain and silly doctrines" equate God with the elements of the world. "But such declarations are simply the startling and erroneous utterances of deceivers" (8.4). The text itself, however, in many places displays linguistic similarities with statements of the Greek philosophers, who relativize the quoted analysis. Themes like the imitation of God and luck (10.3-6) belong to the philosophical tradition of Platonism. The presentation of the place of Christians in the world on the basis of the relationship between body and soul (6.1-9) touches on the seven dissertations of Maximus of Tyrus. In these places and elsewhere the author shows through the quality of his speech his ability to take part in the discourse of the educated in the second century. The common educational foundation offers him the chance to speak to them in "the same language."

The inclusion of some motifs of Greek philosophy does not mean that they are understood in their original sense. The characterization of God as him who "was always of such a character, and still is, and will ever be" (Diogn 8.8) carries the principle of the unchangeability of reality over to God,[12] but this unchangeability applies to the goodness of God, not to the existence of God. His revelation in history and the sending of his Son are incompatible with a God shaped by the statements of Greek ontology. God appears further as "free from wrath" (ἀόργετος), but of this same God it is later said that he "did not regard us with hatred, nor thrust us away, nor remember our iniquity against us" (9.2b). In other words, the God of the Christian faith is not "apathetic" or indifferent regarding fallen humanity.

---

[10] See below under "Authorship, Place of Writing, and Dating."

[11] Cf. Pétrement, "Valentin," 52–55.

[12] Cf. Heraclitus Fr. 30 (FVS I.157-58); Empedocles Fr. 21.9 (FVS I.320); Plato Parm 155d.

The distance from Greek philosophy is expressed most significantly in chapter 9. The image of the deeply fallen person who, incapable of obtaining salvation (9.1), completely entrusts himself to the saving God (9.2) is conceivable and understandable only on the basis of Judeo-Christian tradition. To Greek thought the whole idea is foreign. The sharp criticism of Celsus against such a presentation proves this fact.

6. Theological Profile

6.1 Christianity as a *Tertium Genus*

The fact that Christianity fundamentally differentiates itself from Jewish and Greek religion is an aspect that is first addressed in PrePet 2d: "For that which concerns Greeks and Jews is old; we, however, are the Christians, whom He (God) ennobles as *a third race* in new ways."[13] Therein the awareness expresses itself to form a quantity that has abandoned its origin—Judaism—and holds itself apart from its surroundings—Greek culture. The Christians strengthen their identity by differentiation from their origin and their environment.

The author takes up the motif and formulates it in the first question of Diognetus: Why do Christians not hold those figures to be gods that are viewed as such by the Greeks? Why do they not follow the superstitions of the Jews? The answer to these questions shows the dividing line regarding Greeks and Jews that allows the unique image of Christians to emerge.

The necessary distance from the Greek religion—equated globally with the idols and the veneration thereof—is a given that is never discussed, especially since many arguments had already been given in Jewish apologetics (cf. Philo Decal 65–81). The relationship with Judaism, from which Christianity emerged, is different. The author takes a position in this regard that is unique in the frame of early Christian polemic against Judaism.

In Diogn 3–4 nothing points to the roots of Christianity in Judaism. The overthrow of the Jews is not based on their rejection of Jesus as Messiah but shows itself to be far more fundamental and radical. Although the Jews "worship one God as being Lord of all" (3.2), they think that "by means of blood, and the smoke of sacrifices and burnt-offerings, they offer sacrifices [acceptable] to Him, and that by such honours they show Him respect" (3.5a). This is the fatal error of Judaism, because they imagine "that they can give anything to Him who stands in need of nothing" (3.5b). Thus they place themselves on the same plane as the Greeks, who also believe they honor the gods by their sacrifices. The judgment follows logically: If Jews bring sacrifices, they "appear to me in no respect to differ

---

[13] English translation from the German translation of Schneemelcher, NTApo[5] II.40. Of the text, which belongs to the first half of the second century, only a few fragments have been preserved that Clement of Alexandria passes down.

from those who studiously confer the same honour on things destitute of sense, and which therefore are unable to enjoy such honours" (3.5a).

The criticism offered in Diogn 4 regarding aspects of the Jewish religion—food regulations, Sabbath rest, circumcision, and feast days—adds new elements to the argument, but it does not reach the sharpness and radicalness expressed in Diogn 3 through the equation of Greeks and Jews. Thus it is striking that the criticism on the four aforementioned points agrees to a great extent with the pagan criticisms of Judaism.

The distance of Christians from Judaism is so great that they are too estranged for a relationship to ever have existed. The caricatured presentation of Jewish religious customs is one way of making this distance significant. The position of Christianity itself as *tertium genus* also requires that the dividing line toward the pagans be drawn equally sharply, but both, Judaism and paganism, lie equally far from Christianity.

The fundamental disqualification of Judaism, which is assumed in Diogn 3–4, raises questions. What remains in this view of things of the continuity of salvation history if its historical bearers—Israel, the Jewish people—show in their time through their many sacrifices and religious tradition, of all things, that they, exactly like the pagans, have not known the one true God? What kind of image of God is presented here if the judgment about Judaism appears so negative? The following considerations attempt to give an answer to these questions.

6.2 The Understanding of Revelation

Diogn 7–9 contains the foundational statements in which the author's understanding of revelation is reflected, although Diogn 4.6b ("but you must not hope to learn the mystery of their peculiar mode of worshipping God from any mortal") and 5.3 ("The course of conduct which they follow has not been devised by any speculation or deliberation of inquisitive men; nor do they, like some, proclaim themselves the advocates of any merely human doctrines") already point toward it.[14]

God is "almighty, the Creator of all things," but he is also the invisible God (7.2a) who is ready to complete acts of salvation that are unimaginable for the human reason. From this image of God arises the undeniable need for a revelation to achieve knowledge of God. For "no man has either seen Him, or made Him known, but He has revealed Himself. And He has manifested Himself through faith, to which alone it is given to behold God" (8.5-6).

The clear denial of the ability of reason to know the true God is not the consequence of a cognitive-theoretical opinion of the relationship of reason and faith to one another; rather it results from a "basic certainty" about the God of the faith

---

[14] Eltester, "Mysterium," 290–93, suggests an arrangement of the text in which Diogn 5.3 follows 4.6b directly. Critical of this view: Wengst, *Didache*, 344n36; Lona, *Diognet*, 156–57.

from which one proceeds: "God Himself [. . .] has sent from heaven, and placed among men, [Him who is] the truth, and the holy and incomprehensible Word, and has firmly established Him in their hearts" (7.2a). The Logos as revelator and mediator of creation (7.2c-d) is the medium of God's communication of himself.

If the process of revelation has its origin in God himself, it realizes itself only through the sending of the revelator in the form of the Logos, that is, the Son. In a kind of "prologue in heaven" the point is raised in 8.9: The initiative begins with God communicating his "great and unspeakable conception" to the Son alone. Only after this revelation within the Godhead does the beloved Son reveal everything that was prepared from the beginning, and in this form participation in the divine favor is granted to humans (8.11).

Since the sending of the Son is considered throughout to be historically punctual, it leads to a periodization of history in a time of obscurity and ignorance and a time of revelation and knowledge: "For, who of men at all understood before His coming what God is?" (8.1). This idea does not hide a speculative interest in a time of hiddenness of the mystery about which at one time not even the Son knew. The periodization of history succeeds according to the "once"–"now" scheme that juxtaposes the past as the time of concealment and the present as the time of revelation.[15] Through the assumption of the revelation scheme, the author can give and answer to the question about the late appearance of Christianity (1.1d).[16] The time of obscurity, in which people could have gotten the impression that God did not care about them, that He was indifferent to their fate (8.10), is in reality the period foreseen in God's pedagogy in which humans should experience their own inability to obtain salvation for themselves (9.2a). Through the contrasting structure of the scheme, in which the past is seen as sheer disaster, the author can strengthen his view of Israel and its history already mentioned in 3–4. Based on the scheme, a stage between past and present is ruled out anyway.

God himself remains not far from humanity even in the time of concealment. He "showed great long-suffering, and bore with us" (9.2b), "not that He at all delighted in our sins, but that He simply endured them; nor that He approved the time of working iniquity which then was" (9.1b). This God brought about the turn toward salvation.

The radical nature of the understanding of revelation rests on the Christology and on the saving work of the Son that exceeds all expectations. God sent him into the world (10.2); he gave his only Son as a ransom for us (9.2c); through the

---

[15] The temporal antitheses in Colossians 1:26-27 and Ephesians 3:5, 3:9 are present as elements of the revelation scheme. A traditional connection with Diogn 9 is very likely. Cf. Brändle, *Ethik*, 106–12.

[16] The question that Diognetus asked was actually the question of Greek thought, which held a revelation in history to be nonsense. In jest, Celsus

formulates it clearly: "After so long a period of time, then, did God now bethink himself of making men live righteous lives, but neglect to do so before?" (Or Cels 4.7b). The image of the forgetful God is complemented elsewhere by the image of the sleeping God who awoke from a long slumber and decided to save the human race from evil (Or Cels 6.78). Cf. Lona, *Lehre*, 225, 387.

Son the Father justified the evildoers and the godless (9.4). All of this is unapproachable to the reason. The believer, however, may ask by way of confession: "Who of us would ever have expected these things?" (8.11) or cry: "O unsearchable operation! O benefits surpassing all expectation!" (9.5a).

6.3 The Image of God

The section Diogn 7–10 contains the most important statements on this theme. The understanding of revelation outlined above reveals a dynamic that, going out from God, culminates in the sending of the Son. God is not only the "Almighty and Creator of all" (7.2a); he is also the "sending" God (7.2a-6). God's revelation of Himself completes itself through the sending of the Son. To express this immediacy, the author uses expressions that apply sometimes to God, sometimes to the Son, without specifying the relationship between them in the equal references. As mediator of creation, the Son is "Creator and Fashioner of all things" (7.2c: τὸν τεχνίτην καὶ δημιουργὸν τῶν ὅλων), but God remains "the Lord and Fashioner of all things, who made all things, and assigned them their several positions" (8.7: ὁ γὰρ δεσπότης καὶ δημιουργὸς τῶν ὅλων θεός, ὁ ποιήσας τὰ πάντα καὶ κατὰ τάξιν διακρίνας). God himself has given his Son as "a God" to humanity (7.4: ὡς θεὸν ἔπεμψεν). The sending of the Son reflects the reality of the invisible God. Through the Son it becomes clear that the Father is a saving God who persuades and does not use force: "for violence has no place in the character of God" (7.4: βία γὰρ οὐ πρόσεστιν τῷ θεῷ).

Two predications in Diogn 8.7 state fundamental facts about the author's image of God: God is "not merely a friend of mankind (φιλάνθρωπος), but also long-suffering (μακρόθυμος)." The first term has a long history as a statement about the nature of God (cf. Plato Leg 713d; Symp 189d; Wis 1.6, 7.23 [on the wisdom of God]; Philo Opif 81; Abr 137, 203; etc.) and becomes explicit in the statements that follow, especially in 9.2 ("O overflowing kindness and love of God toward man!"[17]). The second term fulfills a twofold function: For one, it introduces the list of God's attributes in 8.8; for the other, it prepares the presentation on the "patience" of God in the "time of unrighteousness" (9.1–2): "[He] did not regard us with hatred, nor thrust us away, nor remember our iniquity against us, but showed great long-suffering, and bore with us [. . .]" (9.2b).[18]

God loves people because it is his nature:[19] "kind and good, and free from wrath, and true, and the only one who is [absolutely] good" (8.8). Only the good God could make people worthy of life after they had proven themselves to be unworthy by their own works. Only by the power of God is anyone enabled to enter the kingdom of God (9.1c). The emphasis on the goodness of God has

---

17 Translation by Eugene R. Fairweather from Richardson, 220.
18 The long-suffering and the goodness of God are the factors that ensure the continuity of salvation history, even if Israel is left out. The patient and good God is one and the same God who brings about the time of salvation but also ruled over the time of disaster.
19 On "He was ever so, and is and will be," see above: "Greek Philosophy."

parallels in Old Testament texts.[20] The possibility that the author thus turns polemically to address the Marcionites[21] cannot be excluded, but it is still more likely that the phrasing can be traced back to his interest in the known Platonist view—long received in Middle Platonism—connected with the goodness of God, who is free from all envy (cf. Tim 29e; Philo Abr 203; Clem Al Paed I.63.1).

The long list of characteristics of God at the end of chapter 9 concludes the preceding presentation. First: God has in times past proven the inability of human nature to reach life. Second: Now he has revealed the Savior who can save even the powerless. Hence the command that we trust God's goodness on the basis of his deeds and that we "esteem Him our Nourisher, Father, Teacher, Counsellor, Healer, our Wisdom, Light, Honour, Glory, Power, and Life, so that we should not be anxious concerning clothing and food" (9.6b).[22] The eleven statements can be divided into two groups. The first five are metaphors that have to do with the care and maintenance of human life: nourisher, Father, teacher, counselor, and healer. If Christians are not to worry themselves over clothing and food, it is because God is the true preserver of life. How much God has given humanity in his love is listed in 10.2: "on [their] account He made the world, to [them] He rendered subject all the things that are in it, to [them] He gave reason and understanding, [. . .] [them] He formed after His own image." The remaining six metaphors contain properties or attributes that are especially suitable—the breadth of the traditional background supports this—to bring the mystery of the divine to speech: wisdom, light, honor, glory, power, and life.

6.4 Christology

The christological statements can be traced back to five themes:

1. The sending of the Son (υἱός), that is, the Logos (λόγος), by the Father:[23]
   7.2a: "[. . .] God himself, who from heaven established the truth and the holy, incomprehensible word among men, and fixed it firmly in their hearts."
   7.2b-c: "[. . .] he (God) sent the Designer and Maker of the universe himself [. . .]."
   7.2d: "This [messenger] He sent to them."
   7.4: "As a king sends his son, who is also a king, so sent He Him; as God He sent Him; as to men He sent Him; as a Saviour He sent Him [. . .]."
   7.5: "As calling us He sent Him, not as vengefully pursuing us; as loving us He sent Him, not as judging us."

---

[20] Cf. Psalm 86:5: "For you, O Lord, are good and forgiving, abounding in steadfast love to all who call on you"; Psalm 145:8-9a: "The Lord is gracious and merciful, slow to anger [LXX: long-suffering, μακρόθυμος] and abounding in steadfast love. The Lord is good to all. . . ." Cf. further Psalm 25:8; 2Macc 1.24; PsSol 5.2, 5.12, 10.7.

[21] Cf. Tibiletti, "Aspetti," 372.
[22] Some authors choose a christological interpretation: Blackeney, *Epistle*, 72–73; Lorenz, *Brief*, 85–86; Mara, "Osservazioni," 275.
[23] The English translations from 7.2a-c and 7.6 are from Richardson, 218–22; all others are from Roberts/Donaldson/Coxe.

7.6: "Yet he will indeed send him someday as our Judge [. . .]."

10.2: "[. . .] to whom He sent His only-begotten Son [. . .]."

11.3: "For which reason He sent the Word, that He might be manifested to the world [. . .]."

The sending is expressed in the verbs πέμπω and ἀποστέλλω, which are used indiscriminately. The message of the statements quoted above can be quickly summarized: The revelation and saving work of the Father through the sending of the Son belong together in the closest possible way.

2. God's revelation to the Son (παῖς): Only in 8.9 and 8.11 is παῖς used and not υἱός. The Son thus fulfills a twofold function as the recipient (8.9) and media-tor (8.11) of revelation.
3. The giving of the Son (υἱός) by the Father:

   9.2c: "He himself (God) gave up his own Son as a ransom for us—the holy one for the unjust, the innocent for the guilty, the righteous one for the unrigh-teous, the incorruptible for the corruptible, the immortal for the mortal."[24]

The key statement rests on the New Testament terminology (cf. Mark 10:45 par; Acts 7:35; 1 Pet 1:18; Titus 2:14). The following contrasts clarify the distance between the Savior and the saved and emphasize the soteriological meaning (ὑπέρ) of the sacrificial gift of the Son.

4. The saving work of the Son: In his capacity as the Father's emissary, the Son can-not work independently. The consummation of the work of salvation through the Son follows God's initiative (9.1-2b, 9.2c-5). The righteousness of the Son makes the evildoers and the godless righteous by covering their sins (9.3-4).
5. The work of the Logos in the Christian community: The Logos is not only the mediator of creation (7.2). Over and above this function, he also works as the teacher of the believers. As he previously worked with the disciples (11.2, 7), so he enriches the church (11.3-5), and by his teaching he glorifies the Father (12.9).

In the sending statements—they presume the concept of preexistence—the influence of the New Testament tradition is easily recognizable (John 3:16-17; 1John 4:9; Gal 4:4). The words on the dedication of the Son recall Romans 8:32, 5:18-19. In comparison to other authors of the second half of the second century, such as Justin and Athenagoras, the Logos statements are less speculative and philosophically colored. The concise statement about the gift of the Savior (9.2c) differentiates the Christology in *Ad Diognetum* from other outlines that say noth-ing about it (Tatian, Athenagoras, Theophilus).

In many places the actions of God and of the one he sent are presented con-gruently: Both are "Author of all" (7.2c, 8.7); God shows himself in that he has

---

[24] Richardson, 220.

come to the people (8.1, 5); both forgive sins (9.2b, 9.3-4); the Son is sent as God (7.4). In the sending of the Son, God remains the one who saves, persuades, calls, and loves (7.4), though his saving work is completed only through the Son (9.5).

The classification of the Christology of *Ad Diognetum* depends on the prior understanding in the point of view. The statements cannot be understood as being harmonized in light of the doctrine of the two natures or the *communicatio idiomatum* without lapsing into a gross anachronism. Yet categories like "Monarchianism" are also not readily helpful, since they assume a clarity in the language about God that was not at all present at this time.[25] The issue at hand is the ability of language to express the Savior's belonging to the divine realm. The Christology treated here presents an attempt at doing so. The fact that it seems enigmatic and ambivalent corresponds to its dependence on the conditions of the period.

6.5 The Individual in the World on the Way to Salvation

In the author's answer to the questions of Diognetus and in the text as a whole, a picture of humanity emerges, the outlines of which will be brought out in this section.

1. The human as the being that inquires after God and is capable of learning: *Ad Diognetum* presents a roleplay in which the author plays the teacher and Diognetus plays the eager-to-learn student. In the course of the presentation, the author has shown by his words the *habitus* of the teacher (2.1, 10; 4.6a; 7.1); at the conclusion he speaks openly in the form of a self-presentation (11.1) in order to relinquish the role at once to the Logos as the only true Teacher (11.2-5).[26] The questioning Diognetus is asked to prepare himself to receive "a new doctrine" by freeing himself of all that could diminish his understanding (2.1). On the way toward the knowledge of the truth, he will also have to accept the limits of reason: The mystery of the Christian truth (4.6b, 7.1) can be approached only by faith (8.5-6). Metaphorically he is compared at the end to a sweet paradise in which the tree of knowledge is planted (12.1). The wish of the author, "Let your heart be your wisdom; and let your life be true knowledge inwardly received" (12.7), points to the goal placed before the man that he can reach if he entrusts himself to the instruction of the text.

2. The fallen person before the *kairos* of salvation: To knowledge of the truth necessarily belongs the truth about humanity, and it is relentlessly revealed. The individual of his own accord is handed over to his own will and thus to danger "to be borne along by unruly impulses, being drawn away by the desire of pleasure and various lusts" (9.1a). Moreover, on its own, human nature is incapable of reaching life (9.1c, 6a). Yet this fact is only the dark background that stands in contrast to the brightness of the unexpected goodness of God (9.2a, 5). The

---

25 Foundational on this Brox, *Terminologisches*.

26 The structural analogy to the work of Clement—the *Paidagogos* follows the *Protrepticus*—is obvious.

chronological juxtaposition "Once"–"Now" (9.1b-c, 6a) affirms the present as the "time of righteousness" (9.1b), which God has initiated at a precise point in time through the sending of the Son.

3. The individual in the world: If one considers the literary quality of the text, it becomes apparent that the people addressed by *Ad Diognetum* belong to the educated class. The question about the reality of the faith must therefore go into the position of Christians in society (Diogn 5–6). With constantly changing stylistic media, the author presents variations on three motifs: the world as the dwelling place of the Christians in which both their integration with it (5.1-2, 4; 6.2) and their distance from it (5.5-9; 6.3b, 4c) play out; the world as the place of hostility and temptation (5.11, 17; 6.5b, 6b); and the superiority of Christians in the world (5.10, 12, 14-16; 6.7-9). The statement formulated thetically in the language of political metaphor, "what the soul is in the body, Christians are in the world," (6.1) is not substantiated. The following chapters will supply the basis for this evaluation.

4. The individual as imitator of God: The classic question about the way to happiness receives a clear answer, first in a delineation, then in a positive definition: Happiness does not consist of the oppression of the weak, nor of possessions and wealth or of the exercise of power, for thereby no one can imitate God (10.5). Happiness is achieved only by the person who imitates God by taking on the burden of his neighbor and passing on to the needy what he has received from God (10.6). Thus he becomes an imitator of his goodness (10.4). Superiority and distance from the world do not make the believer "unworldly." His purpose as an imitator of God leads him to assume God's conduct as a principle of action. The plan presented here for achieving happiness by the *imitatio Dei* is an inspired example of the reception of a classical theme of the philosophical tradition that is reinterpreted and integrated as a component of the Christian message.

5. The believer in the church under the leadership of the Logos: As a protreptic text, *Ad Diognetum* intends to lead the reader to full inclusion in the church. The thematic sequence and the persuasion-minded argumentation aim toward that goal. To this scheme also belongs the suggestive presentation of a goal already reached, in which the reader is depicted as one who is "begotten by the loving Word" (11.2a) and thus can be sure of his guidance and instruction (11.4-5). The cheering prospect of becoming a delightful paradise in which the tree of knowledge is planted (12.1-2) also contains the admonition to put the knowledge into practice with fear (12.6b) so that the story of the beginning (Gen 3) does not repeat itself (12.6a). The abundance of detached metaphors in the last two chapters gives no concrete information about the indicated fellowship, but it is questionable whether the author cared about that. The process of conversion, Christian instruction, and integration into the church are anticipated here literarily. The necessary decisions of the audience to become involved in this process are in no way diminished. On the contrary, they were prepared and positively influenced.

7.　Authorship, Place of Writing, and Dating

There are few works of early Christian literature that have given rise to as many divergent opinions about the author, place of composition, and time of origin as has the text *Ad Diognetum*. As long as Justin was held to be the author of the work, the remaining information was secured with small variations. Apart from a few exceptions,[27] this state of affairs did not change until the middle of the nineteenth century.[28] After the authorship of Justin was rejected, the suggestions of names of the supposed author piled up.[29] The time and place of origin could be determined to a great extent in connection with the suggested figure of the moment, assuming that the suggestion of the moment was able to persuade.[30] That is sadly not the case.

It makes little sense to assume one of the supposed authors as the writer of *Ad Diognetum* or to suggest yet another new name, if that were possible. More than a certain plausibility cannot be reached in that way. A more methodically sensible way presents itself when one begins from the text itself to sketch the contours of the author. The time and place of origin must follow from that. One can hardly expect to reach a certain conclusion by this method, given the precarious nature of the sources, but the suggestion can be stimulating in the further discussion of the question.

Whoever writes a text that begins with the questions of a student takes on the role of a teacher. The entire explanation confirms him in this role regardless of whether one also takes the self-portrait in 11.1 as evidence for it. Greater precision with which to rescue the figure from anonymity cannot be obtained.

However, the similarities to the work of Clement of Alexandria can be clearly determined.[31] Of course, any comparison between the Alexandrian's extensive body of work and the few pages of *Ad Diognetum* must take this disparity into account, but the points of contact in style and content cannot be disputed. In no other suggested place of origin, such as Asia Minor or Rome,[32] is anything similar present. The issue is naturally not a literary dependency of whatever kind but the

---

[27] E.g., Böhl, *Opuscula*, and Hefele, *Patrum Apostolicorum*.

[28] E.g., Otto, *Epistola*, and Hollenberg, *Brief*.

[29] Donaldson may have gone furthest, as he suspected at first that the author could have been Robertus Stephanus—the father of the editor of the 1592 edition, Henricus Stephanus. However, the age of the manuscript convinced him that this opinion was untenable, after which he supported a very late date for the text: "I am inclined to think [. . .] that some of the Greeks who came over to Italy when threatened by the Turks may have written the treatise, not so much from the wish to counterfeit a work of Justin's as to write a good declamation in the old style" (*History* II:142).

[30] As an example of the disparate states of scholarship, a few of the suggestions can be referred to: Hippolytus of Rome (Connolly, 1935), Pantaenus (Marrou, 1951), Valentinus (Pétrement, 1966), Melito of Sardis (Jossa, 1969/70). The most recent attempt undertaken by Hill, *Teaching*, to prove the authorship of Polycarp of Smyrna without thorough linguistic analysis does not represent any kind of progress.

[31] See above.

[32] Cf. Norelli, *Diogneto*, 56–61.

belonging to a common cultural milieu. Thus, the assertion that the text originated in Alexandria is not unfounded.[33]

In the attempt to determine the date of origin, the heretofore halfway firm
foundations—an anonymous teacher who worked in Alexandria as the author—
become shaky, and any assertion can claim no more for itself than the rank of a
plausible hypothesis.

The figure of Clement offers itself as a point of departure for the timeframe
in which *Ad Diognetum* could have been written. Geffcken might be right in his
observation about the author: "In the main he shines only as a satellite of the
star of Clement."[34] That means that the only vaguely discernable teacher worked
in the last decades of the second century in the same open cultural setting in
which Pantaenus had already worked, which has been called the "Alexandrian
school." The fact that his little text remained in obscurity is not surprising when
one places it beside the vast work of Clement. Nevertheless, it was preserved and
at some point connected to the writings of Justin. This connection protected it
from destruction. Its literary history truly begins again only in the fifteenth century, when it was found in Constantinople.

8.   Bibliography

Alfonsi, L. "Il 'Protretico' di Clemente Alessandrino e l'Epistola a Diogneto." *Aevum* 20
   (1946): 100–108.

Barnard, L. W. "The Epistle Ad Diognetum: Two Units from One Author." *ZNW* 56
   (1965): 130–37.

Baumeister, T. "Zur Datierung der Schrift an Diognet." *VC* 42 (1988): 105–11.

Blackeney, E. H. *The Epistle to Diognet.* London 1943.

Böhl, G. *Opuscula Patrum selecta.* Berlin 1826.

Brändle, R. *Die Ethik der "Schrift an Diognet": Eine Wiederaufnahme paulinischer und
   johanneischer Theologie am Ausgang des zweiten Jahrhunderts.* ATANT 64. Zurich
   1975.

Brox, N. *Terminologisches zur frühchristlichen Rede von Gott.* SBAW.PH 1. Munich 1996.

Connolly, R. H. "The Date and Authorship of the Epistle to Diognet." *JTS* 36 (1935):
   347–53.

Donaldson, J. *A Critical History of Christian Literature and Doctrine.* 2 vols. London 1866.

Eltester, W. "Das Mysterium des Christentums: Anmerkungen zum Diognetbrief." *ZNW*
   61 (1970): 278–93.

Geffcken, J. "Der Brief an Diognet." *ZKG* 43 (1924): 348–50.

———. *Der Brief an Diognetos.* Heidelberg 1928.

---

33 This view has been supported often. Cf. Geffcken, "Brief," 349–50; Marrou, *Diognète*, 251–53,
263–65; Brändle, *Ethik*, 230; Baumeister, "Datierung," 108–10; Rizzi, *Questione*, 170–73.

34 "Brief," 350.

Hefele, C. J. *Patrum Apostolicorum opera.* Tübingen 1839.

Hill, C. E. *From the Lost Teaching of Polycarp: Identifying Irenaeus' Apostolic Presbyter and the Author of Ad Diognetum.* WUNT 186. Tübingen 2006.

Hollenberg, W. A. *Der Brief an Diognet herausgegeben und bearbeitet.* Berlin 1853.

Jossa, G. "Melitone e l'*A Diogneto.*" *AIIS* 2 (1969/1970): 89–109.

Lindemann, A. "Paulinische Theologie im Brief an Diognet." In *Kerygma und Logos: Beiträge zu den geistesgeschichtlichen Beziehungen zwischen Antike und Christentum (FS C. Andresen)*, edited by A. M. Ritter, 337–50. Göttingen 1979.

Lona, H. E. *An Diognet.* KfA 8. Freiburg i. B. 2001.

———. "Das Gottesbild des Ad Diognetum." In *Ein Gott für die Menschen (FS O. Wahl)*, edited by L. Bily et al., 131–42. Benediktbeurer Studien 9. Munich 2002.

———. *Die "Wahre Lehre" des Kelsos.* KfA Erg. 1. Freiburg u.a. 2005.

Lorenz, B. *Der Brief an Diognet.* CMe 18. Einsiedeln 1982.

Mara, M. G. "Osservazioni sull' 'Ad Diognetum.'" *SMSR* 38 (1964): 267–79.

Marrou, H. I. *Á Diognète: Introduction, édition critique et commentaire.* SC 33. Paris [1]1951 [2]1965.

Meecham, H. G. *The Epistle to Diognetus: The Greek Text with Introduction, Translation, and Notes.* Manchester 1949.

Noormann, R. "Himmelsbürger auf Erden: Anmerkungen zum Weltverständnis und zum 'Paulinismus' des Auctor ad Diognetum." In *Die Weltlichkeit des Glaubens in der Alten Kirche (FS U. Wickert)*, edited by D. Wyrwa, 199–229. BZNW 85. Berlin 1997.

Norelli, E. *A Diogneto: Introduzione, traduzione e note.* LCPM 11. Mailand 1991.

Otto, I. C. T. *Corpus apologetarum christianorum saeculi secundi: III: Iustini philosopi et martyri opera quae ferantur omnia: II: Opera Justini addubitata.* Jena [1]1843 [2]1849 [3]1879.

———. *Epistola ad Diognetum Justini philosophi et martyris nomen prae se ferens.* Jena 1845. Leipzig [2]1852.

Pétrement, S. "Valentin, est-il l'auteur de 'Épître à Diognet?" *RHPhR* 46 (1966): 34–62.

Rizzi, M. *La questione dell' unità dell' "Ad Diognetum."* SPMed 16. Mailand 1989.

Schneemelcher, W., ed. *Neutestamentliches Apokryphen, I: Evangelien; II: Apostolisches, Apokalypsen und Verwandtes.* Tübingen [5]1987–1989 (= NTApo[5]).

Stephanus, H. Ἰουστίνου τοῦ φιλοσόφου καὶ μάρτυρος Ἐπιστολὴ πρὸς Διόγνητον καὶ λόγος πρὸς Ἕλληνας: *Iustini philosophi et martyris Epist. Ad Diognetum, et Oratio ad Graecos, nunc primum luce et Latinitate donatate ab Henrico Stephano: Eiusdem Henr. Stephani annotationibus additum est Io. Iacobi Beureri de quorundam locorum partim interpretatione partim emendatione iudicium: Tatiani, discipuli Iustini, quaedam 1592.*

Tibiletti, C. "Aspetti polemici dell' Ad Diognetum." *AAST* 96 (1961–1962): 343–88.

Thierry, J.-J. *The Epistle to Diognetus.* Textus Minores. Leiden 1964.

Wengst, K. *Didache (Apostellehre), Barnabasbrief, zweiter Klemensbrief, Schrift an Diognet: Schriften des Urchristentums II.* Munich 1984.

Wilamowitz-Moellendorff, U. von. *Griechisches Lesebuch II.* Berlin 1906.

The Shepherd of Hermas

David Hellholm

In the *Pastor Hermae* (PH) we have not only the longest book of the so-called "Apostolic Fathers" but also the most extensive apocalypse of early Christianity, with the goal of producing legitimacy for a second opportunity for penance after baptism through supernatural revelations.

1. Textual Tradition

The textual tradition of the Hermas text is very complex,[1] on one hand through the scattered attestation in the Greek, Latin, Coptic, Ethiopian, and Middle Persian languages, on the other through the numerous fragments in most of these languages.

The greatest part of PH is preserved in two Greek manuscripts: in Codex Sinaiticus (? from the 4th c. [Vis I.1–Mand IV 3.6]) and in Codex Athos (A from the 15th c. on ten leaves, though the tenth leaf [Sim IX 30.3–X 4.5] has gone missing). In Latin translation the text exists in two manuscript variants: the Versio Vulgata (L[1] in more than twenty medieval manuscripts) and the Versio Palatina (L[2] in two complete manuscripts from the 15th c.). In the Ethiopian language the complete text exists in one manuscript from the sixteenth century (Ä).

The numerous, mostly very short papyrus fragments are overwhelmingly in the original Greek (P. Oxyrh. 3528 [late 2nd to early 3rd c.], 3527, 1828, 5, 404, 1783, 1172, 3526, 1599; P. Mich. 130 [oldest textual witness: 3rd quarter of the 2nd c.], 129 [2nd half of the 3rd c.]; P. Berlin 5513 [3rd c.]; P. Bodmer XXXVIII [4th–5th c., contains Vis I–III]),[2] but they also survive in Coptic translation: the Achmimic translation (K[a] papyrus codex from the 4th c.) and the Sahidic (K[s] fragments from two pergament codices [A and B] from the 5th, 6th, or 7th c.). A Middle Persian translation appears in the Manichaean fragment M97 (undated).

Among the quotations and allusions made by the church fathers, Clement of Alexandria (? before 215/221), Origen (185–254), Didymus (313–396), Tertullian (ca. 160–220), and especially Pseudo-Athanasius, *Praecepta ad Antiochum* (5th–6th c.) and Antiochos Monachos, *Homiliae* (7th c.) deserve to be

---

[1] See the listing in Whittaker, *Hirt des Hermas*, IX–XX; Joly, "Le Pasteur,"58–68; Leutzsch, *Hirt*, 117–22; further Osiek, *Shepherd*, 1–3.

[2] Only a selection of the most important papyri can be detailed here.

mentioned.[3] It is striking that the overwhelming majority of the fragments contain no portions of the text of the "Book of Visions"; the primary exception is P. Bodmer XXXVIII, but it comes from a later period.[4]

Noteworthy among recent editions of the text (some with translations) are those by M. Whittaker ([2]1967), R. Joly ([2]1968), A. Lindemann and H. Paulsen (1992), M. Leutzsch (1998), B. Ehrman (2003), and M. W. Holmes ([3]2007).[5]

2.   Literary Composition

The methodical reasoning for the compositional development of the Hermas text has as a starting point the evidence, partly internal but partly external to the text, for a caesura between Vis IV and V.[6]

2.1 Evidence within the Text

1. *The change in the mediators of revelation.* In the so-called "Book of Visions" (Vis I–IV) the "presbytress" is the predominant revelation-bearer; after that she does not appear again, for she is replaced in the Mandates and the Similitudes by the "shepherd."

2. *The author.* In the Book of Visions the author is addressed by the presbytress in all four visions with Ἑρμᾶ, while in the "Book of the Shepherd," which is more than five times as long, he is addressed neither by name nor by title.

3. *The persons addressed.* In the Book of Visions the author addresses his readers multiple times with ἀδελφοί; in the Book of the Shepherd, by contrast, this direct address never appears.

4. *The message of penance,* proclaimed in the Book of Visions, appears not to have had complete success, since Sim VI 1.3 discusses a penance done in vain (εἰς μάτην ἐστὶν ἡ μετάνοια αὐτῶν) because the penitents subsequently did not follow the Lord's commands and even blasphemed the divine name.[7] (Cf. also Sim VIII 6.6.) This statement may refer to the repentant sinners who, according to the message of penance in the Book of Visions, had sinned again despite their repentance. For this reason the Book of the Shepherd and the "Addendum" must have been added to the Book of Visions. This addition is justified in Sim IX 1.2-3 by the necessity of a second tower-building allegory: "then accordingly was the building of the tower shown you by the Church [. . .] but now you see [them] through the same Spirit as if shown by an angel. You must, however, learn everything from me with greater accuracy (ἀκριβέστερον)."

---

3   Given by Whittaker, *Hirt des Hermas,* XIX–XX. Quotations by Ps.-Athanasius and Antiochus are thoroughly detailed in Dibelius, *Hermas.*
4   See Carlini (ed.), *Papyrus Bodmer XXXVIII.*
5   See the bibliography.

6   Dibelius, "Offenbarungsträger," 80; Reiling, *Prophecy,* 160; Vielhauer, *Geschichte,* 516–17; Vielhauer/Strecker, "Apokalypse: Hermas," 539–40.
7   Cf. Dibelius, *Hermas,* 580.

5. *Different groups of rich people.* In Vis III 6.5-7 the topic is minor landowners who denied being Christians during persecution; by contrast, Sim VIII 9.1 deals with very wealthy Christians who, though they do not recant because of possible persecution, have nevertheless turned away from the church.[8]

6. *Anaphoric and cataphoric references.*[9] In the Book of Visions there are in several places cataphoric hints toward the following vision(s) (Vis II 4.2, III 13.4b). Anaphoric hints also appear within the Book of Visions (Vis III 10.7–13.4, IV 3.6b). The remarkable thing is that none of the metatexutal references point beyond the Book of Visions. On the other hand, the presbytress gives an anaphoric conclusion signal that the Book of Visions has reached its end with her admonition to Hermas: "σὺ οὖν μὴ διαλίπῃς λαλῶν εἰς τὰ ὦτα τῶν ἁγίων. [...] μνημονεύετε τὰ προγεγραμμένα" (IV 3.6).

The significantly longer Book of the Shepherd (Mand I–Sim VIII), however, contains no anaphoric hints drawn from the Book of Visions. By contrast, there are references back to the Book of Visions in Vis V 5 and Sim IX 1.1. Both of these references, as M. Dibelius and P Vielhauer have shown, are to be interpreted as "addenda."[10] In that case, the enigmatic complex sentence in Vis V 5: "First of all, then, write down my commandments and similitudes (πρῶτον πάντων τὰς ἐντολάς μου γράψον καὶ τὰς παραβολάς), and you will write the other things (τὰ δὲ ἕτερα) as I shall show you (τὰ δὲ ἕτερα καθώς σοι δείξω οὕτως γράψεις)," can be explained as follows: The Book of Visions (I–IV) was first published separately; then the Mandates and the Similitudes were written as a separate book (Mand I–Sim VIII) and probably published;[11] when the bodies of these two texts were connected, τὰ δὲ ἕτερα (Vis V 5b) and τὰ δὲ λοιπά (Sim VIII 11.5) were added in the form of Sim IX–X. This idea is supported by the phrasing of Sim IX 1.1, which reads:

> After I had written down the commandments and similitudes (ἐντολαί καὶ παραβολαί) of the Shepherd, [...] he came to me and said, "I wish to explain to you (θέλω σοι δείξαι) what the Holy Spirit (τὸ πνεῦμα τὸ ἅγιον) that spoke with you in the form of the Church (ἐν μορφῇ τῆς ἐκκλησίας) showed you, for that Spirit is the Son of God (ἐκεῖνο γὰρ τὸ πνεῦμα ὁ υἱὸς τοῦ θεοῦ ἐστιν).

---

[8] Cf. Dibelius, *Hermas*, 599.

[9] Hellholm, *Visionenbuch*, 12; Hilhorst, *Sémitismes*, 19–31; idem, "Hermas," 684–85; Brox, *Hermas*, 32–33; Leutzsch, *Hirt*, 130–32; Osiek, *Shepherd*, 10.

[10] Dibelius, *Hermas*, 493, 602; Vielhauer, *Geschichte*, 517.

[11] The formula "ἐντολαί καὶ παραβολαί" is an expression of unity and does not indicate the arrangement of the "Shepherd of Hermas"; see Dibelius, *Hermas*, 493–94, 536, 543, 546, 578: "The first Similitudes are in no way substantially different from the Mandates" (493); the transition in Sim VI 1.1-4 "upholds the hypothesis presented regarding Vis V 5 Mand XI 1 XII 3.2, that ἐντολαί καὶ παραβολαί was originally the common name of the entire second portion of the book, the actual Shepherd" (578). Vielhauer, *Geschichte*, 517: "[I]n Vis. V 5-6 both the terms ἐντολαί and παραβολαί are connected only by the personal pronoun and article, each used only one time, and are thus understood as belonging together most closely (likewise Sim IX 1.1)."

In this context Vis V was added as an introduction to the Book of the Shepherd and completed by Sim IX–X. The insertion of the Addendum created the full text PH.[12] We thus have to deal with a compositional development in three stages, which probably has its foundation in varying religious and social circumstances within the Roman church, or rather the Roman house churches.[13]

2.2 The Extratextual Evidence

1. The superscript of Vis V. The superscript of the fifth vision shows a certain confusion: A and the Ethiopian translation (Ä) read ὅρασις ε′, L[1] *uisio quinta initium pastoris*. L[2] *incipiunt pastoris mandata duodecim*. The superscript in ℵ: ἀποκάλυψις ε′, appears to point to a specific difference between this vision and the previous ὅρασεις.[14]

2. The Michigan codex (M) does not contain the *Visiones* 1–4, as Bonner has shown. From this fact he concludes that the Mandates and Similitudes with their introduction (Vis 5) circulated in Egypt as a complete work.[15] The Coptic translations (K[a] and K[s]) also appear not to know Visions 1–4,[16] and the same is true of most of the minor papyrus fragments.[17] Athanasius, by contrast, would have it that the Book of the Shepherd begins with Mand I 1 and quotes only from the "Mandates and Similitudes." However, Clement of Alexandria, Origen, and Didymus, all of whom worked, like Athanasius, in Alexandria, also quote from the "Book of Visions." The only unfragmented manuscripts that know the text of the Book of Visions and the Book of the Shepherd inclusive of the Addendum are L[1], L[2], and Ä as well as ℵ and A.

3. From these results, very different conclusions have been drawn: Giet reckons with a timespan between 100 and 140 C.E. and three authors:[18] the first Vis I–IV; the second Sim IX; and the third Vis V + Mand I–XII + Sim I–VIII + X, while Coleborne pleads for a very complex history of origin in seven stages between circa 60 and 117.[19] On the basis of the attestation of the full text in the East, P. Henne[20] and C. Osiek[21] declare for a later division of the full text PH; however, that hypothesis cannot explain either the pattern of the anaphoric and cataphoric references or the further development of the doctrine of penance or of the Christology. In an earlier study I came to the conclusion that in all likelihood

---

[12]   So more or less also Brox, *Hermas*, 25–28, following Hellholm, *Visionenbuch*, 11–13; similarly already Dibelius, *Hermas*, 421, 493, 601–2; Vielhauer, *Geschichte*.

[13]   On the church relationships, see especially Osiek, *Rich and Poor*; Leutzsch, *Wahrnehmung*. With reference to the house churches in Rome, see Lampe, *Stadtrömischen Christen*, 10–52, 124–300, 301–45; idem, *From Paul to Valentinus*, 19–66, 153–355, 359–408.

[14]   Whittaker, *Hirt des Hermas*, XIIn6.

[15]   Bonner, *A Papyrus Codex*, 14; cf. Whittaker, *Hirt des Hermas*, XII–XIII with n6.

[16]   See Whittaker, *Hirt des Hermas*, 116; Leutzsch, *Hirt*, 130.

[17]   See Leutzsch, *Hirt*, 130.

[18]   Giet, *Hermas et les pasteurs*; idem, "Les trois auteurs"; so also earlier Osiek, *Rich and Poor*, 7.

[19]   Coleborne, *Linguistic Approach*; idem, "Shepherd of Hermas."

[20]   Henne, *L'unité*, 18–21.

[21]   Osiek, *Shepherd*, 4, 8.

this extensive work was composed by one author, but not at the same time, rather on three subsequent occasions.[22]

Before the question of the theological result of this history of the origin of PH can be raised, the phenomenon of text and intertext must be discussed.

2.3 Intertextuality: Pretext, Parallel Text, and Amplification

In his article "Arten des Kommentierens—Arten der Sinnbildung—Arten des Verstehens," W. Raible treats the phenomenon of "code conversion as the basis for generic intertextuality,"[23] or as A. J. Greimas puts it, "une operation de trans-codage" that can be called "une nouvelle version de 'la même chose.'"[24] In this process, the original text becomes a "'pretext' for a creative adaptation or further development in the act of understanding."[25] A text can therefore be reduced, replaced by a parallel text, or even amplified.[26]

With regard to PH we have a threefold development of a macrotext composed by a single author to work with: First a "pretext," consisting of the Book of Visions (Vis I–IV); second a "parallel text" (i.e., the Book of the Shepherd), consisting of the ἐντολαί καὶ παραβολαί (Mand I–Sim VIII); third an "amplification," consisting of a) the pretext (Vis I–IV), b) the parallel text (Mand I–Sim VIII), and c) the Addendum (Vis V + Sim IX–X). The end result is the text corpus PH found in ℵ and A as well as L[1], L[2], and Ä.[27] As far as the Hermas text is concerned, Leutzsch determines correctly that Hermas' mode of operation consists of "correcting and reinterpreting what was already written."[28]

3.   Theological Profile

3.1 Ecclesiology

"At the center of the 'Shepherd' stands ecclesiology."[29] Because of the composition history of PH presented above, it is necessary to look at the statistical breakdown of the ecclesiological terminology in the three parts.

---

[22] Hellholm, *Visionenbuch*, 12. Further Dibelius, *Hermas*, 493, 602; Reiling, *Prophecy*, 23; Vielhauer, *Geschichte*, 517; Vielhauer/Strecker, "Apokalypse: Hermas," 540; Hilhorst, *Sémitismes*, 19–31; idem, "Hermas," 684–85; Brox, *Hermas*, 32–33; Leutzsch, *Hirt*, 130–32; so now also Osiek, *Shepherd*, 10.

[23] Raible, "Arten des Kommenteriens," 51–73.

[24] Greimas, "La structure sémantique," 39–48: 43.

[25] Raible, "Arten des Kommentariens," 53.

[26] Raible, "Arten des Kommentariens," 59; idem, *Kognitive Aspekte*, 6–10.

[27] Examples of this kind of amplified macrotext appear often in antiquity, as Raible, "Arten des Kommentariens," 54–56, has emphasized; Leutzsch, *Hirt*, 131, points to Artemidorus, who "in Books IV and V of his *Oneirocriticon* [repeats] for the sake of precision much of what he had already said in the first three books."

[28] Leutzsch, *Hirt*, 132.

[29] Leutzsch, *Hirt*, 141. See especially Perveden, *Concept of the Church*, and Schneider, *Propter sanctam ecclesiam suam.*

The Statistics of the Ecclesiological Terminology

The lexeme ἐκκλεσία appears nine times in the Book of Visions (Vis I 1.6, 3.4; II 2.6, 4.1, 4.3; III 3.3, 9.7; IV 1.3, 2.2), in the parallel text, the Book of the Shepherd (Mand I–Sim VIII) only once (Sim VIII 6.4); in the Addendum ἐκκλεσία appears six times, all in Sim IX (IX 1.1, 1.2, 13.1, 18.2, 18.3, 18.4). The church is called ἁγία ἐκκλεσία three times, all in the Book of Visions (Vis I 1.6, 3.4; IV 1.3).

These observations establish first that the lexeme ἐκκλεσία is absent from the Mandates; second that the word ἐκκλεσία appears only one time in the Book of the Shepherd; and third and finally that the term appears frequently in the Addendum as it does in the Book of Visions.

Other lexemes that belong to the semantic field and were used as self-definitions by Christians are:

1. Saints (ἅγιοι): Vis I 1.9; II 2.4; III 3.3, 6.2, 8.8-9, 8.11; IV 3.6; Sim VIII 8.1.
2. Elect [chosen by God] (ἐκλεκτοί): Vis I 3.4; II 1.3, 2.5, 4.2; III 5.1 v.l., 8.3, 9.10; IV 2.5, 3.5.
3. Righteous (δίκαιοι): Vis I 1.8, 3.2, 4.2; II 2.5; Mand IV 1.3; XI 3, 9, 13–15; Sim III 2-3; IV 2-3; VIII 3.8, 9.1; Add. IX 15.4, 17.5.
4. Servants (δοῦλοι): Vis I 2.4; III 5.1 v.l.; IV 1.3; Mand III 4; IV 1.2, 3.4; V 2.1-2; VI 2.4, 2.6; VIII 4–6, 10; IX 9; X 1.2; XI 1; XII 1.2-3, 2.1-2, 3.1, 5.2, 5.4; Sim I 1, 10; II 2, 4; V 2.2-3, 2.5-9, 2.11, 4.1, 4.3, 5.2-3, 5.5-6, 6.4; VI 2.1, 5.6-7; VIII 6.5, 10.3; Add. IX 13.7, 15.3, 19.1, 19.3, 20.2, 24.2, 26.3, 27.2, 28.4, 28.8.
5. People [of God] (λαός): Sim V 5.2-3; V 6.2-4; VIII 1.2, 3.2-3; Add IX 18.4.

A compilation of the data clarifies the distribution of the lexemes through the three parts of PH:

Lexeme	Book of Visions	Book of the Shepherd			Addendum
		Mand	Sim I–VIII	Total	
ἐκκλεσία	9	0	1	= 1	6
ἅγιοι	8	0	1	= 1	0
ἐκλεκτοί	9	0	0	= 0	0
δίκαιοι	4	5	6	= 11	2
δοῦλοι	3	20	20	= 40	10
λαός	0	0	9	= 9	1
Total	33	25	37	= 62	19

The overall total is thus not very meaningful because the different lengths of of the three parts of the text are considerable. However, what is decisive is the distribution of the various lexemes, all of which except for ἐκκλεσία and λαός are in the plural, which means that even when the unity of the church is a central theme, individuals are being addressed.[30] This idea is supported by the fact that the parenetic requests are directed at the individual members but often followed by generalizations in speeches to Hermas (e.g., Vis I 1.9; II 2.2-4, 3.2; III 8.10; Mand III 5; IV 3.7, 4.4; V 2.8; VI 1.5; X 1.2, 3.4; XII 6.5; Sim IV 8; V3.4, 5.1, 6.7; VI 1.1; VII 7; VIII 11.1; IX 31.4–32.5; X 1.3; 2.3; 4.2, 4).[31]

1. The use of ἐκκλεσία is concentrated in the Book of Visions and the Addendum; in the Book of the Shepherd, it never appears in the Mandates and only once in the Similitudes.

2. All the terms except λαός appear in the Book of Visions, which is not surprising since this book was written first. The statistical distribution is especially striking in reference to the terms ἅγιοι and ἐκλεκτοί: neither appears in the Addendum; ἅγιοι appears only once in the Book of the Shepherd; and ἐκλεκτοί occurs only in the Book of Visions.

3. Of special interest is the overwhelming frequency of the term δοῦλοι in the Book of the Shepherd.

4. δίκαιοι is used more often in the Book of the Shepherd than in the other portions of the text. The same is true of λαός, which does not appear in the Book of Visions at all.

5. No church-related term appears in Vis V. This fact, together with the change of the revelation-bearer from the presbytress as the "Ideal Church" to the shepherd as the "angel of penance" to whom Hermas was handed over (Vis V 3-4, 7), speaks decisively for the idea that this vision is to be understood as an introduction to the Book of the Shepherd and the second part of the Addendum (Sim IX–X). Anaphoric references to the giving over appear in Sim IX 1.1-3 as well as in X 1; therefore these passages form an *inclusio* between the two parts of the addendum. The transfer, as one might expect, is never referred to in the Book of Visions.

6. There are also no church-related terms in Sim X. This fact is connected with the fact that in this closing portion of PH the shepherd's superior, the Son of God, enters to effect the authorization not only of Hermas but also of the shepherd and to entrust Hermas with the news of the possibility of penance after baptism.

As a consequence of these statistical observations, it is necessary to examine a possible difference in the understanding of the church within PH.

---

[30] Cf. Dibelius, *Hermas*, 485–86; Leutzsch, *Wahrnehmung*, 207; idem, *Hirt*, 143; Staats, *Hermas*, 102. Otherwise Osiek, *Shepherd*, 30.

[31] With respect to the generalizations, see Dibelius, *Hermas, passim*.

Different Themes Connected with the Understanding of the Church

With regard to the understanding of the church, not only the direct formation of the concept is important; rather, other elements that belong here include the initiation requirements of the church like baptism, the ordering of life in the church such as ethics, and the future conditions like eschatology.

"Ideal" versus "Empirical" Church

The understanding of the church within the full text rests for the time being on the basis of a distinction between "Ideal Church" and "Empirical Church."[32]

Evidence from the Book of Visions

The Ideal/Preexistent Church		*The Empirical Church*	
Vis I 1.6	Rhoda coming from heaven as holy church		
Vis I 3.2	God created his holy church	Vis II 2.5-6	Call to penance addressed to the saints and the leaders of the church
Vis II 4.1	Complementary disclosure of the presbytress as the church by a youth as revelation-bearer	Vis II 4.2-3	Commission to make copies of a letter from heaven: one for Clement, one for Grapte; Hermas should read it to the presbyters
Vis III 3.3	The tower is the church	Vis III 9.7	Invitation to the wealthy and to the leaders of the church
Vis IV 1.3	Request for completion of the revelation given by holy church		
Vis IV 2.2	Reacknowledgment of the church as revelation-bearer		

The main revelation-bearer to Hermas in the Book of Visions is the preexistent holy church. As such she—the Ideal Church—is concerned about the Empirical Church. This fact is evident from her exhortations to the saints and to the leaders as well as from the tower allegory and its interpretation by the revelation-bearer.

Since the Book of Heaven with the offer of penance is to be transcribed and separately given to the fellowships in the area as well as to the house churches in Rome itself, it is understandable that not only the Ideal Church stands at the center here but that also the Empirical Church and its situation are addressed.

---

32 See Dibelius, *Hermas*, 466; Leutzsch, *Hirt*, 142.

Evidence from the Book of the Shepherd (Mand I – Sim VIII)

The Ideal/Preexistent Church	*The Empirical Church*	
	Sim VIII 6.4	Apostates and traitors to the church

The only place in the Book of the Shepherd in which the church is explicitly referenced is Sim VIII. Here clearly only the Empirical Church is meant, because the Shepherd's judgment of the apostates and traitors to the church is announced in his interpretation of the analogy of the willow tree.

Even though the lexeme "church" does not appear in the rest of the Book of the Shepherd,[33] it does not mean that this parallel text contains no church-related material, for here there is overwhelming parenetic material with the goal of introducing the catechumens into the instruction "in the strict moral requirements of being Christian."[34] Probably we have here a "parallel text" to the pretext of the Book of Visions that was later incorporated into the macrotext of PH as catechetical instruction.

Evidence from the Addendum (Sim IX)

The Ideal/Preexistent Church		*The Empirical Church*	
Sim IX 1.1	The Holy Spirit in the form of the church—the Spirit = the Son of God		
Sim IX 1.2	The church as revelator of the tower allegory		
Sim IX 13.1	The tower is the church	Sim IX 13.1	The tower is the church
		Sim IX 18.2	The church of God should be purified
		Sim IX 18.3	The church of God should be clean
		Sim 18.4	The church of God should be one body, one mind, one Spirit, one faith, one love

The new bearer of revelation, the Shepherd, first identifies the church as the Holy Spirit and reinterprets what the Ideal Church announced to Hermas as the first revelation-bearer. The Ideal Church is established as the revelation-bearer and interpreter of the first building of the tower (Vis III; Sim IX 1.1). The purpose is

---

[33] Brox, *Hermas*, 524: "The Mandates and Sim I–VIII address the theme of the church only indirectly."

[34] Hartman, *Into the Name*, 179; Leutzsch, *Hirt*, 132.

an authorizing of the church as the heavenly bearer of revelation. In this way the revelation in the Book of Visions is confirmed by an independent heavenly revelator, who is named as ὁ ἄγγελος τῆς μετανοίας. A second request of the second tower allegory is given explicitly: Hermas should be instructed about everything "with greater accuracy" (ἀκριβέστον) by the Shepherd, the man "sent [. . .] by the glorious angel" (ὑπὸ τοῦ ἐνδόξου ἀγγέλου) (IX 1.2-3). When it is said in Sim IX 13.1 that the tower represents the Ideal Church, it is stated at the same time that this church is also to be understood as the Empirical Church. Later in the interpretation of the allegory (Sim IX 18.2-4), the weight lies significantly on the Empirical Church with the goal of steering it toward coinciding with the preexistent Ideal Church in the eschatological completion (Sim IX 12.3–29.2),[35] as is clear from the unity formula: ἕν σῶμα, μία φρόνησις, εἷς νοῦς, μία πίστις, μία ἀγάπη!

Baptism as a Basis for Initiation into the Church

Fundamental for assimilation into the church is baptism because it clearly appears as *conditio sine qua non* for salvation (Sim IX 16).[36] Vis III 3.5 states: "Hear then why the tower is built *upon* the waters (ἐπὶ ὑδάτων). It is because your life has been, and will be, saved (ἐσώθη καὶ σωθήσεται) *through* water (διὰ ὕδατος)." This section is of special interest because of the fusion of two aspects: first the tower as the Empirical Church, built ἐπὶ ὑδάτων, and then the individual Christian, who is and will be saved διὰ ὕδατος.

Christians have been saved from their sins by baptism, but baptism is at the same time the sacrament of faith, for "when we descended into the water and received remission of our former sins" (Mand IV 3.1) is parallel to "those who have now believed, and those who are to believe, [. . .] have remission of their previous sins" (Mand IV 3.3).[37]

How important baptism is for Hermas is also apparent in the statement made in Sim IX 16.7, where we are told that "these apostles and teachers [. . .] preached [the seal of baptism] not only to those who were asleep, but themselves also gave them the seal of the preaching. [. . .] For [the righteous and the prophets] slept in righteousness and in great purity, but only they had not this seal" (μόνον δὲ τὴν σφραγῖδα ταύτην οὐκ εἶχον).[38] On the basis of this passage as well as the overall statements about baptism in PH, Kühneweg can rightly determine "what

---

[35] Brox, *Hermas*, 531–32; Leutzsch, *Hirt*, 142.
[36] See Hartman, *Into the Name*, 117, 179, 185: "Baptism is integrated in a whole, i.e., in the process of leaving death for life (Sim. 8.6.6, 9.16.2-3), of being saved (Vis. 3.3.5; Mand. 12.3.6; Sim. 8.6.1), and of entering the kingdom of God (Sim. 9.12). This all explains why baptism is so necessary." Leutzsch, *Hirt*, 141; Kühneweg, "Gesetz,"

65. Otherwise Staats, *Hermas*, 104: "Baptism is mentioned in passing."
[37] Hartman, *Into the Name*, 178–79: "Baptism is the sacrament of faith" (178).
[38] Kühneweg, "Gesetz," 72. Definitely not as "vicarious baptism for the dead," as Staats, *Hermas*, 104, understands it.

foundational meaning baptism has for Hermas" and finally declare: "The only sufficient requirement for insertion into the tower, however, is baptism itself."[39]

The Offer of the Possibility of a Second Penance after Baptism

"The tendency of the book is thoroughly parenetic and directed toward penance."[40] This statement applies not only to the Book of Visions (Vis I–III), but also to the Book of the Shepherd (Mand *passim*; Sim I–IV) and to the Addendum (Sim IX–X).

The penance terminology, including the lexemes ἐπιστρέφειν, *recurro*, and *paenitentia*, are distributed through the three portions of PH as follows:[41]

Lexeme	Book of Visions	Book of the Shepherd			Addendum
		Mand	Sim I–VIII	Total	
μετάνοια	7	14	20	34	16
μετανοεῖν	15	16	43	59	20
ἐπιστρέφειν	2	5	0	5	2
recurro	0	0	0	0	1
paenitentia	0	0	0	0	4/5
Total	24	35	63	98	43/4

The penance terminology is somewhat evenly distributed, when one takes the differing lengths of the three sections into account. A certain comparison is obvious, however. In all three sections penance stands at the center. The main interest of PH thus appears to be the announcement of a one-time penance after baptism and the purification of the church that works through said penance.[42]

Within the house churches in Rome there were differing opinions about the possibility of receiving forgiveness for past sins after baptism. A lax position apparently dominated in the Roman fellowships, especially among the rich,[43] but we know from texts like Hebrews 6:4-6, 10:26-31, 12:16-17,[44] and somewhat softened 1 John 3:6, 5:13-21,[45] that in the early church a minority, especially

---

39 Kühneweg, "Gesetz."

40 Vielhauer, *Geschichte*, 520; Dibelius, *Hermas*, 510–13, 576; Joly, *Le Pasteur*, 22–30; Leutzsch, *Hirt*, 129, 142–43.

41 The enumeration follows the version by Leutzsch, *Hirt*, where the Greek fragments are examined; cf. the distribution studies (minus ἐπιστρέφειν, *recurro*, and *paenitentia*) in Goldhahn-Müller, *Grenze*, 245; quoted in Osiek, *Shepherd*, 28n218.

42 So Dibelius, *Hermas*, 576; Brox, *Hermas*, 476–85.

43 Osiek, *Rich and Poor*; Lampe, *Stadtrömischen Christen*, 72–75; idem, *From Paul to Valentinus*, 90–93.

44 See Braun, *Hebräer*, 170–73: "Excurs: Die Ablehnung der zweiten Buße"; "Hermas modifies the Hb-rigorism, perhaps deliberately antithetically, expressly" (172).

45 See Strecker, *Johannesbrief*, 299–304: "Excurs: Zweite Buße."

among the church leadership, took a strong stand for a rigorous attitude. This tendency toward refusal of a second chance at penance can also be observed in PH, as Mand IV 3.1 makes clear: "I heard, sir, some teachers maintain that there is no other repentance than that which takes place, when we descended into the water and received remission of our former sins."

What Hermas reports as being disclosed by two bearers of revelation, first by the presbytress as the Ideal Church, who transmits a letter from heaven to be transcribed (Vis II 2-3), and afterward by the Shepherd as the "angel of penance" (ὁ ἄγγελος τῆς μετανοίας; Vis V 7; Mand XII 4; Sim IX 1.1, 14.3, 23.5, 24.4), who brings the offer of God's mercy (Mand IV 3.4-5; Sim IX 32.5), is a compromise between the lax and the rigorist positions within the Roman churches and their surroundings: Postbaptismal forgiveness is possible, but only once and only for a limited time (Mand IV 1.8, 3.5; Vis II 2.4-5).[46] For Hermas this is not a restricting, but rather a relieving offer (Mand IV 3.7: ἐζωοποιήθην).[47] However, or rather therefore, the time of penance moves itself ever further into the distance (Vis II 2.4-5; Sim VIII 2.7; IX 32.1; X 4.4).[48]

The Tower as the Church in Vis III—The Tower as the Church in Sim IX

The question of whether there are different central themes with regard to the understanding of the church in PH can best be answered by a comparison between the two tower allegories with their individual interpretations: Vis III and Sim IX. This comparison allows the possibility of following a code conversion of the "pretext" (the Book of Visions) through a creative development via adaptation and adjustment to an altered form (Addendum). This amplification is, as shown above, performed by one and the same author.

1. There is a christological foundation in Sim IX (1.1-2; 12.1-8; 13.2-3; 14.5; 15.2; 16.3-7; 17.1, 4), while there is not one in Vis III. Without the christological basis the allegory in Sim IX cannot be retold, as Brox rightly points out (Sim IX 5.2, 6-7; 6.1–7.3; 12.1-4).[49]

2. In Vis III the tower is built on the water, that is, baptism, but in Sim IX 14.4 the tower is built on a rock with a gate, both of which are identified as the "Son of God" (cf. already IX 12.1).[50] In this way the christological foundation is presented clearly.

---

[46] Lampe, *Stadtrömischen Christen*, 447–48; idem, *From Paul to Valentinus*, 95; Dibelius, *Hermas*, 510–13; Brox, *Hermas*, 476–85: "Exkus: Die Buße": "H[ermas] gains a great advantage with his concept: According to the preaching of the Shepherd, all Christians, from the catechumens to the mature Christians, are in the same situation, namely one unique saving chance to be able to grasp their life, here baptism, there penance. And all stand under the same obligation, which in one case is: no sin after baptism! and in the other: no sin after penance!"; Leutzsch, *Hirt*, 141–42; Osiek, *Shepherd*, 28–30.

[47] So rightly Lampe, *Stadtrömische Christen*, 448.

[48] Cf. Dibelius, *Hermas*, 453, 589, and *passim*.

[49] So also Brox, *Hermas*, 531.

[50] Osiek, *Shepherd*, 220.

3. In Vis III the tower is carried by seven women (8.2), but in Sim IX the twelve virgins are named with their names together with the name of the Son of God (15.1-2). Once again, therefore, the importance of the Christology is raised.

4. In Sim IX 6.1ff. a continual inspection of the tower by the "Lord of the whole tower" (ὁ κύριος ὅλου οὖ πύργου [6.7]) takes place,[51] which is not the case in Vis III. In Vis III Christians who already belong to the church through baptism are pressed to repent and to live according to God's commands. Sim IX, by contrast, deals with people among the nations, including the pagans, who have become believers and entered the church through baptism. In both cases the completion of the tower is still outstanding and will be reached only in the eschatological future, when the Empirical Church covers herself with the Ideal Church.[52] In the present applies: As the bad Christians in Vis III had to be expelled (2.5–7.6), so also in Sim IX must the rash and halfhearted converts again be taken out of the tower, that is, the church (1.4-10; 3.3-4, 8; 5.2; 6.3–9.6; 13.3–14.2; 15.4–31.2). With N. Brox we can therefore determine: "The identity of the groups had changed, but not the concept of the Church."[53]

5. The allegory of the twelve mountains (Sim IX 1.4-10) and its interpretation (Sim IX 17.1-29) is a secondary addition to the allegory of the stones.[54] First the shepherd gives an explanation of the mountains as such; afterward the explanation of the stones is supplied.[55] The number twelve is an allusion to the twelve tribes of Israel. Hermas, however, explains these tribes as twelve nations: τὰ ὄρη ταῦτα δώδεκά εἰσι φυλαὶ αἱ κατοικοῦσαι ὅλον τὸν κόσμον.[56] In this way a universal perspective is introduced that appears only occasionally in PH: the world mission (Sim IX 25),[57] but that is already referenced in Sim VIII 3.2.[58] After the converts are integrated into the tower, which appears like a single stone, and thus become one body, "certain of these defiled themselves, and were expelled from the race of the righteous, and became again what they were before, or rather worse" (Sim IX 17.5).[59] The difference in perspective in Sim IX in comparison

---

51 Dibelius, *Hermas*, 609ff.; Brox, *Hermas*, 398ff.
52 Dibelius, *Hermas*, 609: "[5].1-[6], 8 The testing of the tower building. With [5].1-2 begins the portion of Sim. that serves the special interest of Hermas. For he wants here indeed, spinning the concepts of Vis. III further, to show that the Tower of the Church is not yet so pure and flawless as is described in Vis. III, that therefore the empirical Church does not yet match the ideal." This is true, although the Church in Vis III is not only to be described as the ideal.
53 Brox, *Hermas*, 531.
54 Brox, *Hermas*, 441ff.; Dibelius, *Hermas*, 628; Osiek, *Shepherd*, 244ff.
55 Cf. Dibelius, Hermas, 604–6: Excurs: "Der Fels und die Berge."
56 Dibelius, *Hermas*, 626–27; Brox, *Hermas*, 530–31; Osiek, *Shepherd*, 244: "The church is

founded on its biblical and Jewish heritage, but has moved on further."
57 Brox, *Hermas*, 441; Kühneweg, "Gesetz," 55–56: "In the revelation that Hermas is granted, the world mission that the *Kerygma Petrou* wanted to prove as being fortold by Isa 2:3 is already assumed to be complete."
58 Sim VIII 3.2: "This great tree (= the willow tree) that casts its shadow over plains, and mountains, and all the earth, is the law of God that was given (δοθείς) to the whole world; and this law is the Son of God, proclaimed (κηρυχθείς) to the ends of the earth. . . ."
59 On this see Brox, *Hermas*, 433, 443, 450–51; Dibelius, *Hermas*, 466, 626, 634. Cf. von Campenhausen, *Amt*, 103 with n4.

with Vis III points to the fact that the Addendum comes from a further developed situation within Roman Christianity and beyond.

6. The romance motif in the form of an erotic story about the virgins, that is, the virtues, in Sim IX 10.6–11.8 has no parallel in Vis III;[60] but see Vis I with Rhoda! The goal is twofold: to establish the relationship between Hermas and the virtues (Ἑρμᾶς ὁ ἐγκρατής, Vis I 2.4)[61] and to show the "sexual honor [. . .] with or without celibacy."[62] These virgins represent the opposite of the twelve wild women in black clothing, that is, the vices (Sim IX 13.6-9)! This fact is clarified in the interpretation in the form of catalogues of virtues and vices (Sim 15.1-3; cf. Mand VIII 5).

3.2 Christology

The Christology in PH is distinguished on the one hand by the connection with the pneumatology and on the other hand by the shift in emphasis among the three parts.

Christological Titles

With regard to Christology it is striking that neither the name Jesus nor the title Christ appears.[63]

With one exception (Vis II 2.8) the christological title ὁ υἱὸς τοῦ θεοῦ appears exclusively in the Book of the Shepherd (Sim V 2.6-8, 11; 4.1; 5.2-3, 5; 6.1-2, 4, 7; VIII 3.2; 11.1) and the Addendum (Sim IX 1.1; 12.1-2, 4-6, 8; 13.2-3, 5, 7; 14.5; 15.2, 4; 16.3, 5, 7; 17.1, 4; 18.4; 24.4; 28.2-3 [31.4: *filius dei*]). The *pneuma* in connection with the Son of God is spoken of only in the Book of the Shepherd (Sim V 5.5-6) and the Addendum (Sim IX 1-2).[64]

Lexeme	Book of Visions	Book of the Shepherd		Addendum
		Mand	Sim I–VIII	
υἱὸς τοῦ θεοῦ	1	0	18	30
πνεῦμα = υἱὸς τοῦ θεοῦ	0	0	2	2

---

[60] Cf. Lampe, *Stadtrömische Christen*, 191; idem, *From Paul to Valentinus*, 227; Dibelius, *Hermas*, 618–19; Joly, *Le Pasteur*, 48; Brox, *Hermas*, 405–10; Osiek, *Shepherd*, 227–29.

[61] Dibelius, *Hermas*, 619; Luschnat, "Jungfrauszene," 64; Brox, *Hermas*, 410.

[62] Osiek, *Shepherd*, 228.

[63] As *varia lectio* (a) in Vis III 6.6 only in Codex A: τῷ Χριστῷ instead of τῷ κυρίῳ; (b) in Sim

IX 18.1 in Codex A: τὸν Χριστόν instead of *dominum* (L¹), *deum* (L²), *dominum* (Ä; trans.); in Vis II 2.8 τὸν Χριστόν in Codex ℵ instead of τὸν κύριον (ℵ^c, A, L², E); υἱόν (L¹). Conclusion: A contains many "improvements," so that Χριστός is certainly one of those and the title Christ does not appear in PH. See on this Nijendijk, *Christologie*, 75–76.

[64] Cf. Kühneweg, "Gesetz," 62.

The connection of the title κύριος, which appears about 340 times, is difficult to determine for the whole of PH, since there is not always a clear distinction between κύριος in reference mostly to "God" (e.g., Vis II 2.8; Mand VII 1; X 1.6; Sim VI 3.6; IX 12.6), but also to "Christ" (e.g., Vis III 5.2; 7.3; Sim V 6.1-2, 4; VIII 1.1; 6.4; IX 5.2; 7.1; 10.4; 12.4-5, 8; 13.3; 14.3, 5-6; 15.2; 16.3, 5, 7; 28.2, 6; 30.2) or even to the "Holy Spirit" (e.g., Mand III 1; X 1.6).[65] However, in many cases the title "Lord" (κύριε) in the mouth of Hermas refers to the Shepherd (e.g., Sim IX 16.1, 5).

Christology and Law

Hermas knows only the law of God (Sim VIII 3.2), but no law of Christ: "The Son of God as the Spirit of God is the Giver of the Law and at the same time, as a man, the obedient Servant and the example of fulfillment of the commandments."[66] However, righteousness by works is not the issue,[67] for even though the keeping of the commandments is given a major role in PH, it must be established that only after the purification from earlier sins by faith and baptism are Christians enabled to live by the commandments of the Law (Vis III 7.3; Sim IX 16): "Baptism and Law, that is for Hermas the whole Gospel."[68]

The Correspondence between the Son of God–Spirit–Church–Law

With regard to the correspondence between the Son of God, the Holy Spirit, the Church, and the Law, it appears that all four entities underlie a variation of the revelation scheme.[69]

	Before the World and Hidden		*Within the World and Revealed*	
1	Vis II 2.8; Sim IX 12.1-2	Son of God: old rock	Sim IX 7.1; Mand V 1.7, 12.3	Son of God: new gate
2	Sim V 6.5	Holy Spirit: Creator of the world	Sim V 6.5	Holy Spirit: dwelling in the flesh
3	Vis I 1.6; II 4.1, 7.7-10	Ideal Church: older than the creation	Vis II 2.5-6; Sim VIII 6.4; IX 13.1, 18.3-4	Empirical Church: now made manifest
4	Sim V 5.3, 6.3[70]	Law: given before or with the creation	Sim VIII 5.2; IX 12.3[71]	Law: made known in the "last days"

---

65 See esp. Nijendijk, *Christologie*, 77–80.
66 Kühneweg, "Gesetz," 62.
67 So Dibelius, *Hermas*, 565.
68 Kühneweg, "Gesetz," 53, 64; 65: "Baptism is the foundation of the Church and precedes the Law. [. . .] The keeping of the commandments does

not win him (i.e., the baptized person) salvation, but only secures it."
69 Cf. Hellholm, "Revelation-Schema"; Dibelius, *Hermas*, 619; Kühneweg, "Gesetz," 62–64.
70 I.e., the law of the Ideal Church.
71 I.e., the law of the Empirical Church.

As there is a hierarchy of revelators in PH (see below), so there is also one in the revelation of the Law: A) the *originator* of the Law is God (Sim V 3.2, 5.3, 6.3); B) the *mediator* is the Son of God (Sim V 5.3, 6.3); C) the *mediator of the revelation* is the shepherd (Vis V 5; Vis V–Sim X); D) the *transmitter* to the audience is firstly Hermas (Vis V 6; Sim X 4.1 and *passim*), but afterward also Clement and Grapte (Vis II 4.3);[72] E) the *addressees* are all Christians in Rome and its surroundings (Vis II 4.3; Sim X 4.1).

4.   Intertextual Relationships

Characteristic of PH is the absence of quotations from not only Christian, but also Jewish and even pagan texts. The only text that is referred to is, significantly, the lost apocalypse "Eldad and Modat" with the quotation relevant to PH: "The Lord is near to them who return unto Him (ἐπιστρεφομένοις)" (Vis II 3.4).

In his detailed study of the history of scholarship on the use of Scripture, J. Verheyden comes to the conclusion that the highest plausibility can be assumed for the use of Matthew and one of the letters to the Corinthians;[73] this applies especially to Mand IV with reference to Matthew 5:27-32 and 1 Corinthians 7:10-11.[74] A series of scholars have remained skeptical about use and allusion,[75] mostly with reference to Christian parenetic tradition. The same applies to the common parenetic tradition in PH and in the Epistle of James. The most important points of contact are recorded by W. Popkes, but he declares: "The points of contact are on the whole too seldom specific, too sporadic, and form-critically too insignificant to allow one to go beyond a general knowledge of diverse traditional materials."[76]

Far more confidently remarks É. Massaux, among others, who reckons with the influence of the synoptic parables, especially from Matthew,[77] but less from Mark and Luke. This also applies to John, especially Sim IX 12–16,[78] the Pauline Epistles,[79] such as 1 Corinthians 7:8-9, 28, 38-39; 2 Corinthians 7:10 as well as Ephesians 4:30; 4:3-7,[80] but also for James, with ten examples of literary dependency.[81]

The christological meaning of Isaiah 2:3 with the "equation of Christ and Law" has a significant parallel in *Kerygma Petrou*.[82]

---

[72] Cf. Kühneweg, "Gesetz," 63.

[73] Verheyden, "Shepherd," 329.

[74] Verheyden, "Shepherd," 322–29: "In three ways [. . .] Hermas goes beyond the teaching as found in Matthew and Paul. All three have to do with his specific interest in offering an opportunity for repentance."

[75] Dibelius, *Hermas*, 424; Köster, *Synoptische Überlieferung*, 242–56; Osiek, *Shepherd*, 26.

[76] Popkes, *Jakobus*, 41–42; similarly Konradt, *Existenz*, 330–32; Brox, *Hermas*, 46–47.

[77] Massaux, *Influence*, 265.

[78] Massaux, *Influence*, 293: "Le texte johannique fait figure de leitmotiv du passage."

[79] Massaux, *Influence*, 312: "Hermas connaissait certainement des épîtres pauliniennes."

[80] Massaux, *Influence*, 306.

[81] Massaux, *Influence*, 310ff. Criticism of Massaux by Joly, *Le Pasteur*, 414–15.

[82] Kühneweg, "Gesetz," 55, 57, 64.

The absence of scriptural quotations is explained by the classification of PH as an apocalypse, since quotations are extremely rare in this genre.[83] A more precise explanation can be substantiated by a passage in a letter from Mani to the city of Edessa, in which he writes: "The truth and the mysteries of which I speak, [. . .] I have not received from men or from fleshly creatures, but also not through the reading of the Scriptures (ἐκ τῶν ὁμιλιῶν τῶν γραφῶν)."[84]

Hermas also cites neither oral nor written traditions, although such sources were probably known to him, but relies exclusively on supernatural revelations for legitimacy.

5. Different Categories of Christians

5.1 The Social Relationship between Rich and Poor in the Church

If baptism offers forgiveness of sins and thereby the possibility of leading a pure and spotless life, then sins committed after baptism create a serious problem within the church. Here a discrepancy between the True/Ideal Church and the Empirical Church becomes clearly visible. Hermas focuses completely on this discrepancy and its solution because "the main interest of the book is aimed at the announcement of penance and the purification of the Church that it brings about."[85]

One cause for the problems that appear to threaten the social life of the churches was obviously the discrepancy between the rich (πλούσιοι) and the poor (πτωχοί/πένητες).[86] That distinction concerned not only the economic situation of the poor, but also "the morality of the wealthy Christians [. . .]. Into their business practices crept fraud (παραχαράσσω Sim I 11, cf. Mand III 3) and rapacity (Sim I 11; VI 5.5; Vis III 9.2 κατάχυμα)."[87]

5.2 The Constitution of the Church

The Roman house churches were long governed by a college of presbyters (cf. Vis II 4.3: σὺ δὲ ἀναγνώσῃ εἰς ταύτην τὴν πόλιν μετὰ τῶν πρεσβυτέρων τῶν προϊσταμένων τῆς ἐκκλησίας) and indisputably only circa 190 by a monarchical bishop (Victor).[88] Within the college members occasionally quarreled over precedence (Vis III 9.7-10; Sim VIII 7.4-6). Bishops were presbyters with approximately the same function as deacons (Vis III 5.1, 9.2; Mand VIII 10; Sim I 8; IX 27.2-3; cf. 1Clem). The presbyterial college also had a "church publicist" or

---

[83] E.g., Leutzsch, *Hirt*, 133, 401n206; Staats, *Hermas*, 102.

[84] CMC 64.8-15 (Henrichs/Koenen). Cf. Galatians 1:12.

[85] Dibelius, *Hermas*, 576.

[86] Osiek, *Rich and Poor, passim*; Leutzsch, *Wahrnehmung*, 113–37.

[87] Lampe, *Stadtrömische Christen*, 71–78: quotation from p. 73; idem, *From Paul to Valentinus*, 90–99. See further Osiek, *Rich and Poor, passim*; Plümacher, *Identitätsverlust*, 33–34, 44–46; Leutzsch, *Wahrnehmung*, 192–214.

[88] Lampe, *Stadtrömische Christen*, 334–40; idem, *From Paul to Valentinus*, 397–408; Brox, *Hermas*, 533–41; Osiek, *Shepherd*, 59.

"minister for external affairs" as well as a female "minister for internal affairs" for the widows and orphans (Vis II 4.3).[89]

6.   Genre

Establishing the genre is determinative for the understanding of a text in its entirety as well as for the interpretation of its parts.[90]

6.1 Definition

The definition of the genre "apocalypse" consists of differentiating features of the text's syntactic structure, semantics, and pragmatics.

1. Among the textual syntactic structural characteristics for an apocalypse with vision reports are reports of visions, dream-visions, heavenly voices, revelatory monologues and dialogues, letters from heaven, and interpretive discussions with *angeli interpretes*.

2. Among the text's semantic characteristics are the hierarchy of revelations, the mediators of revelation, societal disorder, and eschatology.

3. Some of the text's pragmatic characteristics are of a generative, others of a final nature. Among the generative are: presentations of crises and problems like emergencies, threats, and controversies of a political, social, or religious sort; the final includes the introduction of solutions through warnings or calls to repentance, as well as through encouragement and comfort. There is in addition the authorization of the announced offer of the overcoming of the crisis.[91]

6.2 Apocalyptic Characteristics

The genre not only of the Book of Visions but of the entire PH is in my opinion that of the apocalypse.[92] This evaluation is supported by the following criteria.

1. The *syntactic* characteristics found in the full text of Hermas are first and foremost *visions*:[93] above all the four main visions in the Book of Visions (ὄρασις [α´[94]], β´, γ´, δ´) as well as the two additional visions in both Vis II (4.1, 4.2-3) and in Vis III (10.6b-d, 10.7–13.4); further in the connecting portion of the Addendum (ἀποκάλυψις ε´ [in ℵ]). Even if these metaterms appear only in the Book of Visions and the Addendum, revelations exist throughout both the

---

89 Gamble, *Books*, 108–9, 288nn83–84; Lampe, *Stadtrömische Christen*, 336ff.; Eisen, *Amtsträgerinnen*, 207–9.
90 Cf. Raible, "Gattungen," 334.
91 Cf. Hellholm, Apokalypse, 586–87.
92 So also Collins, "Apocalypses," 74–75; Leutzsch, *Hirt*, 129; Staats, *Hermas*, 102; Osiek,

Shepherd, 10–12. Classified as pseudo-apocalypse by Vielhauer, *Geschichte*, 522; Vielhauer/Strecker, "Apokalypse: Hermas," 541–44.
93 For more details on the revelation analysis of the Book of Visions, see Hellholm, *Visionenbuch*, 135–39, 140–89, 191–95.
94 Cf. Vis III 11.2: τῇ μὲν πρώτῃ ὁράσει.

rest of the Book of Visions (e.g., Vis III 8.1-7; III 10–13) and in the Book of the Shepherd (Mand XI;[95] Sim IV–VIII) as well as in the Addendum (Sim IX 1.4–11.8), especially in its concluding section, where "that messenger [*nuntius ille*, i.e., the "Son of God"] who had delivered me to the shepherd" appears (Sim X 1.1; cf. Vis V 2). According to Vis V both the Book of the Shepherd and the Addendum were written at the direct instruction of the shepherd: "First of all, then, write down my commandments and similitudes, and you will write the other things (τὰ δὲ ἕτερα) as I shall show you [. . .]. All these words did the shepherd, even the angel of repentance (ὁ ἄγγελος τῆς μετανοίας), command me to write" (V 5–6).

Within the visions there are A) dialogic and B) monologic revelations.[96] Revelatory dialogues and monologues can be divided in a meaningful way into a) narrative and b) interpretive, but at the same time caution is required because they constantly coincide, a straightforward classification is not always possible, or they change their character within a dialogue sequence.[97]

(A:a) Narrative and invitational dialogues and dialogue sequences appear in the Book of Visions (e.g., Vis I 1.5-9, 2.2–3.2; II 4.1; III 1.2-3, 1.9–2.1; IV 2.2-6), in the Book of the Shepherd (e.g., Mand III 3–5; IV 1.4-11, 2.1-4, 3.1-6, 4.1-4; VI 1.5–2.10; Sim V 1.2-5; VI 1.2-4; VII 1–7; VIII 1.1-4; 2.6-9), and also in the Addendum (e.g., Vis V 1–7; Sim IX 5.3-5, 7.3-6; X 1.1–4.4).

(A:b) Interpretive dialogues and dialogue sequences appear in the Book of Visions (e.g., Vis I 14.2; II 4.1; III 3.5–4.2, 4.3–7.6, 8.3-10), in the Book of the Shepherd (e.g., Mand VII 5; VIII 2–6, 7–11; Sim II 2–4; III 2–3; V 4.1-4, 5.2-4, 6.1-4; VI 2.1-4, 3.1-3, 4.1–5.7; VIII 3.1-8, 6.1-2), and also in the Addendum (Sim IX 11.9–31.3, 33.1-3).

(B:a) Narrative monologues appear in the Book of Visions (e.g., Vis I 3.1-2), in the Book of the Shepherd (e.g., Vis IV 1.4, 3.6; Mand I 1.f; II 1–7; III 1–2; IV 1–2; V 1.1-6; VI 1–4; VII 1–4; IX 1–11; Sim I 1–11; II 5–10; IV 2–8; V 2.1-8, 2.9-11; VIII 1.5–2.5, 4.1–5.6), and also in the Addendum (Sim IX 1.1-3; 31.4–32.5).

(B:b) Interpretive monologues appear in the Book of Visions (e.g., Vis III 11.1–13.4; IV 3.2-5) and in the Book of the Shepherd (e.g., Mand V 1.7–2.8; X 1.4–3.3; XI 1–6, 7–16; Sim V 6.5-8; VI 3.4-6; VIII 6.4–10.4).

Revelatory auditions appear in the Book of Visions (e.g., Vis IV 1.4). Revelations from heavenly books occur in the Book of Visions within the individual

---

[95] Cf. Reiling, *Prophecy*, see especially the methodical conclusion.

[96] For more details on the dialogic analysis of the Book of Visions, see Hellholm, *Visionenbuch*, 136–39, 140–89, 196. Cf. already Dibelius, *Hermas*,

554: "[. . .] this question-and-answer play belongs to the established elements of the vision style."

[97] With regard to the entire PH, this is a first analytic attempt that does not strive for completeness. A further analysis would appear yet more differentiated.

visions, once in a revelation read aloud from a small book (Vis I 3.3-4), another time in the transcribing of a heavenly letter with subsequent revelation of the knowledge in it (Vis II 1.3-4, 2.2–3.4).[98]

2. There are various *semantic* characteristics: As in other apocalypses (e.g., Rev 1:1-3[99]) there is a hierarchy of revelation: A) Giver of commission: the Son of God (Vis V 2 and Mand V 1.7: σεμνότατος ἄγγελος; Sim V 4.4 und VII 1: ἔνδοξος ἄγγελος; IX 1.1: ὁ υἱὸς τοῦ θεοῦ; 7.1: ὁ ἀνὴρ ὁ ἔνδοξος καὶ κύριος ὅλου τοῦ πύργου; X 1.1: *nuntius ille qui tradiderat me pastori*). B) Revelation mediator of the first rank: a) the presbytress (ἡ πρεσβυτέρα/ἡ πρεσβῦτις) as the Ideal Church in the Book of Visions (*passim*); b) the shepherd (ὁ ποιμήν; *pastor*) as the angel of penance (Mand XII 6.1 and Sim IX 1.1: ὁ ἄγγελος τῆς μετανοίας) in the Book of the Shepherd and the Addendum (*passim*). C) Revelation mediator of the second rank: a beautiful youth (Vis II 4.1: νεανίσκος εὐειδέστατος); a youth (Vis III 10.7: νεανίσκος);[100] the twelve virgins (Sim IX 2.3, 10.6–11.8: παρθένοι [δώδεκα]). D) The transmitters: Hermas throughout, but also Clement[101] and Grapte[102] (Vis II 4.3). E) Addressees: all Christians in Rome and its surroundings (Vis II 4.3; Sim X 4.1).

Interpretive discussions with *angeli interpretes*: sometimes as the angel of interpretation (presbytress Vis III 3.1ff.; Shepherd Sim IX 11.9–31.2 and *passim*), sometimes as the angel of penance (Shepherd Vis V 7; Mand IV 2.2, 3.5; XII 3.3, 4.7, 6.1ff.; Sim VI 3.6; VIII 3.5, IX 7.1–X), sometimes as the angel of protection (Shepherd Vis V 2-3; Mand IV 2.1, 4.2; Sim V 6.2; X 1.2, 3.5).[103]

Apocalyptic motifs occur in the eschatology (Vis III 9.5; IV;[104] Mand IX 12; Mand III 3.5; Sim I 1–6, 12.3), in the description of the plagues (Sim VI 2.6-7; 3.1–4.7),[105] and in the verdict of the Son of God (Sim X 4.1-4; cf. Rev 21:5-8[106]). The apocalyptic eschatology is not cosmologically aligned, although Hermas knows of a universal Last Judgment (Vis IV 3), but overwhelmingly individualized.[107]

3. The *pragmatic* characteristics are sometimes of a generative, others of a final nature: The cause for the revelations in PH is the crisis situation within the Roman churches due to sinful behavior, especially of the rich members toward the poor (esp. Sim II);[108] the goal of the offer of a second chance at penance is—thanks to

---

98 See Dibelius, *Hermas*, 443.

99 Cf. Hellholm, "Vision He Saw," 120.

100 Cf. Leutzsch, *Hirt*, 401n209 with rich comparative material.

101 On Clement, see Gamble, *Books*, 108–9, 288nn83–84; Bakke, *Concord*, 3

102 On Grapte as διάκονος or ἐπίσκοπος, see Leutzsch, *Wahrnehmung*, 161; idem, *Hirt*, 402n220; Eisen, *Amtsträgerinnen*, 207–8.

103 Cf. Dibelius, "Offenbarungsträger"; idem, *Hermas*, 494–96.

104 Cf. Dibelius, *Hermas*, 485.

105 Cf. Hellholm, "Religion und Gewalt."

106 Cf. Hellholm, "Problem," 44–46.

107 Cf. Dibelius, *Hermas*, 485–86, 490; Leutzsch, *Wahrnehmung*, 207; idem, *Hirt*, 143; Staats, *Hermas*, 102.

108 Cf. Osiek, *Rich and Poor*, 78–90, 142–45; Leutzsch, *Wahrnehmung*, 113–37; Lampe, *Stadtrömische Christen*, 71–78; idem, *From Paul to Valentinus*, 90–99.

the goodness of God—the restoration of a right relationship through the renewed opportunity to repent and the keeping of God's commandments (Sim IX 32.5 and *passim*).[109]

6.3 The Authorization of Hermas' Offer of Repentance

But why did Hermas choose this of all genres to impart his offer of the possibility of a second penance? The answer can be sought in the same text-pragmatic function that consists of the authorization! One of the fundamental pragmatic characteristics of the apocalyptic genre is the authorization of the offer. Hermas, who was not one of the leaders of the church[110] and could assert no authority of his own (Vis III 3.1; Mand IV 2.1; Sim V 4.2),[111] had to legitimate his new offer of the middle position with regard to the second and only possibility of penance with the help of a higher heavenly authority:[112] the revelation from heaven through visions and auditions; the preexistent Ideal Church in the instruction of the rulers (ὁ δεσπότης; Vis II 2.4) as mediatrix of revelation to Hermas and to the Empirical Church (Vis III 3.3; IV 2.5, 3.6; Sim IX 1.1); a shepherd sent to Hermas from the "most glorious angel" (i.e., the Son of God) as a second mediator of revelation (Vis V; Sim IX 1; X 1.1).

Hermas himself is given a legitimization by the immediate instruction first by the presbytress (Vis II 8.11), second by the heavenly letter (Vis II 2.2–4.6), but also third by the Shepherd, with the help of the gathering of the switches (Sim VIII 4.1-2), as well as by a direct instruction (Sim VIII 11.1; X 2.4).

Aside from these events, legitimacy comes from: the appearance of the presbytress in shining clothes with a book in her hand, who sits on a great white chair covered with snow-white cloths;[113] the reading of the presbytress from a heavenly book (βιβλίον; Vis I 2.2, 3.3-4); a little heavenly book and a heavenly letter (βιβλαρίδιον/βιβλίδιον[114]) brought by the revelation mediatrix and transcribed

---

[109] Cf. Osiek, *Shepherd*, 12.
[110] Cf. Leutzsch, *Hirt*, 134–35.
[111] Especially Mand IV 2.1: ἐπεὶ οὐ συνίω οὐδέν, καὶ ἡ καρδία μου πεπώρωται ἀπὸ τῶν προτέρων μου πράξεων ("for I understand nothing, and my heart has been hardened by my previous mode of life").
[112] Cf. Lampe, *Stadtrömische Christen*, 76; idem,

From Paul to Valentinus, 96; Vielhauer/Strecker, "Apokalypse: Hermas," 545–46.
[113] Cf. Dibelius, *Hermas*, 436, 451–52.
[114] On the terminology, see Stirewalt, *Epistolography*, 67–87: "Byblion and deltos are words of Eastern origin" (68–69, 84); White, *Light from Ancient Letters*, 192.

by Hermas,[115] sent to the churches in the neighborhood and read by the presbyters in Rome (Vis II 4.2-3).[116]

There are further complementary visions with reference to the mediatrix of the revelation by other mediators: "Now a revelation was given to me, my brethren, while I slept, by a young man of comely appearance, who said to me, 'Who do you think that old woman is from whom you received the book?' And I said, 'The Sibyl.'[117] 'You are in a mistake,' says he; 'it is not the Sibyl.' 'Who is it then?' say I. And he said, 'It is the Church'" (Vis II 4.1).[118] Further: "I asked her (i.e., the presbytress) to reveal to me the meaning of the three forms [as an old woman, as fairly young, as yet younger and fairer] in which she appeared to me. In reply she said to me: 'With regard to them, you must ask another to reveal their meaning to you.' [. . .] That very night there appeared to me a young man [. . .] 'Hear then,' said he, 'with regard to the three forms, concerning which you are inquiring'": she is in Vis I the church as old because "your spirit is now old," in Vis II as rejuvenated because the Lord has "renewed your spirit," in Vis III as happy, younger, and more beautiful because "ye also have received the renewal of your spirits" (Vis III 10.2–13.4).[119]

---

115 Cf. Stübe, *Himmelsbrief*; Dibelius, *Hermas*, 443, with parallel texts; Leutzsch, *Hirt*, 395n154. The definition restricted by Speyer, *Bücherfunde*, 17, and again in his *Literarische Fälschung*, 67: "The heavenly letter is disclosed, not transmitted," is too narrow in light of the whole range of texts, and the transmitted texts receive no designation; cf. 1En 81.1-2; OdesSol 23.5-7; Revelation 5:1-5; ActsThom 110–11 (the Song of the Pearl); CMC 49.3: "I am Balsamos, the greatest angel of the light (ὁ μέγιστος ἄγγελος τοῦ φωτός). Receive from me and write what I reveal to you on pure papyrus (ἐν χάρτῃ καθαρωτάτῳ) that is indestructible and repels worms" (quotation from and unknown "Apocalypse of Adam"); text and German translation in Henrichs/Koenen, "Kölner Mani Kodex," 49.

116 See Gamble, *Books*, 109: "We glimpse in Hermas's description of Clement's function what might almost be called an ecclesiastical publisher, a standing provision in the Roman church for duplicating and distributing texts to Christian communities elsewhere. [. . .] The churches in Rome, Antioch, Caesarea, and Alexandria [. . .] were probably centers almost from the beginning for the composition of Christian writings and also for the confluence of Christian writings composed elsewhere. [. . .] In fact, copies of Hermas's Shepherd spread quickly:

the work was in circulation in Egypt, both in Alexandria and in provincial regions, well before the end of the second century and was known at the same time in Gaul and North Africa"; 108: "This is one of the few early Christian texts that offer an explicit notice about the dissemination of a piece of Christian writing."

117 Cf. O'Brian, "The Cumaean Sibyl"; Dibelius, *Hermas*, 451–52; Brox, *Hermas*, 104–5; Leutzsch, *Hirt*, 401–2 with n210 (Lit.!).

118 Completely misunderstood by Brox, *Hermas*, 154, when he criticizes, "It is not made clear why he should even receive the revelation, never mind from the old woman, although it deals with her herself. But everything works very awkwardly."

119 On the rejuvenation motif see Leutzsch, *Hirt*, 180–81, 426–31n452; Brox, *Hermas*, 154n77: "The idea of the allegorical polymorphy"; Klauck, *Apokryphe Bibel*, 368–69: "The angel of interpretation correlates this differently appearing image with the periodic state of the believers on earth and their powers of comprehension. In other words: things look bleak at the moment, but there is still hope" (369). On the motif of hope in the apocalyptic, see the summery in Widengren, "Leitenden Ideen," 156: "Even if the current world suffers under the lordship of Ahriman, the final victory will indeed come, and with that all contemplation of the world ends in an optimistic hope."

As mentioned previously, the Book of Visions is attested in the Addendum by an independent revelator, the Shepherd, who is no less a being than the angel of penance (ὁ ἄγγελος τῆς μετανοίας, Sim IX 1.1) and the shepherd himself is charged by his superior, "The glorious man, the lord of the whole tower" (ὁ ἀνὴρ ὁ ἔνδοξος καὶ κύριος ὅλου τοῦ πύργου), with purifying the stones that lie beside the tower (Sim IX 7.1).

At the very end of PH we are told: "After I had fully written down this book, that messenger (*nuntius ille*) who had delivered me to the Shepherd came into the house in which I was, and sat down upon a couch,[120] and the Shepherd stood on his right hand" (X 1.1). Here this heavenly figure, who is apparently the Son of God himself, gives his authorization not only to the full text of PH (X 2.2: *tu autem ceteris haec uerba dices*), but also to the present Shepherd: "To him alone throughout the whole world is the power of repentance assigned" (X 1.3: *huic soli per totem orbem paenitentiae potestas tribute est*).[121]

The legitimization of the new offer of a second, but one-time offer of repentance is as complete as one can imagine it being in an apocalypse.

7. Place and Date of Writing

Despite the good Eastern evidence, Rome (Vis I 1.1; IV 1.2; Sim II) is, contrary to E. Peterson,[122] the scholarly consensus on the place where PH was written.[123]

To determine the date of composition, the history of the origin of PH must be considered. The presbyterial leadership in Rome lasted until circa 160–190.[124] The first quotation appears in Irenaeus (ca. 180). Origen identifies Hermas with the Hermas named in Rom 16:14 (ca. 58), while *Canon Muratori* identifies him as the brother of the Roman bishop Pius (142–175).[125] Both aim at different interests: securing or disputing apostolicity.

---

[120] Cf. Vis V 2: "I have been sent by a most venerable angel to dwell with you the remaining days of your life."

[121] When Dibelius, *Hermas*, 641 states that Sim X "[must be] actually [. . .] the climax of the book; in truth, however, we encounter absolutely nothing new," it is a mistaken assessment because here the semantic content of revelation and admonition is repeated in a summary while the function lies on the illocutionary aspect, i.e., on the pragmatic legitimation of this offer of penance in the closing Similitude with the final empowerment of the Shepherd as bearer of revelation (ὁ ἄγγελος τῆς μετανοίας) and of Hermas as the transmitter of the offer on the part of the Giver of the commission

Himself, i.e., the σεμνότατος ἄγγελος, who is no less a figure than the Son of God.

[122] Peterson, *Frühkirche*, 274–75, 282–84. He changes his opinion in "Giudaismo," 381: in Rome!

[123] Dibelius, *Hermas*, *passim*; Reiling, *Prophecy*, 24; Brox, *Hermas*, 22–23; Osiek, *Shepherd*, 18ff., 59; idem, *Rich and Poor*, 146–53; Leutzsch, *Hirt*, 135; Lampe, *Stadtrömischen Christen*, 182ff.; idem, *From Paul to Valentinus*, 218ff.; Hilhorst, *Hermas*, 683; Staats, *Hermas*, 103; Köster, *Introduction*, 263.

[124] See above.

[125] Reiling, *Prophecy*, 24: "Möglicher Zeitpunkt der Endveröffentlichung."

The ecclesiastical publicist or "minister for external affairs" Clement (Vis II 4.3) is often identified with the author or secretary/correspondent (cf. Rom 16:22: Tertios) of 1Clem.[126] The composition of 1Clem lies in the time frame 95–110.[127] The part of PH written first, the Book of Visions, could have been written at this time.[128] The final publication of the full text would then lie before around 140, since PH makes reference neither to Valentinus (140–160 in Rome) nor to Marcion (ca. 85–ca. 160).[129] The publication of the second part, the Book of the Shepherd, may lie—if at all—shortly before the final publication.

The question of persecution and of martyrdom is complicated for the dating: The main references appear on one hand in the Book of Visions (Vis III 1.9, 2.1, 5.2) and on the other in the Book of the Shepherd (Sim I 3; VIII 3.6) as well as the Addendum (Sim IX 21.2-3, 28.3-5).[130] The fact that in 1Clem "the preparedness for martyrdom of the women of Rome as well as that of the men is praised (6.1-2; 55.3)"[131] does not stand in the way of the early dating of the Book of Visions. Hermas gives the impression of living between two periods of persecution: On one hand the persecutions are over (Vis III 1.9, 2.1, 5.2), on the other hand persecutions are expected in the present (Sim I 3; IX 21.1-2, 28.3-5).[132] The present persecution situation might have occurred under Trajan and Hadrian, that is, before 138.[133] In that case, the Book of Visions would have been written at the beginning of the first quarter and PH around the middle to the end of the second quarter of the second century.

8.   Bibliography

Bardenshewer, O. *Geschichte der urchristlichen Literatur I: Vom Ausgang des Apostolischen Zeitalters bis zum Ende des zweiten Jahrhunderts.* Freiburg i. B. 1902.

Bonner, C., ed. *A Papyrus Codex of the Shepherd of Hermas (Similitudes 2–9) with a Fragment of the Mandates.* UMS.H XXII. Ann Arbor 1934.

Braun, H. *An die Hebräer.* HNT 14. Tübingen 1984.

Brox, N. *Der Hirt des Hermas.* KAV 7. Göttingen 1991.

Campenhausen, H. von. *Kirchliches Amt und geistliche Vollmacht in den ersten drei Jahrhunderten.* BHT 14. Tübingen ²1963.

Carlini, A., ed. *Papyrus Bodmer XXXVIII: Erma: Il Pastore [Ia-IIIa visione].* Bibl. Bodm. Cologny-Genève 1991.

---

[126] Cf. Dibelius, *Hermas*, 423; Lampe, *Stadtrömischen Christen*, 172n157; idem, *From Paul to Valentinus*, 206n1; Köster, *Introduction*, 263; Gamble, *Books*, 109.

[127] Cf. Bakke, "Concord," 3, 8–11.

[128] Cf. Osiek, *Shepherd*, 19; Staats, *Hermas*, 103–4; Gamble, *Books*, 109: "Yet the earliest parts may belong to the early second century and so perhaps to Clement's lifetime."

[129] Cf. Osiek, *Shepherd*, 19; Leutzsch, *Hirt*,

136–37; Staats, *Hermas*, 103–4; Brox, *Hermas*, 24–25.

[130] See Hilhorst, *Hermas*, 688–90.

[131] Lampe, *Stadtrömischen Christen*, 120; idem, *From Paul to Valentinus*, 147.

[132] Cf. Dibelius, *Hermas*, 630, 636; Hilhorst, *Hermas*, 689; Leutzsch, *Wahrnehmung*, 79–82. Unhelpful: Brox, *Hermas*, 471–76.

[133] Staats, *Hermas*, 104; Reiling, *Prophecy*, 24: ca. 125.

Chadwick, H. "The New Edition of Hermas." *JTS* 8 (1957): 274–80.

Coleborne, W. *A Linguistic Approach to the Problem of Structure and Composition of the Shepherd of Hermas.* Ph.D. Diss. University of Newcastle (NSW Australia) 1965.

———. "The Shepherd of Hermas: A Case for Multiple Authorship and Some Implications." In *StPatr* 10/1, 65–70. TU 107. Berlin 1970.

Collins, A. Y. "Early Christian Apocalypses." In "Apocalypse: The Morphology of a Genre," edited by J. J. Collins. Special issue, *Semeia* 14 (1979): 61–121.

Deemter, R. von. *Der Hirt des Hermas: Apokalypse oder Allegorie?* Delft 1929.

Dibelius, M. *Der Hirt des Hermas.* HNT Erg. 5. Tübingen 1923.

———. "Der Offenbarungsträger im 'Hirten' des Hermas." In *Botschaft und Geschichte*, 2: 80–93. Tübingen 1956.

Ehrman, B. D. *The Apostolic Fathers I–II.* LCL 24–25. Cambridge, Mass. 2003.

Eisen, U. E. *Amtsträgerinnen im frühen Christentum: Epigraphische und literarische Studien.* FKDG 61. Göttingen 1996.

Fuchs, E. *Glaube und Tat in den Mandata: 1. Teil der Inaugural-Dissertation.* Marburg 1931.

Gamble, H. Y. *Books and Readers in the Early Church: A History of Early Christian Texts.* New Haven 1995.

Giet, S. *Hermas et les pasteurs: let trois auteurs du Pasteur d'Hermas.* Paris 1963.

———. "Les trois auteurs du Pasteur d'Hermas." In *StPatr* 8:10-23. TU 93. Berlin 1966.

Greimas, A. J. "La structure sémantique." In *Du sens.* Paris 1970.

Harris, J. R. *Hermas in Arcadia and Other Essays.* Cambridge 1896.

Hartman, L. *"Into the Name of the Lord Jesus": Baptism in the Early Church.* Edinburgh 1997.

Hellholm, D. "Apokalypse: Form und Gattung." *RGG*[4] I:585–88. Tübingen 1998.

———. *Das Visionenbuch des Hermas als Apokalypse.* ConBNT 13. Lund 1980.

———. "Deliberations on the Nature of the Church in the Shepherd of Hermas." *TTKi* 78 (2007): 283–97.

———. "Religion und Gewalt in der Apokalyptik." In *Religion, Politik und Gewalt*, edited by F. Schweitzer, 413–38. VWGTh 29. Gütersloh 2006.

———. "The Problem of Apocalyptic Genre and the Apocalypse of John." In "Early Christian Apocalypticism: Genre and Social Setting," edited by A. Y. Collins. Special issue, *Semeia* 36 (1986): 13–64.

———. "The 'Revelation-Schema' and Its Adaptation in the Coptic Gnostic Apocalypse of Peter." *SEÅ* 63 (1998): 233–48.

———. "The Vision He Saw or: To Encode the Future in Writing: An Analysis of the Prologue of John's Apocalyptic Letter." In *Text and Logos: The Humanistic Interpretation of the New Testament*, edited by T. W. Jennings Jr., 109–46. SchPHS. Atlanta 2000.

Henne, P. *L'unité du Pasteur d'Hermas.* CahRB 31. Paris 1992.

Henrichs, A., and L. Koenen. "Der Kölner Mani-Kodex [CMC] (P. Colon. Inv. nr. 4780): Edition der Seiten 1–72." *ZPE* 19 (1975): 1–85.

Hilgenfeld, A. *Hermae Pastor: Veterem latinam interpretationem e codicibus.* Leipzig 1973.

Hilhorst, A. "Hermas." *RAC* 14 (1998): 682–701

————. *Sémitismes et Latinismes dans le Pasteur d'Hermas.* GCP 5. Nijmegen 1976.

Holmes, M. W. *The Apostolic Fathers: Greek Texts and English Translations.* Grand Rapids ³2007.

Joly, R. "Hermas et le Pasteur." *VC* 21 (1967): 201–18.

————. *Hermas le Pasteur: Introduction, texte critique, traduction et note.* SC 53. Paris ²1968.

Klauck, H.-J. *Die apokryphe Bibel.* Tria Corda 4. Tübingen 2008.

Knopf, R. "Die Himmelsstadt." In *Neutestamentliche Studien: Georg Heinrici zu seinem 70. Geburtstag dargebracht,* 213–19. Leipzig 1914.

Köster, H. *Introduction to the New Testament, II: History and Literature of Early Christianity.* New York 2000.

————. *Synoptische Überlieferung bei den Apostolischen Vätern.* TU 65. Berlin 1957.

————.Konrath, M. *Christliche Existenz nach dem Jakobusbrief: Eine Studie zu seiner soteriologischen und ethischen Konzeption.* SUNT 22. Göttingen 1998.

Kühneweg, U. "Christus als Gesetzgeber und Gesetz in den Schriften der sog. Apostolischen Väter II: Der Hirt des Hermas." In *Das Neue Gesetz: Christus als Gesetzgeber und Gesetz,* 53–75. MThSt 36. Marburg 1993.

Lampe, P. *Die stadtrömischen Christen in den ersten beiden Jahrhunderten.* WUNT 2/18. Tübingen ²1989.

————. *From Paul to Valentinus: Christians at Rome in the First Two Centuries.* Minneapolis 2003.

Leutzsch, M. *Die Wahrnehmung sozialer Wirklichkeit im "Hirten des Hermas."* FRLANT 150. Göttingen 1989.

————. *Hirt des Hermas.* SUC III. Darmstadt 1998.

Lindemann, A. *Paulus im ältesten Christentum.* BHT 58. Tübingen 1979.

Lindemann, A., and H. Paulsen, eds. *Die Apostolischen Väter: Griechisch-deutsche Parallelausgabe.* Tübingen 1992.

Luschnat, O. "Die Jungfrauenszene in der Arkadienvision des Hermas." *ThViat* 12 (1973/1974): 53–70.

Massaux, É. *The Influence of the Gospel of Saint Matthew on Christian Literature before Irenaeus.* Macon, Ga. 1990.

Musurillo, H. A. "The Need of a New Edition of Hermas." *TS* 12 (1951): 382–87.

Nijendijk, L. W. *Die Christologie des Hirten des Hermas: Exegetisch, religions- und dogmengeschichtlich untersucht.* Dr. theol. Diss. Utrecht 1986.

O'Brian, D. P. "The Cumean Sibyl as the Revelation-bearer in the Shepherd of Hermas." *JECS* 5 (1997): 473–96.

O'Hagen, A. P. "The Great Tribulation to Come in the Pastor of Hermas." In *StPatr* 4, edited by F. L. Cross, 305–11. TU 79. Berlin 1961.

Osiek, C. "The Genre and Function of the Shepherd of Hermas." In "Early Christian Apocalypticism: Genre and Social Setting," edited by A. Y. Collins. Special issue, *Semeia* 36 (1986): 113–21.

————. "The Oral World of Early Christianity in Rome: The Case of Hermas." In *Judaism and Christianity in First-Century Rome,* edited by K. P. Donfried and P. Richardson, 151–72. Grand Rapids 1998.

————. *The Shepherd of Hermas*. Hermeneia. Minneapolis 1999.

————. *Rich and Poor in the Shepherd of Hermas: An Exegetical-Social Investigation*. CBQMS 15. Washington, D.C. 1983.

Pernveden, L. *The Concept of the Church in the Shepherd of Hermas*. STL 27. Lund 1966.

Peterson, E. "Beiträge zur Interpretation der Visionen im 'Pastor Hermae.'" In *Frühkirche*, 254–70.

————. "Die Begegnung mit dem Ungeheuer." In *Frühkirche*, 285–309.

————. "Die 'Taufe' im Acherusischen See." In *Frühkirche*, 310–32.

————. *Frühkirche, Judentum und Gnosis*. Rome 1959.

————. "Giudaismo e Cristianesimo: culto giudaico e culto cristiano." *RSLR* 1 (1965): 367–91.

————. "Kritische Analyse der fünften Vision des Hermas." In *Frühkirche*, 271–84.

Plümacher, E. *Identitätsverlust und Identitätsgewinn*. BThSt 11. Neukirchen-Vluyn 1987.

Popkes, W. *Der Brief des Jakobus*. THKNT 14. Leipzig 2001.

Rahner, K. "Die Buße im Hirten des Hermas." *ZKT* 77 (1955): 385–431.

Raible, W. "Arten des Kommentierens—Arten der Sinnbildung—Arten des Verstehens: Spielarten der generischen Intertextualität." In *Text und Kommentar*, edited by J. Assmann and B. Gladigow, 51–73. ArchLK IV. Munich 1995.

————. *Kognitive Aspekte des Schreibens*. SPHK.HAW 14. Heidelberg 1999.

————. "Was sind Gattungen? Eine Antwort aus semiotischer und textlinguistischer Sicht." *Poetica* 12 (1980): 320–49.

Reiling, J. *Hermas and Christian Prophecy: A Study of the Eleventh Mandate*. NT.S 37. Leiden 1973.

Schmid, W. "Frühchristlichen Arkadienvorstellungen." In *Convivium: Beiträge zur Altertumswissenschaft*, 121–30. Stuttgart 1954.

Schneider, A. *Propter sactam ecclasiam suam: Die Kirche als Geschöpf, Frau und Bau im Bußunterricht des Pastor Hermae*. SEAug 67. Rome 1999.

Speyer, W. *Bücherfunde in der Glaubenswerbung der Antike: Mit einem Ausblick auf Mittelalter und Neuzeit*. Hyp. 24. Göttingen 1970.

————. *Literarische Fälschung im heidnischen und christlichen Altertum*. HAW I.2. Munich 1971.

Stirewalt, M. L., Jr. *Studies in Ancient Greek Epistolography*. SBLRBS 27. Atlanta 1993.

Strecker, G. *Die Johannesbriefe*. KEK 14. Göttingen 1989.

Ström, Å. V. *Der Hirt des Hermas: Allegorie oder Wirklichkeit?* AMNSU 3. Uppsala 1936.

Stübe, R. *Der Himmelsbrief: Ein Beitrag zur allgemeinen Religionsgeschichte*. Tübingen 1918.

Treu, K. "Ein neuer Hermas-Papyrus." *VC* 24 (1970): 34–39.

Verheyden, H. "The Shepherd of Hermas and the Writings That Later Formed the New Testament." In *The Reception of the New Testament in the Apostolic Fathers*, edited by A. F. Gregory and C. M. Tuckett, 293–329. Oxford 2005.

Vielhauer, P. *Geschichte der urchristlichen Literatur*. Berlin/New York 1975.

Vielhauer, P., and G. Strecker. "Apokalypsen und Verwandtes: 6. Der Hirt des Hermas." In *Neutestamentliches Apokryphen in deutscher Übersetzung, II: Apostolisches, Apokalypsen und Verwandtes*, edited by W. Schneemelcher, 537–47. Tübingen ⁵1989.

White, J. C. *The Interaction of Language and World in the Shepherd of Hermas*. Tempel University 1973.

White, J. L. *Light from Ancient Letters*. Foundations and Facets. Philadelphia 1986.

Whittaker, M. *Der Hirt des Hermas*. GCS.AV I. Berlin [2]1967.

Widengren, G. "Leitende Ideen und Quellen der iranischen Apokalyptik." In *Apocalypticism in the Mediterranean World and the Near East*, edited by D. Hellholm, 77–162. Tübingen [2]1989.

Wilson, J. C. *Five Problems in the Interpretation of the Shepherd of Hermas: Its Date and Pneumatology*. Lewiston, N.Y. 1993.

Windisch, H. "Die Bußverkündigung im Hirten des Hermas." In *Taufe und Sünde im ältesten Christentum*, 356–82. Tübingen 1908.

The Apostolic Fathers Yesterday and Today

Jörg Ulrich

In the year 1672 Jean-Baptiste Cotelier published in Paris an edition of early Christian texts that had previously been printed mostly individually. He gave it the title *Ss. Patrum, qui temporibus apostolicis floruerunt, Barnabae, Clementis, Hermae, Ignatii, Polycarpi Opera edita et inedita, vera, & suppositicia.* This collection contained the Epistle of Barnabas, both epistles of Clement, the letters of Ignatius and of Polycarp of Smyrna, the Martyrdom of Polycarp and the Shepherd of Hermas. With the description "Works of the Holy Fathers who flourished in apostolic times," Cotelier had not only smoothed the way to the term "Apostolic Fathers" that is still used today, which first appeared explicitly in the 1693 edition by William Wake; Cotelier had also further cleared the way for a relative canonization of the "Apostolic Fathers" as a coherent group of texts, for in the editions since the seventeenth century, the texts mostly appear as a common corpus.[1] Through the years, supported and in part first enabled by the discovery of new manuscripts in the nineteenth century, the Didache, the letter to Diognetus, and the fragments of Papias and of Quadratus have made their way into this corpus. The present collection of introductions to the "Apostolic Fathers" uses both a long-established title and the long-collected canon of texts assembled under this title.

There have always been questions about the fittingness of the term "Apostolic Fathers" and the homogeneity of the group of texts insinuated by its collection.[2] They direct themselves, for instance, toward the claim, implied in the title but not supportable historically, that the texts assembled here go back to the apostles or that their authors supposedly knew witnesses of the apostolic period. Over and above that, the critics point to the heterogeneity of content and the widely varying time of origin of individual pieces of the corpus as well as to the sometimes considerable variations in content of the same "teaching of the apostles." Through the title and the juxtaposition, a claim was made for the texts in the collection that they neither can redeem nor even intend, namely for a continuity with and authoritative continuation of a supposedly homogenous ecclesiastical tradition

---

[1] See Pratscher's introduction to this volume.
[2] See Pratscher's introduction to this volume.— Bardenhewer already expressed criticism (*Geschichte* I, 80), attesting to the disunity of the texts and the lack of coherence of content and time period. Altaner/Stuiber, *Patrologie*, 43–44, preferred to speak of the "oldest Christian writers." In the same tradition, the lexicon of ancient Christian literature edited by Siegmar Döpp and Wilhelm Geerlings does not use the lemma "Apostolic Fathers" but treats the texts individually.

from the time of the apostles. According to the critics, however, the "Apostolic Fathers" as a collection of texts are in reality simply an example of a seventeenth-century editorial decision that appears in hindsight to be problematic, that was used in the following years out of habit, but that is not actually plausible.

This criticism cannot be dismissed out of hand. However, there are notable reasons that suggest that the established title and the collected canon of texts that appears under it should be retained. Common characteristics of the texts labeled as "Apostolic Fathers" include[3] the common period of origin in the first half of the second century (despite a considerable gap of a good fifty years); their theological structure, not aiming at "scientific" reasoning for Christianity and its teachings, that is recognizably different from the writings of the apologists; their orthonymous or anonymous authorship (none of the texts uses an early Christian author's name); and finally their unquestionably great importance as reference texts of biblical tradition of the Old Testament and the emerging New Testament and as a connecting piece to the Christian writings of the emerging catholic church in the second half of the second century and in the third century.[4] There are also common characteristics in the theological profiles, such as the dissociation from Gnostic adversaries or from a docetic Christology,[5] so that the collection, for all its internal plurality, still has indisputable inner congruities. In addition, the great significance of this group of texts for our ability to reconstruct early Christian history deserves to be underscored: Without the Apostolic Fathers our otherwise fragmentary image of the early congregations and their theologies would still have far more blank spots.

This fact leads to the question of why the Apostolic Fathers are still worth using. The answer is twofold:

For one thing, these texts make possible a more precise perception of and a better understanding of the earliest Christian history. In this regard their primary interest is historical and theological: Reading the Apostolic Fathers is worthwhile for the reader of the New Testament who wishes, above and beyond familiarity with the biblical text, for more information on their surroundings and the period directly following theirs. It is exciting for the scholar whose interest lies in the historical figure of Jesus of Nazareth and who asks how and with what consequences His life, teachings, death, and resurrection were understood in the early Christian fellowships. It is interesting for someone who inquires about the self-understanding of early Christians, their conflicts and problem-solving and their self-location in the religious, societal, and political environment of the second-century Roman Empire. It is appealing for the church historian and the historian of theology who

---

3 See on this Lindemann, "Apostolische Väter," 692–93.

4 Altaner/Stuiber, *Patrologie*, 43, speaks of "middle links between the apostolic time, i.e., the New Testament writings, and the later Christian texts."

5 See below.

look for continuities and discontinuities in the development of Christian teaching and practice. For in the Apostolic Fathers there are the first signs of developments that have led on a long-term and in no way simply continuous course all the way to the great dogmatic determinations of the ancient church, for example in the doctrine of the Trinity (Nicaea 325 and Nicaea-Constantinople 381) or Christology (Chalcedon 451), or that marked the stations along the way that ran, likewise in no way unbroken, to the strengthening and building up of the congregational offices in the ancient church. Reading the Apostolic Fathers is further worthwhile for the ancient historian, for whom early Christianity is part of the history of the Roman Empire and who may find the social history of the second century interesting. It is also worthwhile for someone interested in religious history who seeks to better understand the relationship of the contemporary Christianity to the other religions and the view of other religions toward early Christianity.

Interest in the Apostolic Fathers is not confined to the wide field of history, however. These texts are also thoroughly suited to give many a stimulating impulse for today's religious, theological, and ecclesiastical debates. Naturally, that does not mean that they hold direct or indirect answers to modern questions. But the situation is nevertheless such that, with their historical distance of about 1,900 years, they can offer an outside perspective that can be stimulating and enriching for today's debates. In the process of orientation and discovery, the decisive advancing moments are sometimes those in which one succeeds in finding the right questions. The Apostolic Fathers raise a complex tableau of theological questions, and it may be that these questions can also be meaningfully raised today, under conditions that are oddly similar in many ways and completely different in many other ways, and must be pursued to new answers while respecting the answers of earlier times.

The following remarks are ordered toward this double direction.

1.   The Apostolic Fathers in Early Church History

The Apostolic Fathers are witnesses of Christian history from (mostly) the early second century and allow the process of creating Christian identity in any time to be better understood. They highlight the reality of Christian communities in any age, their theological and organizational problems, and their efforts to solve these problems. The historically motivated involvement with the "Apostolic Fathers of yesteryear" requires patience in reading texts that are not always user-friendly. However, it also brings about a rich gain in insight and furthers the understanding of the early days of Christianity.

1.1 Central Doctrinal Content and Ethical and Moral Positions as Factors of the Formation of Christian Identity

The identity creation of early Christianity succeeded through the establishment of certain consensuses of conviction with regard to doctrine and ethics. In the center of Christian identity on the doctrinal side stands the understanding of Jesus as the Son of God and the Messiah.[6] In this respect the Apostolic Fathers show both an impressive multiplicity of christological statements and starting points and a consensus with respect to the rejection of certain forms of Christology, primarily Docetism.[7] For Ignatius of Antioch, Christ is God who truly became human, was crucified, died, and rose again (IgnEph 7.2; IgnRom 3.3; IgnTrall 9). The same position is advocated, evidently reinforcing an already established tradition, in the Epistle of Polycarp (PolPhil 7). As a sermon, 2 Clement asserts the reality of Christ's passion at the outset of the remarks (2Clem 1.2). The reality of the incarnation and the real suffering and death are at the heart of the christological interest of the Apostolic Fathers. They have such great importance because they are requirements for believers' deliverance by Jesus, who brings about grace and salvation and fulfills God's mission to destroy death and establish hope in the resurrection (Barn 7.11). Along with the emphasis on the reality of the incarnation (and thus the true humanity of Jesus), there is also a constant affirmation of the divinity of Jesus, which is the central tenet of faith in early Christianity (cf. John 20:28b). Where it does not appear explicitly in the texts, the title of God is implicitly assumed to apply to Christ. In this coherence the title of *Kyrios* plays an important role in many of the texts. Thus on one side there is a consensus that includes both the reality of the incarnation and the divinity of Jesus, while on the other there are sometimes prominent, sometimes still tentative and ambivalent attempts to express the membership of the human Savior in the divine realm appropriately through suitable figures of speech.[8] An important model for this process in the Apostolic Fathers is the preexistence and mission Christology that quickly gained popularity among Gentile Christians. Thereby the "way to Chalcedon" and to the christological confession of 451 is neither pursued nor directly pointed to. But the problem that gave rise to the conclusion that one must speak of one and the same Jesus of Nazareth both in the full sense as a man and in the real sense as God is already present in the Apostolic Fathers. Later years required further conceptual and "factually" logical clarity, the beginnings of which are numerous in later theological history, including the idea that, at the end of a long period of development, gained acceptance at Chalcedon in 451 as a broad, workable compromise.

Christology and soteriology are parenetically accentuated to a conspicuously high degree in the Apostolic Fathers: The salvation that God works through Jesus

---

[6]   On ancient Christian Christology as a whole, see the presentation in Grillmeier, *Jesus der Christus*.

[7]   See below.

[8]   On this, see Brox, *Rede von Gott, passim*.

Christ aims at a kind of "service in return" from the believer—the soteriology is, so to speak, "ethicized" (PolPhil 10.1-11; Diogn 10.6). The life lived in "justice" based on the belief in salvation though Christ becomes the token of Christian identity par excellence in the early twentieth century. The work expected from the saving God is seen by many Christians as a guarantor of prior salvation in the Last Judgment.

Next to His saving function as God incarnate, who sets free a life in virtue and righteousness, the person of Jesus Christ is also connected quite directly to the role of a teacher of virtuous life (2Clem 15.5; Diogn 11). Jesus' life serves as a model (1Clem 16; MartPol); his words and admonitions are authoritative instructions for life for those who believe on him. Next to the words of the Lord, the texts of Holy Writ and traditions with Hellenistic pagan and Hellenistic Jewish provenance, such as the quickly adapted form of a Two Ways teaching (Did; Barn), catalogues of virtues and vices, and *Haustafeln* became sources of urgent instruction for the conduct of the Christian life. Materially there arise mostly very general demands for peace and harmony; for love and love for enemies; for alms, prayer, and fasting; for political loyalty; for righteousness and the doing of the Lord's will. The ethic has an ascetic, world-distancing bent without demanding radical denial. On this point they do not distinguish themselves from the "mainstream" of contemporary Hellenistic Jewish or pagan philosophical ethics.[9]

With regard to the asserted relationship between Jesus as the Son of God and God himself, there is a clear tendency to place both directly next to each other; admittedly, the attempts to resolve the terminology are still very varied. Methodologically one should take care not to apply later categories to individual texts of the Apostolic Fathers and instead better emphasize the experimental character of early Christian theology and try to evaluate the terminological attempts of the time on their own merits and in relation to the texts that are their immediate neighbors. In the Apostolic Fathers there are the first tentative attempts to adequately express the relationship between God and his incarnate *Logos*-Son. They are still quite far from a "Monarchianism" like the later prominent model of that relationship.[10] Nowhere is there anything like a doctrine of the Trinity. But the problem has arisen that, after a long theological-historical development, found a solution in the Niceno-Constantinopolitan Creed of 381 that the Christianity of the fourth century and later times saw as satisfactory.

The special teaching about God in the Apostolic Fathers also displays tensions in the terminological details, but it is drawn from an anti-Gnostic consensus, that the one God is he who acts in the past, present, and future. As such he is the Lord and the Creator of the world, which is why his action in salvation and new creation stand in continuity, not in discontinuity, with his act of creation in the

---

9   On early Christian ethics in their context in intellectual history, see Mühlenberg, *Altchristliche Lebensführung, passim.*

10   On this, see Hübner, *Der paradox Eine, passim.*

beginning. The traits predicated of God arise from different lines of tradition that were still received with a certain degree of naturalness, but they all point toward God's unlimited power and goodness: God heals, is caring and kind, omniscient, living and one, friendly toward humans and patient; God is Provider, Father, Teacher, Lawgiver, and Physician; he is Understanding, Light, Honor, Glory, and Power (Diogn 9.6). Some titles of God in mid-Platonic philosophy, which have an important function in the theology of the early Christian apologists,[11] already appear in the Apostolic Fathers: God is invisible (2Clem 20.5), and he is always the same (Diogn 8.8) and thus unchangeable. The center of the statements about God is admittedly his saving, turning toward fallen humanity, and liberating action that makes up the *proprium* of the Jewish-Christian imagination and that must have seemed strange, almost "secular," from the perspective of Greek religious thought.[12] The differentiation from the pagan philosophers on this decisive point explains the emergence of the Christian self-image as a *tertium genus* between Jews and Gentiles.

Common to the texts of the Apostolic Fathers is a future-oriented eschatology that reckons with a future judgment in which those who believe on Christ and avoid evil deeds will be saved.[13] In most of the texts (and in contrast to 1 Thess 4:17, 1 Cor 15:51-2) there is no (more) immediate expectation of the nearness of Christ's return, but the phenomenon of the delay of the second coming is still virulent and demands interpretation (2Clem 11.1–5) in order to maintain the certainty of faith. Contrariwise, other texts prove the existence of an expectation of nearness even far into the second century (Herm). Chiliastic good in the tradition of John's Apocalypse[14] appears occasionally in the Apostolic Fathers (Pap, Barn) and played a considerable role specifically in Asia Minor in the second century; it appears at this time within (Justin) and outside (Montanism) the "great church," and supposedly, new versions in different guise also appeared, if mostly as a particular phenomenon, in later epochs of church history.[15] The idea of the coming judgment carried out by Jesus as judge that can be commonly found in the Apostolic Fathers includes the passing of heaven and earth, the resurrection, and the entrance into the kingdom of God. The ignorance of the exact timing of the judgment requires a constant vigilance. Occasional references to the shortness of the time or to the idea that the Day of the Lord is nigh (IgnEph 11.1; Barn 21.3) receive emphasis in the exhortation and sharpen the earnestness of the call to repentance. Discussion of the

---

[11] On this, see the collection by Jacobsen/Ulrich/ Kahlos, *Continuity and Discontinuity, passim.*

[12] The idea that the eternal God would send Himself, that is to say his *Logos*, into the sphere of the worldly must have seemed from a pagan perspective to be removing God from the divine sphere and thus to be a secularization. On this, see Brennecke, "Jesus der Christus," 207–19.

[13] On the circles of eschatological ideas in the immediate past and at the time of the Apostolic Fathers, see the instructive collection by Labahn/ Lang, *Lebendige Hoffnung— ewiger Tod?! passim.*

[14] On this, see Bauer, *Messiasreich, passim.*

[15] The monograph by Nigg, *Das ewige Reich*, is always worth reading.

individual resurrection, except in the Ignatian letters that are heavily influenced by the theme of martyrdom, is sometimes underscored, but in these texts it is also not questioned critically but taken from tradition where they give rise to the topic of the resurrection (MartPol 2.3).

The Apostolic Fathers display a complex way of dealing with the handing down and safeguarding of oral and written tradition. For the writings collected in the corpus, the Old Testament is Holy Writ, to which the Gospels and the Pauline tradition join themselves. There is not yet a firm canon of the developing New Testament, and the number of gospels in use is not yet determined; not once is the thought of a fixed written canon of New Testament texts made explicit. But there are the first hints and steps toward development of such a canon (Pap).[16] The Pauline Epistles belong partly to a self-evident matter of tradition (1Clem) but must also partly be held up specially as "orthodox" (PolPhil), which may have been made necessary by their misuse by "heretics."[17] The Old Testament quotations mostly follow the Septuagint, free restatements of which in various forms are constantly to be reckoned with. While some of the texts contain a large number of biblical quotations (1Clem), their number in other texts is significantly lower (Diogn). That Holy Writ self-evidently forms the basis for Christian statements of faith is shown impressively in such early sermons as 2 Clement. Oral traditions about Jesus were collected and interpreted, as the Papias fragments show, wherein the instructional saying of Jesus and the miracle stories stand at the center of attention. All together there are tendencies to differentiate "authentic" elements of tradition from "inauthentic" (Pap), to which the adversaries used to appeal. The early years did not yet know a distinction between "Scripture" and "tradition," and an actual rule of faith (which, in contrast to *disciplina*, does not understand itself as an interpretation of canonized texts) first appears around 200.[18] The exegesis of the texts of the Old and the emerging New Testament knows both a "historical" grasp and the use of the allegorical interpretation beloved of contemporary Judaism, especially Philo of Alexandria (Barn). The question of the proper method of interpretation of Holy Writ deals with a fundamental problem that would accompany ancient and late ancient Christian history for a long time yet.

1.2 Conflict and Demarcation

The Christianity of the Apostolic Fathers is intensively concerned with conflicts with adversaries from without and within. Judaism stands out among the non-Christian opponents, which is obvious because Christianity arose out of Judaism. This conflict shows how early Christianity adopted Jewish sources and traditions,

---

16 On this, see the monograph by Campenhausen, *Entstehung der christlichen Bibel*, originally published in 1968 and recently republished without changes and with a new afterword by Christopher Markschies, which is still worth reading.

17 On the whole complex question of the reception of Paul in the earliest Christian times, see Lindemann, *Paulus, passim.*
18 On this whole problem, see Ohme, *Kanon ekklesiastikos, passim.*

for example the way it took the Jewish Holy Scriptures as its own Holy Scriptures, as the Christian Old Testament; received forms of Jewish-Hellenistic interpretations of the texts; and adopted elements of Jewish tradition such as the model for the Two Ways teaching (Did, Barn). By contrast, the adoption of Jewish ceremonial law was mostly refused, although this remained a controversial theme in many congregations for a long time. Obviously induced both by a rivalry with the synagogue and by "Judaizing" tendencies in their own ranks, there are in some texts of the Apostolic Fathers (Barn, Diogn) open polemics and stark rejections of Judaism, which became a problematic inheritance of Christian history from the early and many later times.[19]

The conflict with Judaism is dominated by the accusation of misunderstanding Scripture and, deduced from that, the inability to obey God. In some cases the justification for Jewish forms of existence and belief are challenged fundamentally (Diogn 3.5). With respect to daily contact, however, there appears to have been rather a suspenseful mix of coexistence and conflict; only isolated incidents of aggression by Jews against Christians and vice versa are attested (MartPol 13.1). These multifaceted relationships between church and synagogue continued in the third century and lasted well into the reign of Constantine[20] until, after the decisive political victory of the imperial church, a Christian-initiated oppression of the Jews subsided. The goal of the polemical distancing of Christians from Jewish tradition is always to test whether they are *de facto* directed against Christians, attribute to Israel and the Jewish cult any significance for salvation, and thus undermine the exclusivity of salvation in Christ (Barn). Such polemic is systematically to be located in the realm of intra-Christian conflicts, even when they display a condescending attitude toward Judaism.

Polemic against the *pagan* cults[21] and Greek philosophy appears in the texts only in passing: Philosophy is derisively called "empty and silly talk" in the letter to Diognetus (Diogn 8.2), the proponents of which spread the error of swindlers. The veneration of elements of the world falsely equated with God or of the dead idols is a very common standard accusation against the heathen that was already well-worn in the early Christian period (2Clem 3.1), but its regular use still shows a certain self-evidence of the differentiation from the religion of the Greeks. The polemic assumes some Jewish but also some pagan contemporary critics of philosophy and owes its interest to the profiling of Christianity as a separate entity between Judaism and paganism; the formation of Christian identity succeeded not only through the establishment of positive agreements of belief among the young fellowships but also through firm differentiation from its origin (Judaism) and its

---

[19] To this context belong the Christian *Adversus Iudaeos* texts that form an actual genre in Christian literature that from today's perspective is highly problematic. See Schreckenberg, *Die christlichen Adversus-Judaeos-Texte, passim.*

[20] Among the multitude of secondary literature, see only Noethlich, *Judentum, passim.*

[21] On the cultic complexity of the pagan Greco-Roman religion, see the description in Kloft, *Mysterienkulte, passim.*

surroundings (paganism). The differentiating polemic does not change the fact that early Christianity did not develop in a vacuum and plainly received structures of thought and argumentation from its pagan (and Jewish) environment, though it admittedly did not adopt them in their original sense but reshaped them and advanced them in a new direction.[22] One can ask whether such cases show a certain syncretistic potential in Christianity and question the legitimacy of such occurrences.[23] Tendencies toward an uncramped reception of pagan philosophical figures can be observed in the texts of the great apologists of the second and third centuries (Justin, Clement of Alexandria, Origen). At the same time, these questions remained a recurring theme in later theological history—in contrast to the "mainstream" of the discriminating reception of pagan philosophy (Justin, later Eusebius of Caesarea, or Augustine) always stood a faction that at least from the outside rejected and voiced criticisms of the use of philosophy (in the late 2nd c., e.g., Tatian or Tertullian).

In the process of differentiation from both Judaism and pagan philosophy, there appears in the Apostolic Fathers, as in other Christian texts from the early years, a moment that is typical of Christian history and must have had a highly strange effect on the world surrounding early Christianity: Christians begin as a matter of course from the assumption that the way of salvation on which they believe is the only possible way to God and deny any legitimacy to competing offers of salvation.[24]

The differentiations from Judaism on the one hand and from Greek philosophy on the other plays a significantly smaller role in the Apostolic Fathers than the conflicts with opponents who were themselves Christians. This conflict with adversaries from within is primarily directed against *Gnostics* (2Clem), proponents of a *docetic Christology* (Ign; PolPhil 6.3–7.1), and Judaizing Christians (Ign, Barn, Diogn). The more precise identification of individual Gnostic groups is often difficult.[25] Relevant attempts sometimes reveal the holes in our knowledge of the oldest Christian "heresies." Attempts to establish a relationship between Gnostics and Docedist highlight the problem that Gnostic groups often supported a docetic Christology, but not all Gnostics were Docedist and not all advocates of a docetic Christology were notably Gnostic. The sharpness of the surviving polemic shows indirectly the highly attractive nature that Gnosticism and Docetism must have had, especially for educated people in the early second century, for whose Platonized image of God the idea of an actual entrance of God into the world was completely foreign. Often the polemic does not speak directly to the false teachers of Gnosticism or Docetism but directs itself to Christians in

---

[22] On the mutual influence and the critical distancing, see now the volume by Jacobsen/Ulrich/Brakke, *Critique and Apologetics, passim.*

[23] On this, see Brennecke, "Synkretisumus," 157–78.

[24] On this, see Brenneke, "Absolutheitsanspruch," *passim.*

[25] On gnosis, see Markschies, *Die Gnosis, passim.*

the same congregation whom the author wants to protect from the temptation of the "heretics."

Content-wise, the antidocetic polemic of the Apostolic Fathers not only warns generally against denial of the Iincarnation but also points positively to the soteriologically decisive meaning of the crucifixion and to the "fleshly" resurrection (PolPhil 6.3–7.1). The fact that the Son of God's becoming human in an unlimited way is seen as the unrenounceable prerequisite, for the saving work of Christ explains the sharpness of the conflict. For Ignatius of Antioch, Christianity stands or falls with the belief in the suffering of the Lord Jesus Christ *for us*. The passion of Christ precedes the suffering of the Christian martyr and strengthens him (IgnSmyrn 4.2). He cannot see the adversaries who "blasphemously" teach that Christ only appeared to suffer (IgnSmyrn 2, 4.1-2, 5.2; IgnTrall 10–11) as Christians. He calls them "unbelievers" and "wild beasts in human form."

In the polemic against Gnostics there are further theological aspects beyond the problem of Christology. These include the ecclesiology in which the "sarcic" present-day church is seen as an antitype of the spiritual church (2Clem 14), whereby the Gnostic distinction between pneumatic and psychic Christians is avoided. The pneumatology objects to the Gnostics' primarily present-focused understanding of the spirit; the eschatology brings up the hope for the future in criticism against the Gnostics' more present-focused eschatology. The emphasis on bodily resurrection also belongs in this context (e.g., 2Clem 9.1-5). Anthropologically the Gnostic-Docetic denigration of the physical is criticized by all insistence on a moderate-abstinent interaction with the things of the world.

Next to the polemic against Gnostic and docetic Christians, another important line of intra-Christian differentiation appears in the criticism of "Judaizing" Christians, who place such importance on the continuity of salvation history between Israel and the church that they want to maintain the Jewish cult because they assign to it lasting relevance for salvation. This idea is judged in some of the texts to be a soteriological limiting of the meaning of Christ for salvation and thus sharply disputed (Barn). The Ignatian letters also polemicize against the Judaizing powers among early Christians (IgnMagn 10.3; IgnPhld 6.1). In comparison to the massive polemics against the Docedists and Gnostics, this aspect plays a more subordinate role in the texts. With regard to all reception of Jewish tradition and forms of thought in early Christianity, both the external differentiation from the synagogue and the internal differentiation from Christians who wanted to hold on to Jewish ceremonial regulations or at least regular contact with the synagogue must be regarded as widely complete in the second century, even though the latter question long remained a theme in the history of Christianity,[26] as the "Jewish homilies" of one John Chrysostom at the end of the fourth century prove.

---

[26] See Kretschmar, "Kirche aus Juden und Heiden," *passim*.

The conflicts with the Gnostic-Docetic positions and with Judaizing tendencies have weight that has increased with distance. Only very marginally are there also polemics against other Christian "deviationists" such as the *Montanist* Christians. The criticism of them succeeds less because of their problematic understanding of the Holy Ghost than because of their all too radical readiness for martyrdom. In the Martyrdom of Polycarp the author seeks to portray the courageous steadfastness as a "catholic" compromise between the shirkerhood of lukewarm Christians and the sharply criticized fanaticism of the Montanists (MartPol 4).[27] The controversy with Marcion and his church that so strongly burdened the history of second-century Christianity does not (yet) play a role in the Apostolic Fathers.

1.3 Praxis and Reality of the Fellowship

We find much about the praxis and reality of the early Christian congregations in the Apostolic Fathers. For all the sketchiness of information caused by transmission, a real living, multifaceted picture of the form of Christian existence in the early phase of Christendom arises from them when taken together.

The Christian congregations are local fellowships that understand themselves at the same time to be part of the "catholic church" in the sense of a church of Christ-believers. This fact gives rise to the task of interchurch communication. The congregations of the Apostolic Fathers know one another and take an interest in one another. Our texts direct themselves to Christian fellowships or to individuals in Christian fellowships. Letters serve the exchange of information about events and problems in the individual congregations but also, as 1 Clement shows, intervene most spiritedly in the affairs of other congregations. Here we see on the one hand early Christianity's claim to universal fellowship within reach, while on the other hand the problem of unity of the Christian congregations presents itself yet again with special clarity (Ign).

As witnesses of Christianity in the first half of the second century, the Apostolic Fathers reveal a considerable geographic spectrum. As always one may judge here or there in the introductory questions of the individual texts: The Apostolic Fathers present a regionally broad palette of spotlights from Rome and Alexandria/Egypt, from Syria-Palestine, from Asia Minor, and from the Greek realm, and thus include a broad portion of the Mediterranean world.[28] The astonishing mobility in the Roman Empire in the time of the Caesars[29] also promoted a considerable fluctuation of personnel in the young congregations. Socially the spectrum that is recognizable to us is remarkably broad: The texts know the problem of poverty just as they address themselves to well-to-do members of

---

27 On this, see in detail Butterweck, *Martyriumssucht, passim.*

28 On the astonishingly fast spread of Christianity in the first centuries, see generally the not uncontroversial but highly stimulating monograph by Stark, *The Rise of Christianity, passim.*

29 Giebel, *Reisen, passim.*

the congregation with the request for material support. And if one takes into account the language, the literary level, and the possible groups that wrote and received the texts, considerable differences in the level of education of Christians in the congregations of the Apostolic Fathers can be deduced.

With regard to liturgical praxis, the texts show a quite colorful complexity while at the same time showing concern for a relative standardization. The reading of certain texts as revelatory documents, the formulating of certain core statements of faith, and the reciting of fixed prayers find their place in the practice of worship. Homilies as genre and elements of worship events are documented. Baptism, for all the differences in baptismal theology and practice, is foundational from the beginning as an initiation. The Didache proves that the congregation, recitation of the formula from Matthew 28:19, carried out baptism in the name of the Trinitarian God (Did 7.3), but the three-membered baptismal formula naturally does not assume any elaborate doctrine of the Trinity. In the completion of the act of baptism we see a concern for fixed forms and for unity, but also the pragmatic acceptance of reasonable differences. A constitutive element is the connection with water. A preceding instruction and a fast before the baptism are required (Did 7.1-4). Generally the requirement of fasting (e.g., the weeklong fast, Did 8.1) and prayer (Did 8.2) played a great role in the praxis of the fellowships. Collective prayers for God's mercy in the congregational meetings have the function of a recognition of sin and request the reconciliation granted by God (1Clem 60.1-2; Did 14.1-3). As much as the sinners in the congregations were urged to repent, which is evident in many exhortations, admonitions, and liturgical formulations (Did 10.6; IgnSmyrn 5.3; 2Clem 13; 1Clem 57.1), there is very little evidence of an institutionalized sacrament of penance. The Shepherd of Hermas represents an attempt—admittedly minimally effective—in this direction, which entitles all believers a one-time, temporary opportunity for penance (HermVis II 2.1-8), but it also does not provide for any firm procedural rules. The problem of penance would remain virulent until well into the time of the imperial church. Even in the earliest times there is evidence of the Eucharist or the *agape* meal (Did 9.1–10.7), but the boundary between a congregational meal that served to satisfy and was mostly called *agape* and a eucharistic meal celebration in a strict sense is not always clearly recognizable. As far as the precise course of the Eucharist in the second century goes, there are still uncertainties in reading the suggested, sometimes disputed sources. In an express differentiation from the keeping of the Jewish Sabbath, the sanctification of Sunday as the Lord's Day (Did 14) as a Christian congregational practice is clearly reflected in the sources.

The Apostolic Fathers display a strong engagement with social welfare in the young fellowships. The theme of "almsgiving" is as prevalent in the texts (2Clem) as the hospitality that was praised even among the opponents of Christianity with gnashing of teeth, which got around so quickly that the fellowships had to make themselves understood on the defense against abusive demands from freeloaders (Did 12.1-2).

A theologically and organizationally decisive question is that about the leadership in the Christian congregations. The conflict in Corinth, in which 1 Clement intervened, hinged on the dismissal of the previous bishop by a rival group; this dismissal is in the author's view unjust, since the previous officeholders had received their legitimation from the apostles and thus indirectly from Christ (1Clem 42–44) and it goes against the divine order to drive them away. The thought of "apostolic succession" appears here for the first time. Bishop Ignatius of Antioch presents a steep concept of hierarchical church leadership in his letters, at the top of which stands the God-ordained bishop, followed by the presbyters and deacons. The unity of the church and its function as custodian of the truth against the false teachers should be preserved by the subordination of Christians under the bishop "as under Christ." The monarchical episcopacy that Ignatius vehemently supports should be divinely authorized in all events in the fellowship. As much as this concept was accepted in the medium view, it seems strangely anachronistic in the theological and historical context of the Apostolic Fathers, which we know has given rise to forgery hypotheses about the Ignatian letters that have been prominently promoted to this day: In the Didache, 1 Clement, and the relatively late Shepherd of Hermas we find namely no bishopric as the pinnacle of a hierarchy but rather collegially organized forms of leadership.

An important role is played by the question of martyrdom,[30] by which Christians in the Roman Empire were all threatened under the political-judicial conditions of the second century: The texts reflect the attempt at an encouragement of martyrdom through the example of important martyrs' personalities (Ignatius, Polycarp) as well as the beginnings of a corresponding veneration of martyrs. The Ignatian letters alone emphasize the martyr's imitation of Christ's suffering, which shows the immediacy of his relationship with Christ and God and so develops consoling action. Numerous exhortations encourage the members of the congregation to perseverance and steadfastness not least in view of the threat of martyrdom.

2. The Apostolic Fathers and the Questions of Christianity in the Twenty-first Century

The present of our still young twenty-first century shows a newly awakened interest in religions and things religious. Tendencies toward collective and individual uncertainty have given rise to a new need for orientation and in this context a new turning to religion as well. This new interest is reflected in the central areas of our societies. Literature and the plastic arts, theater, film, and television all engage religion anew. In the situation of the globalized world, the religions of the world have the task of articulating and positioning themselves anew and at the

---

[30] On the greater context, see the volume by Ameling, *Märtyrer, passim*.

same time taking the chance to engage with the others and have a constructive influence on them.[31]

If one wants to take up this task with a view to success, the new interest in religion and things religious must be accompanied by a progressive process of mutual self-assertion and awareness of others that arises from the foundations of the religion in question. Occupation with these foundations is a requirement for the success of the process, already in progress and to be dealt further with in the future, of the meaningful shaping of their interaction. Most of the world religions, especially Judaism, Christianity, and Islam, already develop themselves from their self-understanding through their great foundational texts recognized as divine revelation and through the central texts of their historical tradition. The knowledge of these central texts is indispensible for any meaningful interaction with the religion. Anyone who wants to take part in the current discourse among religions and the discourse on religion must therefore read the important texts that lie at the heart of the religion in the past and present and have been handed down as an element of its self-expression.[32] The language and thought of religions are formed by their constant recourse to the texts of their earliest history, which in the case of Christianity are the writings of the Old and New Testaments.[33] To be sure, the Apostolic Fathers have produced none of the New Testament's power of impression or even a distant approximation of it, but as complementary texts settled close by the New Testament, they are instructive both for the better understanding of the New Testament and for insight into the earliest phase of its history of effectiveness. Thus the Apostolic Fathers can be recommended to any modern reader for thoughtful reading as central sources for the Christian religion. A better understanding of the earliest phase of Christianity that rests on a thorough knowledge of the New Testament in its earliest literary witnesses serves the better understanding of the Christian religion as a whole, including its present form.

In certain respects, however, the reading of the Apostolic Fathers could also prove profitable for everything that has to do with the concrete questions and problems of Christianity in our day, and that for a double reason:

For one thing, because it can also prove helpful for answering current questions to look at the origins.[34] Doing so is admittedly only meaningful if one is able to build as detailed, nonjudgmental, and source-oriented an image of the origins as possible. The *ad fontes* of humanism and the Reformation could also apply, with a grain of salt, to the Apostolic Fathers.

---

31 On this, see the ambitious program that Verlag der Weltreligionen has undertaken: Simm, *Die Religionen der Welt, passim.*
32 On this, see Simm, *Die Religionen der Welt,* 10–11.
33 On the self-understanding and identity of Christianity with regard to its history, belief, and

ethics, see the brilliant, concise presentation by Nowak, *Das Christentum, passim.*
34 It is worth noting in this context that in early 2007, Pope Benedict XVI held a catechism course on the Apostolic Fathers on the occasion of the general audience on St. Peter's Square in order to assure the pilgrims who were there of their origins.

For another, an interest in the Apostolic Fathers for ecclesiastical and theological questions of the present could be due to the fact that we in the twenty-first century in many respects stand before mental, religious, and social constellations that strongly resemble the colorful, intricate, religiously highly complex world of the second century. Conversely, the pluriform world of the second century that asks after orientation and is shaped by seeker movements seems in many ways more similar to our current situation than the periods that are purely chronologically closer to us—the Middle Ages, the Reformation, the Enlightenment, or the nineteenth century. That does not mean that one should examine positions and suggested solutions from the second century for the potential for orienting our current formulation of questions. They do work with fundamental problems that are very similar to ours, but they do so under the conditions of *their* time and not those of our time. On the other hand, however, it stands so well that one can embrace suggestions from the reading of any of the texts arising from the earliest phase of Christianity that are thoroughly stimulating for today's theological thought and questions, precisely because their impulse comes from a distant time and are thus "from the outside." A few aspects may be instructive here:

— The problem of self-definition of Christianity in its relationship to the non-Christian religious environment and the question of the self-understanding of Christianity with respect to its doctrine and its ethics.
— The phenomenon of the identity formation of Christianity that finds itself in permanent construction in a religiously pluralistic environment.
— The phenomenon of the laboratory character of Christian theology in the context of the permanent conflict with its own tradition and with others.
— The question of the conflict between Christianity and syncretism and of the syncretistic tendencies within Christianity itself.
— The question of the conflict between Christianity and the secular environment and the secularizing potential of Christianity itself, that is, of the possible secularizing effect of Christianity on its surroundings.
— The question of the content and form of the conflict between Christianity and non-Christian religions and the question of the criteria for engagement.
— The problem of communications and missions strategies with respect to sometimes hostile, sometimes misinformed or disinterested dialogue partners.
— The question of the factual and timely formulation of the relationship between Christianity and the world and its ethical consequences.
— The question of the factual and timely formulation of a Christology as the central truth of Christian belief.
— The problem of a legitimate intra-Christian complexity of convictions and teachings that at the same time contains boundaries that identify as "foreign" or "illegitimate" teachings that view themselves from their own perspective as Christian.

— The question of directing, leading, and "steering" within the church(es) and of the criteria thereof.

— The problem of the unity of Christendom and its global/universal claim in light of the simultaneous complexity and diversity of the churches.

These are only a few spheres of questions and thought that according to reason accompany the whole of Christian history to this day but that in the present may be newly virulent to a higher degree than the Christianity of previous centuries was accustomed to—and that nevertheless once played a central role in the time of the Apostolic Fathers. This fact does not change the historical distance and sometimes irritating strangeness of content in these texts that are not less than about 1,900 years distant from us. But under the aforementioned points of view, these genuine treasures from the Christian and religious history of the second century are even more than just a treasure house for specialists interested in historical theology and dogmatic history. They show a multifaceted panorama of Christianity as it was once lived in its internal complexity and in its outward conflict with alternative religious offerings. So they merit the patient reading but also require a circumspect introduction. To prepare such an initiation and to illuminate the approach to these texts that are interesting in many respects is the intent of the scholarly introductions collected in this volume. They seek to present the Apostolic Fathers and help draw conclusions, but not to replace reading the texts themselves, but rather to lead directly to it. Then as now, the Apostolic Fathers entice their readers.

3. Bibliography

The bibliography for this chapter is limited to general, wide-ranging literature. For special questions and problems, consult the bibliographies of the preceding chapters on the individual writings of the Apostolic Fathers.

Ameling, W., ed. *Märtyrer und Martyrerakten*. Altertumswissenschaftliches Kolloquium 6. Stuttgart 2002.

Altaner, B., and A. Stuiber. *Patrologie: Leben, Schriften und Lehre der Kirchenväter*. Freiburg ⁹1980.

Bardenshewer, O. *Geschichte der urchristlichen Literatur I: Vom Ausgang des Apostolischen Zeitalters bis zum Ende des zweiten Jahrhunderts*. Darmstadt 2007. (Reprint of the 1962 special ed.)

Bauer, T. J. *Das tausendjährige Messiasreich in der Johannesoffenbarung*. BZNW 147. Berlin 2007.

Brennecke, H. C. "Der Absolutheitsanspruch des Christentums und die religiösen Angebote der Alten Welt." In *Ecclesia est in re publica*, 125–44. Edited by U. Heil, A. von Stockhausen, and J. Ulrich. AKG 100. Berlin 2007.

———. "Frömmigkeits- und kirchengeschichtliche Aspekte zum Synkretismus." In *Ecclesia est in re publica*, edited by U. Heil, A. von Stockhausen, and J. Ulrich, 157–78. AKG 100. Berlin 2007.

———. "Jesus der Christus: Inkarnation und Säkularisierung." In *Religious Turns—Turning Religions: Veränderte kulturelle Diskurse—neue religiöse Wissnsformen*, edited by A. Nehring and J. Valentin, 207–19. ReligionsKulturen 1. Stuttgart 2008.

Brox, N. *Das frühe Christentum: Schriften zur Historischen Theologie*. Edited by F. Dünzel, A. Fürst, and F. R. Prostmeier. Freiburg 2000.

———. *Termiologisches zur frühchristlichen Rede von Gott*. SBAW.PH 1. Munich 1996.

Butterweck, C. *Martyriumssucht in der Alten Kirche? Studien zu Darstellung und Duetung frühchristlicher Martyrien*. BHT 87. Tübingen 1995.

Campenhausen, H. von. *Die Entstehung der christlichen Bibel*. Reprint of the 1968 ed. with a new afterword by Christoph Markschies. BHT 39. Tübingen 2003.

Döpp, S., and W. Greerlings, eds. *Lexikon der antiken christlichen Literatur*. Freiburg ³2002.

Giebel, M. *Reisen in der Antike*. Darmstadt 1999.

Grillmeier, A. *Jesus der Christus im Glauben der Kirche I: Von der apostolischen Zeit bis zum Konzil von Calkedon (451)*. Freiburg ³1990.

Hübner, R. M. *Der paradox Eine: Antignostischer Monarchianismus im zweiten Jahrhundert*. VC S 50. Leiden 1999.

Jacobsen, A.-C., J. Ulrich, and D. Brakke, eds. *Critique and Apologetics: Jews, Christians, and Pagans in Antiquity*. ECCA 4. Frankfurt/Main 2009.

Jacobsen, A.-C., J. Ulrich, and M. Kahlos, eds. *Continuity and Discontinuity in Christian Apologetics*. ECCA 5. Frankfurt/Main 2009.

Kloft, H. *Mysterienkulte der Antike: Götter—Menschen—Rituale*. Beck'sche Reihe 2106. Munich 1999.

Kretschmar, G. "Die Kirche aus Juden und Heiden." In *Juden und Christen in der Antike*, edited by J. van Amersfoort and J. van Oort, 9–43. Kampen 1990.

Labahn, M., and M. Lang, eds. *Lebendige Hoffnung—ewiger Tod?! Jenseitsvorstellungen im Hellenismus, Judentum und Christentum*. Arbeiten zur Bibel und ihrer Geschichte 24. Leipzig 2007.

Lindemann, A. "Apostolische Väter." RGG⁴ I (1998): 692–93.

———. *Paulus im ältesten Christentum*. BHT 58. Tübingen 1979.

Nigg, W. *Das ewige Reich: Geschichte einer Hoffnung*. Munich ²1967.

Noethlichs, K. L. *Das Judentum und der römische Staat: Minderheitenpolitik im antiken Rom*. Darmstadt 1996.

Nowak, K. *Das Christentum: Geschichte—Glaube—Ethik*. Beck'sche Reihe 2070. München 1997.

Markschies, C. *Die Gnosis*. Munich 2001.

Mühlenberg, E. *Altchristliche Lebensцührung zwischen Bibel und Tugendlehre: Ethik bei den griechischen Philosophen und den frühen Christen*. AAWG.PH 272. Göttingen 2006.

Ohme, H. *Kanon ekklesiastikos: Die Bedeutung des altkirchlichen Kanonbegriffs*. AKG 67. Berlin 1998.

Schreckenberg, H. *Die christlichen Adversus-Judaeos-Texte und ihr literarisches und historisches Umfeld (1.–11. Jh.)*. EHS.T 172. Frankfurt/Main 1990.

Simm, H.-J., ed. *Die Religionen der Welt: Ein Almanach zu Eröffnung des Verlags der Weltreligionen*. Frankfurt/Main 2007.

Stark, R. *The Rise of Christianity: A Sociologist Reconsiders History*. Princeton 1996.

Tröger, K.-W. *Das Christentum im zweiten Jahrhundert*. KGE I/2. Berlin 1988.

Editions and Translations of the Apostolic Fathers

Balthasar, H. U. von. *Die Apostolischen Väter*. CMe 24. Einsiedeln 1984.

Bihlmeyer, K. *Die Apostolischen Väter: Neubearbeitung der Funkschen Ausgabe, I: Didache, Barnabas, Klemens I und II, Ignatius, Polkcarp, Papias, Quadratus, Diognetbrief*. SAQ 2.1.1. Tübingen 1924. [Referred to in the text as Funk/Bihlmeyer.]

Bosio, G. *Padri Apostolici: Introduzione, traduzione, note*. CPS.G7. Turin 1940.

Cotelier, J.-B. *Ss. Patrum, qui temporibus apostolicis floruerunt, Barnabae, Clementis, Hermae, Ignatii, Polycarpi Opera, edita et inedita, vera, & supposititia: Una cum Clementis, Ignatii, Polycarpi Actis atque Martyriis*. Paris 1672.

Dressel, A. R. M. *Patrum Apostolicorum Opera. Textum ad fidem cordicum et Graecorum et Latinorum, ineditorum copia insignium [. . .] instruxuit*. Leipzig 1857.

Ehrman, B. D. *The Apostolic Fathers: Edited and Translated, I–II*. LCL 24–25. Cambridge, Mass. 2003.

Fischer, J. A. *Die Apostolischen Väter [1Clem, Ign, Pol, Quadr]: Eingeleitet, herausgegeben, übertragen und erläutert*. SUC I. Munich 1956.

Frey, J. L. *Epistolae sanctorum Patrum apostolicorum, Clementis, Ignatii, et Polycarpi, atque duorum posteriorum martyria. Omnia graece et latine cum variorum annotationibus et praefatione*. Basel 1742.

Funk, F. X. *Die Apostolischen Väter*. SAQ 2.1. Tübingen/Leipzig 1901.

————. *Opera Patrum Apostolicorum: Textum recensuit, adnotationibus criticis exegeticis historicis illustravit, versionem Latinam, Prolegomena, indices addidit, I–II*. Tübingen 1878–1881.

Gallandi, A. *Bibliotheca Veterum Patrum Antiquorumque Scriptorum Ecclesiasticorum, postrema Lugdunensi longe locupletior atque accuratior cura et studio, I–XIV*. Venice 1765–1781.

Gebhardt, O. de, A. Harnack, and T. Zahn. *Patrum Apostolicorum Opera: Textum ad fidem codicum et Graecorum et Latinorum adhibitis praestantissimis editionibus, I–III*. Leipzig 1875–1877.

————. *Patrum Apostolicorum Opera: Texum ad fidem Codicum et Graecorum et Latinorum adhibits praestantissimis editionibus, Editio minor*. Leipzig 1877.

Glimm, F. X., J. M.-F. Marique, and G. G. Walsh. *The Apostolic Fathers*. FC 1. Washington, D.C. 1947.

Goodspeed, E. J. *The Apostolic Fathers: An American Translation*. New York 1950.

Grant, R. M., et al. *The Apostolic Fathers: A New Translation and Commentary, I–VI.* London 1964–1968.

Hefele, K. J. *Patrum Apostolicorum Opera: Textum ex editionibus praestantissimus repetitum recognovit annotationibus illustravit, versionem Latinam emendatiorem, prolegomena et indices.* Tübingen 1839.

Hemmer, H., et al. *Les pères apostoliques, I–IV.* TDEHC 5, 10, 12, 16. Paris 1907–1912.

Hennecke, E. *Handbuch zu den Neutestamentlichen Apokryphen.* Tübingen 1904.

Hilgenfeld, A. *Novum Testamentum extra canonem receptum, I–IV.* Leipzig 1866.

Holmes, M. W. *The Apostolic Fathers: Greek Texts and English Translations.* Grand Rapids 1999.

Hoole, C. H. *The Apostolic Fathers: The Epistles of S. Clement, S. Ignatius, S. Barnabas, S. Polycarp. Together with the Martyrdom of S. Ignatius and S. Polycarp. Translated into English, with an Introductory Notice.* London 1872.

Ittig, T. *Bibliotheca partum Apostolicorum Graeco-Latina, qua continentur I. S. Clementis Romani prior et posterior ad Corinthios epistulae, II. S. Ignatii epistolae [. . .], III. S. Polycarpi Epistola [. . .]. Praemissa est dissertation de patribus apostolicis.* Leipzig 1699.

Kleist, J. A. *The Didache; The Epistle of Barnabas; The Epistles and the Martyrdom of St. Polycarp; The Fragments of Papias; The Epistle to Diognetus.* ACW 6. Westminster, Md. 1948.

Klijn, A. F. J. *Apostolische Vaders: Vertaald, ingeleid en toegelicht, I–II.* Kampen 1981–1983.

Körtner, U. H. J., and M. Leutzsch. *Papiasfragmente, Hirt des Hermas: Eingeleitet, herausgegeben, übertragen und erläutert* SUC III. Darmstadt 1998.

Lake, K. *The Apostolic Fathers: With an English Translation, I–II.* LCL. London 1912–1913.

Lightfoot, J. B. *The Apostolic Fathers, I–II, A Revised Text with Introductions, Notes, Dissertations and Translations.* London ²1889–1890.

Lightfoot, J. B., and J. R. Harmer. *The Apostolic Fathers: Revised Texts, with Short Introductions and English Translations.* London 1891.

Lightfoot, J. B., J. R. Harmer, and M. W. Holmes. *The Apostolic Fathers.* Leicester ²1990.

Lindemann, A., and H. Paulsen. *Die Apostolischen Väter: Griechisch-deutsche Parallelausgabe auf der Grundlage der Ausgaben von Franz Xaver Funk/Karl Bihlmeyer und Molly Whittaker: Mit Übersetzungen von M. Dibelius und D.-A. Koch.* Tübingen 1992.

Louvel, F., L. Bouyer, and C. Mondésert. *Les Écrits des Pères Apostoliques.* Paris 1963.

Mayer, J. C. *Die Schriften der Apostolischen Väter nebst den Martyr-Akten des hl. Ignatius und hl. Polykarp nach dem Urtext übersetzt.* BKV. Kempten 1869.

Quéré, F. *Les Pères apostoliques: Écrits de la primitive Église: Traduction et introduction.* Paris 1980.

Richardson, C. C., et al. *Early Christian Fathers: Newly Translated and Edited.* LCC 1. Philadelphia 1953.

Ruiz Bueno, D. *Padres Apostólicos: Edicion Bilingüe Completa: Introducciones Notas y Version Española.* BAC 65. Madrid 1950.

Russel, R. *Ss. patrum apostolicorum Barnabae, Hermae, Clementis, Ignatii, Polycarpi, opera genuina. Una cum Ignatii & Polycarpi martyriis, versionibus antiquis ac recentioribus, variantibus lectionibus, selectisque variorum notis illustrate. Accesserunt s. Ignatii Epistolae, tum interpoatae, tum supposititiae, I–II.* London 1746.

Sparks, J. *The Apostolic Fathers.* Nashville 1998.

Wake, W. *The Genuine Epistles of the Apostolic Fathers: S. Barnabas, S. Ignatius, S. Clement, S. Polycarp, the Shepherd of Hermas, and the Martyrdom of St. Ignatius and St. Polycarp [. . .]. Translated and publish'd.* London 1693.

Wengst, K. *Didache (Apostellehre), Barnabasbrief, Zweiter Klemensbrief, Schrift an Diognet: Eingeleitet, herausgegeben, übertragen und erläutert.* SUC II. Darmstadt 1984.

Zeller, F. *Die Apostolischen Väter: Aus dem Griechischen übersetzt.* BKV² 35. Kempten/Munich 1918.

A new Oxford edition with introduction, translation, and commentary by A. F. Gregory and C. M. Tuckett is in preparation.

Contributors

Gerd Buschmann, Senior Lecturer in Evangelical Theology and Religious Pedagogy at the Pädagogische Hochschule Ludwigsburg, Baden-Württemberg.

Boudewijn Dehandschutter, Emeritus Professor of Church History and History of Theology at the Theological Faculty of the Catholic University of Löwen.

Jonathan A. Draper, Professor of New Testament in the School of Religion and Theology of the Faculty of Humanities, Development, and Social Sciences of the University of KwaZulu-Natal.

David Hellholm, Emeritus Professor of New Testament at the Theological Faculty of the University of Oslo.

Ulrich H. J. Körtner, Professor of Systematic Theology at the Evangelical Theological Faculty of the University of Vienna.

Andreas Lindemann, until his retirement in 2009, Professor of New Testament at the Ecclesiastical Hochschule Bethel (since 2007: Ecclesiastical Hochschule Wuppertal/Bethel).

Hermut Löhr, Professor of New Testament at the Evangelical Theological Faculty of the Westphalian Wilhelms-Universität Münster.

Horacio E. Lona, Professor of New Testament Exegesis and History of Early Christian Literature at the Philosophisch-Theologische Hochschule der Salesianer, Theological Faculty, Benediktbeuern.

Wilhelm Pratscher, Professor of New Testament Studies at the Evangelical Theological Faculty of the University of Vienna.

Ferdinand R. Prostmeier, Professor of New Testament Literature and Exegesis at the Theological Faculty of Albert Ludwig University in Freiburg im Breisgau.

Jörg Ulrich, Professor of Church History at the Theological Faculty of Martin Luther University in Halle-Wittenberg.

Index